Improving Compliance with International Environmental Law

JAMES CAMERON JACOB WERKSMAN
&
PETER RODERICK

FIELD

E·S·R·C
ECONOMIC
& SOCIAL
RESEARCH
COUNCIL

Routledge
Taylor & Francis Group
LONDON AND NEW YORK

First published 1996 by Earthscan

2 Park Square, Milton Park, Abingdon, Oxon OX14 4RN
711 Third Avenue, New York, NY 10017, USA

Routledge is an imprint of the Taylor & Francis Group, an informa business

First issued in hardback 2016

A catalogue record for this book is available from the British Library

ISBN: 978-1-85383-261-1 (pbk)
ISBN: 978-1-138-16327-0 (hbk)

Typeset by JS Typesetting, Wellingborough, Northants.

CONTENTS

ACKNOWLEDGEMENTS

The editors and authors at FIELD would like to thank the FIELD programme assistants, and the many students and interns who contributed their time and energy to every stage in the preparation of this volume and the work related to the ESRC project. Marion Bloom and Louise Rands, FIELD programme assistants, and Frances Connelly, our then Administrator, were crucial in supporting the project in its early stages, and Maria Adebowale provided invaluable assistance in the completion of this volume for publication. Alexandra Keutsch, Melinda Baas, Banni Pootschi, and Ellen-Sophie Lokholm – interns at FIELD during this period – contributed their time, energy, and in Alexandra's case, research and editorial skills.

Clearly, none of this work would have been possible without the support of FIELD's funders. The project was undertaken with financial, intellectual and administrative support from the United Kingdom's Economic and Social Research Council (ESRC) through their programme on Global Environmental Change, and was bolstered by funding for FIELD's related projects and programmes in Climate Change and Energy, Trade and Sustainable Development, and the International Law of Sustainable Development, generously provided by; the Ford Foundation, the W Alton Jones Foundation, the Rockefeller Brothers Fund, the John Merck Foundation, the Conservation, Food & Health Foundation, and the German Marshall Fund.

Thanks must also go to Blackwell publishers, for their kind permission to reprint contributions from the Review of European Community and International Environmental Law (RECIEL).

Finally, FIELD gratefully acknowledges the members of the Climate Change Secretariat, and the diplomats, policymakers, academics and civil servants who participated in the FIELD/ESRC Seminar on Improving Compliance, who contributed their invaluable time and expertise in making this publication possible.

LIST OF CONTRIBUTORS

Chowdhury R Abrar is a Professor in the Department of International Relations at Dhaka University, Dhaka. He holds an MA from Sussex University and a PhD from Griffith.

James Cameron is a practising barrister and Director of the Foundation for International Environmental Law and Development (FIELD) at the School of Oriental and African Studies (SOAS), University of London, and is Visiting Professor at the College of Europe in Bruges.

Annabella Gualdoni is a JD Candidate, Boston College, and was a research assistant with FIELD.

Martin Hession is a Research Scientist at the Environmental Change Unit, Oxford University.

Leesteffy Jenkins is an Attorney in Washington, DC, specializing in international environmental law. She is counsel to various animal welfare conservation groups specializing in wildlife issues.

Andrew Jordan is a Research Associate at the ESRC–funded Centre for Social and Economic Research on the Global Environment (CSERGE), located jointly at the University of East Anglia and University College London, where he specializes in the politics of global environmental protection.

Alexandra Keutsch is a trainee solicitor with the firm Cameron Markby Hewitt and was a research assistant with FIELD.

Zen Makuch is a Canadian barrister. He holds a BA (York), MSc (LSE), LLB (Osgoode Hall), LLM (London) and is a member of the Law Society of Upper Canada. He is a member of the board of advisers to the European Institute of Public Law and lectures in environmental and international trade law at both the Universities of Hull and London.

Ronald B Mitchell is an Assistant Professor in the Department of Political Science at the University of Oregon. He holds a PhD in Public Policy from Harvard University.

George Paleokrassis is a solicitor with the London-based shipping firm Watson Farley & Williams and was a research assistant with FIELD.

Peter Roderick is a barrister who has worked in private practice, industry and academia. He now primarily advises international, national and local environmental organizations.

Gregory Rose is head of the Environmental Law Unit of the Legal Office of the Australian Department of Foreign Affairs and Trade, and visiting lecturer at the Australian National University. Previously he was Director of the Marine Resources Programme of FIELD, and editor-in-chief of RECIEL.

Philippe Sands is a practising barrister and Legal Director of the Foundation for FIELD at SOAS, University of London. He is also Visiting Professor of Law, New York University. His chapter is drawn from the author's *Principles of International Environmental Law*, published by Manchester University Press in 1995.

Jacob Werksman is a Staff Lawyer and Co-Director of the Climate Change and Energy Programme with FIELD at SOAS, University of London, where he is a visiting lecturer in International Law.

Farhana Yamin is a Staff Lawyer and Co-Director of the Climate Change and Energy Programme with FIELD at SOAS, University of London, where she is a visiting lecturer in Comparative and International Environmental Law.

Wang Xinxia was a member of the Chinese Delegation to the Eighth COP of CITES. She has worked in the Treaty and Law Department, Ministry of Foreign Affairs, China, and has been seconded as the legal adviser by the CITES Management Authority of China.

INTRODUCTION

by James Cameron, Jacob Werksman and Peter Roderick

This volume is the fruit of two major efforts at the Foundation for International Environmental Law and Development (FIELD), both aimed at improving understanding of how international environmental agreements operate, and how compliance with their provisions might be improved.

Six chapters have been drawn from the *Review of European Community and International Environmental Law* (RECIEL), FIELD's quarterly publication of thematic articles contributed by lawyers and lay persons working in the area of environmental protection from the governmental, non-governmental, academic and private sectors. The then Editor-in-Chief Gregory Rose commissioned these articles for RECIEL's volumes on *Implementation of International Environmental Law* (vol 2:4) and on *Financial Mechanisms for the Protection of the Environment* (vol 3:2/3). The articles republished here were selected for their continuing relevance to the areas they cover, and to include contributions from those outside of FIELD.

The larger part of this volume is the product of two years of research work undertaken by FIELD with the support of the United Kingdom's Economic and Social Research Council (ESRC), aimed at 'Improving Compliance with International Environmental Regimes for the Protection of the Global Commons'. The FIELD/ESRC project proceeded in three stages. Stage I involved identifying and analyzing existing compliance mechanisms and dispute settlement provisions in international agreements relating to the environment, a review of the latest literature in law and political science on implementation and compliance, and the commissioning of a paper to provide the basis for a common analytical approach to implementation and compliance issues. Stage II required members of FIELD staff to identify areas of their work directly relevant to the issue of implementation and compliance and to produce in-depth research papers using the common analytical approach developed in Stage I. The project culminated with Stage III, a seminar during which FIELD staff and other project participants presented their conclusions and exchanged ideas with policy makers and civil servants involved in the development and implementation of international environmental agreements.

One of the objectives of the project was to facilitate a better understanding not only across different international environmental agreements, but across the two main – and often competing – academic disciplines that address and seek to influence the design of international environmental agreements: law and political science. Ronald Mitchell, an academic and political scientist, leads off Chapter 1 with a theoretical approach to analyzing compliance and effectiveness. The project coordinators and contributors, most of whom are lawyers, sought to follow the approach and the vocabulary offered by the political science community, and to apply these concepts to concrete challenges.

The project revealed that the shared aim of both lawyers and political scientists in analyzing an international environmental regime is to improve the regime's effectiveness, to help ensure that the substantial time and effort devoted to the negotiation of these agreements can be assessed as worthwhile. As this project developed it became, in part, an attempt to bring closer together lawyers and political scientists, as well as academics and practitioners, as they work towards this common aim.

One immediate impediment to this union was a significant difference in vocabulary. In their effort to make sense of the world, political scientists seek to systematize, describe and, in the process, often rename what they observe. International agreements and institutions become 'regimes', treaty breaches are 'non-compliant behaviour', binding commitments become 'primary rules' and negotiators find themselves classified into 'epistemic communities'. Lawyers, also obsessed with words, often resent this nomenclatural intrusion. But by following Mitchell's lead and, if only temporarily, adopting his vocabulary, many of the lawyers contributing to the project found they had benefited from a clearer and more structured approach to the issues they addressed.

There can be little doubt, however, that the language of law and the culture of legal discourse are a central part of international negotiations, and are used by states themselves to describe and predict behaviour. In a world in which it is often difficult to make any unitary assumptions about what motivates state behaviour (this is especially true in the context of multilateral conventions which have implications for a broad scope of interests), the language and culture of international law may be one of the few unifying factors. Among these are the force of precedent, the sanctity of the text, and the respect for sovereignty. As the inevitable cross-fertilization of ideas between political scientists, lawyers, academics and practitioners continues, words and concepts from each discipline will either survive or be abandoned, on the basis of their demonstrated utility.

Lawyers seem intensely interested in what states say (or write), while political scientists claim to be more concerned with what states actually do. For example, Mitchell's approach tends to test the analyst's faith in the text, and in the institutions and procedures that support it. Our attention is directed away from the agreement, to concentrate instead on the exogenous 'real world' factors that influence state behaviour. Compliance with international agreements may in certain circumstances be more attributable to a convergence of international goals and domestic self-interest than to a respect for international law. The legal character of the text, ie whether it is binding, and whether there are mechanisms to enforce its obligations as a matter of law, seems of little relevance.

Sands, operating in the legal tradition, leads us back to the agreements themselves. He suggests that the best response to failures to comply with international law is to strengthen the legal character of obligations, and the institutions, and the procedures that enforce them. His arguments focus on the ability of a complainant, relying on rights derived from an agreement to obtain a judgment from an appropriate tribunal.

But Sands, Cameron, and many of the authors of the chapters that follow, suggest that the distinction between the approaches is largely one of emphasis. Although expressed in different ways, both the political scientist and the lawyer are calling for well-designed rules, clearly expressed, with institutions and procedures that allow non-compliance to be discovered and exposed. Whether the result is described as 'opprobrium' or a 'breach' of the rule of law, both disciplines acknowledge the strengths and the limitations of such a system with regard to its impact on the behaviour of states.

As Mitchell points out, the criticism is often made that while '[p]olitical science research provides a systematic methodology for testing theories of the relationship between treaties and behaviour against the empirical evidence', lawyers too often fail to inquire into the relevant facts. The selection of contributions in this volume seeks to respond to these criticisms by relying on the filter of first hand experience to place empirical data into the context and culture of international negotiations. James Cameron, Philippe Sands, Jacob Werksman and Farhana Yamin each served on government and NGO delegations during the negotiation of the 1992 United Nations Framework Convention on Climate Change; Gregory Rose and James Cameron have participated in meetings of the International Whaling Commission and the Convention on the International Trade in Endangered Species; Philippe Sands has advised governmental and non-governmental clients before national, European and international tribunals; Farhana Yamin worked with UNEP on the drafting of the Lusaka Agreement; and Jacob Werksman was a consultant to UNDP during the negotiations on the restructuring of the Global Environment Facility.

The reader will notice that in addition to the broad scope of the contributions, there is a strong focus on the challenges associated with the design and implementation of the Climate Change Convention. This focus can be explained, in part, by FIELD's long time involvement in the negotiation of the Convention, which began with the Second World Climate Conference in November 1990, and which has continued through the 11 sessions of the Intergovernmental Negotiating Committee which drafted the treaty and prepared for its entry into force. The focus can be further justified by the emergence of the Convention as a regime of major importance with the support of almost 140 Parties. The Convention's potential to influence nearly every aspect of human activity that relies on the production and the consumption of fossil fuel raises unprecedented challenges in relation to implementation and compliance. It is hoped that the issues raised in this volume will help this regime and others to anticipate and respond to these and similar challenges.

A summary of the seminar convened at the close of Stage III of the project will help give the reader a sense of the complexity of the issues raised by the chapters that follow. The summary has been made without reference to the speakers, and the opinions expressed should not be attributed to any of the participants. A list of participants follows on p.xvii.

A Regime and Compliance Theories

The seminar opened with a discussion of the interrelationship of regime theory, compliance theory and international law. A regime has been understood as including norms, standards, principles, rules and decision-making procedures – traditionally the domain of lawyers. Over the last 10 years a link has been made between regime theorists and international lawyers in the field of international relations. Theorists now see the limits of realism in explaining international affairs and lawyers have seen that creating legally binding obligations cannot alone solve problems ahead. A number of participants agreed that compliance procedures within international environmental regimes and agreements will have to assimilate the idea that punitive sanctions alone will not provide solutions. Focus should instead be on an intensified political persuasive process – negotiations through what have become known as non-compliance procedures. Non-compliance does not focus on the intentional or criminal violation of international norms. Other reasons such as lack of resources, ignorance, and the need for capacity building can all lead to non-compliance. Compliance with complex and challenging obligations can require elaborate scientific and administrative programmes on a national level, and big changes have to be recognized as being unlikely to happen quickly.

It was felt unlikely that the development of a general theory of non-compliance for international environmental agreements was possible, necessary or even desirable. There is a set of ideas from past agreements which can be used as a starting point. While domestic law offers some lessons on the effectiveness of strong rules, a trend was noted in US domestic law away from coercive activities, and towards education and incentives.

B Value of Sanctions

Agreements made by consensus are the best hope for ensuring compliance, and it was emphasized that there must be political will behind such agreements in order for them to be effective. The empowerment of a regime with the ability to impose sanctions does reflect, in part, the seriousness with which states take their obligations. Some felt comfortable with the sanctioning function only in a climate in which they would rarely, if ever, be used. Instead of solving the problem, the imposition of sanctions would serve only to exacerbate tensions. One of the political scientists present pointed out that sanctioning can take place on various levels, and international law may not be necessary; there may be other ways to achieve behaviour modification (eg the consumer response to eco-labelling of dolphin-safe tuna). The important issue is to check that the tools used give the desired results; an international strategy must go beyond behaviour modification to the achievement of desired results.

It was generally agreed that if a stick (sanctions) was not to be used, then international law must use a carrot (incentives to change). The issue then becomes how to better define the carrots, and make them as appetizing as possible. A soft approach carries risks, however, as many environmental issues contain a temporal element, an irreversibility, which must be considered in negotiations. A number of lawyers sided with political scientists in arguing that less time should be spent creating formal coercive sanctions and more time on other issues. All sorts of pressures are mobilized by the international community other than sanctions; the cooperative process needs to be built up, and sanctions will not enhance this. Issues such as learning, confidence-building, and capacity-building are all important within compliance regimes. Compliance can often come from threats of exposure, facilitated by verification monitoring procedures.

A non-compliance procedure which reveals blockages in the process is important. In the past, states have been conditioned to accept their own and others' poor performance. When expectations are increased then standards are driven up. What matters is establishing, and following through with, the institutions and procedures necessary to ensure transparency in the process.

A number of participants agreed that financial incentives are not enough on their own. Financial assistance may encourage compliance in developing countries but such mechanisms are ineffective or unworkable as incentives for developed countries even if they are currently the principal cause of the problem.

C Non-Compliance and Primary Rules

Though each regime is situation-specific, some suggested that the process of developing non-compliance procedures could follow a standard rule of development, linked to the level of specificity achieved in the negotiation of the agreements' primary rules. Begin with soft law, then move to creating a framework convention, next create specific obligations (clear targets), and *then* supervise compliance of obligations. Most recognised a danger in jumping straight from a framework to a non-compliance procedure.

D Regional Agreements

Sophisticated control regimes have been more successful at a regional level because of common culture shared by the limited number of parties. On a global level things become more complicated, and mandatory systems are used less frequently.

The Lusaka Agreement was introduced as a regional arrangement amongst several African countries designed to deal with the issue of illegal poaching in Southern Africa. Hopes for its success have been pinned on the involvement in the negotiations of the agreement of those who will be responsible for its implementation. National law officers and local NGOs worked with the CITES Secretariat and government delegates under the auspices of the Zambian Minister for Tourism to draft provisions for a permanent independent task force that will be empowered, among other things, to investigate cross-border incidents of illegal trade.

Another regional approach was used in the Long Range Transboundary Air Pollution (LRTAP) Convention. This framework Convention has, to date, spawned four specific protocols, and Parties have been able to learn from previous efforts. It was pointed out that this means involvement of states *and* the local authorities, and private actors who have to comply with the measures. If all actors affected are not involved at Stage 1 there will be no interest later. Local governmental officials have difficulty accepting the reality of these international agreements. Regional regimes seem to allow Parties to remain in closer contact with real problems and potential solutions; the Parties' interests tend to be less disparate and their concerns more immediate. Often more creative responses can be tried, outside the restrictive legal and political precedents that seem to dominate global negotiations.

E Global Regimes (the Climate Change Convention)

The final topic of discussion dealt with the specific challenges associated with the Climate Change Convention. Two familiar lines of approach for responding to non-compliance were identified as having been raised during the negotiations of the Convention. Though neither have had their effectiveness truly tested in practice, a number of terms or characteristics have come to be associated with them; (1) consultative, amicable, political non-compliance procedure (Article 13: Multilateral Consultative Process), and (2) traditional, coercive bilateral procedure aimed at breaches (Article 14: Settlement of Disputes). Many agreed that the procedures developed for the Montreal Protocol, which has provided a number of important precedents for the climate negotiators, might not at present be applicable to the Climate Change Convention. The Convention is very general and there is a question of whether the commitments it currently contains would warrant such a regime. Those involved in the negotiations also stressed that the Parties deliberately chose *not* to use the term 'non-compliance procedure'. The term 'multilateral consultative process' was used deliberately instead of 'compliance' because monitoring and verification is not built into the Convention. Its drafters did not prejudge the need for any procedure, but instead provided only for the *consideration* of a process.

The vagueness of the Convention was stressed by many. Even if commitments were refined, the implementation of these goals will be, technically, very difficult to monitor. There may be little point in developing a compliance system that looks at State efforts if you cannot effectively monitor them; effective monitoring and verification schemes would play an important role, once the Parties had agreed to adopt specific targets, in building the Parties' confidence in their own and others' efforts at implementation. Parties should seek ways to ensure that implementation could be measured by establishing standards of behaviour.

F Conclusion

Most of the lawyers and political scientists present stressed the importance of ensuring that the Climate Change Secretariat (and perhaps all secretariats of international environmental agreements) be strengthened, and be given a greater role in monitoring Parties' compliance as well as the authority to initiate non-compliance procedures. The example of the European Community was offered to demonstrate that national governments, left to their own devices, will rarely initiate enforcement proceedings; only one case had been brought before the European Court of Justice under Article 170 of the Treaty which entitles States to bring claims against each other, while more than 80 cases had been brought under Article 169 which entitles the Commission to adjudicate compliance with the Treaty. The group's attention was called to two new developments in the area – the NAFTA Environmental Side Agreement and the World Bank Inspection Panel – both of which establish procedures that allow citizens to seek review of compliance with International Law and Policy.

The seminar closed with others remaining unconvinced of the need for formal judicial proceedings to maintain the rule of law. International regimes should instead be allowed to tinker with the rules, as is often done through domestic judicial processes. One participant stressed that compliance procedures should not be entrusted to the International Court of Justice (ICJ). He felt that Parties to an agreement might try to seek an advisory opinion from the ICJ, or another tribunal, if they are just looking for an answer to a specific question; but it is preferable for Parties to reach accommodation on important interpretation issues through multilateral negotiation, not bilateral confrontation.

THE ESRC SEMINAR ON IMPROVING COMPLIANCE; LIST OF PARTICIPANTS

Dr Barbara Adam
School of Social and Administrative Studies
University of Wales Cardiff
62 Park Place, Cardiff CF1 3AS
United Kingdom
fax 44 222 874436

Andronico Adede
Deputy Director
COD/Office of Legal Affairs
Room 3450A, United Nations
New York, NY 10017
USA
fax 1 212 963 1963

Nassrine Azimi
Coordinator, Environmental Training Programme
UNITAR
Palais des Nations, 1211 Geneva 10
Switzerland
fax 41 22 733 1383

Sonja Boehmer-Christiansen
Senior Fellow
Programme on Environmental Policy and Regulation
Science Policy Research Unit
Mantell Building, University of Sussex
Falmer, Brighton BN1 9RF
United Kingdom
fax 44 273 685865

Jo Butler
Climate Change Secretariat
11 Chemin des Anemones
Chateline, CH 1209 Geneva
Switzerland
fax 41 22 979 9034

James Cameron
Foundation for International Environmental Law and Development (FIELD)
46–47 Russell Square
London WC1B 4JP
United Kingdom
fax 44 71 637 7951

Professor Abram Chayes
Harvard University Law School
Cambridge, Massachusetts
USA
fax 617 492 1919

Pedro Motta Pinto Coelho
Chief, Divisao do Meio Ambiente
Ministry of Foreign Affairs, Itamaraty
Brasilia DF, Brazil
fax 55 61 223 7362

Ambassador Raul Estrada-Oyuela
Ministro Plenipotenciario
Director of International Institutions
Ministry of Foreign Affairs
Reconquista 1088/7
Buenos Aires, Argentina
fax 54 1 312 3539

Owen Greene
IIASA
A-2361 Laxenburg, Austria
fax 43 2236 73 147

Gabriela Kutting
Cardiff Law School
PO Box 427
Law Building Museum Avenue
Cardiff CF1 1XD, United Kingdom
fax 44 222 874097

David Lanchbery
Project Director, Environment, VERTIC
Carrara House, 20 Embankment Place
London WC2N 6NN
United Kingdom
fax 44 71 925 0861

Linda Rae Legault
Research Administrator
Centre for the Study of Environmental Change
Lancaster University, Lancaster LA1 4YF
United Kingdom
fax 44 524 846339

Rudi Lewanski
Dipartmento di organizzazione e sistema politico
Universita degli studi di Bologna
Strada Maggiore 45, 40125 Bologna
Italy
fax 39 51 234 036

Ambassador Robert van Lierop
Permanent Representative of Vanuatu to the United Nations
416 Convent Avenue
New York, NY 10031
USA
fax 1 212 926 4131

Nick Mabey
Centre for Economic Forecasting
London Business School
Sussex Place, Regent's Park
London NW1 4SA
United Kingdom
fax 44 71 724 6069

George Peleokrassis
Watson Farley Williams
16 Appold Street
London EC2 1XX
United Kingdom
fax 44 71 814 8141

Professor Jyoti Parikh
Indira Gandhi Institute (IGIDR)
Gen Vaidya Marg
Goregaon (E), Bombay 400 065
India
fax 91 22 8402752/8402026

Professor Michael Redclift
ESRC GEC Programme
Wye College
University of London
Wye, Kent TN25 5AH
fax 233 813 187

Elizabeth Rowbotham
CSERGE
University of East Anglia
Norwich, Norfolk
United Kingdom
NR4 7TJ
fax 44 603 250 588

Dr Julian Salt
Department of Peace Studies
University of Bradford
West Yorkshire BD7 1DP
United Kingdom
fax 44 274 385240

Philippe Sands
FIELD
(Details as above)

Hugo Maria Schally
Permanent Mission of Austria to the United Nations
9–11 Rue de Verembe, Geneva 20
Switzerland CH-1211
fax 41 22 734 45 91

Dr Clare Smith
Centre for Economic Forecasting
London Business School
(Address as above)

Detlef Sprinz, PhD
Global Change and Social Systems
Potsdam Institute for Climate Impact Research
PO Box 60 12 03, 14412 Potsdam
Germany
fax 49 331 288 2600/39 51 234 036

Patrick Szell
Solicitor's Office
Department of the Environment
Room P6/106, 2 Marsham Street
London SW1P 3EB
United Kingdom
fax 44 71 276 6658

Dr Barbara Tomlins
National Foundation for Educational Research in England and Wales
The Mere, Upton Park
Slough, Berkshire SL1 2DQ
United Kingdom

David Victor
IIASA
A-2361 Laxenburg, Austria
fax 43 2236 73 147

Jake Werksman
FIELD
(Details as above)

Dr Chris Williams
Norah Fry Research Centre
3 Priory Road, Bristol BS8 1TX
United Kingdom
fax 44 272 466553

Farhana Yamin
FIELD
(Details as above)

PART 1

Compliance Theory

1 COMPLIANCE THEORY: AN OVERVIEW[1]

Ronald B Mitchell

INTRODUCTION

> Too many people assume, generally without having given any serious thought to its character or its history, that international law is and always has been a sham. Others seem to think that it is a force with inherent strength of its own . . . . Whether the cynic or sciolist is the less helpful is hard to say, but both of them make the same mistake. They both assume that international law is a subject on which anyone can form his opinions intuitively, without taking the trouble, as one has to do with other subjects, to inquire into the relevant facts.[2]

Five decades after Brierly made this insightful comment, empirical understanding of the impact of international law on behaviour, at least by political scientists, remains in its infancy. Very recently, however, political scientists have taken a renewed interest in identifying the links between treaties and international behaviour. This chapter provides an introduction to the current state of debate among political scientists on questions of treaty compliance, with special attention to how theories of international relations clarify the relationship of compliance to treaty provisions.

Do nations and their citizens adjust their behaviour to comply with environmental treaties? Can we improve environmental treaties to make compliance more likely? If so, how? Reliable answers to these and related questions require careful evaluation of past experience with efforts to improve such treaties. Such evaluation, in turn, profits from understanding the factors – treaty-based and otherwise – that previous research suggests are sources of international behaviour. Three different schools of thought – what I shall call pragmatist, realist, and institutionalist – provide different though not uncomplementary answers to these questions.

Policy interest in the relationship of treaties to behaviour stems from a pragmatic concern that treaty goals are not always achieved as completely and effectively as possible. Government diplomats and international lawyers spend considerable resources drafting and redrafting treaties to resolve international environmental problems. Environmental groups commonly support these efforts, pressing governments to negotiate more new treaties and to strengthen and refine existing environmental treaties. Business groups regularly oppose provisions of environmental treaties as excessively costly and burdensome. Policy analysts and pundits regularly highlight the problems with existing treaties and propose new treaty provisions to address them. All these actions reflect a belief that better law can remedy bad behaviour. The actions simultaneously illustrate an assumption that treaties can influence behaviour and the fact that they do not always do so. Indeed, for many lawyers, 'the assumption that legal texts drive changes in behaviour is second nature.'[3] The number and variety of proposals to improve environmental treaties suggest, however, that we still lack a solid understanding of what factors facilitate, and which impede, compliance with a treaty. Partly because these actors' involvement in the treaty process often is in response to concerns particular to a given treaty, they frequently fail to identify sources of failure or success common to other treaties.

Political science research provides a systematic methodology for testing theories of the relationship between treaties and behaviour against the empirical evidence. While these linkages have received only limited attention historically, they are currently the focus of much attention. In international relations, issues of compliance quickly enmesh one in a larger and long-standing debate over why nations behave the way they do. The realist school of thought, developed after World War II, views the pursuit and use of power and the anarchic structure of modern international relations as the primary determinants of international behaviour.[4] Realists consider international law as having little significant impact on nations' international policies. 'Considerations of power rather than of law determine compliance' in all important cases.[5] Law only influences behaviour, if at all, when relatively unimportant, non-security issues are at stake. The conformance of state behaviour to treaty rules reflects spurious correlation rather than true causation: structural factors that lead states to certain actions also lead them to negotiate treaties codifying those actions. Aspiring to explain 'a small number of big and important things,' realists have shown little interest in evaluating treaties as a source of international behaviour.[6] Nevertheless, realism encourages a bias against assuming that treaties cause behaviour to change, and provides an essential set of alternative explanations of why nations might take actions that conform to treaty provisions.

Institutionalists and international lawyers agree with Hans Morgenthau that 'the great majority of the rules of international law are generally observed by all nations.[7] Disagreement arises over whether we can attribute such behaviour to the treaty. International institutions, regimes, organizations, and treaties 'appear to be major determinants of collective behaviour . . . at the international level.'[8] Given this assessment, institutionalists have sought to identify the conditions under which treaties can influence behaviour and the types of norms, principles, rules and processes that do so most effectively.[9] While realists see states as dominating international affairs, non-state actors also play important roles in institutionalist theories as targets of regulation and as participants in the effort to elicit compliance.[10] While institutionalists look for cross-treaty generalities regarding the causal links between behaviour and treaties, they often fail to convert these into the practical advice demanded by policy-makers.

Drawing on each of these three outlooks on compliance – pragmatist, realist, and institutionalist – the following chapter develops a synthetic framework for subsequent analysis of the degree to which treaty rules influence behaviour and the causal mechanisms by which they do so. Pragmatists demand that our framework be sufficiently well-defined that it allow empirical analysis of past experience and prescriptive advice for future policy. Realists suggest a healthy scepticism that forces us to question rigorously whether political and structural factors more readily explain, or at least condition, any correlations between treaty provisions and behaviours. Institutionalists identify the means by which treaties may influence behaviour, demanding empirical validation of which ones prove more or less effective. Together they provide propositions regarding the sources of compliance and non-compliance, the means by which treaty rules can increase compliance, and the exogenous factors that may also increase compliance.

This chapter begins by delineating various possible sources of 'first-order' compliance, for example, the reasons why national and subnational actors often comply even in the absence of any efforts to elicit compliance. The opposing forces that may lead an actor to fail to comply are discussed. An outline is then provided on how these pressures for non-compliance can be countered by the unilateral actions of governments and non-governmental actors. This is followed by developing a framework for thinking about the various factors that institutionalists argue can improve compliance; I identify three components of a treaty compliance system – a primary rule system, a compliance information system, and a non-compliance response system – that form the basis for subsequent empirical analysis.

DEFINITIONS

I define compliance as an actor's behaviour that conforms to a treaty's explicit rules.[11] As a subset of compliance, I distinguish treaty-induced compliance as behaviour that conforms to such rules *because of* the treaty's compliance system. Since this chapter seeks to set forth a pragmatic framework for thinking empirically about the relationship of treaties to compliance, the definitions laid out here should not be taken as either representative of, or contradictory to, broader theoretical conceptions. Rather, I offer these definitions to be empirically useful, rather than theoretically comprehensive. Using these definitions, then, the realist-institutionalist debate becomes a question of whether treaty-induced compliance ever occurs. The term 'compliance' is commonly applied in comparing behaviour to specific treaty provisions, a treaty's broader spirit and principles, implicit international norms, informal agreements, and even tacit agreements.[12] While ambiguous and non-explicit rules, like principles and norms, may well influence behaviour, empirically evaluating these influences usually founders on the inability to get agreement, often among the parties and certainly among analysts, regarding whether a given action constitutes compliance or not. In contrast, restricting study to *explicit* treaty provisions allows replicable evaluation of compliance against clearer and less subjective standards. While recognizing that treaties may induce positive behavioural change that nonetheless fails to achieve an established standard, I exclude from my definition the notion of 'compliance with the spirit of an agreement' which introduces unnecessary subjectivity into empirical analyses.

Evaluating compliance against treaty provisions also makes more sense than speaking of compliance with the treaty as a whole. Parties often comply with some treaty provisions while violating others. Within a nation, different actors – governments, industry and non-governmental organizations (NGOs) – may well be responsible for implementing different treaty provisions.[13] To speak of 'treaty compliance' therefore loses valuable empirical information by aggregating violation of one provision with compliance with another. It also deserves mention that measuring compliance by strict reference to legal standards suggests that compliance is binary, either one complies or one violates; in fact, treaties can induce considerable beneficial behavioural change that either falls short of actual compliance, *strictu sensu*, or goes beyond minimum treaty requirements.[14] Compliance also needs to be kept distinct from the related concept of effectiveness. While I discuss the distinction at length at the end of this chapter, compliance can be thought of as exclusively a question of altering behaviours without consideration of whether these behavioural changes are necessarily sufficient to accomplish the stated or unstated aims of the treaty. In most instances, compliance will correlate sufficiently with effectiveness to make *more* compliance preferable to *less*.

For any given treaty provision, the actual compliance level across countries and across time is likely to reflect compliance due to a combination of sources. Compliance levels will reflect the underlying structure of the environmental problem, the relationship of the treaty's requirements to existing behaviour and future interests, as well as the structure and decision-making processes of the governments, corporations and other organizations involved. A single environmental problem may pose different problems for developed countries and developing countries. For many environmental treaty rules, some actors will unilaterally decide to comply, others will decide to violate, and others' decisions will depend upon whether, and how many, other actors comply. This section focuses on the factors that produce compliance even in the absence of a system for identifying and responding to non-compliance, thereby highlighting both the exogenous forces for compliance and the important role that corporate as well as governmental actions play in international environmental treaties.

SOURCES OF COMPLIANCE

Regulatory treaties' proscriptions of undesirable actions and prescription of desirable ones are often fulfilled. Determining whether the subsequent absence of proscribed actions or presence of prescribed ones is evidence of treaty-induced compliance would be simple if no other potential explanations for these behaviours existed. But, as noted above, the contention is not about whether nations comply, but why. Governments and private actors face a wide variety of incentives and constraints in undertaking any action. Acts that the treaty defines as compliance (or violation) may occur for numerous reasons having little to do with treaty dictates. Enumerating the treaty-independent, first-order sources of compliance and non-compliance provides a valuable means of avoiding falsely characterizing compliance as treaty-induced.

Compliance as independent self-interest

The simplest explanation of why a government or other actor regulated by a treaty undertakes a given behaviour is because they believe it furthers their interest. Nations often negotiate treaties precisely 'for the promotion of their national interests, and to evade legal obligations that might be harmful to them.'[15] As consensual agreements between nations, treaty provisions reflect the relative success of the different signatories in promoting their interests. Obviously, a key determinant of the willingness to comply is the degree of behavioural change the treaty requires. The degree of required change varies across treaties and across rules and actors within a single treaty.

Actors may comply because the treaty rules require no change in behaviour. Through successful negotiation a country may place all the burden for adjustment on other states. 'Leader' states negotiating an environmental accord may already have established and implemented legislation that goes well beyond the requirements to which 'laggard' states will agree. Industries already meeting a specified pollution standard may support treaties that require their foreign counterparts to do the same as a means of improving competitiveness without changing their behaviour. Especially when agreements reflect lowest common denominator policies, many states and companies will find themselves already in compliance. Some states may simply not be engaged, or only minimally engaged, in the activity regulated by the treaty, as is the case with Switzerland's membership in the oil pollution and whaling regimes.

Compliance is not surprising when agreements proscribe undesirable actions that no one currently has incentives to undertake, in hopes of restraining future economic, political or technological pressures for such actions. As in the Antarctic Treaty's constraints on mining, such agreements codify existing behaviours to 'protect against changes in preferences'.[16] Compliance to date has been perfect because the availability of lower-cost sources elsewhere has meant that incentives to mine in Antarctica remain low.[17]

States can also facilitate their own compliance by negotiating vague and ambiguous rules. Ambiguity may reflect agreements reached despite sincere differences about a specific rules content – 'papering over' – or efforts to accrue environmental praise by agreeing to terms that appear to require behavioural change, but that prove sufficiently vague to allow business as usual. The absence of an international court to interpret such ambiguities authoritatively 'naturally' leads states to interpret treaty rules so they can behave as their interests dictate while claiming their behaviour is in compliance.[18] While excessively self-serving interpretations may well elicit international and domestic criticism, ambiguous treaty language makes charges of outright violation difficult.

When treaties require new behaviours, they may only require signatories to take actions they already know they want to take. Unilateral compliance may be a preferred option. In some such case, the state would have behaved as it did in any event, compliance being strictly coincidental. In others, the agreement provides international legitimacy which increases domestic political support enough to enable the government to implement a desired but otherwise unattainable policy. For example, a climate change agreement may provide some governments with the impetus necessary to adopt energy taxes. Treaties may also reflect 'suasion' games where one or more powerful states benefit from unilateral compliance but benefit more if others also comply.[19] While it will seek to get others to comply, such a state will comply whether or not those strategies succeed. DuPont's phase-out of CFCs and Conoco's installation of double-hull tankers before internationally required suggests these companies decided to comply independently of other companies' decisions, though they preferred that others comply.

The preceding sources of compliance show how actors may comply out of self-interest even if they define that interest myopically and independently of others' actions.[20] However, the calculus leading a state to comply may involve more expanded notions of independent self-interest than realist scholars would concede. Institutionalists point to states adopting broader and longer-term views of self-interest, including joint gains and empathy, for example, that lead them to comply in a wider range of situations than realism would predict.[21] States and corporations may fear the unknown and unintended side-effects of their current non-compliance on the future of the treaty and on a range of other relationships.[22] They may fear adverse public opinion, domestically or internationally. Parties may comply with rules viewed as fair and legitimate even if costly at times.[23] Even when dominant, powerful (hegemonic) states coerce weaker states to accept a treaty, legitimate social purposes and changes in perceived self-interest may cause nations to continue complying past the point that immediate self-interest can explain.[24] These conceptions of self-interest veer away from strictly independent decision-making: rather than making worst case assumptions that no others will comply, the decision-maker forecasts compliance by others based on past experience to calculate the expected benefits of their own compliance.

Even if a treaty rule requires change, bureaucratic procedures, group think, and bounded rationality may make the choice of compliance – once initiated – hard to revisit.[25] Governments and corporations deal with some compliance problems through standard operating procedures and habits, thereby foregoing potentially beneficial opportunities to violate in order to reduce overall decision-making costs, even in issues involving national security.[26] Even realists admit that habit sometimes drives states to actions contrary to immediate self-interest because states do not constantly reassess their interests and power.[27] Businesses promulgate and train personnel in corporate procedures that reflect domestic and international laws, even in cases where the likelihood of opportunistic violations being detected is minuscule. International rules allow actors to simplify or reduce the number of decisions they must make in a complex environment.[28]

While compliance is calculated independently of other actors' behaviours, it is not a static decision. Over time, economic and technological changes can 'cause national governments to change their minds about which rules or norms of behaviour should be reinforced and observed and which should be disregarded and changed.'[29] Reductions in the price of alternatives to chlorofluorocarbons (CFCs) have increased the likelihood that the Montreal Protocol's phase-out deadlines will be met.[30] Oil price shocks in the 1970s explain some of the increase in compliance with oil pollution treaty rules in effect at the time. Economic recession will reduce environmental compliance if countries redirect resources from environmental to developmental goals, but could increase compliance if it reduces the economic activities creating the environmental externalities. Whether economic or technological shifts make compliance more or less attractive depends on the type of shift and government responses to it.[31]

Powerful non-state actors, including multinational corporations, non-governmental environmental groups and scientists, often influence international politics directly and by helping to define state interests.[32] New scientific knowledge or greater environmental activism can cause increases in the perceived costs of an environmental externality and lead to greater compliance.[33] Elections or larger social or political factors often change the bargaining positions of domestic bureaucratic and political groups, altering how a state assesses its interests in compliance. Domestic environmental groups may become increasingly powerful and concerned; treaties provide them with 'a stronger case for constraint than would be possible in the absence of such obligations'.[34] Such developments not only increase the domestic costs of violation but often constrain even efforts at retaliatory non-compliance.[35] International agreements generate inertia which supports compliance once it has begun.[36] Such changes may increase overall compliance if they reflect transnational social shifts toward greater environmental concern.

At any given time, however, for those governments or non-state actors basing compliance decisions on self-interests independently defined, compliance proves robust and concerns over non-compliance are minimal. Indeed, the behaviour of these actors is not treaty-induced compliance. For these actors, treaty rules have been brought in line with existing or intended future behaviours, and not vice versa. When most parties to a treaty have such interests, the rule will exhibit high compliance even absent positive inducements or negative sanctions. Power plays little role in determining whether a state complies or not. In situations like those just delineated, we can expect considerable compliance. Efforts to manipulate interests are unnecessary because treaty rules reflect pre-existing interests, the rules require little change in current behaviour patterns, or the actors fail to recalculate their interests constantly. In these cases, compliance is not caused by the treaty but merely coincides with it.

Compliance as interdependent self-interest

Compliance can arise from interactive as well as independent decision-making.[37] States and corporations can not only include broader and longer-term concerns in their calculus of self-interest, but also can include their expectations regarding the impact their own compliance will have on others. Coordination and collaboration game models help clarify the operation of such interdependent conceptions of self-interest.

In coordination games, each actor prefers compliance so long as enough other actors comply. While 'enough' varies from actor to actor, each assesses whether to comply based on the actions, or expected actions, of others. Realists see such complementarity of interests in compliance as explaining why most treaties require so little enforcement.[38] Like Schelling's 'meeting' games, treaties can avert dilemmas of common aversion by coordinating action: the rule allows expectations to converge on an equilibrium behaviour that, once achieved, no one has incentives to violate.[39] The distribution of the benefits of compliance depend on the form of coordination, but once others choose to comply, the dominant strategy for all lies in complying.[40]

Coordination games do not face the 'sanctioning problem' that plagues collaboration problems.[41] First, actors are self-deterred because while my non-compliance hurts others, it hurts me enough to deter me. Second, since non-compliance is always a public effort 'to force the other actor into a different equilibrium outcome', detection problems do not arise.[42] Third, since other actors' most effective retaliation for non-compliance is continuing to comply, the desire to sanction reinforces rather than undermines the incentives to comply. For example, once nations agree on an allocation of the limited number of possible satellite orbits, no country has incentives to destroy its own satellite by placing it in the same orbit as another nations, and if it were to do so, it could not do it clandestinely.[43] The distribution of power among nations determines which behavioural equilibrium nations agree to, with the strong dictating to the weak, but not in determining whether the equilibrium is maintained. Treaties will tend to codify the equilibriums that provide benefits to the strong, but they will not face the subsequent task of inducing compliance from weak states.

Situations involving public goods can exhibit similar properties for some actors involved. If enough actors recognize that they can be better off collaborating to produce a public good and can trust each other enough to 'jump' to this joint outcome, a subset of all actors can negotiate and comply with an agreement even though other nations continue to violate.[44] Actors willing to tolerate non-compliance by others may achieve joint gains, even though those gains are less than they would be if all actors complied. Actors who fail to consider how their decision to comply encourages others to comply see the costs of compliance outweighing the benefits. Actors who recognize that their decision to comply may convince enough others to comply to make the benefits outweigh the costs, will attempt to assure others of their good faith. Common to both these scenarios is the fact that, given what one actor can dependably expect others to do, that actor's best strategy is to comply.

Unfortunately, environmental problems more often resemble collaboration games in which joint compliance is preferred to joint violation but in which each actor's dominant strategy is to violate, even if others comply. The literature on prisoners dilemma, multi-person prisoners dilemma, and on free-riding in such situations is extensive.[45]

Realists point out that such conditionality of benefits on compliance by others coupled with the fear and uncertainty underlying international relations make collaboration essentially impossible. For example, as desirable as it collectively may be to reduce international industrial pollution, the anarchic international arena produces fears of free-riding that lead states to define interests on unilateral, unconditional bases, thereby preventing agreement or compliance.[46] Despite the benefits of mutual compliance, the absence of international enforcement and risks of relative gains by others leads all parties to violate.[47]

Under such circumstances, compliance requires enforcement. International collaboration problems, in contrast to coordination problems, 'must specify strict patterns of behaviour and insure that no one cheats'.[48] Unfortunately, if anything best characterizes the weakness of international law, it is the lack of an effective central enforcement system. Realists, like Morgenthau, note that 'there can be no more primitive and no weaker system of law enforcement'.[49] The institutionalists recognize that coordination games often face significant 'sanctioning problems', where the lack of ability and incentives to detect and respond to violation in turn hinder achievement of compliance. Enforcement itself poses a collective action problem in which even states that comply may not monitor or enforce against others.[50]

Compliance in collaboration problems can arise from enforcement by a dominant or hegemonic state with system-wide concerns that sees what may be a collaboration problem for others as a suasion game. The dominant state manages the problem because it is capable of, and perceives sufficient benefits from, complying itself and/or enforcing compliance by others. Weak states are forced to comply with these 'imposed orders' by 'coercion, cooptation, and the manipulation of incentives'.[51] The economic and technological changes mentioned earlier can alter compliance levels by increasing a dominant state's power for, and interest in, enforcing such treaties. Growth in international economic interdependence will increase a dominant state's desire and capacity to exercise control of the international system.[52] Improved satellite surveillance could aid a dominant state's ability to monitor activities, impose sanctions more swiftly, and thereby increase compliance. Such changes may correlate with treaty amendments if they also lead to compliance system changes, such as less ambiguous wording. In such cases, however, tighter wording is simply another indicator of the changed interests that caused improved compliance, rather than being an independent cause of improved compliance.

Fears of free-riding can also be overcome if states view the benefits they derive in other existing and future international agreements as conditional upon a record of compliance.[53] Such caution is fostered when states detect violations and either reciprocate with their own violation or 'discount the value of agreements on the basis of past compliance'.[54] Even if compliance in a given instance may be costly when narrowly construed, the costs in other areas and on one's reputation can persuade a state to comply. Compliance under such conditions is possible but will be more fragile and more difficult to establish than when actors have independent interests in compliance.

Since such cooperation depends on some degree of international trust, decreases in underlying rivalries and competition, such as the end of the Cold War, will likely increase compliance levels.[55] As with changes in power, such a change may produce changes to treaty rules as well as compliance levels, leading to spurious correlations. However, the regime itself can increase trust by improving knowledge and reducing misperceptions of other states.[56] Over time, such trust, reputations, rule legitimacy, and habitual practice grow and can reinforce incentives for compliance.

SOURCES OF NON-COMPLIANCE

Having noted several reasons for compliance, we can now turn to the reasons for non-compliance. Especially in collaboration situations, unless some parties encourage compliance or discourage violation, other parties may find it preferable to violate a given treaty rule. Other factors may also lead to non-compliance. To understand how actors elicit compliance in the face of such preferences, the various sources of non-compliance need to be delineated.

Non-compliance as a preference

An actor may prefer non-compliance simply because the benefits of compliance – absent coercive efforts, simply do not outweigh its costs. This situation may arise for several reasons. Some actors may consciously sign treaties to garner the political benefits of membership, never intending to comply.[57] Others may feel strong domestic and international pressures to sign an agreement regardless of the compliance costs. For example, the 178 countries in attendance at the 1992 United Nations Conference on Environment and Development (UNCED) faced strong pressures to sign climate change and biodiversity agreements; few countries refused to sign, based on claims that compliance did not serve their interests. Other states may view most but not all rules in a treaty as in their interests, leading them to sign with the intention of complying with most but not all rules.

Assumptions that because states sign they will comply ignore the fact that a state's material interests may include signature but not compliance. At least three scenarios can account for this. First, a state may be a classic free-rider, valuing the benefits of compliance by others, but seeking to avoid the costs of its own compliance. Second, a state may value compliance by itself and by others and even deem that the benefits of compliance outweigh the costs, but may nonetheless prefer to devote the compliance-related resources to more pressing social problems. Third, a state may view compliance as having no real benefits. A state may not value actions that they admit would improve the environment. It is tempting to view environmental problems as global commons or 'prisoner's dilemma' problems with the implicit assumption that all actors prefer mutual compliance to mutual violation. Yet, this ignores basic disagreements over man's relationship to the environment. The Iraqis' intentional dumping of oil during the Gulf War, the controversy over commercial whaling, and the general debate over environment versus development reflect such disagreements.

Even when total social costs make compliance a preferred strategy, the incidence of those costs usually means that those being asked to comply will have continuing incentives to violate. Environmental treaties frequently seek to remedy industrial pollution externalities; by definition, therefore, compliance involves companies incurring costs that they had previously imposed on other social groups. Compliance with the Long-Range Transboundary Air Pollution Convention's sulphur dioxide emission restrictions required private power plants to install scrubbers and otherwise increase costs so that citizens in other countries could enjoy a cleaner environment.[58] The resources that targeted industries use to oppose international regulatory efforts attest to the costs they view as involved in compliance. Whether dealing with reluctant nations or reluctant industries within a nation, benefits from compliance arise only when others link compliance to other issues through positive or negative inducements.

Non-compliance due to incapacity

Even actors who perceive compliance as beneficial may fail to comply for lack of the necessary resources. In economic terms, the willingness to pay need not equate to an ability to pay. Violation can be due to financial, administrative or technological incapacities, rather than any unwillingness to comply.[59]

While developing country governments may not value environmental improvement because of the lack of domestic constituencies or because of more pressing concerns, even those that do may simply not have sufficient resources to meet the costs of compliance. Growing attention to this source of non-compliance has led nations to establish mechanisms to finance compliance in both the London Amendments to the Montreal Protocol and the Framework Convention on Climate Change.[60]

Environmental non-compliance also occurs because of a lack of administrative capacity.[61] Even if we assume that governmental decisions to comply with treaty rules will bring government actions into compliance, that assumption comes into serious question when compliance requires a government to alter successfully the actions of myriad sub-national actors. This two-level quality of environmental treaty compliance can lead to non-compliance when a government lacks informational or regulatory infrastructures adequate for eliciting compliance. Even using its best efforts, the Brazilian government may fail to communicate successfully restrictions on tree clearing to the peasant farmers responsible, leading to non-compliance. Even if the informational infrastructure exists, an effective regulatory infrastructure that can induce behavioural change by these actors may be absent. Tankers registered in Liberia and Panama rarely enter those countries' ports, making inspections for compliance with international marine pollution standards difficult.

Negotiators may even establish standards that current technologies are unable to meet. Hopes that regulatory necessities will lead to technological inventions do not always prove well-founded, leaving companies with no, or only prohibitively expensive, means of complying. While these problems often boil down to variants of financial incapacity problems, cultural and social contexts may make compliance significantly more difficult to elicit from the companies and citizens of one country than another.[62]

Non-compliance due to inadvertence

Finally, states may take actions sincerely intended and expected to achieve compliance but nonetheless fail to meet treaty standards. Environmental rules establishing aggregate national targets for pollution reduction by specified deadlines may pose particular problems in this regard.[63] For example, a carbon tax established in good faith at a level deemed sufficient to achieve a 20 per cent reduction in carbon dioxide emissions by a specified date might reduce emissions by only 15 per cent by that deadline.[64] This problem is not restricted to developing states; inherent uncertainty in the impacts of most policy strategies mean even developed states efforts to alter their citizens' and companies' behaviours may fail to achieve their intended results.[65] And programmes that bring one country into compliance may fail to have the same results elsewhere. Whether due to misguided policy or to the inherent uncertainties in the outcomes of certain policies, the two-level nature of environmental compliance may make compliance due to inadvertence especially common.

ELICITING COMPLIANCE IN THE FACE OF PRESSURES FOR NON-COMPLIANCE

To this point, the discussion has largely been restricted to first-order sources of compliance and non-compliance, ie, those incentives that governments and private actors have to comply with treaty rules prior to efforts by other actors to directly influence their choices. Whether their predisposition to non-compliance actually leads a government or company to violate depends on how willing and able other actors are to manipulate incentives to make compliance both possible and preferable. Such manipulation can involve positive inducements or negative sanctions that take the treaty framework as given or they can involve refining various components of the treaty compliance system itself.

Positive inducements

Giving positive rewards for compliance provides one means of increasing incentives for compliance. To the extent that non-compliance is due to inadvertence or incapacity, other actors can respond in two ways to those who appear likely to, or already have, failed to comply with a treaty rule. Efforts at education clarify treaty requirements and identify strategies for compliance. Educational efforts can involve diplomatic discussions between government officials or can directly target the private actors responsible for the environmental problem. Industry groups in one country often conduct seminars to educate their own personnel as well as those of companies in other countries as new regulations are promulgated. Such efforts help avoid non-compliance due to lack of knowledge or inadvertence. Such seminars can demonstrate and disseminate information on cheap alternative means of complying that help increase the ranks of compliers. Private corporations seeking to increase sales may seek out and promote compliant technologies, independent of any governmental or inter-governmental efforts. As environmental concerns increasingly influence overseas development aid, policy advisers are helping devise programmes to address or avoid the administrative incapacity problems that plague many developing nations.

Beyond educational efforts, financial transfers can elicit greater compliance when non-compliance arises from any of the factors mentioned above. In essence, one actor pays for another's compliance. Inter-governmental side-payments outside of formal treaty procedures for environmental treaty compliance have been infrequent to date. However, NGOs have paid debts for, and pharmaceutical companies have negotiated deals with, developing countries to create environmental preserves. Finland has paid the USSR to clean up a nickel smelting plant.[66]

The fact that these actions have not been linked with specific environmental treaty provisions suggests two problems. First, governments prove reluctant to pay not only their own compliance costs, but those of other governments who are obligated under the treaty to comply in any event. Second, such efforts, whether taken within or outside the treaty context, face the 'mundane problem of funding'.[67] Financing proves difficult to organize because it poses collective action problems for the fund providers.[68]

Negative sanctions

The more traditional remedy for non-compliance has involved deterrence through the threat or use of sanctions. To be effective these sanctions must be both credible and potent. Actors hoping to encourage compliance must convince reluctant actors that the likelihood that a violation will be detected and stiffly sanctioned make the expected costs of violation exceed those of compliance.

Governments, corporations, NGOs, and general publics can all impose sanctions. Actors targeted for sanctions can similarly include governments, corporations or even individuals.[69] Social opprobrium and world public opinion can pressure such actors to comply through several channels.[70] Diplomats are 'called to account by other participants in the international system, either through bilateral diplomacy or in international forums'.[71] NGOs and the publics they mobilize can prompt letter-writing campaigns, consumer boycotts of imports and tourism, corporate cancellation of contracts, and government trade restrictions, as evident in the response to Norway's resumption of commercial whaling.[72] Whether these actions are adequate to force a reluctant business or government to comply, however, is open to interpretation. Realists contend that public opinion exerts no 'restraining influence upon the foreign policies of national governments'; institutionalists hold it 'can have unexpectedly powerful results . . . help[ing] to bring about far-reaching [human rights] changes in powerful and entrenched regimes'.[73]

Realists see collective goods as supplied when 'the interest of pre-eminent powers in the consumption of collective goods is strong enough to cause them to undertake the provision of those goods without being properly paid'.[74] A dominant state must both establish and enforce treaties resolving collective action problems.[75] Depending on its own commitment to the issue, which may vary over time, the dominant state may choose to

(1) tolerate violations,
(2) expend resources to force others to comply, or
(3) expend resources to force others to both comply with and enforce the treaty.

In such cases, weaker states comply to the extent that stronger states actually, or credibly threaten to, force compliance via political and economic sanctions for violation.[76] Compliance does not require explicit enforcement: the reputation for power, or 'prestige', of stronger states leads weaker states to comply with rules that conflict with short-term self-interest even absent explicit enforcement.[77] Powerful states, and they alone, use sanctions to enforce those international rules that suit their immediate interests.[78] In essence, states do not enforce international law but command obedience from weaker states.[79]

Compliance under such a model of hegemonic enforcement will tend to decline as powerful states lose their power monopoly and other states with different interests gain power.[80] Also, the costs of maintaining international agreements tends 'to rise faster than the financial capacity of the dominant power to support its position'.[81] Thus, enforcement demands increase at the same time that the power to enforce decreases.[82] Since states violate treaty commitments whenever they have the interest and power to do so, decreased hegemony increases non-compliance as weaker states gain relative power.

An alternative view of the influence of hegemonic power on compliance levels suggests that as extreme power asymmetries decrease compliance increases because no actor possesses sufficient power 'to ignore the dictates of the resultant institutions with impunity'.[83] Likewise, weaker states can no longer expect a public good to be provided without their contribution, and therefore comply. While predicting different effects of reduced asymmetries of power on compliance, both theories suggest that changes in power distribution will produce changes in compliance.

Reciprocity has been the dominant factor institutionalists have used to explain the 'potential anomaly' of why governments comply 'with rules that conflict with their myopic self-interest'.[84] In collaboration problems, each party has immediate and continuing incentives to violate and few incentives to enforce the rules against others. Rather than general concerns over reputation, discussed above, specific reciprocity – promising to comply if others comply and threatening to violate if others violate – provides an enforcement strategy. If actors have long-term views, regular and continued interactions, and rapid and reliable information about the actions of others, reciprocity strategies can overcome the non-compliant free-rider problem.[85] For example, reciprocity strategies have been used to explain compliance with arms control treaties.[86]

While working well bilaterally, reciprocity 'may not prove compelling in a multilateral situation'.[87] The initial violation may not impose sufficient costs on any single actor to provide incentives for retaliation. At the same time, those retaliatory violations that do occur can not be targeted directly at the initial violator. They impose costs on compliers and violators alike, leading the retaliator to 'suffer the opprobrium' of compliant actors, while failing to impose sufficient costs on the initial violator to induce compliance.[88] These disincentives to retaliation reduce the credibility essential to the strategy, and can lead to escalatory violations that undermine compliance by all parties.[89]

Actors can skirt the problems inherent in retaliatory non-compliance through sanctions that link environmental compliance to other issues. In some instances, the gains of mutual compliance are sufficiently large that some actors undertake enforcement. Governments can use a wide range of unilateral or coordinated efforts to impose trade or other economic sanctions. Such sanctions, whether undertaken by states or other actors, allow costs to be targeted at the initial non-complier and avoid the risks outlined above of retaliatory non-compliance. NGOs and publics often prove more willing than governments to sanction violations by corporations or other governments. Governments can avoid retaliation by targeting sanctions against violating nationals or corporations of other countries; governments that might defend their own wrongful actions often care less about defending those of their nationals. This allows governments to induce compliance by foreign nationals without harming intergovernmental relationships on other issues by pressuring the other government directly.

In short, even taking the treaty context as given, many different actors can take a wide array of actions to induce actors to comply despite their pre-disposition to violate.

Compliance system design[90]

Given the realist scepticism regarding the impact of treaties on behaviour, we must rely on institutionalists and pragmatists to identify principles for designing a treaty compliance system that will elicit high compliance. The institutionalists' disagreement with realists is not that other factors do not cause changes in compliance. Rather, they make the narrower claim that treaty rule changes also can increase compliance. While regimes and treaty rules reflect power and interests, they can have an independent effect on compliance. Power and interests sometimes provide inadequate explanations of observed correlations between international rules and actors' behaviour.[91] International behaviour can reflect not only compliance, but treaty-induced compliance. However, whether a particular treaty actually induces compliance depends on how its compliance system is designed. Critical to this argument is the notion that the structure of international power and interests underdetermines a treaty's compliance system; it assumes that at a given point in time, nations could have agreed to more than one compliance system design.

A 'compliance system' is that subset of the treaty's rules and procedures that influence the compliance level of a given rule.[92] Building on this concept, three subsystems of any compliance system can be distinguished: a primary rule system, a compliance information system, and a non-compliance response system. If variance in compliance exists across treaties that can not be explained by factors exogenous to the treaty regimes, these three systems provide a framework for identifying the source of such variance in inducing compliance.

The primary rule system consists of the actors, rules and processes related to the behaviour that is the substantive target of the regime. By its choice of who gets regulated and how, the primary rule system determines the degree and sources of pressures and incentives for compliance and violation. The compliance information system consists of the actors, rules and processes that collect, analyze and disseminate information regarding the instances of, and parties responsible for, violations and compliance. The self-reporting, independent monitoring, data analysis, and publishing activities that comprise the compliance information system determine the amount, quality, and uses made of data on compliance and enforcement. The non-compliance response system consists of the actors, rules, and processes governing the formal and informal responses undertaken to induce those identified as in non-compliance to comply. The non-compliance response system determines the type, likelihood, magnitude, and appropriateness of responses to non-compliance.

An environmental treaty's primary rule system generally attempts to alter the actions of private, sub-national actors through the implementation activities of national governments. In contrast to arms control or human rights treaties, environmentally activist governments must elicit behavioural change by the primary target of regulation, either directly or by prompting the responsible national governments to implement and enforce treaty terms. Frequently, the rules and procedures comprising all three components of the compliance system can address either governmental, non-governmental, or sub-national level entities.

What factors endogenous to the treaty could increase compliance? What treaty compliance system changes would make compliance more likely for a given set of actors when addressing a given environmental problem? What attributes of treaty rules and processes should we look for as the basis of its impact? Compliance system design involves two distinct elements. First, the selection of the primary rules determines how many actors are predisposed towards compliance and how many towards non-compliance. Whether made consciously or not, choices of how the treaty defines compliance and who must change their behaviour becomes a major determinant of compliance. It sets the bounds on how many actors will comply voluntarily and the efforts needed to get others to comply. Second, having selected certain primary rules, the system must maximize the likelihood that actors will respond to non-compliance through means that redress the source of non-compliance. This element of design involves attempting to achieve the highest compliance possible by improving the compliance information and non-compliance response systems, to make the detection of, and response to, non-compliance more likely, credible, and potent.

Primary rule system

The preceding discussion has highlighted how the incentives of actors to comply or violate depend critically on the structure of the problem the treaty is attempting to solve. Collaboration problems fascinate analysts precisely because their resolution requires jointly desirable compliance that proves hard to generate internationally.[93] Different approaches to such resolution greatly influence who bears what costs under what conditions and the degree to which benefits depend on actions by other actors. Given this, 'choices of strategies and variations in institutions are particularly important, and the scope for the exercise of intelligence is considerable'.[94]

Some analysts have explored how institutions can alter payoff structures, ie, the benefits and costs that actors incur in each of the potential outcomes of the strategic game. Yet, a less developed implication is how nations can choose between *different solutions* to the *same problem* that have different payoff structures. Payoff structures may vary by solution as well as by problem. Even if international institutions prove too weak to alter payoff structures, they may be able to increase compliance by selecting from an array of possible solutions those that increase the likelihood of compliance.[95] For a given problem, several alternative solutions may exist. Even if, under conditions of perfect compliance, these solutions provided equal environmental benefits, they might exhibit different likelihoods of compliance because they regulate different actors. What kind of activity is being regulated? How many actors with what interests must change their behaviour? How large and costly a change is involved? What exogenous incentives to comply do these actors have? By answering these questions, through the process of selecting the point for regulatory intervention and defining the standards for compliance, negotiators may take a large step towards determining the degree of treaty compliance. Claims that inducing compliance with the Framework Convention on Climate Change will be harder than with the Montreal Protocol rest on the notion that more people and industries must make much bigger behavioural changes in the former case. Regional agreements seek to increase cooperation by increasing the frequency of interaction between actors. Agreements that put greater burdens on developed countries may generate more compliance because those countries have the incentives and resources to do so. In short, the selection of primary rules may prove the most powerful lever international policy-makers have over the level of compliance elicited.

One key feature of the selection of a regulated activity involves its transparency. Some activities are highly visible and involve transactions between actors while others are autonomous acts conducted largely out of view. While transparency's main contribution to compliance comes through making detection of violations easier, as discussed below, it also facilitates compliance by reassuring each actor about others' behaviour. Actors predisposed to comply but concerned about non-compliance by others will violate under conditions of uncertainty. The ranks of 'nice' actors – those actors who will comply initially with a treaty rule before having information about the actions of others[96] – can be swelled by reducing this uncertainty. By regulating more transparent actions, treaties assure actors that others' non-compliance will be immediately visible and thus permit them to protect their interests accordingly. Reducing such fears that produce initial non-compliance allows compliance to develop.

Besides strategic choices of who and what to regulate, primary rules can increase compliance through greater specificity.[97] Chayes urges 'more concrete and quantitative performance criteria as they become politically and empirically validated'.[98] Increasing specificity increases compliance in at least two ways. First, for actors disposed to comply, specific rules make compliance easier by reducing the uncertainty about what they need to do to comply.[99] Specific rules also reassure actors that others will not dispute the compliance of a given act. The actor can therefore act without fear of facing sanctions for non-compliance despite a good faith effort to comply. Second, for actors predisposed to non-compliance, precise treaty language removes the excuse of inadvertence and misinterpretation from actors when they must account for non-compliance.[100] This will not change the actions of any actor facing significant compliance costs but may alter the choices of actors at the margin of compliance.

The notion that greater specificity improves compliance assumes that specificity can be increased without any change in the willingness to agree among the parties. At any given point in time, it may prove impossible to agree on more precise language. However, a rule's current level of precision need not always reflect the maximum possible level of precision for the existing level of common interest. Even within a context of nations seeking to avoid major constraints on their behaviour, the range of negotiable outcomes may include some rules that are less vague than others, making the choices between rules important to subsequent compliance levels.

Compliance information system

The major goal of any treaty's compliance information system is to maximize transparency. Transparency refers to both the amount and quality of the information collected on compliance or non-compliance by the regulated actors as well as the degree of analysis and dissemination. Increasing transparency is seen as an essential component in any prescription to increase compliance.[101] Transparency is as essential to hegemonic states enforcing compliance and to states resolving coordination problems as to the reciprocity needed to elicit compliance in collaboration problems.[102] To make the threat of a retaliatory violation – or linkage via sanctions or inducements – credible, the regulated actors must know that their choices will not go unnoticed.

If power and interests leave more than one rule in the zone of possible agreement, then negotiators' choices between rules will effect how easy verification is.[103] The choice of primary rules plays a crucial role since the choice about what acts to regulate implicitly includes a choice about how transparent compliance and non-compliance will be. The Montreal Protocol regulated CFC production because it was far easier to monitor a very few producers than thousands of consumers.[104] While numerous activities contribute to climate change, technological capabilities will make verification of point-source polluters, like power plants, far easier than areal polluters, such as logging or rice farming. Previously regulated activities may already have data collection and dissemination systems on which a treaty can piggyback, much as the LRTAP Convention has used economic fossil-fuel usage data to estimate emissions.[105]

Treaties usually provide for self-reporting by national governments, and the wide variance in levels of self-reporting suggests that some reporting systems work better than others.[106] Transparency can be increased by making rewards for compliance conditional on supplying such reports or allowing inspections. The human rights experience suggested to drafters of Agenda 21 that NGOs and industry had the ability and incentives to provide valuable compliance information.[107] On-site monitoring has been authorized in an international convention on wetlands as well as in nuclear weapons treaties.[108] Such measures skirt the self-incrimination problems that deter self-reporting and improve both the quantity and quality of data available. Treaty rules and procedures can also enhance information flow between parties, increase resources dedicated to monitoring, and finance the development of improved verification technologies.[109]

For the collected data on behaviour to lead to an appropriate response, treaty staff, governments or NGOs must analyze and interpret the data to identify both the cases and sources of non-compliance. Often this may require a forum to inquire further into actions taken and the reasons behind them.[110] By increasing both the actors and means authorized to collect, analyze and disseminate information, a treaty can increase the likelihood that those tasks occur. By improving the ability for, and likelihood of, detecting violations, transparency fosters all parties' abilities to invoke reciprocity, sanctioning, and inducement strategies.[111]

Non-compliance response system

If the treaty's compliance information system succeeds at developing information about non-compliance and non-compliers, successful alteration of their behaviour also requires some response. While responsive actions available to actors were discussed above, the following sections discuss three strategies by which treaties can increase the likelihood that such responses occur and are effective.

Facilitating compliance

Treaty organizations and secretariats can increase the likelihood and effectiveness of the positive inducements that states can take unilaterally. They can provide mechanisms for burden-sharing for financing, making it feasible to fund projects that are larger than a single country ordinarily would fund. These arrangements also establish a set of commitments and correlated expectations regarding contributions from various states to such a fund. While the International Monetary Fund (IMF) and World Bank have funding problems, nations in general are willing to make funds available for project funding. International organizations may also be able to fund projects that would be too controversial for individual donor countries to fund. Whether such cooperative funding ventures will succeed in environmental affairs remains to be seen, as the Montreal Protocol and the Framework Convention on Climate Change are the first to include significant financial transfer mechanisms.

Facilitating compliance may also involve international education efforts targeted at clarifying rules and the means to compliance. For example, Sweden and the International Maritime Organization created the World Maritime University to provide courses on marine pollution requirements and how to comply with them. Technology transfers also help. The Montreal Protocol requires technology assistance to address non-compliance due to technical incapacity. The convention's highlighting of the fact that compliance by developing states depends upon these financial and technology transfers may help press developed states to fulfil these commitments.[112] Financing and technology transfers provide useful levers to induce compliance when sanctions may be politically difficult to impose, as among allies. Inducements themselves ease the non-compliance detection problem since a government that might ignore a free-standing reporting requirement might well prove more forthcoming if providing the information opened up new funding sources.

These inducements can influence actors who want, but are unable, to comply as well as providing incentives for countries to re-examine the costs of, and priority given to, compliance. Even states planning to violate may reconsider if the financial transfers are large enough. Inducements have their own problems, however: joint funding itself has to overcome inherent free-rider problems. Also, inducements cost more than sanctions. For the country seeking to motivate compliance, the promise of inducements is costly if they succeed while the threat of sanctions is costly only if they fail.[113] Inducements are also vulnerable to problems of moral hazard, in which those who would otherwise comply strategically misrepresent that fact to convince others to pay their compliance costs. While international funding, technology, and education programmes may prove difficult to enact and small in magnitude, they may nonetheless make compliance more likely.

Sanctioning violations

Proponents of sanctions contend that 'compliance can be obtained efficiently by making violation unattractive rather than by altering the costs or benefits of compliance'.[114] While sanction strategies face major constraints on their effectiveness in the international environment they remain a recurring theme in efforts to strengthen compliance systems.[115] As one example, Gro Harlem Brundtland, the Norwegian Prime Minister, has recommended ensuring compliance with carbon dioxide emission targets by establishing 'an international authority with the power to verify actual emissions and to react with legal measures if there are violations of the rules.'[116]

Sanctioning often proves ineffective because it involves costs for the sanctioner as well as the sanctionee. It can be made more effective through several means. Regular international meetings of treaty parties increase the opportunities for actors to bring diplomatic and public pressures on non-compliant actors to explain and change their behaviour.[117] Treaty rules that allow publication and dissemination of self-reported and independently-gathered information provide a 'basis for a wider critique and evaluation of a party's performance and policies' by countries, companies, and NGOs that have incentives to respond to non-compliance.[118] For example, Greenpeace and Sea Shepherd have frequently taken action to identify and prevent whaling.[119] Media reports of non-compliance and pressures from domestic NGOs do not evoke the same questions of sovereignty that governmental sanctions often raise. NGOs may also be more likely than governments to impose political and economic costs on non-compliant governments and corporations. By fostering such diffuse but influential pressures, improved transparency can increase compliance even absent formal sanctions.[120]

Treaties that formally authorize and 'assign responsibility for applying sanctions' increase the expectation that 'a given violation will be treated not as an isolated case but as one in a series of interrelated actions'.[121] As Morgenthau notes, 'nobody at all has the obligation to enforce' international law.[122] Few countries even have incentives to do so. To address the concerns over sovereignty that counteract a desire to sanction another government for treaty violations, treaties can redefine what constitutes infringement of sovereignty by authorizing certain actions in the event of treaty violations.[123] Treaties can remove the international legal barriers, such as those in the General Agreement on Tariffs and Trade (GATT), that constrain those countries with incentives to enforce.

Finally, incentives to sanction can be increased by 'privatizing' the benefits and costs of enforcement activity.[124] The 1911 Fur Seal Treaty between Japan, Canada, the US and the USSR strictly curtailed killing seals at sea while leaving the US and USSR in exclusive control of kills on the seals' breeding islands. The latter countries annually compensated Japan and Canada with a share of the kills in exchange for their halting the wasteful at-sea killing. The seal population recovered from 300,000 in 1911 to its pre-exploitation level of 2.5 million by the 1950s.[125]

Privatization can also involve authorizing governments to enforce directly against nationals of other countries caught violating treaty rules, as in the Convention on International Trade in Endangered Species' provisions for penalizing and confiscating specimens.[126] This 'use of domestic enforcement procedures is likely to be possible in an increasing range of cases, like environmental treaties, where international regimes are aimed ultimately at influencing the private activities rather than state behaviour'.[127] By authorizing and establishing standards for second-level enforcement, treaties can increase their frequency. Governments balk less at sanctioning individual and corporate nationals of other governments than at sanctioning those governments directly. Whether such a strategy can work depends on whether states with enforcement incentives have effective jurisdiction over the regulated activity, but treaties that are aimed at such opportunities to focus sanctions on individual actors provide one means of increasing compliance.

Preventing violations

Besides positive inducements and negative sanctions to elicit compliance, treaties, like domestic regulations, have a third potential strategy. Some international standards rely on efforts to raise obstacles to, and otherwise prevent, non-compliance in the first instance. If primary rules can be established which succeed at coercing compliance in the first place, the demands placed on those responsible for monitoring and enforcing treaty regulations can be dramatically reduced. To implement such a strategy requires greater attention to 'pre-monitory' control measures, ie, efforts to inspect and survey behaviour before violations occur, rather than to detect and investigate them afterwards.[128]

A coerced compliance system relies on finding regulatory chokepoints where limits can be placed on the ability to violate a treaty's terms, thereby restraining actors who might otherwise be inclined not to comply. Careful selection of the point for regulatory intervention can allow treaties to target actors who have fewer incentives to violate rules, or target transactions between actors with differing incentives. Often it entails restricting the most transparent activity in the train of actions that preceed an environmentally harmful action; an activity that is not environmentally harmful itself may nevertheless provide the most effective point for preventing violations from occurring. Domestic examples include requiring manufacturers to install catalytic converters on automobiles, or banning handgun sales. In switching from limiting intentional oil discharges to requiring oil tankers to install expensive pollution-prevention equipment, the International Convention for the Prevention of Pollution from Ships elicited compliance from tanker owners with strong economic incentives not to comply because non-compliance would have required the cooperation of a ship-builder, a classification society, and an insurance company in constructing what all knew to be an illegal tanker.[129] Any one of these actors could prevent a violation from occurring.

A deterrence-oriented approach underlies the use of sanctions, which require successfully detecting, prosecuting, and sanctioning violations after they occurred to deter them from occurring in the future. In contrast, a coerced compliance model greatly reduces the need for 'post-monitory' control that can identify violations after they have occurred. Post-monitory control efforts face the common problems of detecting violations that violators desire to keep hidden, identifying the perpetrator of a detected violation which may not always be obvious, collecting legally legitimate proof of the violator having perpetrated the violation, and ensuring that the sanctions imposed are sufficient to deter others. A preventive orientation can be designed into treaty provisions by ensuring that the actors responsible for preventing violations have both the incentives and authority to do so.

Time and treaty process

Finally, beyond the instrumental compliance policies involved in the compliance systems discussed above, treaties can reflect longer-term, less direct efforts to induce compliance. Compliance systems are nested among broader norms, principles, and processes that may play far greater roles in altering behaviour. Treaty processes can seek to influence the ways governments and other actors perceive and define their interests so they increasingly see compliance as furthering their interests. 'Soft law', involving norms, principles and guidelines, informal agreements, and tacit bargaining strategies may all wield considerable influence over behaviour. Larger 'behavioural alteration systems, of which treaties and their compliance systems form only a part, may exercise influence not only through altering behaviour in an instrumental sense but by successfully changing the values and interests of the actors involved. Many theorists contend that treaties alter behaviour by leading states to adopt broader and longer-range views of their interests, providing new scientific information that clarifies policies to achieve existing goals, or causing governments to learn new goals.[130] As Alexander Wendt argues, 'international institutions can transform state identities and interests' and through so doing change their behaviour.[131] Treaties that establish exclusively hortatory goals may have significant behavioural impacts, even when 'compliance' proves impossible to measure. This chapter decidedly does not exclude such transformation as an important pathway by which institutions change behaviour – it has simply sought to identify how treaties can mitigate international environmental problems through the less ambitious means of changing the behaviour of nations and their citizens even when it proves impossible to alter their identities and interests.

Parties previously inclined to non-compliance may come independently to prefer to comply. A treaty can authorize and fund scientific research and information-sharing to clarify the benefits and costs of a state's own behaviour to its independent self-interest. Compliance becomes more attractive if new knowledge shows greater benefits to compliance, such as higher costs of environmental degradation. Efforts to foster open-ended knowledge creation can increase domestic political pressures for compliance.[132] The Long-Range Transboundary Air Pollution Convention provided scientific exchanges and a joint database on transborder fluxes of pollutants that convinced some states to change their behaviour.[133] Such international exchanges were essential in showing states the degree to which their environmental fate depended on the actions of their neighbours, increasing incentives for both compliance and enforcement. Research and development into cheaper means of complying provides a long-term solution to incapacity and high compliance costs as sources of violations.

Treaty processes can also encourage a process of social learning by which governments and other actors come to alter their values and objective functions.[134] The negotiation and re-negotiation process can change the value actors place on certain goals. Thus, treaties can increase environmental concern simply through regular discussions that increase the understanding and perceived importance of the issue. This involves more than re-assessing costs or discovering new ways to achieve existing goals; it involves changing those goals. International organizations can consciously shape perceptions of self-interest. Developing and disseminating information regarding pollution and helping place scientists in domestic policy positions altered interests which increased compliance with treaty rules regulating Mediterranean pollution.[135]

COMPLIANCE AND EFFECTIVENESS

A final word is in order regarding the relationship between compliance and effectiveness.[136] While this chapter argues for better evaluation of whether and how treaties alter behaviour, such behavioural change is an important, but essentially intermediate goal. We are most interested in whether treaties produce the environmental improvements that motivate their negotiation in the first place. Compliance and behavioural change are valuable only if they lead to accomplishment of treaty goals. In Oran Young's terms, we are interested in a treaty's problem-solving, as well as behaviour-changing, impacts.[137] Some recent scholars have proposed three indicators of effectiveness that go beyond compliance, namely, the degree to which

(1) parties achieved treaty goals,
(2) actual decisions corresponded with expert advice, and
(3) the environmental resource improved relative to what would have happened in the absence of the treaty.[138]

Evaluating effectiveness defined as problem-solving requires making an often-subjective choice among various possible definitions of the problem. First, 'sharp statements of objectives seldom are achieved' in international environmental treaties, making it difficult to find the yardstick against which to measure effectiveness.[139] Second, even if one defines effectiveness as the degree of environmental improvement, the multiple causes of most environmental phenomena and the generally poor quality of data make identification of causal links extremely tenuous.[140]

Greater compliance is neither a necessary nor sufficient condition for effectiveness. First, high compliance is not necessary. Non-compliance with an ambitious goal may still produce considerable positive behavioural change that may significantly mitigate, if not solve, an environmental problem. Second, high compliance is not sufficient. High compliance levels with rules that merely codify existing behaviour, or rules that reflect political rather than scientific realities, will prove inadequate to achieve the hoped-for environmental improvement. For example, compliance with the Montreal Protocol may prove perfect but too late to avoid irreversible harm from stratospheric ozone loss.[141]

Even a treaty that can be empirically identified as the cause of compliance may fail to lead to the desired environmental improvement. Most environmental problems have three different types of sources: the regulated human behaviour, other non-regulated human behaviours, and non-human sources. A treaty that successfully brought a halt to an environmentally harmful behaviour might not preserve the environmental resource if other human behaviours and natural factors influencing environmental quality caused the resource to be depleted.

Having said that, however, compliance can provide a valuable proxy for effectiveness, since greater compliance will produce more environmental improvement so long as the rules do not have perverse effects, although the improvement may still be insufficient to mitigate the problem. In most cases negotiated rules have a positive relationship to better management, if not resolution, of the environmental problem.[142] In these conditions, higher levels of compliance will lead to higher levels of effectiveness, *ceteris paribus*. In some cases, under assumptions of perfect compliance, two rules will be equally beneficial to the environment. In such cases, the rule that induces greater compliance can safely be inferred as increasing treaty effectiveness. In other cases, however, determining whether a given rule will be more effective in solving an environmental problem will require evaluating the trade-offs between a rule that offers large nominal environmental benefits but is likely to elicit low compliance and another rule that offers smaller nominal environmental benefits but has a high likelihood of compliance. A particularly striking example of such trade-offs is involved in the current choice faced by the International Whaling Commission (IWC) regarding whether to maintain a moratorium on commercial whaling in a treaty to which fewer countries are willing to be parties or allow some commercial whaling to keep countries operating under treaty auspices.

Rules that achieve high levels of compliance may be too costly, economically inefficient, or fail to be cost-effective. Compliance cannot be the sole criteria for making choices among alternative treaty provisions. The argument is that evaluating likely compliance levels must be an important and relevant consideration in policy debates. Nominally cheaper, more 'efficient' policies may simply not be capable of inducing the level of compliance needed to achieve a socially desirable outcome. In contrast, a more expensive, inefficient policy may prove more enforceable or otherwise more likely to elicit high levels of compliance needed to achieve this outcome. Before selecting a particular policy approach, the benefits of the socially desired outcome must be weighed against the costs required to induce high compliance levels. We cannot rule out certain options simply because more efficient options can 'conceivably' achieve the intended environmental end. Policies must be evaluated in terms of compliance, as well as efficiency, cost, and equity. Where they elicit the compliance necessary to achieve the environmental goal, more efficient solutions are clearly preferable. Where compliance with efficient solutions appears significantly less likely than with alternatives, we must examine whether the compliance costs of inefficient solutions are nonetheless outweighed by the benefits that high compliance provides.[143]

FURTHER RESEARCH

This chapter has laid out one view of the theoretical context that informs much of the current research being conducted by international relations scholars into compliance with environmental treaties. This framework suggests a large number of important empirical questions that need to be answered if scholars are to contribute to the important task of advising those who actually negotiate international environmental accords. The study of international environmental politics in general, and issues of compliance and effectiveness in particular, is currently receiving a large and rapidly growing amount of scholarly and policy attention.[144]

Certainly one important task involves identifying whether treaty-induced compliance is common. Specific studies have evaluated compliance with the provisions of particular treaties, such as the International Convention for the Prevention of Pollution from Ships and the Convention on International Trade in Endangered Species.[145] Studies of individual treaties can provide in-depth understanding, especially when they identify variance in compliance across rules within a treaty which allows control of many of the variables that often confound analysis of cross-treaty variation. They suffer, however, from the problem that their conclusions often prove difficult to generalize and, by definition, can evaluate the success or failure only of whatever types of particular institutional and legal arrangements were undertaken in those particular treaties. Such studies also do not address the larger question of whether treaty rules generally do prompt changes in behaviour. Indeed, most such studies document instances of rules failing to influence behaviour, as well as succeeding at doing so. Determining if compliance occurs frequently in international environmental affairs, whether treaty-induced or not, demands study by those evaluating treaty rules and behaviour across a wide range of treaties.

Current research is looking at both national-level factors that influence compliance, as well as at variance across different types of problems to identify the necessary conditions for treaty-induced compliance to arise. Political science scholars are beginning to explore systematically the variance across different environmental treaties in eliciting compliance and achieving desired behavioural changes. Some variance will certainly be shown to arise from differences in how the treaties frame their substantive provisions and design their compliance information and non-compliance response systems. However, several other factors will certainly be shown to play key roles in compliance variance across issue areas. First, different levels of international concern regarding a problem may have large effects on the level of compliance achieved. Second, some types of activities are inherently more difficult to regulate than others. Some environmental remedies need only alter current production processes to eliminate that component causing the environmental externality, as with oil pollution and acid rain. In other cases, achieving treaty objectives may require reducing the level of activity to correspond to the relevant ecosystem's carrying capacity, as with fisheries agreements. In still other problems, treaties may need to ban an activity completely in certain areas or for certain periods, as with whaling, trade in endangered species and atmospheric nuclear testing. Several research teams, involving many international scholars from a wide array of disciplinary backgrounds, are currently probing into these and related questions.[146]

Understanding what limits contextual factors place on compliance, and what factors determine that context, can make it easier to design politically viable, yet successful, environmental compliance systems. One major international team of scholars is conducting a cross-treaty and cross-country evaluation of compliance in ten countries with five environmental treaties.[147] Another study currently underway is evaluating the financial mechanisms in various environmental treaties.[148] Considerable effort is underway to collect more systematic databases on variables related to both the compliance and effectiveness of environmental treaties to facilitate progressively better analysis of the effects of international treaties.[149] Comparisons across different treaties can highlight the impact of contextual factors on the effectiveness of similar compliance systems, or the relative effectiveness of different compliance systems. Factors that are not policy-manipulable in the short run, such as scientific understanding of (and hence governmental concern over) the risks of a particular environmental threat or solutions to it, may be policy-manipulable in the long run. Numerous questions suggest themselves. How do wildlife preservation treaties compare with pollution regulation accords? Do bilateral agreements prove better or worse at eliciting compliance than multilateral agreements? In general, how does the number of parties influence compliance levels?

Political scientists are also just commencing research to determine what valid lessons can be learned from broader international relations research efforts, for example those investigating compliance, verification and enforcement issues in arms control.[150] Comparing and contrasting the arms control experience with that of environmental treaties could shed light on both areas of study.[151] Similar comparisons might usefully be made with compliance provisions and experience in trade and human rights conventions.[152] The Commission on Sustainable Development for monitoring adherence to the principles in UNCED's Agenda 21 was modelled after the UN Commission on Human Rights, yet little close study has documented whether and why the human rights experience should easily and successfully transfer to the environmental realm.[153]

CONCLUSIONS

The preceding discussion provides a foundation for identifying both whether and how treaties induce compliance. Most treaties have parties that combine the different types of motivations outlined. Even in the international environmental issues commonly characterized as collaboration problems, it seems likely that some states comply due to an independent interest in compliance, others are willing to comply if enough other states do, and others will seek to violate, complying only if they receive sufficient sidepayments, face sanctions, or are prevented from violating. Some might act no differently if there were no treaty while others may be complying only under direct threats of sanctions. High compliance levels in general, and increases in compliance levels in particular, may be due to a treaty but may be due to a range of other factors.

The wide array of compliance sources that are exogenous to the treaty suggests a healthy scepticism in attributing a treaty as having caused compliance. More importantly, they provide rival hypotheses of why compliance would increase at the same time as a change in rules. They provide a check-list of 'likely suspects' that will help avoid attributing causation to rules in cases where other factors are responsible for a change in compliance.

Changes in the power and interests of dominant states may lead both to adoption of more stringent rules and to better compliance. Treaty rules and correlated behaviours may often be merely different indicators of the same set of power and interests that drive much of international politics. The existence of deeper causal links, rather than just coincidence, will regularly cause compliance changes to correlate with rule changes. Economic and technological changes might increase incentives and capacities to comply, and domestic political changes may also lead actors to change their calculus regarding compliance. These factors may confound efforts to attribute causally a change in compliance to a particular rule change. Explicitly looking for independent evidence of such changes, however, allows us to confirm this analysis if appropriate evidence is found and to eliminate it if evidence shows no such change occurred. If changes in rules do appear to have caused increased compliance, however, the review presented here delineates the types of changes to the primary rule system, compliance information system, or non-compliance response system that we should expect to see.

Despite the continuing reference to international environmental politics as a new field, many environmental treaties have been in force long enough to begin evaluating their behavioural impacts.[154] While empirical evidence of compliance may take time to develop, many environmental agreements stand ready to be analyzed by those inclined to find data addressing whether international rules effect compliance.[155] Whether the nations of the world succeed at averting the many international environmental threats that loom on the horizon will depend not on negotiating agreements to alter the behaviours that harm the air, land, and water but on ensuring that those agreements succeed in getting governments, industry and individuals to change their behaviour. We can hope and work for a day when all nations and their citizens are sufficiently concerned about the environment that we will not need international law to outlaw pollution and dictate environmentally-benign behaviours. Until then, however, identifying and then implementing those treaty provisions that elicit compliance will provide one valuable means of managing the protection of the global environment.

2 COMPLIANCE, CITIZENS AND NGOS

James Cameron

One of the greatest challenges posed to those involved in the international environmental movement is ensuring compliance with international environmental agreements (IEAs). Central to the task of improving compliance with IEAs is identifying the relationship of the relevant compliance system with the underlying societal context. In essence, the closer that relationship, the better the compliance. Similarly, the closer law is to real world fact, the more likely law can guide behaviour. While, however, this societal context necessarily expresses the complexity of human society, the ability of public international law to reflect that complexity has seemed severely, and arguably intrinsically, limited. The result has been that individuals and non-governmental organizations (NGOs) – an increasingly important non-state manifestation of collective expression of individual will and aspiration – have been formally denied a role in the development of international law in general. Despite the continuing attraction of state sovereignty as the most acceptable representation of collective political will so far invented, it is no longer possible nor even desirable to deny non-state actors access to international law-making with its important consequences for international law, compliance and access to justice in environmental matters.

LAW, POLITICS AND INTERNATIONAL LAW

Law, particularly international law, is the product of the relationship between real world fact and the world of ideas. Law seeks to realize that which begins conceptually. As notions of society and community interaction evolve, law must necessarily evolve as well to reflect this. However, this is easier said than done as new and emerging ideas must, in effect, achieve a certain level of acceptance before the law properly recognizes them and adjusts itself accordingly.

> The foundations of international law rest upon realities, which belong to the world of facts which are observable and at times even measurable ... thus it is inevitable that as the political-cultural context changes, attention arises between the tendency of existing international law and institutions to persist along with their underlying perceptions on the one hand, and on the other the new modes of perceptions, values and convictions to amend, reform or even totally overthrow the existing international order: new convictions, values and perceptions which have not yet had the opportunity to shape the international legal system.[1]

It is difficult to measure the time between the birth of a so-called 'mode of perception, value, or conviction' and the moment of its incorporation into law. It is safe to say, however, that typically this time period is more lengthy than is desired. This lag presents a multitude of problems. For instance, by the time one value becomes reflected in the law (usually having been conceived much earlier), another (or others) may be formulated and ready to take its place. Also consider that this is not a linear process in which one value rears its head to supplant an existing value, only to be later substituted by an altogether different value. The process is instead parallel, involving a conceptual path that may be traversed in any of a different number of ways. The importance of recognizing the relationship between ideas and values and their incorporation into the world of fact relates to the law's ability to modify behaviour effectively.

Law itself is considered part of the social process and admittedly has significant influence over behaviour. This must necessarily be so:

> Being social constructs, both international law and the theory of international law have an impact on actual behaviour. Theory, rules and behaviour are involved in mutually constituted processes. Their 'existence' can be explained by reflexive reference to each other.[2]

Indeed, it is difficult to ignore law's societal roots without denying its validity:

> A jurisprudence of international law that fails to guide the activities that relate to the gathering, storing, retrieval and utilisation of data about the world context will be a declining jurisprudence, a candidate for fossilisation.[3]

Having recognized law's near all-encompassing effect, we also recognize that a number of players – sometimes direct, often indirect – are increasingly responsible for influencing law's evolutionary development.

In the arena of international environmental law, two such participants are individuals and NGOs. As will be discussed, individuals and NGOs have been increasingly fulfilling much-needed roles otherwise neglected. Yet, despite their growing visibility on the international scene and the tremendous impact international legal decisions have on them, individuals and NGOs have systematically been denied a voice in the international legal discourse.

Before suggesting legal means for individuals and NGOs to develop and enforce primary rules in national courts, the reasons for international law's limited recognition of the complexity of human society will be discussed, in the individual/NGO context; followed by consideration of the ways in which developments in international environmental regimes, particularly the UNCED process, have begun to seek to address this complexity more directly by increasing the possibilities of individual and NGO involvement in the compliance system.

THE TRADITIONAL LIMITATIONS OF INTERNATIONAL LAW

The following two factors can be identified to date as having limited the ability of public international law to accommodate NGOs and individuals in any substantive way.

The continuing concept of state sovereignty and its proscription of international law

The first such factor is the notion of state sovereignty, arguably *the* cornerstone of international law. As well as restricting the range of possibilities of international regulation, supervision and control, adherence to the concept of sovereignty poses difficulties for the establishment of a role for non-state actors in helping to develop and enforce primary rules. As Lindborg has said:

> International decision-making is traditionally based on the model of one nation-one vote, which respects national sovereignty. Integrating NGOs into the system as full voting partners challenges this tradition. Difficult questions arise, such as who do NGOs represent, how are they held accountable and how votes be allocated to the tens of thousands of NGOs clamouring to be part of the debate? Furthermore, how should input be weighed against the input of the nation state?[4]

This tension between the legal concept of sovereignty and increased NGO involvement, in fact, becomes particularly evident in the context of environmental and sustainable development issues. The differences of perspective between developed and developing countries provide one example. The increasing number of NGOs in the developing countries is being viewed with suspicion, particularly by those states who are most concerned with expressing their rights to exploit the developing countries' natural resources.5

Yet the foundations for a doctrine of international law whose sole participants are states are slowly being eroded. The ever increasing role played by the individual illustrates this:

> . . . the person (whether an individual or corporation) has become increasingly accepted as an independent actor, subject to and benefiting from international law . . . . The distinctions between public and international law have become increasingly artificial as many states and instrumentalities have entered the market-place in a major way – either as traders themselves or as guardians of industrial policy – and as commerce and foreign policy have become increasingly intertwined. For example, the Iraqi invasion of Kuwait and the resulting UN economic sanctions involve traditional issues of public international law; yet the implementation of the sanctions very much affected US and European banks with Iraqi or Kuwaiti deposits. At much less dramatic levels, the same kind of mixed public-private issues are posed daily by satellites broadcasting daily across national boundaries, by fishes in international waters and by investors trading on foreign stock exchanges.[6]

This paradoxical nature of the relationship between sovereign states and transnational NGOs is felt all the more keenly as it is certainly arguable that the effectiveness of international environmental regimes depends on their success in influencing the actions of transnational non-state actors (namely corporations). Indeed, one can go further. The relationship between non-governmental entities at the international level and national level is simultaneously important for effectiveness. Environmental groups can apply pressure on corporations to improve their environmental performance in support of agreed environmental goals through the focal point of international negotiations for global commons agreements and through the practice of the international organizations responsible for facilitating compliance by states with their obligations.

The difficulty in separating international law from politics

The second limiting factor is the difficulties often encountered in attempting to distance international law from political argument. If law is to maintain a distinction from politics, this will arguably be dependent upon its facility for marshalling legal arguments to manage conflict and to guide behaviour through principles and rules towards agreed ends that can be both invoked and enforced.

As Boyle notes, international law's 'essentially political character may dilute the force of legal standards and merely serve to legitimise practices otherwise unsupportable from an environmental viewpoint'.[7] International environmental institutions are described as being 'fundamentally . . . no more than the expression of their members' willingness to act. In this they are no different from the United Nations itself or from any other political institution'.[8] It is on the basis of this lack of objectivity of international law and its lack of distance from politics which leads Koskenniemi in his customary well-motivated but nihilistic way to question the reality of international law:

> . . . it is impossible to prove that a rule, principle or doctrine (in short, an argument) is both concrete and normative simultaneously. The two requirements cancel each other. An argument about concreteness is an argument about the closeness of a rule, principle or doctrine to state practice but the closer to state practice an argument is, the less normative and the more political it seems. The more it seems just another apology for existing power. An argument about normativity on the other hand, is an argument which intends to demonstrate the rule's distance from state rule and practice. The more normative a rule, the more political it seems because it is less possible to argue it by reference to social context. It seems Utopian and like figures of natural justice, manipulable at will.[9]

While the interdependence of international law and politics is not denied – '[r]ules of law can and do express political values, views and preferences, they are made as a result of political will and behaviour and serve political interests'[10] – Georgiev still maintains the independent existence of law: '[law] is not identical with those views, values and interests'. He stands against Koskenniemi's view by arguing that the basis for such a separate existence is expressed as normativity:

> Once created, they acquire a separate existence and are no longer merely political opinions or social behaviour. Political opinions, interests, will and behaviour may change but the legal rules can only change in conformity with the requirements which the law itself formulates also autopoietically and which do not follow automatically the changes in politics and opinions. The assumption of the existence of international law is based on the very recognition of such existence, and not on the actual observance of its rules. An obligation arises because States say they have undertaken it and international law exists because States and people believe and say so. The 'reality' of international law coincides with its magic.[11]

Once one raises the ideal of organizing human behaviour for the purposes of protecting the environment and meeting the needs of present and future generations in the international legal system, openness to the fullest representation of the beneficiaries of such trust must follow. The limited scope of transparency and accountability in international legal process is particularly alarming in those treaties that deal with resource management and have a restricted state membership. The absence of non-state voices can leave institutions to function as the legitimization of national policies, rather than acting as a fiduciary in the interests of the environment.[12] Increasingly it is precisely this fiduciary role which IEAs are assuming on behalf of international society. The UNCED treaties and other documents support this view.

Following a constitutional model, as my culture and consciousness encourages me to do, it seems to me that separation of powers leads to the accountability in law of holders of public power delegated to them by the people, so that holders of public power in international society are held accountable *where* and when they act. If they act in a form of social organization called a treaty system, or Conference of the Parties, drawing upon resources of information and ideas from all over the world, then their activities must be reviewable in law in that place or context. Furthermore, they enlist the support of those who delegate power to them in the resolution of global problems facing humankind. States alone cannot solve global commons problems because states alone do not possess the sum of the real world power necessary or adequate to solve problems of such scale and complexity. This fact calls for more than just intergovernmental cooperation. It demands a sincere and determined effort to create international institutions which, without denying the essential figure of the sovereign state in institutions which are themselves sovereign, manage to harness the energies of the non-state actor to solve the problems which argue for the existence of the institution in the first place.

UNCED AND THE DEVELOPMENT OF NON-STATE ACTOR INVOLVEMENT

The involvement of NGOs in inter-governmental policy and programme discussions is not new: it was formalized with the establishment of the United Nations in 1945. Article 71 of the UN Charter provides that:

> The Economic and Social Council may make suitable arrangements for consultation with non-governmental organizations which are concerned with matters within its competence. Such arrangements may be made with international organizations and, where appropriate, with national organizations after consultation with the Member of the United Nations concerned.[13]

The arrangements developed to implement this provision have been adopted in a variety of UN conferences, UN subsidiary organs, international treaty processes and the specialized agencies of the UN. The rights accorded to accredited NGOs have not changed from those set forth in the UN Economic and Social Council (ECOSOC) rules but practice has modified them somewhat. First, the distinction between the three different categories of ECOSOC NGOs have tended to blur over time. These organizations have a right to be consulted on provisional agendas, on whether NGO observers may be present throughout the meeting or solely for discussion of agenda items within their field of interest, and have priority speaking rights.

Second, the possibilities for NGOs to speak in meetings and circulate documents has grown. In accordance with UN practice, NGO interventions may only occur with the consent of the body concerned and the discretion of the presiding officer. Brief statements on the subject at hand, however, have been increasingly encouraged, with the limitations that if the number of NGOs requesting to speak is too large, the inter-governmental organ can ask that they organize themselves into constituencies and express their views through spokespersons.

In addition to formal rights, for some time NGOs have played an informal, but effective, role in various IEAs' compliance information systems.[14]

UNCED

The UNCED process – from its inception, through its negotiations to its final products – marked a significant increase in the involvement of NGOs and individuals and focused attention onto their importance in achieving sustainable development. Indeed, it has even been argued that UNCED preparations seem to have shifted the line between acceptable influence and intrusions on sovereign power, bringing NGOs closer to the heart of decision-making.

> At the preparatory sessions for UNCED, NGOs have worked alongside the government delegations to prepare reports, to find issues, provide data and advocate positions. This expanded NGO role is forcing a new examination of the traditional 15 state decision-making process and is stretching the boundaries of the United Nations negotiating structures.[15]

To compensate for the greater number of NGO participants, the UNCED rules of procedure, those governing the Commission for Sustainable Development and those recently adopted for forthcoming UN conferences, require that NGOs make available written presentations through the Secretariat at their own expense and in the official UN languages. The statements are not normally issued as official documents. The United Nations is also becoming increasingly accommodating in helping NGOs make arrangements to distribute documents and publications in the vicinity of meeting rooms. According to a GEF Report:[16]

> 1400 NGOs were accredited to UNCED and are now eligible to be accredited to the Commission on Sustainable Development. The more liberal UNCED accreditation rules, (Rules of Procedure, Rule 65 Decision 1/1 Role of NGOs in the preparatory process for UNCED) and the simpler process for obtaining accreditation have since been followed in the rules for the UN Conferences on Small Island Developing Nations (1994), population and development (1994) and habitats II (1996) UN conference on environmental and development.[17]

For example, as a result of Agenda 21, Chapter 27.9, ECOSOC decided in February 1993 to conduct a general review of current arrangements for consultation with NGOs, with a view to updating them. This review is to be concluded by 1995. The UN Committee on NGOs is working on the modalities for such a review.[18]

This enhanced role for NGOs increases the importance to be given to the kind of NGOs who are allowed to participate. The GEF Report drew attention to the OECD-centric bias of the current ECOSOC accreditations:

With respect to accreditation, the ECOSOC arrangements stress that NGOs seeking consultative status should be international in structure and scope of activities. This can exclude national NGOs and community groups with specialized expertise or extensive knowledge and experience of local and field conditions. It also favours more extensive participation by well-organized, international NGOs based in the industrialized nations. Recognizing the inherent limitations of these arrangements, recently held conferences and treaty processes have placed greater emphasis on the competence and relevance of the NGO in relation to the subject under discussion and sought to encourage balanced representation from both developed and developing nations and regions. For example, the NGO Participation Fund for UNCED permitted representatives from 92 developing nations and four central and Eastern European countries to attend the fourth preparatory session for UNCED, 155 and 8, respectively, to the conference itself.[19]

Since UNCED, the principles supporting wide public participation in environmental problem-solving, the need to involve the non-governmental community, access to information, access to legal remedies and liability for environmental harms have received a significant political boost and some legal and institutional backing. There is something approaching international consensus that the citizen must be given rights that can be directed towards global environmental protection. This poses a significant theoretical and practical difficulty for international organizations – they were created as, and remain in law, organizations of states.

Beckeridge argues that the juxtaposition of documents advocating community rights alongside traditional expressions of sovereignty, necessarily condition the principle of state sovereignty and leads to re-definition of that fundamental concept which facilitates the accommodation of individuals' rights:

> Yet accompanying the apparently absolute pronouncements of these paragraphs are extensive provisions placing sovereign states within a new web of relations and responsibilities to other entities, even with respect to the management of natural resources within sovereign territories. The language of the various documents addressing global and local concerns frames the assertions of sovereignty, conveying a far more complex vision of multiple interactive scales and forms of governance.[20]

Principle 10 of the Rio Declaration marks a significant step in the development of procedural rights for all persons to have access to information, to the decision-making process and to remedies for environmental harm:

> States shall facilitate and encourage public awareness and participation by making information widely available. Effective access to judicial and administrative proceedings including redress and remedies shall be provided . . . .

Agenda 21 is littered with references to the language of participatory rights.[21] Most of these urge adoption at the national level but one is left in no doubt but that an international standard is being set for the attainment of sustainable development.[22]

> Governments will need to promulgate or strengthen, subject to country specific conditions, any legislative measures necessary to enable the establishment by NGOs of consultative groups, and ensure the right of NGOs to protect the public interest through legal action.

This national model of individual and NGO involvement provides a template that can be applied to the international context. On a practical level, concerning among other things efficiency and notions of fairness, this model is undoubtedly apt.

STRENGTHENING THE ROLE OF MAJOR GROUPS

> One of the fundamental prerequisites for the achievement of sustainable development is broad public participation in decision-making. Furthermore, in the more specific context of environment and development, the need for new forms of participation has emerged. This includes the need of individuals, groups and organizations to participate in environmental impact assessment procedures and to know about and participate in decisions, particularly those which potentially affect the communities in which they live and work . . . .[23]

The argument, rather quaintly modified, is extended to international institutions.[24]

Agenda 21 recommends that the UN system, including international finance and development agencies, and all inter-governmental organizations and forums should, in consultation with NGOs, take measures to perform certain functions, including

- review and report on ways of enhancing existing procedures and mechanisms by which NGOs contribute to the international discourse at all levels;
- promote and allow NGOs and their self-organized networks to contribute to the review and evaluation of policies and programmes designed to implement Agenda 21; and
- take into account the findings of non-governmental review systems and evaluation processes.

Chapter 38 continues this pattern of increasing NGO involvement by suggesting measures to design open and effective measures to achieve the participation of NGOs, including those relating to major groups, in the process established to review and evaluate the implementation of Agenda 21 at all levels and promote contribution to it.

Para 38.44 states that:

> Procedures should be established for an expanded role for NGOs including those relating to major groups, with accreditation based on the procedures used in the conference. Such organizations should have access to reports and other information produced by the UN system. The General Assembly, at an early stage, should examine ways of enhancing the involvement of NGOs within the UN system in relation to the follow-up process of the conference.

Post-UNCED anxiety for effective follow-up measures has led some politicians to recognize two fundamental issues concerning compliance and the citizen: firstly, the participation of individuals in environmental decision-making:

> (t)he Agenda 21 follow-up needs a focal point at intergovernmental level to assess performance and sustainable development. Whatever the institutional context this focal point can only fulfil its task if it has the right information from governments and international bodies. It will also need to ensure effective access to non-governmental organizations. Public confidence in environmental management cannot be built without their participation.

And secondly, accountability of the agents implementing and enforcing environmental legislation:

> Globally we need to improve the performance of international institutions. All the UN agencies need to be much more accountable for their activities in the environment and development field.[25]

This latter point has also been recognized by the US Vice-President, Al Gore, in respect of the financing of sustainable development:

> Heads of nations must commit themselves to improving overseas development practices to ensure that the projects are sustainable. One of the best ways of doing this is to increase the transparency of lending practices so that local communities and non-governmental groups have the opportunity to comment on proposals.[26]

Experienced international negotiators, diplomats and Heads of Missions are finding themselves part of striking changes in the way their business is being conducted:

> The Role of NGOs in the negotiation and implementation of Agreements (which has increased dramatically during and since the UNCED process) will continue to grow. (Two weeks ago, in Geneva, I was startled to find the Chairman of a meeting of the *ad hoc* Committee on (*sic*) Parties to the Basel Convention giving the floor to the representative of Greenpeace to negotiate as an equal with Governments on drafting language – something which I have never before witnessed in 20 years of involvement with multilateralism.)[27]

Weiss points to the increasing role of private actors in developing international standards:

> While governments are perceived as the usual route for developing international minimum standards, there are also other important sources, including corporations, industrial associations and professional societies ... as companies become global operators, they are driven for reasons of economic efficiency to adopt relatively comparable standards among themselves. Industrial associations and other non-governmental fora are also increasingly developing common environmental guidelines for particular industries or particular operations. While these are quite general in character they do contribute to the emergence of a minimum standard of environmentally responsible behaviour.[28]

The role of international institutions in global standard-setting would therefore be both facilitated and made more effective if they were to build on an already existing global standard between transnational private actors. To this end they should seek to strengthen the procedures granting access to such non-governmental actors. Indeed, as far as Weiss is concerned, 'Efforts by governments to formalize minimum standards may be unnecessary, or even counter-productive'.

Handl notes the debates within the IAEA Standing Committee on Nuclear Damage as to how to integrate state liability with private liability in a comprehensive liability regime and looks at the transboundary regulatory regimes such as the Paris and Vienna Nuclear Liability Conventions which already evince a private law approach.[29]

Handl underlines the importance of non-state actors' involvement and even proposes new means of formally structuring environmental regulations to achieve this:[30] 'One possibility might be to treat these entities as formally independent of states in recognition of their *de facto* independence in the transnational arena. Another would be to couch international regulations in terms of private legal obligations directly incumbent on the principal actors, instead of in language that focuses on states' international responsibility as the international cardinal principle.' He returns, ultimately, to this cardinal principle to explain further.[31] 'It's unlikely that TNCs' international legal status would be upgraded to the point where they could be both direct claimant and respondent under international law.' The cardinal principle: 'States are the repository of ultimate power to enforce transnational Community standards.'

To return to the sense of my conclusion of the first section, there is a need for a structure for participation for non-state actors that increases their availability to contribute meaningfully to the decision-making processes without so violating traditional (but no less real for that) concepts of sovereignty so that in the midst of chaos born of fear of change, countries refuse to support the structure. In this reformist frame of mind it is vital to recognize that there are constraints to change in the current system arising out of a vested interest in the change-agents (NGOs) to maintain their power bases in public support for radical action.

The danger in bringing NGOs closer to the heart of the decision-making process is that in so doing a compromise results which fails to ensure that their political, scientific, moral, or legal credibility based on their independent 'outside' status is maintained.

RIGHTS ARGUMENTS

There is currently a loose international process evaluating the usefulness of human rights discourse and disciplines in addressing environment and development issues. Because the environment can arguably be shown to fit any of a number of categories of rights, be it civil and political rights or solidarity or third generation rights, and serves a range of functions, it is a delicate and painstaking operation to proceed to isolate the most logically sound and simultaneously effective rights argument.

International organizations, following UNCED in particular, are beginning to grapple with the involvement of non-state actors in their legal processes by using rights language. Ideas drawn from western legal systems are informing this debate. Developing countries are often sceptical or are afraid of the consequences to their sovereignty, but they have found rights language associated with development to interpose with that of the environment in order to stress issues such as poverty and human welfare.

The UNCED process gave significant impetus to this debate, with the Rio Declaration placing human beings at the centre of concern about the environment. Similar language can be found in the Hague Declaration of 1989. The Sierra Club Legal Defence Fund recently organized a meeting of Experts on Human Rights and the Environment to assist the Special Rapporteur on that subject, Madame Fatma Ksentini, and thence the UN Commission on Human Rights. The Draft Declaration of Principles On Human Rights and the Environment emerging from this group of experts adequately represents the current state of the debate on this subject:

I. General Principles

1. Human rights, an ecologically sound environment, sustainable development and peace are interdependent and indivisible.
2. All persons have the right to a secure, healthy and ecologically sound environment. This right and other human rights, including civil, cultural, economic, political and social rights, are universal, interdependent and indivisible . . .
4. All persons have the right to an environment adequate to meet equitably the needs of present generations and that does not impair the rights of future generations to meet equitably their needs.

III. Informational, Participatory and Remedial Rights

15. All persons have the right to information concerning the environment. This includes information, howsoever compiled, on actions and courses of conduct that may affect the environment and information necessary to enable effective public participation in environmental decision-making. The information shall be timely, clear, understandable and available without undue financial burden to the applicant.
18. All persons have the right to active, free and meaningful participation in planning and decision-making activities and processes that may have an impact on the environment and development. This includes the right to a prior assessment of the environmental, developmental and human rights consequences of proposed actions.
20. All persons have the right to effective remedies and redress in administrative or judicial proceedings for environmental harm or the threat of such harm.[33]

The first category of rights is likely to be extremely limited. The second category is more likely to be effective for a variety of reasons. The two categories of rights will be discussed below. Regardless, in addressing these issues several questions are raised. How do the rights arguments extend into international institutions and situations? Where may these rights be expressed? Who can argue convincingly that they do not apply in institutions constructed by international law, deriving authority from international law and subject to international law if those rights are intended to have the same prominence?

Basic human right to environment

Of great controversy is whether an individual has a basic human right to a sound environment. Various entities would contend that such a human right indeed exists. However, the inalienability of such a generic right is in question. This is so for a variety of reasons. Although, it would be an interesting exercise to argue the merits for a generic right to environment, for our purposes it is not necessary.

Right to access of information and decision-making procedures and due process

As opposed to a generic right to environment, it is more apparent why individual rights to access of information and decision-making procedures as well as due process in the international context should be acknowledged. Handl notes:

> Internationally guaranteed, specific environmental rights of individuals, such as information and participatory rights can be understood as a refinement of

> established political or civil human rights or as novel human rights . . . [T]hese rights represent the pivot in a trilateral relationship of individual/human rights, democracy and environmental protection. As such they warrant our unreserved endorsement as internationally protected rights: their normative reach is well-defined, their claim to potential universal validity believable.[34]

Environmental issues present a social problem whose solution necessitates cooperation of society at large. Further, its resolution presupposes broad participation of an open society. Handl continues, 'Citizens must have access to pertinent environmental information as well as to relevant environmental decision-making fora.[35]

Rights of access to information strengthen the institutions' control function of monitoring treaty impact implementation, which function non-governmental organizations can already be seen to be performing. Access to information rights could also be granted to non-governmental observers to international organizations but these would be limited by confidentiality and security provisions. We can already notice a broad consensus on the validity of a right to access of information and decision-making procedures. According to the 1992 Rio Declaration and Agenda 21, all interested members of the international community must have access to information. Accordingly, this is seen as vital to the achievement of the social, economic, and environmental goals of sustainable development.

One example where access of information and the ability to participate in decision-making procedures is essential involves the new GATT agreements and the World Trade Organization (WTO). The Dispute Settlement Understanding (DSU), incorporated in the Final Round of the Uruguay Round of GATT, is a key element in the administration, implementation, and enforcement of the agreements of GATT 1994. Although the new system has some attractive features, the DSU fails to incorporate the procedural mechanisms for effectively delivering sustainable development. Such mechanisms would include those giving individuals and NGOs access to the same information that is transmitted during the course of dispute settlement as well as a means to intervention. A right of intervention for those with a sufficient interest in the dispute would allow greater transparency in the dispute settlement process.

In my view, the most effective rights for use by non-state actors on the international plane or in order to assist compliance with international obligations in legal process at any level are indeed procedural. This view is further supported by the UNCED consensus:

> The generalized right of participation envisioned in the Rio Declaration, Agenda 21, and the Forest Principles is essentially procedural. While decision-making authority is left in the hands of national governments, the clear expectation of these provisions is that government decision-making would be altered through the consideration of information and views that might be otherwise overlooked and furthermore, that the procedural avenues established will provide a forum for holding governments to a substantive standard of sustainability. National proceedings are therefore expected to become vehicles for inducing governments to adhere to international goals. Participants in the process who oppose destruction of biological resources are, in some sense, the allies and agents of global environmental interests.[36]

The ECE Charter on Environmental Rights and Obligations is an international instrument that provides for individual access to administrative and judicial proceedings and participating in the decision-making processes. It invites member states to reflect these rights in their national legislation.

The importance of granting individuals procedural rights at the national level stems from the very nature of environmental protection, defined by Kramer as 'general interest protection'. Legislation that affects vested interests, such as is the case with agricultural, transport or competition legislation, is readily enforceable as society is made up of these vested interest groups 'who will mass up when the legislation does not take care of their interests'. The 'situation is different with environmental law because nobody really cares to what extent groundwater is polluted, or to what extent high seas are contaminated', therefore making environmental legislation considerably more difficult to enforce. Granting procedural rights to individuals or interested groups would remedy this.[37]

Public interest litigation has increased individual participation in the enforcement of environmental standards in America where *locus standi* has been granted, eg *Japanese Whaling Society Association* v. *American Cetacean Society*[38] and in Australia *Australian Conservation Foundation* v. *Commonwealth of Australia*.[39]

The usefulness of this approach can be seen where such litigation can be used to put pressure on governments to comply with the international law obligations, holding public bodies accountable through the exercise of government review, eg *Defenders of Wildlife Inc.* v. *Endangered Species Authority*.[40]

In Pakistan, the nation's Supreme Court in effect acknowledged the fundamental human right to a sound environment and gave to the individual a procedural recourse to protect this right. In the case *Ms Sheila Zia and others* v. *WAPDA*,[41] the Court responded to citizen claims about health risks from electric power installations by ordering that work on construction of a grid station be halted until an independent commissioner was able to evaluate the risks.

This ruling involved the first senior judicial examination of the risks of electromagnetic fields (EMFs) in Pakistan and is also part of a series of environmental cases being taken by the Court under an internationally unusual procedure which allows the Court to institute proceedings without prior hearing in lower courts where it considers that a fundamental human right may be violated and questions of public importance raised. This power provides an alternative mechanism for environmental regulation.

The ineffective enforcement of international law is often due to a combination of lax state commitments and judicial reluctance to review non-implementation of international obligations. The successful realization of international law therefore may ultimately depend on the extension of procedural rights to individuals so that they can initiate review proceedings to enforce international law through the national courts. The United States is an interesting case study. Barton and Carter recommend that the United States 'accept international judicial penetration of its legal system' so that it can 'exemplify global norms of law-based behaviour.' They continue:

> ... it has accepted none of the treaties that permit private suits against the US government ... it must be willing to accept international treaties and executive agreements that can be interpreted and enforced by US domestic courts, thus allowing the US courts to participate fully in the development of international treaties and common law... Not only should the United States move to accept this international form of judicial review, it should also use its own judicial review to ensure that it adheres to international standards ... the court[42] used a surprisingly

> narrow standing test to permit the executive to avoid a possible transnational application of endangered species protections.[43]

Rights to initiate proceedings in international tribunals are most unlikely for the time being. However, the potential does presently exist for some international environmental agreements to connect the dispute procedures to the national legal systems of their member states.

Perhaps we can expect to see rights to intervention in dispute settlement procedures and administrative review – there are equivalent rights in the first Protocol to the statute of the International Court of Justice (ICJ); a circumscribed form exists for the ECJ; GATT panels are being encouraged to head that way.[44]

The World Bank's announcement of the creation of an ombudsperson is welcome in initiating a degree of accountability for international institutions. The new inspection panel is to serve both as a form of ombudsperson for outside complaints and as an internal check on management.

> The panel would set a precedent for international organizations to allow outside complaints, although it falls short of some of the demands of US environmental groups. The panel can only hear complaints about the bank's failure to follow its own procedures or policies, not about the contents of these policies.[45]

Barton and Carter conclude that, 'Individuals and corporations can play an indispensable role in helping to call nations to account. And international norms and rules will obviously mean much more if there are effective mechanisms for enforcing them. When the United States creates international entities, or enters into international agreements, it should take the lead in ensuring that the resulting rules are enforceable and can be invoked by persons as well as States . . .' (see Iran-US Claims Tribunal in 1981, and the Canada-US Free Trade Agreement in 1988) . . . 'Support for the GATT dispute system also reflect progress, although more needs to be done to allow persons to bring actions.'[46]

CONCLUSION

The following points could serve as notes for enlightened leadership towards improving compliance with international environmental agreements:

- Design modern international institutions dealing with global commons issues which are as open as possible.
- Institutions subject to the rule of law with genuine separation of powers where public power-holders are held accountable in law for abuse of power to other states but allowing for non-state actors to be involved in the legal process.
- Guarantee certain procedural rights such as access to information, subject to judicial review in international tribunals.
- Constantly connect legal principles and process at the international (regional) and national level.

APPENDIX – CASE STUDIES

CASE STUDY 1 – ANTARCTICA

It is helpful to look at how far the position of non-governmental organizations has advanced within the Antarctic Treaty System between 1984 and 1992 in order to assess the importance of the role they play in the life of international organizations. In 1984 Barnes proposed that NGOs should be accorded formal rights to observe and participate in meetings; that new institutional mechanisms should be created in order to carry out the 'functions of environmental impact assessment, regulation and enforcement in the Antarctic'; that 'wilderness and scientific values' be given the highest priorities; and that 'a moratorium on mineral exploration and exploitation should be agreed'.[47] Eight years later these ideals seemed close to realization: . . . 'The 1990s [sought] further admissions to the ATCP status . . . the award of observer status to non-ATCPs and various international bodies (eg SCAR, ASOC), the ever-increasing environmental focus of ATCMs and recommendations (eg a stress on the inter-relationship of the Antarctic eco-system and associated eco-systems, waste disposal, Environmental Impact Assessments), SCAR's performance of an advisory role on environmental issues (CCAF, CCAMLRA), the tightening up of CCAMLRA's fishing restrictions, and the adoption of a PREP with a mining ban.[48] How far have such improvements for environmental protection within the Antarctic Treaty System been a consequence of the NGO role? 'NGO environmental groups claim that their activism is primarily responsible for keeping ATPs up to the mark. For them the ATS was hampered by the glacial pace of change consequent upon biennial ATCMs operating according to consensus procedures, lack of relevant expertise in many ATCM delegations, the absence of an expert advisory environmental committee, and weak compliance and enforcement mechanisms' (Beck).

The visible role performed by NGOs in Antarctic matters, is a point recognized formally during and after 1990 when ASOC received observer status at ATCMs/ATSCMs. As a result, NGO environmental groups are now placed in a more central position to make input into the ATS reinforcing the role performed during the past decade or so by such bodies as UNEP and International Union for Conservation of Nature and Natural Resources and the individual environmentalists serving on certain ATCM delegations (eg Australia, Denmark, New Zealand, USA). NGOs have played a vital role of constantly *initiating higher standards* for environmental protection which eventually become incorporated into the regime proper.

January 1987, the first non-government base in Antarctica and the World Park concept which has subsequently been articulated in PREP, 'a natural reserve devoted to peace and science', was set out in Greenpeace's Antarctic Declaration. The NGOs' influence on the regime is marked by Beck: 'During 1990 to 1991 the negotiations conducted by ATPs for a comprehensive environmental protection regime reflected not only change modes of thinking in the international community but also an admission of both the national and ATS levels of existing environmental management weaknesses. From this point of view, the resulting PREP served not only to enhance the level of protection but also to codify and rationalize existing recommendations on this topic.'

An analogous case is the International Union for Conservation of Nature and Natural Resources (RUCN) which started the movement to create the CITES regime by calling in 1963 for worldwide effort to develop a regime to regulate trade in endangered animal and plant species. The vigorous surveillance of the environmental impact which NGOs conduct means that they are in a position to notice details that could otherwise go ignored. To this end NGO environmental groups press the need for 'fundamental change' on the part of scientists – claiming that no longer should any activity be allowed so long as it carried the magical name 'science'. PREP consequently places new responsibilities on scientists. NGOs also perform an important function in their *appraisal of existing legislation*. Phillips, speaking on behalf of WWF points out the deficiencies in the 1991 environmental protocol as being essentially vagueness in the powers of the new Committee for Environmental Protection: 'We would like specific functions to ensure that environmental rules are interpreted consistently by all parties, a forum to discuss such controversial issues as the Dumont D'Urville airstrip or the *Bahai Paraiso* sinking, assisting on the preparation of environmental impact assessment documents and keeping a watch for potential environmental impact. It could also provide objective participation on inspection teams.'[49] Such appraisal functions are increasingly important in the light of the normative indeterminacy which is a consequence of the increasing framework-cum-implementing protocol agreements. Handl refers to the Basel Convention as an example of a case where 'states may leave the definition of the key legal parameters regarding the scope and the very nature of conventional obligations to which they contract to be settled at a later date'.

The Basel Convention finalization of two such concepts – 'Environmentally sound management of wastes' and of 'liabilities' – have been left for decision by the parties until after the Convention formally enters into force. 'By necessity this approach also signals a certain open-endedness of the legislative enterprise'. Such indeterminacy is seen by NGOs as a danger in encouraging lax standards and inconsistency in enforcement and is rightly challenged by Phillips with regard to the Environmental Protocol: 'The environmental impact procedures (EIA) Protocol implementation and interpretation are almost entirely left to each Treaty Party, and are likely to vary widely from Party to Party. We advocate that the committee should have a much greater role in the process, improve the consistency and quality of both initial and Comprehensive Environmental Evaluations since all parties will have access to the committee's expertise and experience within the EIA process. The earlier the Committee is involved in the process the less likely the final CEE will be contentious. CEEs do have to be considered by Treaty Consultative Meetings, but even if the ATCM advised against a proposed activity on environmental grounds, the party can still go ahead with it. We would like to see the procedures in the Protocol strengthened by having more systematic advice and decision-making. The object for this is for the same high standards to apply to all parties as are already being implemented by the best of them.' NGO criticism of existing standards is a necessary component of improvement by international organizations. See Phillips' criticisms of the current practices for the disposal of waste: the Annex on waste disposal and management is seen as 'an improvement for shipping waste out of the Antarctic rather than disposing of it there, yet it still has its faults': however, the Annex is full of phrases such as 'inasfar as is practicable', which are difficult to enforce and it still arrives for incineration, inappropriate in the Antarctic, and sanctions open burning of waste until 1999.

Moreover 'ASOC presented a critique of PREP at the Bonn ATCM on the absence of a permanent mining ban. The 50-year review provision inserted to accommodate governments (eg USA) reluctant to forego permanently the opportunity to undertake mineral resource activities in Antarctica implies that mining might occur in 2040 or thereafter. NGO environmental groups also pointed to the other weaknesses in PREP, including the lack of both the Secretariat and an independent inspectorate as well as the failure to define the area of coverage according to an ecological boundary, like the Antarctican version.

NGOs also play an important role in *enhancing public awareness*: an effective campaign against whaling provided a springboard for action on Antarctica. ASOC Antarctic World Park petition secured several thousand signatures between 1977 and 1982 and subsequently several million people signed the Antarctic declaration. They extend the process of scrutiny in the international organization by entering treaty compliance through state sphere of bad publicity: they made the French Dumont D'Urville airstrip an environmental *cause célèbre* for most of the 1980s and circulated photographs of Adelie penguins killed by explosives to establish serious breaches of Agreed Measures (eg killing birds without a permit and use of explosives).

Perhaps their most essential role is therefore the ability to ensure that international organizations are never able to ignore public concerns. As the medium between the public and the states, NGOs fulfil one of their most important roles which is to *democratize the international legal process*. The initiation of the Montreal Protocol was largely due to NGO mobilization of public opinion.[50]

A parallel case is ASOC's coordination of public opinion over CRAMRA and the subsequent mining moratorium. On 2 June 1988, the signature took place of the Wellington Convention on Exploitation of Antarctic Mineral Resources. France and Australia announced on 18 August 1992 their intention not to ratify the Convention.

The Protocol on Environmental Protection (PREP) designating Antarctica as a 'natural reserve devoted to peace and science' was adopted in October 1991. According to Verhoeven 'there is no objective reason, since no new discovery, scientific or other, occurred to encourage a radical challenge. The fact is however, that public opinion does not support the adoption of Wellington Treaty any more.' As Phillips explains, 'When the environmental NGOs put out publicity material on Antarctica it was like releasing a dam – letters, hundreds of thousands of signatures on petitions, and offers of help all poured in from the public. The NGOs did not manipulate public opinion on the protection of Antarctica as they have been accused of doing, but they were able to challenge the strong feelings that were already there. The Antarctic Treaty Parties are quite open about the strength of this public opinion during the negotiations leading to the 1991 Environmental Protocol, and it was undoubtedly an important influence in persuading them one by one to reject the Minerals Convention CRAMRA, the 1988 Convention on the Regulation of Antarctic Mineral Resources, and then to agree the terms of the Protocol, including its ban on mining, astonishingly quickly. There was no doubt that the Protocol represents a significant move within the Treaty System towards the World Park concept.'

NGOs' expertise and awareness of local conditions makes them valuable in *extending the resources available* in the negotiation process. According to Beck, non-ATPs involved in UN discussions have proved heavily reliant upon briefing documents and information papers furnished by NGO environmental groups. As a result, UN resolutions adopted since 1989 have acknowledged the 'significant importance of Antarctica' in the global environment, advocated a World Park strategy, including a mining ban, and stressed the need for conservation measures to be negotiated with the full participation of all members of the international community.

A primary problem with international environmental treaties is the difficulty of *monitoring* and enforcing treaty requirements. As Handl notes, although the Basel Convention's effectiveness may ultimately turn on various informal monitoring and verification processes involving non-state actors: 'NGOs have been key players in the tracking of hazardous waste export and in alerting both would-be importing companies and the international public of the illegal or unsound waste disposal plans and operations'.[51] Lindborg argues that NGOs can, in effect, sidestep the entire issue 'by enacting treaty goals through public education and mobilization regardless of whether or not the treaty ever enters into force – as in United States' CFC reduction prior to signing the Montreal Protocol. NGOs have officially and unofficially served as environmental treaty enforcers, monitoring results and creating bad publicity that "shames" countries into compliance.'[52]

CASE STUDY 2

The GEF[53] report also states that 'concerns generally expressed about the adequacy of NGO and community participation in the GEF project cycle centre on questions of timing and communication.' The report finds that real communication requires more than access to information. 'Relevant data and information should be made available in the form that is meaningful, including translation into local languages and other means of communication appropriate to the community in question.'

GEF NGO Participation

The GEF Council has since decided to allow 10 NGO representatives to attend or observe its meeting. Council meetings will be preceded by a larger NGO consultation, funded in part by the GEF Secretariat, at which the 10 representatives will be chosen, according to agreed criteria, by NGOs themselves.

GEF information policies

'The GEF is charged with operating transparently and accountably. If the NGOs are to participate effectively in the GEF, access to the documentation under consideration is essential. In keeping with this principle, the Administrator's Office makes available to interested NGOs all GEF documents prepared for the participants. These include the GEF chairman's report to the participants, Parts I and II, the reports of the chairman of STAP, final project documents, and the quarterly GEF bulletin. The Administrator is making arrangements for these documents to be obtained at the UN/World Bank depository libraries around the world. They are already available on Econet and associated electronic databases.'

World Bank

The report is also 'concerned that inadequate information on World Bank projects that are associated with GEF project grants is made available to members of STAP, the participants, or affected community and interested NGOs prior to consideration and endorsement of each tranche by the participants'. In the Bank, access to detailed project preparation and appraisal documents is subject to the acquiescence of the country concerned. Information provided to the Bank by the country on the understanding that access to it will be restricted must be treated in accordance with that understanding. The World Bank review of its information disclosure policy continues under increased pressure to release sufficient information on the associated bank project to permit informed decision-making on the GEF components.

The World Bank's 'monthly official summary' (MLS) provides a monthly progress report on all World Bank projects including GEF projects. In addition, the MLS includes summary environmental data sheets for projects that may have significant adverse environmental impacts (Category A). Environmental data sheets on proposed projects that may have more limited or no environmental impacts (Categories B and C) are available to the public on request from a contact point published in the MLS.

Policies on NGO participation in the project cycle, include EIA, and information disclosure. Bank policy statements (operational directives), previously restricted to Bank staff, are now being made available to interested parties outside the Bank, and a list of World Bank financed projects with potential for NGO involvement is updated and issued twice a year, complementing the monthly operational summary. Economic and sector papers may also be made available, as are environmental working papers. Bank information disclosure points are contained in Administrative Manual Statement 1.10 of June 1989. These policies are currently under review.

Inspection Panel

The World Bank has recently created an Inspection Panel, which will provide people directly and adversely affected by a Bank-financed project with an independent forum through which they can request that the Bank act in accordance with its own policies and procedures. Projects funded by the GEF and implemented by the Bank will be subject to such procedures.

3 COMPLIANCE WITH INTERNATIONAL ENVIRONMENTAL OBLIGATIONS: EXISTING INTERNATIONAL LEGAL ARRANGEMENTS

Philippe Sands

INTRODUCTION

Environmental degradation is a transnational phenomenon. The pattern and scale of industrialization and consumerism to date, and its likely continuation into the foreseeable future, make states demonstrably interdependent in terms of both the continuation and in addressing the effects of global environmental change.

The extent to which protection of the global commons can be assured will depend on the extent and timescale of changes achievable in human behaviour. The challenge is to discover and devise ways in which such changes can be brought about. Effective international environmental agreements creating legal obligations (primary rules) are one means of seeking to bring about these changes.

The effectiveness of such regimes will, in turn, depend on the extent of compliance with such obligations or rules; and this has become a matter of increasing concern in international relations in recent years. This is evident from the attention which the issue of compliance received during the preparations for United Nations Conference on Environment and Development (UNCED), and in the negotiation and implementation of recent environmental agreements, including in particular the 1987 Montreal Protocol, the 1992 Climate Change Convention, the 1992 Biodiversity Convention and the 1992 Convention for the Protection of the Marine Environment of the North-East Atlantic (OSPAR Convention). The growing relevance of environmental concerns to broader issues related to international peace and security was affirmed by the United Nations Security Council in January 1992 when the President and its members declared that 'non-military sources of instability in the . . . ecological fields have become threats to international peace and security'.[1] The response to those concerns has resulted in a number of initiatives relating to the further development of existing mechanisms for implementation, enforcement and dispute settlement, and to the development of new mechanisms, including the decision in July 1993 by the International Court of Justice to establish a Chamber for Environmental Matters. What are the reasons for the increased attention being paid to compliance with international environmental obligations?

Among the various factors at least three appear to be particularly relevant. First, it is evident that the nature and extent of international environmental obligations has been transformed in recent years as states take on more environmental commitments, under treaty and other obligations, which are increasingly stringent and with which they must comply. Second, the growing demands and needs of states and those subject to their jurisdiction for access to natural resources, coupled with a finite, and perhaps even shrinking, available resource base provide the conditions for increasing conflict over access to natural resources. Finally, as international environmental obligations increasingly address fundamental economic interests and needs, states which do not comply with their environmental obligations are perceived to gain unfair, and perhaps unlawful, economic advantage from their environmentally harmful activities in relation to those states which are complying with their obligations. For each of these reasons the focus on compliance in the development and application of international environmental agreements has become increasingly keen.

For the purposes of this chapter, compliance can be defined as the behaviour of a state, ascribed thereto by reason of and derived from the behaviour of its nationals, which conforms to a treaty's primary rules.[2] The failure so to behave – non-compliance – is an important issue because it limits the overall effectiveness of those treaties, undermines commitments which have been made under the international legal process, and can lead to conflict between states and instability in the international order.

According to Mitchell[3] the reasons for states' non-compliance include a lack of institutional, financial or human resources, and differing interpretations as to the meaning or requirements of particular obligations. His discussion of noncompliance reinforces the widely held view that whilst non-compliance is a subject in need of greater attention, existing international legal arrangements and mechanisms may not be adequate. Indeed, such arrangements and mechanisms will never be adequate *in themselves* to achieve such compliance. They can, however, given present day global society and the transnational nature of much environmental degradation, certainly be seen as a necessary part of the 'tool-kit' for achieving compliance.

At UNCED, and in relation to the treaties mentioned above, attention has focused as much on the need to devise mechanisms to *prevent* disputes as on the development and application of procedures to resolve them peacefully when they arise. Recent efforts have also sought to ensure that, where possible, enforcement and the settlement of disputes are addressed in a non-contentious and non-adversarial manner.

From an international legal perspective, compliance raises at least three separate, but closely related, questions.

(1) What formal or informal steps must a state or international organization take to implement its international legal obligations?
(2) What legal or natural person may seek, or has the right, to enforce the

international environmental obligations of a state or international organization? and

(3) What techniques, procedures and institutions exist under international law to resolve conflicts or settle disputes over alleged non-compliance with international environmental obligations?

As this chapter seeks to show, none of these issues is particularly new, and over the years a range of techniques have been adopted and used to improve compliance. Developments in relation to environmental matters have thus drawn heavily on developments in international law and practice in other unrelated areas although techniques and practices specific to environmental matters have emerged and are now being applied. Despite the apparently recent emergence of what has been referred to as 'environmental security',[4] the legal issues relating to the environment which are faced by the international community today concerning implementation, enforcement and conflict resolution are actually remarkably similar to those of one hundred years ago.[5] Since the Pacific Fur Seal arbitration of 1893, environmental disputes have arisen, and been submitted to international dispute resolution arrangements, in the context of a variety of different issues,[6] some of which have threatened international peace and security. The current dispute between Hungary and Slovakia over the construction of the Gabcikovo-Nagymaros dam and the diversion of the Danube illustrates the range of international fora for the resolution of disputes over environmental and natural resources issues. Hungary had explored a range of enforcement and dispute settlement options including unilateral reference to the ICJ, arbitration, conciliation by the EC Commission, and the emergency procedures of the Conference on Security and Cooperation in Europe (CSCE) before it and Slovakia by Special Agreement signed in April 1993 agreed that the differences should be settled by the ICJ.[7]

As will be seen, while the techniques for ensuring compliance and resolving disputes have developed significantly since the Pacific Fur Seal arbitration, the mechanisms available remain are under-utilized and it is unclear whether they are equipped to deal with the growing range of environmental issues which may require resolution. The limited progress achieved at UNCED is unlikely to improve upon existing arrangements in any significant manner in the near future.

THE DEVELOPMENT OF PRIMARY RULES OF INTERNATIONAL LAW: TREATIES

International law may be regarded as 'the body of rules which are legally binding on states in their intercourse with each other'.[8] These rules derive their authority, in accordance with Article 38(1) of the Statute of the ICJ, from four formal sources: treaties, international custom, general principles of law, and subsidiary sources (decisions of courts and tribunals and writings of jurists and groups of jurists).[9] The International Law Commission has identified a number of sources from which the rights (and obligations) of states (and other members of the international community) arise:

- bilateral or multilateral treaty, or a treaty provision for a third state;
- binding decision of an act of an international organization;

- a rule of customary international law;
- the judgement of an international court or tribunal; or
- a right created or established in favour of a particular state.[10]

Treaties (which are also known as conventions, accords, agreements and protocols) are the primary source of international legal rights and obligations in relation to environmental protection. A treaty can be adopted bilaterally, regionally or globally, and is defined by the 1969 Vienna Convention on the Law of Treaties (1969 Vienna Convention)[11] as 'an international agreement concluded between states in written form and governed by international law, whether embodied in a single instrument or in two or more related instruments and whatever its particular designation'.[12]

The treaty-making process

The adoption and entry into force of an environmental treaty is preceded by a series of steps which will frequently take place over a lengthy period of time. Once two or more states have identified an environmental issue as requiring cooperation through international legislation, they will identify the appropriate international forum or institution(s) to serve as a legislative forum. If the subject is already covered by a framework treaty the new legal obligation could be developed in a Protocol or by amendments to an existing Protocol; in such cases the appropriate legislative forum will usually be the Conference of the Parties or equivalent institution established by the framework agreement. If the international legislation can appropriately be dealt with by an international act other than a treaty, it may simply be addressed by a binding decision, or resolution, or other act of an international organization or the Conference of the Parties of an environmental treaty. If a new treaty is required, the states involved will need to determine which international organization provides the appropriate forum for the negotiation of such a treaty. This decision can itself be controversial. By way of example, although the 1992 Biodiversity Convention was negotiated under the auspices of the United Nations Environment Programme (UNEP), developing countries insisted that the UN General Assembly, rather than UNEP, was the appropriate international organization under whose auspices the Climate Change Convention was to be negotiated. This was due to the view that developing countries were better represented in New York at the UN General Assembly than at UNEP and were likely to be able to participate in negotiations. Similar considerations lay behind the failure of the UN General Assembly in December 1992 to agree whether the UN Commission on Sustainable Development (CSD) should meet in Geneva (where many developing countries are not represented) or New York (where all developing countries are represented), or in both places.[13]

Once the forum for negotiations has been agreed, that body will establish a negotiating process. This could be anything from a relatively informal ad hoc group of governmental experts (such as was established by UNEP Governing Council for what became the 1985 Vienna Ozone Convention), to the establishment of a formal institutional structure (such as the Intergovernmental Negotiating Committee for a Framework Convention on Climate Change (INC/FCCC), established by UN General Assembly Resolution 44/212). Similar arrangements apply in the negotiation of Protocols under framework agreements. An alternative approach is for an international organization to establish a subsidiary body to 'prepare' a text for the consideration and adoption by an Intergovernmental Diplomatic Conference (such as the establishment by the Governing Body of the IAEA of a Standing Committee on Nuclear Liability to prepare draft amendments to the 1963 Vienna Convention).

The negotiations may be open-ended or established only for a limited period. Examples of the former include the negotiations of the 1985 Vienna Convention which took place over a five-year period, and the negotiation of the 1982 UNCLOS (UN Convention on the Law of the Sea), which took nearly 20 years. On the other hand, the 1992 Climate Change Convention and the 1992 Biodiversity Convention were negotiated in just 15 months, the negotiators having been asked to prepare a text in time for signature at UNCED. Once the draft text has been negotiated it will be adopted and opened for signature. It will then enter into force in accordance with its provisions on entry into force.

IMPLEMENTATION

With a view to achieving compliance with their treaty and other international obligations, states must firstly adopt national legislation, policies and programmes ('national acts') and must second ensure that such national acts are complied with by those subject to its jurisdiction and control.

National law

Once a state has formally accepted a primary rule, usually following the entry into force of a treaty which it has ratified or the act of an international organization by which it is bound, it will usually need to develop, adopt or modify relevant national legislation, or give effect to national policies, programmes or strategies by administrative or other means. Some treaties expressly require Parties to take appropriate measures to ensure the implementation of obligations,[14] or 'to take appropriate measures within its competence to ensure compliance with [the] Convention and any measures in effect pursuant to it'.[15] It is unclear whether there is any correlation between the existence of such an obligation in the treaty and the level of compliance. The failure expressly to state such an obligation does not necessarily mean that such an obligation does not exist as a matter of general international law. Some agreements also require Parties to designate a competent national authority or focal point for international liaison purposes, including in relation to domestic implementation.[16] The 1982 UNCLOS provides a typical example, its provisions being drawn from a number of different precedents, particularly in the field of marine pollution. UNCLOS provides specifically for the enforcement by states of their laws and regulations adopted in accordance with the Convention and the implementation of applicable international rules and standards.[17] It also requires states to ensure that recourse is available under their legal system for prompt and adequate compensation for damage caused by marine pollution by persons under their jurisdiction.[18]

National compliance

Once an obligation has been domestically implemented the party must ensure that it is complied with by those within its jurisdiction and control. Several treaties expressly require Parties to ensure such compliance,[19] or to apply sanctions or punishment for breaches or violations of national implementing measures.[20] Others specifically provide for the application of criminal penalties or for the 'punishment' of violations.[21] Ensuring compliance at the national level tends to be a matter for the public authorities of each state, although there is much evidence to suggests that domestic compliance of environmental obligations is inadequate and that compliance with international obligations needs to be enhanced.[22]

Recognizing that public authorities in many countries may not be particularly well suited to ensuring compliance, either because of a lack of resources or a lack of commitment, and recognizing also the role which individuals, groups and business can play in ensuring compliance, more and more states are allowing private enforcement of national environmental obligations before national courts.[23] These are sometimes referred to as 'citizen suits', allowing citizens (and businesses) to enforce national environmental obligation in the public interest and without having to show a personal or property interest. The availability of national remedies to challenge acts which are damaging to the environment or in violation of environmental obligations is being addressed internationally. Principle 10 of the Rio Declaration states that '[e]ffective access to judicial and administrative proceedings, including redress and remedy, shall be provided'. The EC has recognized that individuals and public interest 'groups should have practicable access to the courts in order to ensure that their legitimate interests are protected and that prescribed environmental measures are effectively enforced and illegal practices stopped'.[24] The 1993 Lugano Convention, was the first international agreement to elaborate upon the rules governing access to national courts to allow enforcement of environmental obligations in the public interest Article 18 requires standing to be granted to environmental organizations to allow them to bring certain enforcement proceedings before national courts.

The question of which state may or must ensure implementation is a difficult one where the environmental obligation relates to the protection of a shared natural resource or the global commons. This can lead to conflicts between states over which, if any, has jurisdiction over a particular activity or violation. Some treaties allocate enforcement obligations to particular states. The 1982 UNCLOS, for example provides for flag state, port state, or coastal states jurisdiction depending on where the pollution incident occurred.[25] No equivalent treaty rules apply for other matters, such as atmospheric pollution, and under the 1988 CRAMRA (Convention for the Regulation of Antarctic Mineral Resource Activities) each Party would be required to ensure that recourse is available in its national courts for adjudicating liability claims under Article 8 of the Convention (and consistently with Article 7), including the adjudication of claims against any operator it has sponsored.[26]

The rules of UNCLOS are relatively detailed and may provide a basis for the allocation of enforcement jurisdiction in other agreements. Generally the flag state will be responsible for ensuring that vessels flying its flag comply with applicable international pollution rules and standards, and with laws and regulations adopted in accordance with UNCLOS. It will also be responsible for the effective enforcement of such rules, standards, laws and regulations 'irrespective of where a violation occurs'.[27] A port state may investigate and institute proceedings in respect of a vessel voluntarily within its port or at an off-shore terminal for harmful discharges from that vessel outside the internal waters, territorial sea or exclusive economic zone (EEZ) in violation of international rules and standards.[28] A port state must take measures to prevent vessels from sailing where they have ascertained that the vessel is in violation of applicable international rules and standards relating to seaworthiness which may threaten damage to the marine environment.[29] A coastal state may institute proceedings against vessels within its port for violations of its laws and regulations adopted in accordance with the Convention or applicable international rules and standards for environmental violations occurring in its territorial sea or EEZ.[30] Where there are grounds for believing there is a 'substantial discharge causing or threatening significant pollution of the marine environment', the coastal state also has the right, under UNCLOS, to investigate and institute proceedings against vessels navigating in its territorial sea, to obtain information from and to undertake inspections of, vessels navigating in its EEZ.[31]

UNCLOS does not prejudice the rights of states under international law to take and enforce measures to protect their coastlines or related interests from pollution or a threat of pollution. Such pollution may result from a maritime casualty, including collision or stranding, which may reasonably be expected to result in major harmful consequences.[32]

With regard to the sea-bed and ocean floor and its subsoil beyond the limits of national jurisdiction (known as the 'Area' which forms, with its resources, the 'common heritage of mankind'),[33] states' Parties to the Convention are responsible for ensuring that their activities, or the activities of their nationals or those effectively controlled by them or their nationals, are carried out by them in conformity with Part XI of UNCLOS. States' Parties are also subject to any rules to be adopted by the Authority concerning pollution and other hazards to the marine environment, and the protection and conservation of natural resources.[34]

The allocation of detailed obligations providing enforcement powers in order to ensure compliance is not well developed in respect of other environmental media involving shared resources. In the absence of specific treaty provisions the rules governing enforcement jurisdiction remain subject to the general rules of international law in this field.

Compliance Information Systems

Apart from the traditional techniques for achieving compliance with international environmental obligations, which are discussed in detail below, alternative approaches relied upon in international environmental law are, principally:

(1) imposing reporting requirements on states, and
(2) improving access to, and dissemination of, environmental information.

Reporting

States must usually report the measures which they have adopted to give effect to their international obligations to the relevant international institution responsible for implementing a particular treaty or other international act.[35] Most environmental agreements expressly require Parties to report certain other information to the international organization designated by the agreement. The information to be reported typically includes statistical information on production, imports and exports;[36] information on the grant of permits or authorizations;[37] including criteria;[38] details of decisions taken by national authorities;[39] scientific information;[40] and information on breaches or violations by persons under the jurisdiction or control of the Party.[41]

These reports may be required on an annual or bi-annual basis, or according to some other time frame.[42] They provide a means for the international institution and the other Parties to assess the extent to which, and how, Parties are implementing their obligations. It is clear, however, that many states fail to fulfil even the basic reporting obligation, which suggests that other, more substantive obligations may also remain unimplemented. A report prepared for the United States Committee on Environment and Public Works recently considered, *inter alia*, six environmental treaties which require Parties to submit periodic reports, and found wide variations in compliance with reporting requirements.[43] Some treaties revealed a strong record. All six Parties to the International Whaling Convention (IWC)[44] complied with certain information requirements, 16 of the 17 Parties to the 1988 No_x Protocol[45] and 52 of the then 65 Parties to the 1987 Montreal Protocol[46] did so. At the other end of the scale, however, are for example the 1972 London Convention,[47] MARPOL[48] and the 1973 CITES[49] which have a very poor compliance record in relation to reporting requirements. This documents the limited ability of many countries, particularly developing countries, to meet such requirements.

Steps, however, are being taken to address the problem. Under the Biodiversity and Climate Change Conventions financial resources are required to be made available to meet the incremental costs of developing countries of fulfilling their reporting requirements, and this should go some way towards improving compliance. Nevertheless, the scope and nature of the information to be reported under those Conventions will impose significant burdens on all Parties, and it remains to be seen whether and to what extent the increased rigour and extent of reporting requirements can be effectively met, or whether these and other instruments will encourage further participation from international organizations and non-governmental organizations in the reporting process. In this regard the operation of the reporting and information arrangements established for the UNCSD will be of some interest.

Environmental information

There is broad recognition today of the importance of early access to detailed information on matters relating to the environment. Improved access to information may influence the behaviour of both consumers and large-scale actors thereby enhancing implementation, as well as supporting fuller participation of citizens in decision-making processes. A range of international mechanisms and techniques have been developed, including:

- establishing international rights of access to information on the environment;
- creating environmental information labelling and eco-auditing schemes, and
- establishing independent international observation and monitoring programmes.

Most international environmental agreements require states to provide information to national authorities, to other parties, or to international organizations. The objective of improved public access to information on the environment is now reflected in various instruments adopted by the OECD,[50] EC[51] and, to a lesser extent, the World Bank.[52] The EC legislation, for example, which is based on both environmental and economic rationales, attempts to ensure free access to, and dissemination of, environmental information held by public authorities. This model has been followed by other regional agreements.

NON-COMPLIANCE RESPONSE SYSTEMS AND ENFORCEMENT

Facilitating compliance and compliance incentives

A range of techniques has been developed to facilitate and encourage compliance by states with their international obligations. Facilitating techniques include the provision of financial resources and transfer of technology and technical information. However, compliance incentives also include the imposition of liabilities upon those states which violate their obligations, and the use of trade and other economic incentives.

Financial resources

The use of public sector financing to encourage environmentally beneficial activities and projects has become an increasingly important topic in international environmental law. Two types of financial involvement are most important. First, multilateral development and lending institutions are encouraged to incorporate environmental considerations into their activities, applying appropriate international standards. Second, international public sector funds are made available to assist poorer countries in meeting the costs of stringent international environmental protection requirements.

All of the multilateral development banks have recognized the need to integrate environmental concerns into their policy-making, and, to varying degrees, they have adopted measures to achieve that objective. With regard to international public sector funds, the most significant development has been the linkage between the provision of financial resources by developed countries and the fulfilment of treaty commitments by developing countries. The 1990 Montreal Protocol amendment was the first agreement to make treaty fulfilment by developing countries directly dependent upon the provision of cash or credit by developed countries. This led to the establishment of the Global Environment Facility (GEF) which is to provide grants or concessional loans to developing countries for projects addressing ozone depletion, climate change, biodiversity, and the protection of international waters. The facility is capitalized at over $2 billion. Other regional institutions, such as the European Bank for Reconstruction and Development (EBRD), serving Central and Eastern Europe, have also undertaken to commit a significant proportion of their funds to 'environmental' projects.

The 1990 Amendments to the 1987 Montreal Protocol have set an important precedent by establishing a mechanism to 'meet all agreed incremental costs' of developing country Parties 'to enable their compliance with the control measures of the Protocol'.[53] The Climate Change Convention goes even further, by requiring developed country Parties 'to meet the agreed full costs incurred by developing country Parties in complying with their' reporting requirements and the 'agreed full incremental costs' needed by developing country Parties for implementing their substantive obligations under the Convention.[54]

Liability for environmental damage

Creating liability for environmental damage is a way to integrate environmental costs into production processes. International treaties can impose liability upon a state or, as is more frequently the case, directly on the private actor that caused environmental harm. Early agreements establishing liability referred only to personal injury and property damage. Civil liability for environmental damage has only recently started to be addressed in international instruments. The number of international conventions establishing the liability of private actors has increased significantly and seems likely to continue doing so in future. Recent instruments which have addressed civil liability for environmental and other damage have been in the areas of transport of dangerous goods[55] and of hazardous activities generally.[56] Existing agreements are being amended in the light of new environmental concerns, and new liability rules can be expected for the waste trade and the Antarctic.

State liability has proceeded more slowly, and to date no treaty rules of general applicability establish the liability of states for environmental damage, although specific treaties regulate liability for damage caused by space objects, and in the Antarctic.

Economic instruments

The limited effectiveness of traditional 'command-and-control' regulatory approaches has given rise to some support for economic and fiscal measures to protect the environment, particularly because the latter are considered to be administratively efficient and not to require a high degree of 'policing'. Recent agreements and other international acts, including the Rio Declaration, encourage the use of such measures, and there are some signs that the growing interdependence between international economic and environmental law may result in their increased use.

Many recent intergovernmental statements and declarations have called for the international use of economic and fiscal instruments as tools of international environmental protection. Many recent statements and declarations have endorsed the use of taxes, emission charges, and tradeable emission permits, but to date no binding international legal instruments establish or support them. The most important development in this connection is the EC Commission's proposal for a Community-wide tax 'based on an energy component and on a component based on carbon content', designed to limit use of fossil fuels to combat climate change.[57] The EC proposal heralds the introduction of laws making use of economic and fiscal instruments at the international level.

International regulation of subsidies and public investment, like pricing and taxation policy, remain at an early stage of development, with little evidence of hard law outside the EC. The EC has taken a lead in developing the law relating to subsidies to accommodate environmental needs, and the issue seems set to be addressed by the General Agreement on Tariffs and Trade (GATT) following the Uruguay Round.

Trade and competition rules

Multilateral prohibitions on trade affecting endangered animal and plant species date back to at least 1940. Since then, the use of trade prohibitions has been extended beyond nature protection to cover hazardous wastes and substances, such as those which deplete the ozone layer. More recently, the 1987 Montreal Protocol and its 1990 Amendments have used trade prohibitions in an effort to limit production and consumption by states that are not Parties to the Protocol. The Protocol and Amendments attempt this by:

- prohibiting the importation of controlled substances from any non-Party state;
- providing for the eventual prohibition on the import from any non-Party state of products containing controlled substances; and
- providing for the possible prohibition on the import from any non-Party state of products produced with, but not containing, controlled substances.[58]

Complex legal questions have been raised about the compatibility of these measures with free trade obligations under the rules of the EC, GATT and the North American Free Trade Agreement (NAFTA). As a result, cases have been referred to various dispute settlement bodies, some of which are identified below, which have reached different verdicts as to the appropriate balance to be struck between free trade objectives and environmental protection objectives.

International enforcement

Once evidence has become available that a state, or a Party to a treaty, has failed to fulfil an environmental obligation established by international law, the question arises as to which entities or persons, having the requisite degree of international legal personality, may seek to enforce that internationally. In this context 'enforcement' means the right to take measures to ensure the fulfilment of international legal obligations or to obtain a determination by an appropriate international court, tribunal or other body, including an international organization, that obligations are not being fulfilled. The various options which are available include international enforcement by one or more states, by an international organization, or by non-governmental actors. In practice, international enforcement will usually involve a combination of the three, each of which will act in different capacities. The nature and extent of the right which any of these actors may have to invoke enforcement measures, or participate in them, will depend on the nature and legal basis of the alleged violation, the subject matter involved, and the provisions of the international legal rule which is at issue. This aspect of enforcement is really about standing to bring international claims.

Legal enforcement by states

As the principal subjects of international law, states have the primary role in enforcing rules of international environmental law. To be in a position to enforce a rule of international environmental law a state must have standing, and to have standing it must be able to prove that it is, in the words of the International Law Commission, an 'injured state'. This in turn means, according to Article 5 of the International Law Commission's Draft Articles on State Responsibility, that it is 'a state a right of which is injured by the act of another state'.[59] Such rights could include those arising from a number of different sources, including: from a bilateral or multilateral treaty; from a binding decision of an act of an international organization; from a rule of customary international law; from the judgement of an international court or tribunal; from a treaty provision for a third state; or from a right created or established in favour of it as a particular state.[60]

In cases involving environmental damage at least two situations need to be distinguished. The first is where one state is permitting activities which cause damage to the environment of another state, the second where one state is permitting or causing damage to the environment in an area beyond national jurisdiction.

Damage to the environment of a state

In situations involving damage to its environment, or consequential damage to its people or their property or other economic loss, a state will probably not find it difficult to claim that it is an 'injured state' and that it may bring an international claim. In the Trail Smelter arbitration the United States invoked its right not to be subjected to the harmful consequences of transboundary air pollution from sulphur emissions in Canada, and to bring a claim against Canada for having violated its rights. As a riparian state and a party to an international agreement with France, in the Lac Lanoux arbitration Spain relied upon *prima facie* rights to challenge France over proposed works which it alleged would violate its right to use the waters of the River Carol under certain conditions.[61] Similar considerations apply in respect of the Gabcikovo-Nagymaros dispute submitted by Hungary and Slovakia to the International Court for a determination of rights on the basis of a bilateral treaty between those two states and 'principles of general international law'. And Australia, in the Nuclear Tests Case, argued that French nuclear tests deposited radioactive fallout on Australian territory which violated its sovereignty and impaired its independent right to determine the acts which should take place within its territory.[62]

Damage to the environment in areas beyond national jurisdiction

Not all cases will be as straightforward as the Trail Smelter Case, however. Both the Nuclear Tests Cases, brought by Australia and New Zealand against France calling on the latter to halt its atmospheric nuclear testing in the South Pacific region, and the Pacific Fur Seals case[63] raise the issue of whether a state has standing to bring an environmental claim to prevent damage to an area beyond national jurisdiction, even if it has not suffered any material damage. This raises the possibility of bringing an action on the basis of obligations which are owed *erga omnes*, either on the basis of a treaty or on the basis of customary law. As a general matter, where one Party to a treaty or agreement believes that another Party is in violation of its obligations under that treaty or agreement, it will have the right, under the treaty or agreement, to seek to enforce the obligations of the Party alleged to be in violation, even if it has not suffered material damage.[64] In most cases involving a violation of a treaty obligation, however, the applicant state is likely to have been induced into bringing a claim because it has suffered some form of material damage and not because it wishes to bring a claim to protect the interests of the international community. An example of this is the claim brought by Mexico against the United States under the GATT over the latter's import ban on yellow-fin tuna caught by Mexican vessels on the high seas in violation of United States fisheries laws.

With respect to breaches of treaty obligations, the right of a state to enforce obligations will usually be settled by the terms of the treaty. Various human rights treaties permit any Party to enforce the obligations of any other Party by bringing a claim before the relevant treaty organs.[65] Similarly, the EC Treaty allows a member state which considers that any other member state has failed to fulfil an EC obligation, including an environmental obligation, to bring the matter before the European Court of Justice (ECJ).[66] Although this right has been relied upon on numerous occasions to threaten court proceedings, it appears to have resulted in a decision by the ECJ on only one occasion, when France successfully brought proceedings against the United Kingdom for unlawfully having enforced domestic legislation setting a minimum mesh size for prawn fisheries.[67] Under EC law there is also no need to show that the claimant state had suffered damage: the mere violation of EC law is sufficient to allow standing. Thus a failure by a member state to carry out an environmental impact assessment as required under Directive 85/337 would allow any other member state to bring an action to the ECJ in accordance with Article 170 even if the environmental consequences might not be noticed beyond the country required to carry out the assessment. Under EC law, each member state has an actionable legal interest in the proper fulfilment by every other member state of its environmental obligations. Given that the environment is, in many instances, a shared natural resource in respect of which each member of the international community has an interest in its protection, compelling policy arguments can be raised to apply the rationale underlying the EC approach to the international legal protection of the environment generally.

The situation in general international law is less well developed, although there may be a move in the direction taken by the EC under some recent environmental treaties. Thus, a failure by one Party to the 1987 Montreal Protocol to fulfil its obligations under that treaty would entitle any other Party to the Protocol to seek to enforce the obligation by invoking the non-compliance or dispute settlement mechanisms under the Protocol, without having to show that it had suffered environmental damage as a result of the alleged failure.[68] The 1989 Basel Convention similarly provides that any party 'which has reason to believe that another Party is acting or has acted in breach of its obligations' under the Convention may inform the Secretariat and the Party against whom the allegations are made.[69] Most other environmental treaties are less explicit, establishing dispute settlement mechanisms which will settle the question of enforcement rights in accordance with the provisions available under that treaty or related instruments. Some treaties specifically preclude their application to the global commons. The 1991 Espoo Convention, for example, precludes Parties from requesting an environmental impact assessment or other measures in respect to harm to the global commons.

Whether a state has, in the absence of a specific treaty right such-as the Montreal Protocol, a general legal interest in the protection of the environment in areas beyond its national jurisdiction such as to allow it to exercise rights of legal protection on behalf of the international community as a whole (sometimes referred to as *actio popularis*) is a question which remains difficult to answer in the absence of state practice. This might be the situation, for example, where the activities of a state were alleged to be causing environmental damage to the global commons, such as the high seas, the sea-bed beyond national jurisdiction, outer space or perhaps the Antarctic, or to living resources found in or passing through those areas. In such cases, the question is which states, if any, have the right to enforce such international legal obligations as may exist to not cause environmental damage to an area of the global commons?

The matter has been considered in passing by the ICJ on at least two occasions, and by some of the judges in a third case. In the South West Africa (Preliminary Objections) Case the ICJ stated that 'although a right of this kind (*actio popularis*) may be known to certain municipal systems of law, it is not known to international law as it stands at present: nor is the Court able to regard it as imported by the 'general principles of law' referred to in Article 38, paragraph 1 (c), of its Statute'.[70] However, a majority of judges in the Barcelona Traction Case implicitly recognized the possibility of what might be considered to be an *actio popularis* under international law where an obligation exists *erga omnes*. The Court held that

> an essential distinction should be drawn between the obligations of a state towards the international community as a whole, and those arising vis-à-vis another state in the field of diplomatic protection. By their very nature the former are the concern of all states. In view of the importance of the rights involved, all states can be held to have a legal interest in their protection; they are obligations *erga omnes*.[71]

In the Nuclear Tests Cases four judges in their joint dissenting opinion (Judges Onyeama, Dillard, Jimenez de Arechega and Sir Humphrey Waldock) identified the conditions in which the *actio popularis* might be argued:

> If the materials adduced by Australia were to convince the Court of the existence of a general rule of international law, prohibiting atmospheric nuclear tests, the Court would at the same time have to determine what is the precise character and content of that rule and, in particular, whether it confers a right on every state individually to prosecute a claim to secure respect for the rule. In short, the question of 'legal interest' cannot be separated from the substantive legal issue of the existence and scope of the alleged rule of customary international law. Although we recognize that the existence of a so-called *actio popularis* is a matter of controversy, the observations of this Court in the *Barcelona Traction, Light and Power Company, Limited* case suffice to show that the question is one that may be considered as capable of rational legal argument and a proper subject of litigation before this Court.[72]

Despite the fact that the notion of *actio popularis* and rights and obligations *erga omnes* may be treated as distinct but related concepts, this dissenting opinion suggests that the two are, actually, rather closely linked. There has been little judicial consideration of what rights and obligations exist *erga omnes*, although the lists cited usually include obligations arising from the outlawing of acts of aggression and of genocide and relating to the protection of fundamental human rights.[73] Some support has been expressed by commentators for the view that obligations owed *erga omnes* might extend to environmental damage in areas beyond national jurisdiction,[74] and support for this view might also be found in the International Law Commission's classification of a 'massive pollution' of the atmosphere or of the seas as an international crime.[75] It has also been suggested that obligations *erga omnes* could be created by the actions of a limited number of states.[76]

There thus appears to be a tendency towards favouring the right of a state to bring an action in its capacity as a member of the international community to prevent significant damage from occurring to the environment in areas beyond its national jurisdiction. Although most discussion has focused on damage occurring in the global commons, there are equally compelling policy reasons for allowing the *actio popularis* concept to apply also in respect of damage occurring to the environment within another state's jurisdiction. To the extent, then, that a rational legal argument can be made in favour of the *actio popularis*, in respect of which international environmental obligations could it be relied upon? At this stage it is most likely to be successfully invoked in a case involving very significant damage to the environment, perhaps even requiring 'massive pollution' or harm to be shown. Likely candidates would probably include those environmental obligations that have been associated with the 'common concern' or 'common heritage' principles. They might therefore include the protection of the global environment from significant harm (Principle 21 of the Stockholm Declaration and Principle 2 of the Rio Declaration) and rights established by treaty which relate to, *inter alia*, protection of the high seas, the climate system, the ozone layer, biodiversity, plant genetic resources and, to a lesser extent, wetlands and cultural property, as well as in respect of environmental matters which are associated with, or could be couched in the language of, human rights obligations.[77]

On a more cautious note it should remembered that not all international organizations or their non-compliance bodies are likely to favour the *actio popularis* concept. The GATT Dispute Settlement Panel in the Yellow-fin Tuna Case specifically rejected the claim by the United States that it was entitled to take measures to protect dolphins on the high seas, although in that case the Panel applied GATT law and not public international law, and no evidence was presented by the United States that the dolphins were protected under international law.

International law in this respect remains at a stage of early development, and states have not, with only limited exceptions, sought to assert a legal right to act on behalf of the international community as a whole in the protection of environmental issues on the basis of customary law or national law. Where they have, as in the early Fur Seals arbitration and the GATT's Yellow-fin Tuna Case, they have been rebuffed on the grounds that they were seeking to apply *their* laws extraterritorially. In both cases the result may have been different if they had relied upon, and could have proved the existence of, a rule of customary international law, as Australia and New Zealand sought to do in the Nuclear Tests Cases.

In many respects the discussion of actio popularis at the international level is similar to that which is taking place at the national level. In international affairs the function of a state might be compared to that of an attorney-general in national law. These national discussions suggest a further limitation on the likelihood of actions being brought by public authorities to enforce the environmental rights of the community as a whole. The views of one scholar on the clear limitations of an attorney-general's ability to enforce rules to protect the environment on behalf of the community as a whole are equally applicable at the international level:

> Their statutory powers are limited and sometimes unclear. As political creatures, they must exercise the discretion they have with an eye towards advancing and reconciling a broad variety of important social goals, from preserving morality to increasing their jurisdiction's tax base. The present state of our environment, and the history of cautious application and development of environmental protection laws long on the books, testifies that the burdens of an attorney-general's broad responsibility have apparently not left much manpower for the protection of nature.[78]

The unwillingness of states to enforce obligations concerning the protection of the environment is, regrettably, supported by many examples. Perhaps the most notorious is the failure of any state to seek to enforce compliance by the former USSR with its international legal obligations arising out of the consequences of the accident at the Chernobyl nuclear power plant in 1986. This and other failures suggest that it is unlikely that the same states would seek to enforce obligations owed to the global commons, the violation of which may only lead to indirect harm to the state. This suggests the need for an increased enforcement role for international organizations, or other members of the international community, particularly where the mere attempt to enforce obligations can establish a precedent which could subsequently bind the enforcing state.

Enforcement by international organizations

While international organizations play an important legislative role in the development of international environmental law, their executive function in its enforcement is limited. International organizations are international legal persons which may seek to protect their own rights and enforce the obligations that others have towards them.[79] Sovereign interests have, however, led states to be unwilling to transfer too much enforcement power to international organizations and their secretariats, although there are some indications that this reluctance is being overcome.

Early examples of limited enforcement roles granted to international organizations mainly relate to fisheries and to international rivers,[80] and are limited to recommendatory and similar functions. Marginally more ambitious is the obligation of the CITES Secretariat which, if it is satisfied that information it has received indicates that certain endangered species are being affected adversely by trade in specimens, has to communicate that information to the relevant Party or Parties. This may then lead to the matter being reviewed by the next Conference of the Parties 'which may make whatever recommendations it deems appropriate'.[81]

Developments in relation to the protection of the marine environment and the Antarctic environment foresee an enhanced enforcement role for international organizations. The approach of the 1971 Oil Pollution Fund Convention is particularly ambitious, since it establishes and endows the Fund with legal personality in the laws of each Party and gives it rights and obligations, including being a Party in legal and enforcement proceedings before the national courts of that Party.[82] The 1982 UNCLOS also introduces innovative arrangements by endowing some of its institutions with a range of enforcement powers. Thus, the Council of the International Sea-Bed Authority can 'supervise and coordinate the implementation' of Part XI of UNCLOS and 'invite the attention of the Assembly to cases of non-compliance'; institute proceedings on behalf of the Authority before the Sea-Bed Disputes Chamber in case of non-compliance; issue emergency orders 'to prevent serious harm to the marine environment arising out of activities in the Area' and to direct and supervise inspectors to ensure compliance.[83] A Legal and Technical Commission will be entitled to make recommendations to the Council on the institution of proceedings and the measures to be taken following any decision by the Sea-Bed Disputes Chamber.[84]

The Antarctic Mineral Resources Commission, which would have been established under the 1988 CRAMRA, would have been required to draw to the attention of all Parties any activity which affected the implementation of CRAMRA or compliance by any Party with its obligations, as well as of any activities by a non-Party which affected implementation.[85] The Commission would also have had the power to designate observers,[86] and to 'ensure the effective application' of the provisions in the Convention concerning, *inter alia*, notification, reporting of mineral prospecting, and 'keeping under review the conduct of Antarctic mineral resource activities with a view to safeguarding the protection of the Antarctic environment in the interest of all mankind'.[87]

The 1988 CRAMRA is now unlikely to come into force since it has been 'replaced' by the 1991 Antarctic Environment Protocol to the Antarctic Treaty, the main environmental institution for which there will be a Committee for Environmental Protection.[88] The Committee's enforcement role under the 1991 Protocol is more limited than that envisaged for the Commission under CRAMRA: it will provide advice and adopt recommendations, including on the effectiveness of measures taken, the application and implementation of environmental impact assessment procedures, and the state of the Antarctic environment.[89] The advice and recommendations are to be drawn upon fully by the Antarctic Treaty Consultative Meetings in adopting measures under the 1959 Antarctic Treaty for implementation of the Protocol.[90] The Committee is not, however, granted any formal enforcement powers.

The 1992 OSPAR Convention also goes some way towards establishing a role for the Commission it creates in ensuring compliance with obligations. Under Article 23, which is entitled 'Compliance', the Commission has two functions. First, it must 'assess' the compliance by Parties with the Convention and the decisions and recommendations adopted thereunder on the basis of the reports submitted by the Parties.[91] Second, when appropriate the Commission may

> decide upon and call for steps to bring about full compliance with the Convention, and decisions adopted thereunder, and promote the implementation of recommendations, including measures to assist a Contracting Party to carry out its obligations.[92]

Although this provision falls short of expressly empowering the Commission itself to take measures such as court proceedings in national courts or the right to invoke arbitration proceedings under the Convention, it goes significantly beyond the provisions of almost all other international environmental agreements. Other arrangements endow particular organizations with enforcement or quasi-enforcement functions. In relation to weapons agreements the United Nations Security Council has a more or less unlimited right to 'take action in accordance with the [United Nations] Charter' if the consultation and cooperation procedure established under the relevant treaties does not remove doubts concerning fulfilment of obligations under certain nuclear weapons treaties.[93] More generally, many of the institutions established by environmental treaties are required, as their primary task, to keep under review the relevant treaty and promote its effective implementation.[94] This general function could be interpreted, over time and under the right conditions, as allowing these institutions to play a role in the enforcement of treaty obligations.

No discussion of international enforcement powers would be complete without mention of the EC Commission which must, under Article 155 of the 1957 EEC Treaty, ensure that the provisions of the Treaty and the measures taken by the institutions (ie secondary legislation) are applied. This includes ensuring that member states have correctly implemented their EC obligations, including secondary legislation. To enforce the correct implementation of such obligations, the Commission can bring Article 169 proceedings. These begin with the Commission's presentation of case and evidence to the member state concerned which then has the opportunity to make observations. This allows a full airing of the differences between the Commission and the member state and often leads to the matter being resolved without any action being taken before the ECJ. If this is not the case the Commission will deliver a 'reasoned opinion' and may bring the matter before the Court.[95] The number of infringement proceedings brought by the Commission under Article 169 in general has risen dramatically.[96] At any one time the EC Commission is likely to have several dozen pending matters, and it has to date brought more than 50 cases to the ECJ alleging violations of EC environmental laws, often under a controversial use of its powers.

The EC Commission can also apply to the ECJ for interim measures under Article 186 of the Treaty – a form of interlocutory relief well established in Community jurisprudence and quite often employed, for example, in competition and anti-trust cases. The Commission has to show a good arguable case, that the need for relief is urgent and that irreparable damage to the Community interest will be done if the order is not granted. The member state can defend itself by establishing that it will suffer irreparable harm if the order is made. The Commission is in the fortunate position of not having to give a cross-undertaking in damages in the event that it ultimately loses the case. In Case 57/89, *EC Commission* v. *Germany*, the European Court considered the circumstances in which it would be prepared to prescribe necessary interim measures in environmental cases.[97] The case concerned the construction in Germany of a reservoir and related site, and the Commission sought the adoption of interim measures to suspend the work until the Court had given its decision on the main application.

The Court held that for a measure of this type to be ordered, the application must state the circumstances giving rise to the urgency and the factual and legal grounds establishing a *prima facie* case for the interim measures.[98] It rejected the application on the grounds that the Commission had failed to prove urgency: the application had been submitted after the project was well underway and the interim measures had not been sought until 'a large part of the work had already been partially completed', and it could not be shown that 'it [was] precisely the next stage in the construction work . . . which [would] cause serious harm to the protection of birds . . .'.[99]

Enforcement by non-governmental actors

According to traditional rules of public international law, non-governmental actors are not international legal persons except within the limited confines of international human rights law and its associated fields. It is virtually impossible to find a text-book on international law which makes any reference to the role of environmental and other non-governmental actors in the international environmental legal process, although it is widely recognized that they have become in many areas, and particularly in the field of international environmental law, *de facto* international actors who are, in limited circumstances, endowed with *de jure* rights. In practice non-governmental actors play a central role in the development and application of international environmental law. They participate in the negotiation of environmental treaties and other international meetings, most often by participation on official delegations of states, or by the grant of official observer status, or simply by attending the conference in an unofficial capacity.

Among the various non-governmental actors involved in the international legal process associated with environmental issues, environmental organizations have been most involved in the implementation and enforcement process. In the late 1970s and early 1980s environmental organizations developed from being small, under-resourced, and national to being large, well resourced, and international: UNCED was attended by more than 10,000 individuals representing environmental organizations in an official capacity accredited to the conference. These groups have frequently made effective use of the international legal system in their efforts to protect the environment at the national, regional and global level.

Since the 1972 Stockholm Conference, which was to a large extent convened as a result of pressure by environmental organizations, they have played an important role in contributing to the great increase in international environmental legislation and in the enforcement process at the national and international level. In the enforcement process the role of environmental organizations can be formal or informal, and their primary role continues to be at the national level, through political means or by recourse to administrative or judicial procedures for enforcing national measures adopted by a state in implementing its international treaty and other obligations. Increasingly, however, non-governmental organizations are playing a role in the enforcement of international obligations at the transboundary level and in other international contexts.

Enforcement in the national courts

The support which was expressed at UNCED for a stronger role for the non-governmental sector in enforcing national environmental laws and obligations before national courts and tribunals, as reflected in Agenda 21 and the Rio Declaration,[100] must be understood in the context of earlier treaties and agreements which sought to recognize and encourage their role, particularly where individuals were the victims of pollution or environmental damage in a transboundary context. These earlier efforts sought either to establish principles or rules governing equal access to national courts by victims of transfrontier pollution, or to establish the jurisdiction of courts in the event of transboundary incidents.

Several OECD Council recommendations of the mid-1970s identify the constituent elements of a system of equal rights of access. This provides access, for example, in favour of persons who are affected or likely to be affected in their personal or proprietary interests by transfrontier pollution, in the country where the pollution originated, to information, participation in hearings and enquiries and 'recourse to and standing in administrative and judicial procedures' to prevent pollution, have it abated, and/or obtain compensation for the damage caused.[101]

These non-binding OECD instruments are supplemented by a range of treaty and other binding obligations which address equal access or the jurisdiction of courts over transboundary disputes. The 1974 Nordic Environmental Protection Convention allows any person who is affected or may be affected by a nuisance caused by 'environmentally harmful activities' in another contracting state to bring before the appropriate court or administrative authority of that state the permissibility of such activities, including the question of measures to prevent damage and compensation.[102] This Convention also provides for the appointment of a supervisory authority in each state 'to be entrusted with the task of safeguarding general environmental interests in so far as regards nuisances arising out of environmentally harmful activities in another contracting state', including the right to institute proceedings before or be heard by the courts or administrative authority of such a state.[103] The supervisory authority of the state in which damage occurs is also required to facilitate onsite inspections to determine such damage.[104]

An enforcement role for individuals is envisaged by several treaties establishing international rules on civil liability. In relation to the jurisdiction of national courts, these fall into two categories: those treaties requiring victims to bring proceedings before the courts of the state in which the transboundary pollution originated, and those which allow victims to choose the courts of the state in which either the pollution originated or the the damage was suffered. The nuclear liability conventions adopted in the 1960s fall into the former category.[105] The requirement that victims of nuclear damage should have to make their claims before courts which may be several thousands of miles away from the area where damage occurred establishes an onerous burden. Moreover, they do not expressly allow for claims for environmental damage, although negotiations are currently underway to extend the definition of damage to include environmental damage. The oil pollution conventions adopted a decade or so later also provide support for the enforcement role of individuals, and are more accessible to individuals since they allow victims to claim before the courts of any contracting state or states where an incident has caused pollution damage.[106]

The second category of conventions assuring a role for individual enforcement of environmental laws are those establishing private international law rules allocating jurisdiction to national courts over a range of civil and commercial matters, including disputes arising out of the law of tort. These generally fall into the latter category, allowing the victim a choice of courts.[107] Although they were not prepared with environmental pollution and disputes in mind, they are capable of being applied to a broad range of transboundary environmental disputes. The 1968 Brussels Convention on Jurisdiction and Enforcement of Judgements in Civil and Commercial Matters (1968 Brussels Convention), to which EC member states alone may become Parties, has a number of purposes, including the free circulation of judgements throughout the EC, and establishing jurisdiction rules for civil and commercial matters.[108] Under Article 5(3) of the Convention jurisdiction in matters 'relating to tort, delict or quasi-delict' is conferred on the courts of the place 'where the harmful event occurred'.

In *Handelskwekerij GJ Bier v. Mines de Potasses d'Alsace*,[109] a case in which a discharge of pollutant took place in France and damage was suffered in the Netherlands, the ECJ said that the words 'where the harmful event occurred' should be interpreted

> in such a way as to acknowledge that the plaintiff has an option to commence proceedings either at the place where the damage occurred or the place of the event giving rise to it.[110]

This has opened the way for victims of transboundary pollution in EC member states to choose the jurisdiction in which they wish to bring environmental cases which could be classified as tortious, delictual or quasi-delictual in nature. In 1988 the Brussels Convention was supplemented by the Lugano Convention on Jurisdiction and Enforcement of Judgements in Civil and Commercial Matters, which applies broadly similar rules to relations between EC and EFTA countries as those set forth in the Brussels Convention.[111]

International enforcement

At the international level the formal opportunities for non-governmental actors to play an enforcement role are extremely limited. Under some of the regional human rights treaties individual victims, including non-governmental organizations, may bring complaints directly to an international body. Thus, the European Convention on Human Rights allows the European Commission on Human Rights to receive petitions from any person, non-governmental organization or group of individuals claiming to be the victim of a violation by one of the Parties of the rights set forth in the Convention, provided that the Party against which the complaint has been lodged has accepted the competence of the Commission to receive such petitions.[112]

Similar provisions are set forth in the Optional Protocol to the 1966 International Covenant on Civil and Political Rights in respect of communications by individuals to the Human Rights Committee, alleging breaches of the Covenant.[113] The International Covenant on Economic, Social and Cultural Rights, however, does not grant individuals and non-governmental organizations such rights.[114] The UN Commission on Human Rights[115] cannot receive individual complaints concerning human rights violations, although its subsidiary Sub-Commission on the Prevention of Discrimination and Protection of Minorities,[116] can receive communications concerning complaints about a consistent pattern of gross and reliably attested violations of human rights, and then refer them to the Commission on Human Rights.

Non-governmental organizations and individuals have played a particularly active role in supporting the enforcement role of the EC Commission, usually by submitting complaints to that institution concerning the non-implementation by member states of their environmental obligations. In 1991 more than 400 complaints were received by the EC Commission concerning non-compliance with environmental obligations, leading to a number of formal investigations by the Commission.

It is in their informal capacity as watchdogs that environmental organizations play an important role in the development, application and enforcement of international environmental law. Environmental organizations have long been active in monitoring and seeking to enforce compliance by states of international environmental laws and standards. In this context development, application and enforcement may be so closely intertwined that it may be misleading to attempt to separate the tasks, as illustrated by the following two examples.

The ban on international trade in ivory: CITES

There is little doubt that but for the intervention of a large number of environmental organizations, and in particular the British-based Environmental Investigation Agency (EIA), the decision in October 1989 to uplift the African elephant (*loxodanta africana*) to Appendix 1 of 1973 CITES (and thereby ban international trade in ivory) would not have taken place. Environmental organizations raised public consciousness about the issue and, using international law and international legal arguments, as well as their status as observers at the Conference of the Parties of CITES, ensured that the issue was formally addressed on the international agenda. Having raised the issues, including allegations of breaches by the CITES Secretariat of its neutrality and independence, it was an environmental organization (in this case the World Wide Fund for Nature (WWF) which disposed of the international legal argument put forward by certain Parties to the CITES (and supported by the CITES Secretariat)) that the proposed ban would amount to a retroactive application of law, or otherwise constitute a wrongful interference with the legitimate expectations of existing ivory stockpile holders. This the WWF did by obtaining, and then circulating to all 103 Parties present at the CITES meeting in Lausanne, an independent and formal legal opinion challenging the basis of the 'retroactivity' and 'legitimate expectation' arguments. While the effect of the WWF action cannot be quantified with certainty, it is interesting to note that following the circulation of the legal opinion, those legal arguments did not reappear, and a former member of the CITES Secretariat has indicated that this was due to WWF action.

The complex legal saga of the attempt to save the African elephant by uplifting it to CITES Appendix I did not, however, end with the overwhelming vote of the Conference to do so. On 17 January 1990, shortly before the 90-day period for entering reservations to the CITES amendment had expired, the government of the United Kingdom and other states entered a reservation excluding the application of the ban to the territory of Hong Kong. It was left to environmental organizations to consider the legality of that reservation under English law, under CITES law, and under EC law. Immediately after the reservation was entered by the United Kingdom, a group of United States environmental organizations, led by Greenpeace, obtained an independent and formal legal opinion from another non-governmental organization. On 25 April 1990 they formally petitioned the US Secretary of the Interior to certify to the President of the United States, pursuant to the Pelly Act, that China, the United Kingdom (on behalf of Hong Kong), and Zimbabwe were 'diminishing the effectiveness' of the CITES programme for the protection of the African elephant. If successful, the President would have been required to impose appropriate economic sanctions against the countries concerned. When the UK reservation expired after six months it was not renewed.

Subsidies to the UK nuclear industry: EC competition laws

This example concerns the proposed privatization of the electricity industry by the British government, commencing with the 1989 Electricity Act. It illustrates the role of environmental organizations in having recourse to particular rules of international law, as well as the way in which 'economic' laws may be used to assist in the achievement of 'environmental' objectives. Certain environmental groups in the United Kingdom objected to the proposed privatization of the civil nuclear power industry, which accounted for about 18 per cent of domestic electricity production. The manner in which they were able to take steps to prevent the proposed nuclear privatization was provided by European Community law, and in particular its rules on competition law, including 'state aids' (subsidies).

The British government was proposing to subsidize the nuclear sector in three ways: first, by granting up to £2500 million towards decommissioning costs; second, by imposing on electricity distributors a legal obligation to purchase 15 per cent of their electricity from non-fossil fuel sources (the so-called non-fossil fuel obligation) of which the only one available was nuclear; and third, by imposing a nuclear levy, a tax on each consumer bill aimed at lessening the cost to the generator of nuclear electricity, which was accepted by the government to be considerably higher than non-nuclear generated electricity.

A domestic environmental group, the Council for the Protection of Rural England (CPRE) was advised by legal counsel that these proposed governmental subsidies were *prima facie* contrary to Article 92 of the EEC Treaty, which prohibits 'state aids', and ought therefore to be notified to the Commission of the European Communities. Such a notification had not occurred, and in a flurry of publicity in June 1989 the CPRE formally complained to the EC Commission about the proposed governmental subsidies. At the same time, the financial sector and potential investors were becoming increasingly nervous about their potential exposure to long-term financial liabilities associated with the nuclear industry, and made clear that they would only invest in the nuclear industry if provided with firm guarantees of government aid, such as those to be provided in the 1989 Act.

In September 1989 the Commission informed the CPRE that it was to commence a formal investigation of the proposed subsidies to the nuclear sector. This information was widely publicized, adding further apprehension in the financial sector and undermining the Government's assurances of long-term support. In November 1989, under pressure from the unlikely coalition of environmentalists and financiers, the government announced that it was withdrawing the nuclear industry from the privatization programme. In so doing, it made clear that its inability as a matter of law, and indeed lack of desire, to subsidize a private nuclear sector had played a large role in its decision.

For the CPRE, its use of rules of economic law to achieve environmental objectives was considered successful.[117] The final decision of the Commission was not in itself the objective. Rather, the principal objective was to get the EC Commission to commence a formal legal investigation, thereby embarrassing the government by highlighting its potentially illegal act and focusing the City on the uncertainties of governmental support for activities which the CPRE believed to be environmentally harmful.

INTERNATIONAL CONFLICT RESOLUTION (SETTLEMENT OF DISPUTES)

Introduction

A range of international procedures and mechanisms are available to assist in the pacific settlement of environmental disputes arising over non-implementation of international obligations. Article 33 of the United Nations Charter identifies the traditional mechanisms for the pacific settlement of disputes including negotiation, enquiry, mediation, conciliation, arbitration, judicial settlement, resort to regional agencies or arrangements, or other peaceful means of their own choice.[118]

These techniques can be divided into two broad categories: diplomatic means according to which the parties retain control over the dispute insofar as they may accept or reject a proposed settlement (negotiation, consultation, mediation, conciliation); and *legal means* which result in legally binding decisions for the parties to the dispute (arbitration and judicial settlement). Recourse to regional arrangements and international organizations as mediators and conciliators provide something of a middle way: the legal consequences of any decision taken by the institution will depend on the treaty establishing the institution.

Many of the earliest environmental treaties did not provide for any dispute settlement mechanisms, whether of a diplomatic or legal nature, or of a voluntary or mandatory character.[119] Initially, the trend was towards the use of informal and non-binding mechanisms, such as negotiation and consultation, supplemented by the use of more formal mechanisms, such as conciliation, arbitration and judicial settlement. More recently, there has been a move towards the development of new techniques which aim at establishing non-contentious mechanisms which allow the intervention of a third party in an international context. More recently, there has been a move towards the development of new techniques to establish non-contentious mechanisms. Recent treaties provide Parties with a range of options for dispute settlement and encouraging implementation: the 1992 Climate Change Convention envisages at least three mechanisms to assist in dispute resolution or non-implementation: a Subsidiary Body for Implementation, which is intended to provide assistance in implementation; a multilateral consultative process for the resolution of questions regarding implementation in a non-confrontational way; and the settlement of remaining disputes in more traditional ways by reference to negotiation, or submission to arbitration or the ICJ, or to international conciliation.[120]

Diplomatic means of dispute settlement

Negotiation and consultation

The technique of negotiation has been used to resolve a wide range of environmental disputes. In the Fisheries Jurisdiction Case the ICJ set the basic objectives underlying negotiation as an appropriate method for the solution of a dispute. The Court held that the objective of negotiation, should be

> the delimitation of the rights and interests of the Parties, the preferential rights of the coastal state on the one hand and the rights of the Applicant on the other, to balance

> and regulate equitably questions such as those of catch-limitation, share allocations and 'related restrictions concerning areas closed to fishing, number and type of vessels allowed and forms of control of the agreed provisions'.[121]

The International Court also set out conditions establishing that future negotiations should be conducted

> on the basis that each must in good faith pay reasonable regard to the legal rights of the other . . . thus bringing about an equitable apportionment of the fishing resources based on the facts of the particular situation, and having regard to the interests of other states which have established fishing rights in the area. It is not a matter of finding simply an equitable solution, but an equitable solution derived from the applicable law.[122]

Environmental treaties refer, more or less as a matter of standard practice, to the need to ensure that Parties resort to negotiation and other diplomatic channels to resolve their disputes before making use of other more formal approaches.[123] Since negotiations of this type invariably take place behind closed doors it is difficult to identify specific examples involving the successful resolution of claims and disputes by negotiation. One such case involves the settlement between Canada and the USSR concerning damage caused by the disintegration over Canada of Cosmos 954, a nuclear powered satellite launched by the USSR. The negotiated settlement was agreed to in the context of the USSR's consideration of the question of damage 'in strict accordance with the provisions' of the 1972 Space Liability Convention to which both countries were Parties.[124]

Consultation between states is also encouraged by environmental treaties as a technique to avoid and resolve disputes and potential disputes between states. In the Lac Lanoux Case the arbitral tribunal held that France had a duty to consult with Spain over certain projects likely to affect Spain's interests, and that in this context

> the reality of the obligations thus undertaken is incontestable and sanctions can be applied in the event, for example, of an unjustified breaking off of the discussions, abnormal delays, disregard of the agreed procedures, systematic refusals to take into consideration adverse proposals or interests, and, more generally, in cases of violation of the rules of good faith.[125]

Specific examples of environmental treaties requiring consultation relate to numerous diverse situations, including the following non-exhaustive list: development plans which may affect the natural resources of another state;[126] measures to prevent pollution of coastlines from oil pollution incidents on the high seas;[127] prior to the grant of permission for ocean dumping in emergency situations;[128] pollution from land-based sources of certain substances;[129] on the permissibility of environmentally harmful activities;[130] and generally problems in applying a treaty or the need for and nature of remedial measures for breaches of obligation.[131] The 1979 LRTAP Convention requires early consultations to be held between Parties 'actually affected by or exposed to a significant risk of long-range transboundary air pollution' and the Parties in which a significant contribution to such pollution originates.[132]

Mediation, conciliation and international institutions

Where negotiation and consultation fail, a number of environmental treaties provide for the use of mediation,[133] conciliation[134] (or the establishment of a

Committee of Experts)[135] to resolve disputes, both of which involve the intervention of a third person. In the case of mediation, the third person is involved as an active participant in the interchange of proposals between the parties to a dispute, and may even offer informal proposals of his or her own. In the case of conciliation, the third person assumes a more formal role and often investigates the details underlying the dispute and makes formal proposals for the resolution of the dispute. Examples of conciliation include the role of the International Joint Commission established by Canada and the United States in the 1909 Boundary Waters Treaty,[136] which fulfils a combination of quasijudicial, investigative and recommendatory, and coordinating functions. The European Commission on Human Rights also performs conciliation functions: once a petition has been referred to it, it is required to ascertain the facts, place itself at the disposal of the parties concerned with a view to securing a friendly settlement of the matter on the basis of respect for Human Rights as defined in the Convention; and, where no such friendly settlement is reached, draw up a report on the facts and state its opinion as to whether the facts found disclose a breach of obligations under the Convention.[137]

The Dispute Settlement Panels established under the GATT perform a similar function.[138] Under Article XXIII:2 of the GATT they assist the Parties to a dispute to reach a solution and, failing that, to make an objective assessment of the matter before it, including an objective assessment of the facts of the case and the applicability and conformity with the GATT.[139] If requested by the contracting Parties, the Panels make such other findings, including recommendations, as will assist them in making recommendations or in giving rulings. Under the 1985 Vienna Convention and the 1992 Biodiversity Convention, conciliation will be used if the parties to the dispute have not accepted compulsory dispute settlement procedures by arbitration or the International Court of Justice.[140]

The political organs of international institutions and regional agencies also play an important role in the settlement of disputes. Such organs may be granted an express mandate to consider disputes between two or more Parties to the treaty.[141] Alternatively, they may attempt to resolve disputes between Parties absent a specific mandate to do so. Examples of the latter include the 1985 decision of the Conference of the Parties to CITES concerning the application of the Convention to endangered species acquired prior to the entry into force of the Convention,[142] and the 1991 decision of the Executive Committee of the 1971 Oil Pollution Fund Convention to exclude claims by Italy against the Fund for non-quantifiable damage to the marine environment.[143]

A limited number of treaties establish subsidiary bodies to deal with compliance and disputes relating to non-compliance. The most important example is the non-compliance procedure established under the 1987 Montreal Protocol and conducted under the auspices of an Implementation Committee first established by the Second Meeting of the Parties to the 1987 Montreal Protocol.[144] Resort to the non-compliance procedure is without prejudice to the dispute settlement provisions available under Article 11 of the 1985 Vienna Convention, which include negotiation, good offices, mediation, arbitration, submission to the ICJ, and the establishment of a conciliation commission.

Numerous other examples exist. The 1974 Nordic Environmental Protection Convention provides for the establishment of a Commission upon the demand of each Party to give an opinion on the permissibility of environmentally harmful activities which entail considerable nuisance in another Party.[145] The 1985 South Pacific Nuclear Free Zone Treaty establishes a control system which includes a complaints procedure involving the possible convening of a Consultative Committee to consider complaints and evidence of breach of obligations, with certain inspection powers, and the right to report fully to members of the South Pacific Forum and give its decision as to whether a breach of obligations has occurred.[146] Under the 1991 Espoo Convention, if the Parties cannot agree whether a proposed activity is likely to result in a 'significant adverse transboundary impact' any Party involved in the disagreement may submit that question to an Inquiry Commission.[147] The Inquiry Commission, comprising three members, will advise and prepare an opinion based on 'accepted scientific principles' on the likelihood of significant adverse transboundary impact, and may take all appropriate measures to carry out its functions.[148] Finally, the procedure established under the Conference on Security and Cooperation in Europe provides an alternative means of achieving conciliation.[149]

Legal means of dispute settlement

Mediation and conciliations do not produce legally binding decisions. If the Parties to a dispute seek such a result they opt for arbitration or recourse to an international court.

Arbitration

International arbitration has been described as having 'for its object the settlement of disputes between states by judges of their own choice and on the basis of respect for the law. Recourse to arbitration implies an engagement to submit in good faith to the award.'[150] In recent years states negotiating environmental treaties have favoured the inclusion of specific provisions for the establishment of an arbitration tribunal, with the power to adopt binding and final decisions. Early examples providing for the establishment of a body to take binding decisions include the 'special commission' to be established at the request of any of the Parties to disputes relating to high seas fishing and conservation,[151] and the detailed provisions on the establishment of an Arbitration Tribunal in the Annex to the 1969 Oil Pollution Intervention Convention.[152] Other treaties refer simply to the possibility of submitting disputes to arbitration without providing details on the establishment of such a body or its working arrangements.[153] Certain environmental treaties provide for the submission of disputes to arbitration by mutual consent of the relevant Parties[154] or allow a Party to declare, at the time of signature or ratification, that it is not bound by parts of the dispute settlement provisions, including submission to arbitration,[155] or provide for a Party to declare, at time of signature or ratification, or at any time thereafter, its acceptance of compulsory recourse to arbitration and/or the International Court of Justice.[156]

International courts

The settlement of international disputes may also be referred to an international court, which is a permanent tribunal competent to deliver a legally binding decision. In relation to environmental disputes four international courts have played, and are likely to continue to play, a role: the International Court of Justice, the European Court of Justice, the courts established under the various regional human rights treaties, and the courts and tribunals established under the UN Convention on the Law of the Sea. In addition, there are several non-governmental efforts to establish 'international courts' dedicated to addressing international environmental issues. Whilst not creating binding arrangements these provide a useful way to bring to public attention important international environmental issues.[157]

International Court of Justice

The International Court of Justice, sometimes referred to as the World Court or the Hague Court, is the principal judicial organ of the United Nations. It was established as a successor (although not formally the legal successor) to the Permanent Court of International Justice in 1945. Jurisdiction of the International Court of Justice over a particular dispute depends on whether the Court has been invoked in a contentious case between two or more states, or to give advisory opinions on questions of law at the request of states or certain international organizations.[158] In July 1993 the Court established a seven member Chamber for Environmental Matters. This decision followed previous consideration by the Court on the possible formation of such a chamber, and was taken in view of the developments in the field of environmental law which have taken place in the last few years and the need to be prepared to the fullest possible extent to deal with any environmental case falling within its jurisdiction.[159]

Contentious cases

The contentious jurisdiction of the Court in relation to a particular dispute can arise in at least two ways. First, under Article 36(1) of its Statute, the Court has jurisdiction by agreement between the parties to the dispute, either by a special agreement (*compromis*) whereby two or more states agree to refer a particular dispute and defined matter to the Court, or by a compromissory clause in a multilateral or bilateral treaty. The treaty could be a general treaty for the peaceful settlement of disputes, a treaty dealing with the general relations between the states, or a treaty regulating a specific topic, such as environmental protection. Many environmental treaties provide for possible recourse to the ICJ to settle disputes. Occasionally they establish the compulsory jurisdiction of the International Court,[160] but more usually the reference of a dispute to the Court requires the consent, in each case, of all parties to the dispute.[161] Recent practice in environmental treaties allows parties at the time of signature, ratification or accession, or at any time thereafter, to accept compulsory dispute settlement by recourse to arbitration or to the ICJ.[162] In practice few Parties accept this option.

A second way in which contentious cases get to the ICJ is under Article 36(2) of the Statute (the 'Optional Clause') under which Parties to the Statute of the Court may declare that they recognize the compulsory jurisdiction of the Court, in relation to other states accepting the same obligation, in all legal disputes concerning the interpretation of a treaty, any question of international law, the existence of any fact which, if established, would constitute a breach of an international obligation; and the nature or extent of the reparation to be made for the breach of an international obligation.[163] Acceptance of the jurisdiction of the Court under Article 36(2) may be made unconditionally, or on condition of reciprocity, or for a limited period of time.[164] Additionally, the practice of the Court has been to accept reservations or conditions to declarations made under the Optional Clause.

While the ICJ and its predecessor, the Permanent Court of International Justice, has never dealt fully with a major international environmental dispute, it has had the opportunity in a number of cases concerned with natural resource issues to consider matters concerning environment and conservation or to give judgements which establish important general principles. Relevant cases before the Permanent Court include the Diversion of the Waters of the River Meuse[165] and the Territorial Jurisdiction of the International Commission of the River Oder.[166] Cases before the ICJ which have particularly influenced the development of international environmental law include the Corfu Channel Case, where the Court affirmed 'every state's obligation not to allow knowingly its territory to be used for acts contrary to the rights of other states';[167] the Fisheries Jurisdiction Case, where the Court set forth basic principles governing consultations and other arrangements concerning the conservation of shared natural resources;[168] and the Nuclear Tests Cases.[169] The Court currently has one contentious case before it which it considers as having important implications for international law on matters relating to the environment: the Gabcikovo-Nagymaros Project (Hungary/Slovakia), addressing, *inter alia*, whether agreements for the construction of a dam which would result in the diversion of the Danube river may be terminated by one of the Parties on the grounds of, *inter alia*, the adverse environmental consequences of the project.[170] Another case raising environmental issues, concerning Certain Phosphate Lands in Nauru (*Nauru* v. *Australia*), was settled between the Parties in August 1993. It concerned the obligation, if any, of Trustee states for, *inter alia*, the physical destruction of the island as a unit of self-determination accompanied by a failure to rehabilitate the land, as well as the nature and extent of obligations relating to permanent sovereignty over natural resources and entitlement to the costs of rehabilitation.[171] The settlement of the case, three years after it had been filed by Nauru and after the Court had rejected the Australian claim that the case should be struck out on the grounds that it was inadmissible, illustrates the potential role of the Court as a forum for alleging violations of international law.

Advisory opinions

The Charter of the United Nations allows the General Assembly or the Security Council to request the ICJ to give an advisory opinion on any legal question,[172] and allows other organs of the United Nations and specialized agencies authorized by the General Assembly to request advisory opinions of the Court on legal questions arising within the scope of their activities.[173] Advisory opinions are not binding in law upon the requesting body, although in practice they are accepted and acted upon by that body. Although no legal question on an environmental issue has been the subject of a request for an Advisory Opinion, this route could provide a useful and non-contentious way of obtaining independent international legal advice on environmental matters. The Court currently has one request for an Advisory Opinion before it which raises environmental issues: in July 1993 the World Health Organization (WHO) sought an opinion on whether the use of nuclear weapons would be lawful under international law, given the effects on human health and the environment. Although the utility of the request has been questioned on both political and legal grounds, it may present the Court with an opportunity to consider the status of various rules of international environmental law.

Interim measures of protection

If it considers that the circumstances so require, the ICJ also has the power to indicate interim measures of protection to preserve the rights of the parties to a dispute.[174] The irreparability of environmental damage will make interim measures particularly important in cases concerning environmental protection. During the preliminary phase of the Nuclear Tests Cases the Court indicated interim measures of protection, asking that the parties ensure that no action should be taken which might aggravate or extend the dispute or prejudice the rights of another party, and calling on France to 'avoid nuclear tests causing the deposit of radioactive fall-out on Australian territory'.[175] Interim measures of protection were also indicated in the Fisheries Jurisdiction Cases,[176] but were not indicated more recently in the Passage through the Great Belt Case.[177]

European Court of Justice

The European Court of Justice is the judicial institution of the EC and is required to ensure that in the interpretation and application of the EEC Treaty 'the law is observed'.[178] Environmental cases reach the European Court in a number of ways. The most frequent route is under Article 169 of the EEC Treaty, and since 1980 the EC Commission has brought more than 40 cases to the ECJ alleging the failure of a member state to comply with its EEC environmental obligations, in which its is usually successful. Its judgements have been useful to determine, *inter alia,* that member states may not plead provisions, practices or circumstances existing in their internal legal system to justify a failure to comply with an environmental obligation;[179] that mere administrative practices which may be altered at the whim of the administration do not constitute the proper fulfilment of an environmental obligation under a directive;[180] and that the legal obligations imposed on a member state by an environmental directive are limited to those dangerous substances specifically listed in the directive and not to other unlisted dangerous substances as well.[181] More recently the European Court has considered the legality of measures taken in the context of environmental trade obligations[182] and the failure to execute one of its own judgements.[183] Under Article 170 of the EC Treaty a member state which believes another member state has breached its obligations has a similar right to bring a matter before the ECJ, but to date no case concerning alleged breaches of environmental obligations has been brought under this provision.

Under Article 173 of the EC Treaty the ECJ is competent to review the legality of certain acts of the EC Council and Commission on the grounds of lack of competence, infringement of an essential procedural requirement, infringement of the EEC Treaty or any rule relating to its application, or misuse of powers. Actions may be brought by a member state, the Council or the Commission, as well as by any legal or natural person provided that the act concerned is a decision addressed to that person or is of direct or individual concern to it.[184] Under this head the ECJ has considered the legality of the treaty basis of EC environmental legislation,[185] and received an application from two environmental groups alleging violations by the EC Commission of its legal obligations under the EEC Treaty.[186] The ECJ also has jurisdiction under Article 175, under similar conditions as Article 173, to challenge the failure of the EC Council or Commission to have acted in pursuance of its environmental obligations under the EEC Treaty. To date no environmental case appears to have been brought under this provision.

Finally, the ECJ has also considered environmental questions on the basis of its jurisdiction under Article 177, the 'preliminary reference procedure'. Under this provision the national courts of the EC member states may refer to the ECJ questions concerning, *inter alia*, the interpretation of the EC Treaty and the validity and interpretation of acts of the EC institutions, provided that a decision on the question is necessary to enable the national court to give a ruling on the question. Preliminary references from national courts to the ECJ are used when a dispute before the national courts raise a complex question or questions of EEC law or where the dispute turns on the EEC point and no appeal lies against the decision of the national court. The Article 177 procedure has been used on several occasions to allow the EC to rule on matters of an environmental nature, such as the question of compatibility with EEC law of the ban by an Italian municipality on the sale and distribution of plastic bags and other nonbiodegradable packaging material.[187]

The experience of the ECJ might provide a useful basis for judicial developments in other regions which are seeking to put in place regional free trade arrangements, including in relation to the African Economic Community and the North American Free Trade Agreement.

Human rights courts

The human rights courts established under the various regional human rights conventions[188] may also have jurisdiction over environmental matters, although so far only the European Court of Human Rights appears to have had an opportunity to address environmental issues.[189] The European Court has jurisdiction over all cases concerning the interpretation and application of the European Convention provided that the Party or Parties concerned by the case have accepted its compulsory jurisdiction or, failing that, with their consent.[190] The Court may only deal with a case after efforts by the Commission to achieve a friendly settlement have failed,[191] and only the Commission or the Party whose national is the alleged victim, or which referred the case to the Commission, or against which the complaint has been lodged, may bring a case before the Court. The victim therefore has no right to bring a matter to the Court, although in practice the victim will work closely with the Commission in the preparation of the case.

UNCLOS

Part XV of the 1982 UNCLOS, which has not yet entered into force, contains detailed provision on compulsory dispute settlement, allowing states at the time of signature, ratification or accession or at any time thereafter to choose one or more of the following to decide disputes under UNCLOS: the International Tribunal for the Law of the Sea (established in accordance with Annex VI of UNCLOS), the ICJ; an arbitral tribunal (constituted in accordance with Annex VII); and a special arbitral tribunal (constituted in accordance with Annex

VIII).[192] A state which does not designate one of these means is deemed to have designated arbitration in accordance with Annex VII.[193]

The application of the compulsory dispute settlement procedure is limited to certain disputes under the Convention. The exercise by a coastal state of its sovereign rights or jurisdiction under UNCLOS are only subject to the compulsory procedures when it is alleged that a coastal state has violated certain provisions of the Convention concerning rights of navigation, overflights or the laying of submarine cables and pipelines or other internationally lawful uses of the EEZ, or where it is alleged that a coastal state has violated specified international rules and standards for the protection and preservation of the marine environment which are applicable to that state and which are established under UNCLOS or by a competent international organization or diplomatic conference.[194] Certain disputes relating to marine scientific research will also be excluded from the compulsory procedure.[195] Fisheries disputes will be subject to the compulsory procedure, with the exception of disputes relating to the sovereign right of a coastal state with respect to the living resources of the EEZ including the discretionary powers for determining allowable catch, harvesting capacity, allocation of surpluses and terms and conditions of its conservation and management laws and regulations.[196] Such disputes may, however, be submitted to the conciliation procedure if it is alleged, *inter alia*, that the coastal state has manifestly failed to comply with its obligations to ensure that the maintenance of the living resources in the EEZ is not seriously endangered.[197] Parties may also optionally declare that the compulsory procedures do not apply to disputes concerning boundary delimitations, military activities, and those in respect of which the Security Council is exercising its functions.[198]

Disputes relating to the exploration and exploitation of the international seabed and ocean floor (the Area) and its resources are subject to special, and rather complicated, dispute settlement procedures, which will generally involve disputes going to a Sea-Bed Disputes Chamber of the International Tribunal for the Law of the Sea.[199] The Sea-Bed Disputes Chamber will have jurisdiction over a wide range of disputes involving different categories of persons involved in the conduct of activities in the Area, including states, Parties, the Authority, the Enterprise, state enterprises and legal or natural persons, and prospective contractors.[200]

UNCED

Whereas the 1972 Stockholm Conference did not really address the compliance issue, the subject was clearly an important one for UNCED. United Nations General Assembly Resolution 44/228, which convened UNCED, recognized that one of the objectives of the Conference should be 'to assess the capacity of the United Nations system to assist in the prevention and settlement of disputes in the environmental sphere and to recommend measures in this field, while respecting existing bilateral and international agreements that provide for the settlement of such disputes'.

By any standard this task can be considered to have been only partly fulfilled. Principle 10 of the Rio Declaration calls on states to provide 'effective access to judicial and administrative proceedings, including redress and remedy'[201] and on states to 'resolve all their environmental disputes peacefully and by appropriate means and in accordance with the Charter of the United Nations'.[202] Agenda 21 goes a little further in recognizing the limitations of existing arrangements, including the inadequate implementation by Parties of their obligations, the need to involve international institutions and environmental organizations in the implementation process, and the existence of important gaps in the dispute settlement mechanisms. Chapter 39 of Agenda 21 ('International legal instruments and mechanisms') addresses some of the needs. The whole of the international community is called upon to ensure 'the full and prompt implementation of legally binding instruments',[203] and Parties to international agreements are instructed to 'consider procedures and mechanisms to promote and review their effective, full and prompt implementation', including through the establishment of 'efficient and practical reporting systems on the effective, full and prompt implementation of international legal instruments' and consideration of the ways in which international bodies might contribute towards the further development of such mechanisms.[204] The role of international institutions is recognized. UNEP is called upon to promote the implementation of international environmental law;[205] UNDP will play a lead role in support of the implementation of Agenda 21 and capacity building at the country, regional, interregional and global levels;[206] and the UN Commission on Sustainable Development will 'consider, where appropriate, information regarding the progress made in the implementation of environmental conventions which could be made available by the relevant Conferences of the Parties'.[207]

> With regard to dispute settlement, the international community is called upon to study and consider the broadening and strengthening of the capacity of mechanisms, *inter alia* in the United Nations system, to facilitate, where appropriate and agreed by the parties concerned, the identification, avoidance and settlement of international disputes in the field of sustainable development, duly taking into account existing bilateral and multilateral agreements for the settlement of such disputes.[208]

Specifically, this includes

> mechanisms and procedures for the exchange of data and information, notification and consultation regarding situations that might lead to disputes with other states in the field of sustainable development and for effective peaceful means of dispute settlement in accordance with the Charter of the United Nations including, where appropriate, recourse to the International Court of Justice, and their inclusion in treaties relating to sustainable development.[209]

The functions of the UN Commission on Sustainable Development will include reviewing progress in the implementation of Agenda 21 commitments and 'to consider, where appropriate, information regarding the progress made in the implementation of environmental conventions, which could be made available by the relevant Conferences of the Parties'.[210]

CONCLUSIONS

As this chapter shows, the increased attention which is being given to the issue of compliance has generated a broad range of measures in the field of environmental protection which supplement the availability of measures under the rules of general international law. The decision by the ICJ to establish an Environmental Chamber marks a potentially important development to encourage the role of judicial settlement of international environment law disputes, and recognition that the effectiveness of the growing body of principles and rules will require the availability of appropriate dispute settlement mechanisms. The limitations inherent in international arrangements for ensuring compliance with international environmental obligations are clear from this overview. Developments in international law alone will not be sufficient to overcome the political, economic and social reasons which lie behind non-compliance. Nevertheless the law, legal processes and legal institutions can make a difference, and recent developments suggest that important changes in the way states and other members of the international community think of compliance reflect the changing structure of the traditional international legal order.

Addressing compliance will require a comprehensive effort to develop rules and institutional arrangements at three levels: for implementation, enforcement, and dispute settlement. First, with regard to implementation, the provision of technical, financial and other assistance to states, particularly developing states, points to the growing 'internationalization' of the domestic legal situation, and an awareness that international environmental law will not achieve its objectives if it does not also take account of the need to, and techniques available for, improving domestic implementation of international environmental obligations. Second, with regard to enforcement, states remain unwilling, for a variety of reasons, to bring international claims to enforce environmental rights and obligations, and this will further reinforce the supplementary role of international organizations and, to a lesser extent, non-governmental actors in the international enforcement process. Broadening the category of persons formally entitled to identify violations and take measures to remedy them is a process which is underway and which should be further encouraged if states and other members of the international community are to be subjected to the sorts of pressures that will lead them to improve compliance with their obligations. Third, as the dispute between Hungary and Slovakia over the Gabcikovo-Nagymaros Dam has shown, the availability of a broad range of mechanisms for dispute settlement, including the compulsory jurisdiction of certain regional and sectoral courts and other international bodies, suggests an important and growing role for independent international adjudication. Finally, Principle 10 of the Rio Declaration and recent developments in the EC reflect the recognition that ensuring effective access to judicial and administrative proceedings, including redress and remedies, are appropriately matters for consideration by the international community.

PART 2

Global Compliance Systems

PART 2

Global Constraint Systems

4 DESIGNING A COMPLIANCE SYSTEM FOR THE UN FRAMEWORK CONVENTION ON CLIMATE CHANGE

Jacob Werksman[1]

INTRODUCTION

This chapter is an effort to apply 'compliance theory', as summarized earlier in this book,[2] to a concrete challenge. The 1992 United Nations Framework Convention on Climate Change became binding law on 21 March 1994. At their first session in March–April 1995, the Parties to the Climate Change Convention set up a group of experts to study issues related to the designing of a 'multilateral consultative process, available to Parties on their request, for the resolution of questions regarding the implementation of the Convention'.[3] This process could form an important part of the Convention's compliance system, and assist in enabling and encouraging Parties to comply with the Convention's provisions.

A well-designed multilateral compliance system could prove to be of particular importance to both developed and developing country Parties that are concerned about the effective implementation of the Convention, but that may have concerns about their own ability to comply or may not have the political or economic power to act alone in encouraging compliance by fellow Parties.

This chapter provides a general overview of the issues Parties to the Convention will have to address when returning to the negotiation of a compliance system. The second section analyzes the Convention's general characteristics and its primary rules. The analysis highlights the importance of clarifying and strengthening the commitments under the Convention, and suggests that the common but differentiated structure of the Convention will mean that the availability of financial resources will play a crucial role in the Convention's compliance system.

Part 3 will apply the analytical framework suggested by compliance theory to assess the various state interests that may be affected by the implementation of the Convention, and suggest certain principles that could guide the further development of the Convention's compliance system in such a way that takes these interests into account. Part 4 identifies gaps in the institutions, procedures and methodologies for assessing compliance provided for in the existing text of the Convention. In particular, it notes the need to empower the Convention's institutions to review individual Parties' compliance. In Part 5, Articles 13 and 14, which represent alternative approaches to responding to concerns about Parties' non-compliance, are analyzed. The benefits and drawbacks of traditional dispute settlement procedures, and more recently developed non-compliance procedures are discussed.

Part 6 suggests that as traditional dispute settlement procedures are rarely, if ever, invoked, Parties could consider using Article 13 as a basis for establishing a strong non-compliance procedure capable of assessing and responding to individual circumstances of non-compliance.

Finally, Part 7 looks ahead to the effect that future developments in the implementation of the Convention, such as joint implementation and protocols to the Convention, might have on the analysis of compliance with the Convention.

OVERVIEW OF THE CLIMATE CHANGE CONVENTION

General Characteristics

Some have suggested that faith in purely intergovernmental processes to solve global environmental problems is misplaced. Tom Princen argues that the fundamental shifts in human social and economic behaviour necessary to respond to climate change and other global environmental challenges will require a foresight and broad perspective that is beyond the capacity of the traditional, nation-state approach of international diplomacy.[4] The resolution of conflicts over the use of shared natural resources can only be achieved by breaking down the traditional categories of international law and recognizing that decisions must be made at the local level, where those resources are actually being used. International agreements should play a support role, by creating favourable international conditions for local control, and by providing a framework for linking global concerns with local solutions.

Princen's observations raise a legitimate but far more ambitious agenda than this chapter can hope to respond to. Whatever its potential for innovation, the Convention is fundamentally a conservative legal instrument, designed in the image of innumerable previous treaties to protect the sovereign primacy of the nation state. This analysis must therefore recognize the present political, institutional and legal constraints of international law and institutions. Nevertheless, recent developments in international regimes reveal an encouraging trend towards Princen's vision of a more integrated approach to seeking solutions to global environmental issues through the greater involvement of local and non-state actors in the development, implementation, and monitoring of international obligations.[5]

Despite intense academic interest in compliance theory, and progressive policy-making aimed at improving compliance with other international environmental agreements, the term 'compliance' never gained currency in the climate change negotiations. Instead, Parties' behaviour in relation to the Convention is referred to throughout the Convention, more neutrally, as 'implementation'. This gives some indication of the extreme ambivalence many states felt, and continue to feel, towards the issue of climate change. Well-publicized, apocalyptic predictions associated with climate change have spurred political leaders to express concern about global warming. Yet the profound socio-economic implications of responding to climate change have led the same politicians to balk at undertaking concrete commitments backed up by strong compliance systems.

The Convention reflects this ambivalence in at least four ways. The Convention's primary rules are not clearly articulated. The text does not expressly entrust to an international process the review of an individual Party's compliance with these rules. The future development of these rules is linked to a reliance on science to direct policy development. And, finally, consensus on the final text was achieved only through a stark differentiation of obligations between developed and developing countries.

Inchoate rules

The Climate Change Convention was rushed to completion, and many of its substantive, procedural and institutional aspects have yet to take shape. As a result the Convention's primary rules, as well as its systems for generating compliance information and responding to non-compliance, are riddled with inchoate language. These 'constructive ambiguities' can be justified on a number of grounds. They allow a multitude of states to become Parties to agreements while retaining a maximum degree of latitude. Such ambiguities are said to leave open the opportunity for interpretation by state practice and by ongoing negotiations within the framework of the Convention.[6]

In the meantime, the Convention may yet lack the degree of specificity necessary for a thorough analysis in terms of compliance. As has been suggested elsewhere, it is difficult to expect Parties to comply, and the Convention's institutions to assess compliance, without a clear and agreed understanding of what Parties' obligations are, both quantitatively and qualitatively.[7]

A logical prerequisite for assessing and enforcing compliance is that Parties understand and agree, at some level of specificity, on what actions are required of them under the Convention and on the qualitative nature of these requirements, for example, whether or not they are legally binding.[8] While there is no doubt that the Convention as a whole is considered a legally binding agreement, countries continue to disagree over the legal nature of individual aspects of the Convention. Whether non-compliance with a particular provision of the Convention can be considered a breach of international law will have important implications for the design of the Convention's compliance system, which will have a role to play in assessing both the legal and the political implications of non-compliance.

Effectiveness v. compliance

During the negotiations a number of delegations successfully blocked proposals that would have empowered the Convention's institutions to review or assess an individual Party's compliance with its obligations. As a result, the

Convention's text is unclear as to whether the Conference of the Parties (COP), in reviewing the implementation of the Convention, may look beyond the *overall effectiveness* of the Parties' combined efforts to assess an individual Party's compliance.[9]

It was and can still be argued that the modest primary rules contained in the Convention do not require or allow an assessment of individual compliance. As these rules are strengthened, as Parties have agreed they must and will be,[10] the need to hold Parties individually accountable for compliance with their commitments will likewise grow.

Science and politics

In a world where the costs and benefits of the responses to and impacts of climate change will be distributed amongst nations in a profoundly inequitable manner, the Convention reflects the temptation to look to science as an objective arbiter of responsibilities. Climate science will guide the Parties' review of the effectiveness of the Convention and of the adequacy of Parties' commitments in relation to the Convention's objective.[11] The best available scientific knowledge must be used to develop methodologies for calculating Parties' net emissions of greenhouse gases.[12] These provisions represent the broad consensus reached among negotiators to link climate science to the further development of the Convention. It reflects the faith the ambivalent have in science to, in the end, resolve their doubts.

However, the incorporation of science into the decision-making process will lead to an ongoing demand on Parties' abilities to make complex trade-offs between scientific uncertainties and political judgements in assessing both the effectiveness of the Convention and the compliance of individual countries. A recent presentation to the INC by the Chair of the Intergovernmental Panel on Climate Change (IPCC), that has assisted the INC with scientific advice, emphasized that science alone could not resolve issues without political input.[13] Scientific uncertainties with regard to the calculation and verification of a Party's emissions must be resolved at a political level. The compliance regime will have to tap into scientific expertise while maintaining a firm grounding in the moral, economic and political implications of the effects of climate change.

The Convention's Principles direct decision-makers to follow a precautionary approach which acknowledges this dilemma and urges that decisions be made pro-actively in areas of high risk and scientific uncertainty.[14] Parties may consider, at later stages in the operation of a compliance system, whether to develop decision-making tools, such as burdens of proof, that incorporate precaution into the assessment of Parties' compliance.[15]

Differentiated responsibilities

While international agreements are often bargains struck between states on a bilateral and reciprocal basis, the Climate Change Convention imposes differentiated and non-reciprocal obligations on distinct categories of Parties.[16] The dynamic that characterizes this Convention is in a sense bilateral, but between two groups of countries: developed and developing states.[17]

The rationale for this division, which places the bulk of mitigation and financial resource obligations on the developed countries, is set out in the Convention's Preamble and Principles. Parties to the Convention acknowledge that 'the largest share of historical and current global emissions of greenhouse gases has originated in developed countries'.[18] However, the Parties also recognize that while 'per capita emissions in developing countries are still relatively low . . . the share of global emissions originating in developing countries will grow to meet their social and development needs.'[19]

Finally, in a tacit recognition that, while developing countries are concerned about the risk of rapid climate change, the costs and risks of responding to it are more than they are prepared to bear, the Parties note that the economic and social development and poverty eradication are the first and overriding priorities of the developing country Parties. This raises the issue of whether the Convention's compliance system should itself reflect this differentiation. As will be discussed, different types of compliance systems are designed to respond to different sources of non-compliance. The force with which a system should facilitate or coerce compliance, will vary both with the strength of a Party's commitments and with the political and economic resources a Party has available to comply or resist compliance.

To some extent this differentiation has already taken place through the availability of financial assistance to developing countries. The Parties explicitly acknowledge that '[t]he extent to which developing country Parties will effectively implement their commitments under the Convention will depend on the effective implementation by developed country Parties of their commitments under the Convention related to financial resources and transfer of technology.'[20] More relevant, and more challenging, to the short-term development of a compliance system may be the development of mechanisms for ensuring the compliance of developed country Parties, that bear the bulk of the obligations but are not eligible for financial assistance.

Primary Rules

The Convention's primary rules can be divided into three general categories of commitments:

(1) the obligation to communicate information on net emissions of greenhouse gases, and to report on the steps taken to abate those emissions;
(2) the obligation to undertake measures to mitigate and adapt to climate change; and
(3) the obligation to provide financial resources in support of the implementation of the Convention.

Communication of Information[21]

Parties are required to communicate two types of information under the Convention: national inventories of sources and sinks of greenhouse gases;[22] and measures taken by the Parties to implement the Convention.[23] These obligations are then differentiated between developed, developing and least-developed countries with regard to content, timing and the availability of financial resources.

Each developed country Party must provide a detailed description of the policies and measures it is taking as well as a specific estimate of the effects these steps will have towards implementing the Convention.[24] Although developing countries may, on a voluntary basis, propose to the Secretariat projects and response measures for funding,[25] there is no explicit requirement that developing countries undertake and report specific mitigation activities.

While developed countries are obligated to make their national communication within six months of the entry into force of the Convention, developing countries need not report before three years; least-developed countries may report at their own discretion.[26] Finally, the availability of financial resources for the preparation of developing country reports, can be seen as a prerequisite for developing country compliance with reporting obligations.[27] This differentiation in timing, and the link to the availability to financial resources will affect not just the initial stages of the implementation of the Convention, but must be taken into account by the COP in determining the future timetables for communications of information.[28]

Mitigation and Adaptation

All Parties, including developing countries, undertake a series of common obligations, contained in a laundry list of measures in Article 4.1. Among the most significant of these is to 'formulate, [and] implement ... national ... programmes containing measures to mitigate climate change by addressing anthropogenic emissions by sources and removals by sinks of all greenhouse gases ... and measures to facilitate adequate adaptation to climate change'.[29] Developing country Parties' obligation to implement programmes containing measures under Article 4.1 are qualified in three significant ways. Developing countries are spared any indication of the extent and timing of these measures. All of developing country obligations are linked to the provision of financial resources by developed country Parties.

In what is considered by many to be the weak heart of the Convention, all developed country Parties are required, in addition to the above, to adopt policies and take measures that limit their greenhouse gas emissions and enhance their sinks, and to report detailed information on these actions to the COP.[30] Because this commitment does not explicitly bind Parties to meet any particular target or comply with any particular timetable for reducing net emissions, some commentators have described the commitment as being of primarily a political rather than a legal[31] nature, or as representing a 'quasi'[32] or 'soft'[33] commitment.

While some analysts have admired the delicate political balance achieved by Article 4.2(a) and (b), others have recognized it as an impenetrable thicket of qualifications and compromise. After an initial period of debate over the meaning of this paragraph, with some arguing that it contained the elements of a binding target, others asserting it was nothing more than an expression of political will – or the lack of it – it now seems clear that countries will leave the text behind rather than attempt to clarify it into a binding expression of targets and timetables.

The Parties agreed instead, at COP 1, to begin negotiations on a protocol or other legal instrument, aimed at strengthening developed Parties' commitments by elaborating policies and measures and by setting quantified limitation and reduction objectives within specific time frames.[34] This approach may have important implications for the role of compliance procedures under the Convention, as protocols establish separate but related legal regimes – whose Parties need not necessarily overlap.[35] A number of these implications are discussed below.

Financial resources

As has been suggested in the previous discussion, developed country Parties[36] listed in Annex II, must provide new and additional resources to meet the 'agreed full costs' incurred by developing countries in fulfilling their reporting obligations.[37] They must further provide the 'agreed full incremental costs' incurred by developing countries in fulfilling their obligations under the remainder of Article 4.1. Finally, Annex II countries must 'also assist the developing country Parties that are particularly vulnerable to the adverse effects of climate change in meeting costs of adaptation to those adverse effects'.[38]

Although the Convention further requires that the implementation of Parties' financial commitments 'shall take into account the need for adequacy and predictability in the flow of funds and the importance of appropriate burden sharing among the developed country Parties', no set of principles or procedures has been designed to determine what overall amount should be contributed, or how the burden of that contribution should be distributed amongst the donor Parties.[39]

Clarifying commitments and strengthening compliance

Clarifying the qualitative and quantitative character of the Convention's commitments will be an important first step towards enabling Parties to understand and assess their own and each other's compliance with these commitments. Such clarification will affect the way in which Parties further develop the Convention's compliance system.

Logic and domestic law models suggest that more detailed and restrictive legal rules will demand more sophisticated and coercive compliance systems. The successful implementation of more precise commitments under the Convention would appear to require a more exacting monitoring and verification scheme. In practice, however, states will commonly attach well-developed compliance systems to treaties devoid of substantive commitments,[40] and will undertake tougher commitments only with the assurance that the compliance system will remain lenient.[41]

Recent evidence suggests, however, that Parties to international environmental agreements have been willing to strengthen compliance systems gradually in step with their increasing commitments. Specific developments in the context of the Montreal Protocol[42] and the UN-ECE Second Sulphur Protocol[43] will be discussed in greater detail below.

Progress towards a strengthened and equitable compliance system will likely depend on the availability of financial resources for those Parties less able to comply. The Convention goes beyond the provision of resources to developing countries; it links developing country compliance to the compliance of developed countries with their commitments to provide these resources.

Financial assistance under the Convention forms part of the primary commitments of the developed countries and is recognized not merely as an inducement, but as a *pre-requisite*, for developing country compliance. This suggests that a compliance system, whenever it reviews the compliance of a developing country Party must follow a cycle of commitments which will lead it to review developed country Parties' compliance with their financial commitments.

It should be noted, however, that the Convention's differentiated commitments and the flexibility and leniency it affords developing country Parties does not remove such countries from the concern of the Convention's compliance system. Although their compliance is in many ways predicated on the provision of financial resources by developed country Parties, it is possible to imagine situations in which their compliance might be called into question. The mere availability of financial resources does not ensure that the obligations will be carried out to the satisfaction of all Parties. Indeed, the fact that developed countries will be paying for developing countries' compliance will likely increase their interest in monitoring, through Convention procedures, how the money is spent.[44]

RESISTANCE TO COMPLIANCE IN THE CONTEXT OF CLIMATE CHANGE

While certain gaps in the Convention can in part be explained by the strict time deadline imposed on the negotiators,[45] delegates were far from agreeing on an approach to addressing non-compliance when the text was adopted. The negotiations revealed a number of state interests both in favour of and against the further development of a compliance regime for the Convention. These interests can be analyzed on three levels:

(1) why states might resist compliance with the Convention generally;
(2) why states might resist the strengthening of the Convention's compliance response procedures; and
(3) why states might resist taking advantage of such systems, should they be put in place.

The starting point for compliance regime analysis is to identify why states comply or fail to comply with international obligations and then to try to posit conditions in which they will comply. Mitchell suggests that the simplest explanation of why a government undertakes, or fails to undertake, a given behaviour is because it believes it furthers its interest to do so.[46]

Climate change provides a particularly formidable challenge in this regard because it is difficult, at present, for many states to assess accurately their interests, both with regard to climate change and with regard to the Convention. Despite the considerable consensus reached within the scientific community on the urgent need for responses to climate change, considerable uncertainties remain as to the likelihood, timing and extent of the impacts of global warming. This uncertainty, combined with the inchoate nature of many of the Convention's rules makes it particularly difficult for states (as well as political scientists and lawyers) to identify accurately a state's short-term and long-term interests. Nevertheless, during the negotiation of the Convention, states began to reveal initial positions, that will likely prove relevant for the further development of a compliance system.

Barriers to compliance

A compliance system must anticipate the likely 'sources' or motivations for Parties' non-compliance, and design responses that are likely to overcome resistant behaviour. Although climate change implicates a profoundly varied set of interests in different types of states, this analysis will make a number of broad generalizations about categories of developed and developing states. This can in part be justified on the grounds that, as the Convention reflects, states themselves recognize these generalized categories and the commonality of interests they represent, when they negotiate and enter into international agreements.

Political scientists have identified several groups of state interests to explain why states comply or fail to comply with international obligations. States may comply with an agreement because they are ideologically or politically committed to the achievement of the agreement's objective, or to compliance with international law generally. If it has the resources and the domestic political support to carry out its obligations, such a state will develop an 'independent self-interest' in complying.[47] An industrialized country with a strong 'green' lobby and a medium-term interest in reducing its dependence on fossil fuels, may have already developed domestic policies that will lower its emissions of greenhouse gases to levels that will comply with or even exceed the Convention's requirements. Although the Convention's compliance system would not be invoked against such states, it has an important role to play in educating and convincing other Parties that it is also within their independent self-interest to comply.

Certain states may also find themselves in compliance due to policies or circumstances completely unrelated to the Convention's commitments or objective. Germany, which has taken a wavering lead in setting domestic targets, and in calling for international commitments on CO_2 reductions, has seen its national emissions drop dramatically since the treaty was signed, largely as a result of drastic efficiency improvements and plant closures in reunified former East Germany.[48] Similarly, the United Kingdom, which recently called for new OECD CO_2 reduction targets, has experienced a sharp drop in national emissions due to a cost saving switch from coal to oil and natural gas.[49]

States may *fail* to comply in good faith, either through inadvertence or a lack of financial or administrative resources. States may remain in non-compliance during a period of bargaining because they 'believe themselves marginally better off not complying with the treaty so long as no significant costs attend violation, and no major financing is provided for compliance'. Or, finally, states may be beyond the reach of non-compliance regimes due to the strength of political or economic interests fundamentally opposed to the objective of the Convention.[50]

Inadvertence

Given the current state of confusion over the Convention's text, the number of states inadvertent to compliance may prove significantly large. The compliance of these Parties will depend primarily on the effectiveness of the Convention's institutions to clarify the nature of their obligations. The Convention requires Parties to promote the development and implementation of education and training programmes and the strengthening of national institutions, to help ensure that all Parties fully understand their obligations under the Convention.[51]

Lack of financial and administrative resources

In theory this second category of 'good faith non-compliers', will succumb easily to the operation of the Convention's financial mechanisms or to any additional facilitative compliance system as may be adopted by the Convention, as long as adequate resources are provided and applied effectively. The success of the Convention's financial mechanism is currently in the hands of the Global Environment Facility (GEF), which will be finding its feet under a new system of governance, and developing operational policies that will allow it to carry out policies, programme priorities and eligibility criteria established by the COP.[52]

Bargaining non-compliers

A third category of states, 'bargaining non-compliers', will pose greater challenges as the Convention's institutions attempt to assess the correct balance of encouragement and coercion. This balance, again, will differ widely depending upon the economic resources of the state involved. As has been shown, those developed countries that carry the heaviest burden under the Convention are not eligible for financial assistance. The Convention's compliance system must be able to increase the perceived cost – whether political, legal or economic – to them of failing to comply. For those developing country Parties that are eligible for financial assistance, the financing policies agreed by the COP, increased experience in the implementation of the Convention, and the involvement of implementing agencies will help to establish parameters of reasonableness around negotiations with bargaining non-compliers.

Dissenters

In the context of climate change there may well emerge a fourth category of states for whom the costs of complying will always prove higher than the Convention's mechanisms can afford. These states are unlikely to comply, regardless of the resources or sanctions available through the Convention's compliance system. The extreme dependence of both developed and developing countries on fossil fuels may reveal a number of these 'blocking states'.

The United States, conscious of its role in producing some 25 per cent of global greenhouse gas emissions was highly influential in preventing the adoption of specific targets and timetables for the Convention. After the change in administration, the US has officially acknowledged that the Convention's current commitments are inadequate, but has yet to endorse any specific targets or timetables for emissions reductions. Motivated by an interest in maintaining global markets in petroleum, Saudi Arabia has significantly slowed Convention machinery.

Should any country remain steadfast in its resistance to compliance with the Convention, there is probably little a compliance system can do to coerce changes in behaviour directly. In the context of climate change, where the economic and political strength of a Party roughly correlates to its contribution of greenhouse gases to the atmosphere, Parties upon which economic sanctions would have an impact are probably not worth pursuing. A compliance system that analyzes and assesses state behaviour in relation to international commitments can focus public, diplomatic and legal pressure on governments to shift policy and, as a last resort, force violators out from under the umbrella of the agreement.[53]

Resistance to non-compliance systems

During the negotiations, proposals for a strengthened compliance regime were put forward exclusively by a small number of developed country delegations.[54] They saw the purpose of a well-developed non-compliance response system as avoiding and settling disputes between developed country trading partners over compliance with economically sensitive measures foreseen by the Convention. Smaller, environmentally progressive countries that have undertaken unilateral measures to abate greenhouse gas emissions, but that may need the support of multilateral processes to ensure that more powerful countries comply, were particularly vocal in promoting stiffer compliance regimes.

A number of developed country delegates expressed surprise and frustration that developing countries, that would be carrying such a light and subsidized burden under the Convention would resist the establishment of a strengthened compliance system. Hiding behind the ranks of the Group of 77, developing countries, were undoubtedly industrialized countries happy to have their battles fought for them.

Countries' resistance to the development of non-compliance systems in the context of climate change can be explained generally as having at least three sources: a concern over interference with sovereign power to determine domestic economic policy; a concern with regard to future obligations under the Convention; and a concern that resources would be better spent on other priority issues.

Concern for sovereignty

Sovereignty is often seen as the only equalizing principle among states of vastly different size and political, economic and military power. Any erosion of this principle would allow international processes to assess and pass judgement on the activities of a particular state. Such processes would likely be resisted particularly by developing country policy-makers; even if, as under the present Convention, these processes seem less likely to be applied to them.

Adequate financial resources may not alone ensure compliance with detailed reporting obligations. Both developed and developing countries have already demonstrated concern about divulging for public review information about their greenhouse activities.[55] Information related to 'sources' and 'sinks', depending on the level of detail required, may touch upon the essential industrial and agricultural activities of countries, as well as provide a catalogue of its most valuable natural resources. Both developed and developing countries may see this information as sensitive to their national security, economic and trade interests. Although each country will have the reciprocal advantage of access to other countries' reports, many developing countries will suffer a relative disadvantage in not being able to process or take advantage of this information.

Concern with regard to future obligations

Should the review and development of the Convention's obligations continue to be linked, through the Convention's objective, to climate change science, there is every indication that commitments to stabilize and reduce greenhouse gas emissions will have to be increased – for all countries. The further development of a compliance system will continue to meet resistance from those Parties, both developing and developed, that are likely to have difficulty reducing greenhouse gas emissions.

For certain developing countries, these concerns are more pressing, as their growing economies lift them into the range of developed country responsibilities.[56] Already the World Bank and other development institutions have targeted a number of G-77 members for 'graduation' from the roles of countries eligible for developing country concessions and assistance.

Other priorities

As has been noted, developed and developing countries continue to demonstrate ambivalence about their commitment to responding to climate change. Representatives from both groups of countries softened the impact of the Convention's provisions with cautious references to the cost-effectiveness of response measures and the need to monitor carefully the socio-economic impacts of these responses. Developing countries insisted that the Convention's principles reflect that economic development and poverty eradication would remain a priority for their development plans. Strengthening the Convention's institutional mechanisms will necessarily distract resources and attention from other issues on the global policy-making agenda that many may consider of greater importance.

Certain countries particularly dependent on the production, sale and use of fossil fuel have actively pressed for the removal of climate change from the UN agenda. These 'blocking states' have an interest in slowing other Parties' implementation of the Convention and have used their rights as Parties to attempt to erect procedural barriers. They can be expected to obstruct negotiations of a strengthened non-compliance response procedure as well.[57]

Finally, while developing countries are assured, in the short term, that the main weight of the Convention's obligations will be borne by developed countries, long-term solutions will depend upon their involvement. In this context, it must be noted that all the procedures and the sanctions involved in implementation of stronger compliance systems are most burdensome on developing countries. Sophisticated compliance systems require resources and expertise both to initiate and to reply to complaints of non-compliance, resources that may be beyond the means of many developing countries. Coercive sanctions, now being contemplated under other international environmental agreements, such as the withdrawal of treaty benefits and the imposition of trade sanctions, will have a disproportionate impact on fragile Third World economies.

Resistance to the use of non-compliance regimes

Perhaps equally important to a regime that may have difficulty in achieving full compliance without facilitation or coercion, are states' interests in promoting the compliance of other Parties. As has been noted previously, the mere existence of a strong compliance system does not ensure compliance. Compliance regimes will depend in part on the willingness of Parties to initiate procedures against other, non-complying Parties, or to entrust the right to do so to intergovernmental or non-state actors. An individual state's commitment to climate change issues, and its relative political and economic influence will affect its willingness to raise questions regarding other Parties' non-compliance or to promote compliance with the Convention generally.

A reason often given for states' unwillingness to initiate procedures against other states, whether under a particular treaty, or institution or court, is the fear of retaliation, and the threat that an equally vigorous enforcement might be aimed at themselves. The differentiation of commitments under the Convention may, however, encourage certain developing country 'enforcer' states to initiate proceedings against developed states without the fear of having the fulfilment of their own commitments questioned. It is not inconceivable, for example, that should commitments under the Convention be strengthened and an industrialized country begin to fall behind in its commitments, a small island country, concerned about predicted rises in sea level, may decide to trigger a compliance procedure.

A number of other interests have been revealed during the negotiations that may motivate certain Parties to seek enforcement of other Parties' commitments. As has been mentioned previously, states may use the Convention's compliance provisions as a means of ensuring that their trading partners do not attract market share and browner industries through slack enforcement of climate related regulations.[58]

Those countries that have developed an edge in climate friendly technologies may have an interest in keeping a close watch on other Parties' compliance to stimulate market demand for their products. France, a major exporter of nuclear technology, may have revealed a long-term commercial interest in the wide implementation of the Convention, when during the Convention negotiations it battled with Saudi Arabia over whether technology transferred under the Convention should meet certain 'safety' standards. Similarly, the Japanese government has shown interest in benefiting commercially from the implementation of international environmental agreements through the sale of highly efficient technologies.[59]

Evidence from the ozone regime

A review of the experience of the Montreal Protocol Implementation Committee (MPIC) suggests, for that regime, the most commonly given reason for non-compliance is a Party's lack of financial and administrative resources. It is important to note that thus far the MPIC has dealt only with concerns raised by the Ozone Secretariat[60] which have focused primarily on the completion of relatively non-controversial reporting requirements. Neither the Secretariat nor a Party has yet raised a 'reservation' against another Party regarding implementation of substantive obligations to reduce or eliminate consumption or production of ozone depleting substances.

At a recent meeting, the MPIC received a report from the Ozone Secretariat that identified six Parties that had consistently failed to comply with reporting requirements under the Protocol. These six represented a fairly broad mix of countries, each with a different explanation for non-compliance. Costa Rica, reported that it had made best efforts but had fallen behind due to delays in funding from one of the Protocol's Implementing Agencies. Italy hoped to come into compliance through the implementation of new legislation that would enable it to clear up the 'bureaucratic problems' that had prevented it from reporting sooner. Iran's and Syria's failure to comply was somewhat more difficult to discern, but efforts were clearly underway to satisfy the Secretariat with further information. Belarus and the Ukraine were both suffering from political and economic upheaval, and have sought financial assistance through the Protocol's financial mechanisms.[61]

INSTITUTIONS AND PROCEDURES FOR COMPLIANCE

Compliance information and review processes

The Convention currently provides a skeletal framework of institutions and procedures that allow for two types of implementation review:[62]

(1) a review of the 'overall aggregated effect' of steps taken by Parties[63] and
(2) an examination of Parties' commitments in light of the Convention's objective[64] including, in particular, the review of the adequacy of the developed country Parties' commitments.[65]

Both of these processes will be carried out by the Conference of the Parties with assistance from two of its subsidiary bodies, the Subsidiary Body for Implementation (SBI) and the Subsidiary Body for Scientific and Technical Advice (SBSTA).

As this skeleton framework is filled out by decisions of the Parties, these review processes have the potential to generate the information necessary to conduct a review of an individual Party's compliance with its commitments to mitigate greenhouse gas emissions. The Convention's institutions will be provided with data on each Party's sources and sinks of greenhouse gases, and on the measures taken by Parties to control their net emissions.

Each Annex I Party will further be required to provide a specific estimate of the effects its policies have on its net emissions.[66] Scientific assessments of the effects of these measures will be provided by the SBSTA.[67] Further information may be made available to the COP by competent intergovernmental and nongovernmental organizations.[68]

While the text of the Convention does not explicitly empower any of its institutions to review the extent to which an individual Party has complied with its commitments, Parties have already moved beyond the text to allow for individual, in depth reviews of developed country national communications. The purpose of such reviews, which may include in-country visits, will be to

> provide a thorough and comprehensive technical assessment of the implementation of the Convention commitments by individual Annex I Parties and Annex I Parties as a whole. Its purpose is to review, in a facilitative, non-confrontational, open and transparent manner, the information contained in communications from Annex I Parties to ensure that the Conference of the Parties has accurate, consistent and relevant information at its disposal to assist it in carrying out its responsibilities . . .[69]

Nonetheless, the more specific responsibilities assigned to this review process carefully reflect the Convention's insistent focus on the assessment of 'overall' and 'aggregated' performance, and away from individual Party's compliance. The strong resistance from a number of countries to the review of individual compliance may well become the most formidable barrier to the establishment of an effective compliance system.

Methodologies for assessment

Should the Parties chose to establish a process for reviewing individual compliance with the Convention, such a process will ask and seek satisfactory answers to the following three specific questions:

(1) Has a party complied with its commitments to communicate information?
(2) Has a party complied with its commitments to mitigate net emissions of greenhouse gases?
(3) Has a party complied with its financial commitments?

Agreed upon methodologies, that would provide a uniform reporting procedure and an objective standard for assessing the completeness and accuracy of a Party's submissions, will need to be developed to answer each of these questions. At present, the Convention calls for the COP to develop comparable methodologies for preparing inventories of net greenhouse gas emissions, and for evaluating the effectiveness of measures to limit these net emissions.

Although the IPCC and the OECD have been working to develop comparable reporting methodologies, a number of Annex I Parties that had ratified the Convention by or near the time it entered into force, have begun to submit reports in advance of agreement upon methodologies. As a result, challenges, primarily from NGOs, have already begun to be made to the accuracy of the economic assumptions and emissions calculations presented in a number of developed country action plans.[70]

While Annex II Parties are required to incorporate 'details of measures' taken in accordance with financial resource and technology transfer commitments under Article 4,[71] there is as yet no requirement to demonstrate the nature and extent of these resources according to an agreed methodology. This will make the assessment of compliance with financial resource commitments difficult. Given the close link between Annex II Parties' financial resource commitments and the commitments of developing country Parties, further elaboration of the Convention's financial commitments may be necessary.

ARTICLES 13 AND 14: NON-COMPLIANCE PROCEDURE AND DISPUTE SETTLEMENT PROCEDURE

An opportunity to develop procedures under the Convention that will scrutinize an individual Party's compliance, has been left open by Article 13, which anticipates the establishment of a process for resolving questions regarding the implementation of the Convention; and by Article 14, which allows Parties, under certain circumstances, to invoke dispute settlement procedures for the resolution of disputes between two or more Parties 'concerning the interpretation or application of the Convention'.[72] These Articles represent two distinct types of processes for addressing Parties' non-compliance: noncompliance procedures (NCP) and traditional dispute settlement procedures (DSP).

Article 13: A multilateral consultative process

The brief text of Article 13 belies the detailed discussions held during the negotiations on the need for, and the nature of, a compliance system for the Convention. Delegates weighed a number of specific proposals for the development of such a system including an elaborate model proposed by the Co-Chairs of Working Group II.[73] Article 13's text, which is a legacy of the Co-Chair's proposal (entitled 'Resolution of Questions Regarding Interpretation and Implementation of the Convention'), acknowledges that questions regarding the implementation of the Convention may arise and that they should be resolved, to the extent possible, through multilateral (as opposed to bilateral) consultative (as opposed to confrontational) processes. Article 13 does not prejudge to which of the Convention's institutions such a process should be assigned.

Article 14: Traditional dispute settlement

Article 14 provides for a hierarchy of procedures designed to respond to a situation where a disagreement between two or more Parties to the Convention has ripened into a dispute.[74] Should Parties fail to settle their dispute through negotiations 'or other peaceful means' Parties may avail themselves of either judicial dispute settlement through the ICJ, arbitration or conciliation under the auspices of the Convention.

The main questions raised during the negotiations of these provisions were whether jurisdiction over the disputants should be compulsory or voluntary; and whether the outcome of the procedures should be considered legally binding upon them, or merely recommendatory.[75] The Convention allows any Party to declare in writing 'when ratifying, accepting, approving or acceding to the Convention, on any time thereafter' that it recognizes as compulsory either or both the jurisdiction of the Court, or the jurisdiction of an arbitral tribunal set up under the Convention, over any dispute concerning the interpretation of the Convention in relation to any other Party making the same declaration.[76] Any decision taken by the Court would be legally binding upon the Parties to the dispute.[77] The COP has yet to elaborate arbitration procedures but, should it decide to follow the precedent established by other international environmental agreements, decisions of the arbitral tribunals set up under the procedure would also be binding upon Parties to the dispute.[78]

If a disputing Party has not subjected itself to the compulsory jurisdiction of either of these procedures it cannot be forced to do so. However, if the dispute remains unsettled after a year has passed, any of the Parties to the dispute can submit the dispute to an *ad hoc* conciliation commission[79] composed of an equal number of members appointed by each of the disputants. The jurisdiction of the conciliation commission is compulsory for all Parties. Its decisions, however, are 'recommendatory' in nature and the disputants are required only to 'consider' the award 'in good faith'.

This flexible, multitrack approach, which allows states to select effectively from the three formal dispute settlement procedures, anticipates that multilateral treaties cover a wide range of state interests. Any particular situation may require a different institutional or procedural response, tailored to meet the concerns of the states involved. This flexibility, however, also provides loopholes. Those states unwilling to comply with the Convention can escape legal censure either by declining to declare themselves subject to the binding adjudication of the Court or tribunal, or by rejecting the recommendatory decisions of the conciliation commission.

Non-compliance and wrongfulness[80]

Non-compliance procedures and dispute settlement procedures are beginning to appear side by side in an increasing number of agreements.[81] Parties appear to recognize the need for both, without having thought carefully about how the two processes relate. The two approaches differ not only in their procedures, but in their purpose. Although both NCPs and DSPs seek to resolve questions and to encourage compliance, they are designed to respond to different types of noncomplying behaviour.

Koskenniemi suggests these types of behaviour can be distinguished as 'noncompliance' and 'wrongfulness'. NCPs provide a political process for seeking 'amicable' responses to non-compliant behaviour that falls short of wrongfulness, behaviour that could be categorized as 'good faith noncompliance' and 'bargaining non-compliance,' as outlined above. DSPs are designed, instead, to deal with a wrongful breach amounting to an ascertainable violation of binding treaty obligation,[82] which might describe the behaviour of a dissenting or blocking non-complier. The distinction is based both on the nature of the primary rule being violated (ie, whether or not it is legally binding and sufficiently precise) and the motivation of the Party's behaviour.

Each procedure can be seen as designed to offer the appropriate institutional and procedural response to the target behaviour. NCPs, run by a body under the control of the Parties and composed of their representatives, offer a less formal, political response aimed primarily at 'facilitating' compliance. DSPs take place outside the direct supervision of the COP, and are designed to settle a dispute with a determination of which disputant is right. Finally, Koskenniemi distinguishes the two processes on the basis of the types of remedies legally available to them, suggesting that it would not only be inappropriate, but an unlawful *exces de puvoir*, for an NCP supervised by a COP to take binding decisions that purported to determine the legal wrongfulness of a Party's behaviour or to suspend treaty rights as a result of such a determination.[83]

The initial judgement as to where a Party's behaviour lies on the spectrum of non-compliant behaviour, between non-compliance and wrongful breach, is made by whatever entity has the standing to trigger either process. NCPs have been designed to be initiated by Parties with concerns about their own inability to comply, by Parties concerned about each other's behaviour and by the Secretariat. DSPs, traditionally, have been open only to states.[84]

Comparing DSPs and NCPs

Comparisons of DSPs and NCPs continue to form part of a largely theoretical exercise: DSPs have long been included in international environmental agreements, but have never been invoked. NCPs have only recently been adopted and have yet to demonstrate their value in practice. Nevertheless certain generalizations about each type of procedure can be made. Traditional dispute settlement procedures, such as those contained in Article 14, can provide a formal and structured process for resolving legal disputes between two or more Parties to an international agreement. Through litigation, arbitration or conciliation, Parties entrust the settlement of their differences to a limited and putatively impartial group of qualified individuals, external to the Convention's institutions, who consider evidence, adjudicate and render a final decision or award.

These procedures are often criticized as confrontational and adversarial, intended primarily to 'look backward' at past behaviour in order to assess blame and impose sanctions on an offending party. The complex and formal procedures needed to initiate and pursue a dispute, which require Parties to identify specific breaches of commitments by other states, have come to be regarded as unnecessarily hostile, and as having an adverse effect on state relations that is thought to discourage states from initiating procedures.[85] Indeed, to date, no Party to an international environmental agreement has taken advantage of formal dispute resolution procedures of the type contemplated in Article 14, even though implementation of these agreements has been less than complete.

It was, in part, in response to what negotiators viewed as the shortcomings of traditional dispute resolution, that the Convention anticipates the establishment of an NCP under Article 13. Multilateral NCPs, which are to be supervised by a convention's governing body, offer a less confrontational approach, that is said to 'look forward' for ways in which the Convention's collective resources can be used to facilitate Parties' compliance. Multilateral NCPs are designed to preempt and avoid confrontations that might trigger more formal dispute resolution. They are thought to be particularly well-suited to global environmental regimes, where many Parties share an interest in the effective implementation of the Convention's objectives.

Multilaterally negotiated solutions encourage states to act as trustees of global interest and to resist or escape the strictures of pre-existing bilateral relationships.[86] Finally, NCPs that aim to facilitate compliance, rather than to reprimand failures to comply, suit multilateral agreements which involve a wide range of Parties with differing abilities.

NCPs such as those in the MPIC and the Second Sulphur Protocol Implementation Committee (SSPIC) are, however, a new development in international environmental law, and not enough practice is available to judge their effectiveness accurately. Nevertheless, the multilateral, facilitative approach has been criticized in principle, as leading to 'least common denominator', negotiated solutions governed by the politics of expediency, rather than the principles of law. If the resolution of conflicts over the interpretation or application of rules is always subject to the flexibility of multilateral negotiations, the binding quality of the rules themselves can be called into question. Under such a system, rules would never reach a point of stasis, and the Convention would be open to constant renegotiation.

The success of such a process will depend upon Parties developing a common interest in the success of the Convention, so that the resolution of questions would be based on agreed principles rather than on a bargain struck between states with very different priorities and interests.[87]

Standing alone, purely facilitative approaches appear to be able to respond effectively only to a limited category of non-compliance. They are designed, primarily, to identify instances of non-compliance and to assist Parties willing but unable to comply with their commitments. The treaty's financial mechanism can be alerted to cases of non-compliance by the NCP or by the Party in need of assistance. However, the common but differentiated nature of the Convention's mitigation and financial commitments leaves the developed countries, that bear the bulk of the treaty's substantive commitments, ineligible for financial assistance. Furthermore, countries simply unwilling to comply, regardless of their eligibility and the availability of financial resources will not likely be swayed by efforts to facilitate their compliance.

STRENGTHENING NON-COMPLIANCE PROCEDURES

It is tempting to view the two approaches represented by Articles 13 and 14 as complementary rather than as alternatives, as a carrot and stick for facilitating and coercing compliant behaviour. Although a number of international environmental agreements now contain both types of procedure, any relationship between the two has been discouraged rather than elaborated.[88]

The general characteristics of Article 13 and 14, and their sequential positioning in the text suggests that NCPs should be used as a means to avoid the need for DSPs. Should a Party remain in non-compliance after the NCP had exhausted its efforts to encourage compliance, traditional dispute settlement techniques would be available to coerce compliance by adjudicating a final judgement, and offering a specific remedy to the complaining Party.

However, the formalities of a DSP, which require states to lodge an accusation based on breach of international law, appear to have proved an insurmountable political obstacle to the use of traditional dispute settlement procedures. Under these circumstances it seems unlikely that the coercive benefits of formal dispute resolution will have any more force than a symbolic and unarticulated threat.

Certain procedural and substantive improvements can be made to the primarily political, facilitative approach of NCPs, give them the more adjudicatory character necessary to assess non-compliance, and to bring to bear the most pressure possible on resistant Parties to comply. Thus, instead of relying on traditional dispute resolution procedures to provide the coercive element to compliance systems, the climate change Parties may chose to revisit a number of innovative proposals[89] put forward during the negotiation of the Convention, or that have gained acceptance in other international agreements. These proposals can be roughly separated into two groups distinguished by their use of either ad hoc panels or standing implementation committees.

Ad hoc panels: The co-chairs' text[90]

Confronted with the challenge of finding a middle ground between traditional dispute settlement and non-compliance procedures, the Co-Chairs of Working Group II[91] of the INC proposed, during the negotiation of the Convention, a process that would avoid the open-ended political debate within the Conference of the Parties by assigning specific questions of non-compliance to an *ad hoc* panel.[92]

The Co-Chairs' proposal focused on developing the Convention's institutional capacity to carry out the adjudicatory functions and legal analysis that might otherwise be provided by traditional dispute resolution. They proposed that the process be designed to resolve questions regarding both implementation and the *interpretation* of the Convention, suggesting that the process could take up issues not yet ripened into formal legal disputes and subject them to an analysis that extended into the legal aspects of Parties' commitments.

The power to accept or reject the Panel's recommendation, to thereby determine the outcome of the question, and the power to take actions appropriate to that outcome in order to 'advance the objectives of the Convention' would rest with the COP. The legal backbone to the COP's analysis could be provided to an otherwise largely political process, through requests from the COP or the Ad Hoc Panel, for the establishment of a parallel Panel of Legal Experts (also established on an *ad hoc* basis); or through requests for advisory legal opinions from the ICJ.

Ad hoc panels, which require a formal request from a Party or Parties and the selection and convening of a body for the specific purpose of reviewing an individual Parties' compliance, raises some of the same concerns about political costs as raised by traditional dispute settlement procedure. The power to initiate such high profile procedural initiatives would unlikely be entrusted to the Secretariat. Finally, the members of *ad hoc* panels would have no opportunity to develop the institutional experience that seems essential for consistent decision-making, and for building the confidence of Parties in the Convention's noncompliance procedure.

All that remains of the Co-Chairs' proposal in the final text of the Convention, is a narrowed version of the proposed scope of the procedures' mandate (ie, the resolution of *questions*, but with regard only to the implementation and not the *interpretation* of the Convention) and a slightly *ad hoc* aftertaste (ie, the process may be available to Parties *on their request*).

A standing implementation committee

In order to avoid the difficulties of relying on ad hoc procedures, the Parties may wish to consider borrowing from the achievements of negotiations of the Implementation Committees under the Montreal Protocol and the draft Second Sulphur Protocol, and assign a non-strengthened compliance procedure to the Convention's existing institutions.

Although the text of Article 13 provides an invaluable procedural foothold for Parties wishing to develop further the Convention's compliance procedure, all it ensures is that the first COP will consider the issue. By the same token, however, Parties need not feel restricted by Article 13 when developing institutions and procedures for non-compliance. The COP's broad mandate[93] and the existence of a Subsidiary Body on Implementation ready to 'assist the COP in the assessment and review of the effective implementation of the Convention' provides Parties with more than adequate leeway to develop a compliance system, and to assign its functions to the Convention's existing institutions.

In effect, a number of the adjudicatory functions that might have been carried out by external courts or tribunals, or ad hoc panels, could be assigned to an internal, subsidiary body operating under the authority of the Convention's COP. Under such a procedure the traditional dispute settlement procedures of Article 14 would remain available to help ensure the stability and integrity of the Convention's primary commitment while recognizing that they are unlikely to be involved with any frequency. The opportunity to seek advisory opinions from the ICJ, *ad hoc* panels of legal experts, or the UN Office of Legal Affairs would allow Parties to explore the meaning and extent of the Convention's commitments, without effectively reopening the text.

ELEMENTS FOR INCLUSION IN A COMPLIANCE SYSTEM

Some assessment of the legal and political possibilities for developing the Article 13 process, and assigning its functions to the Convention's institutions, can be drawn from the precedent of other agreements, and from the experience of the negotiation of the Convention itself, during which a number of delegations submitted innovative proposals.

Institutions

The duties at present assigned to the Convention's institutions are inadequate to provide for even a rudimentary compliance system. However, the Convention's general framework, and the COP's broad mandate allows ample room for institutional and procedural growth.

Conference of Parties[94]

The Conference of the Parties has the dual mandate to keep under regular review the implementation of the Convention, and to make the decisions necessary to promote the effective implementation of the Convention. As the Convention's 'supreme body' all final decisions regarding compliance will likely rest with the COP.

Although the detailed task of reviewing individual communications may be passed to a smaller subsidiary body, meetings of the COP will play a central role in focusing media and NGO attention on progress being made in the implementation of the Convention. Meetings of the COP will be open to any body or agency qualified in matters covered by the Convention. The COP may take into account information from the widest variety of sources, including intergovernmental and non-governmental sources, as well as information gathered through the systematic observation anticipated in Article 5.

Secretariat[95]

The Secretariat's powers with regard to implementation appear to be limited to compiling and transmitting reports submitted to it, and to facilitating assistance to the Parties in preparing and communicating information. Staffed by international civil servants, the Secretariat will provide intersessional continuity to the work of the COP. It will act as a neutral screen for information reported by Parties, by aggregating information designated as confidential by Parties before passing it on to the subsidiary bodies engaged in reviewing compliance.[96] The secretariat will also serve as the interface for coordination of all agencies involved in implementation. This will be particularly important in light of the central role the Global Environmental Facility (GEF) and its implementing agencies will have in the implementation of the Convention.

Under the MPIC and the SSPIC, parties have found it essential that their respective Secretariats, as the focal points for reporting on commitments, have the power to initiate NCPs. The Secretariats of these agreements will also serve as a point of diplomatic contact for resolving misunderstandings. Although these powers to the Climate Change Secretariat would appear to expand considerably those enumerated in the Convention's Article 8,[97] a similarly narrow mandate, given to the Secretariat in the original text of the Montreal Protocol, was expanded by decision of the Parties to include the types of functions outlined above.[98]

Subsidiary body for implementation[99]

At present the SBI has an open-ended membership of government representatives 'who are experts on matters related to climate change'. These broad parameters suggest that the SBI could have a membership identical to the COP itself, and were included in the Convention at the insistence of less powerful developing countries concerned about being excluded from a smaller, representative body. While such an arrangement appears to promote transparency and democracy, careful analysis of individual Parties' compliance might prove impossible in the unfocused and politicized debate in an SBI the size of the COP. As a result, democratic principles might well be thwarted by deals brokered away from the open forum, through informal negotiations.

The experience of the MPIC suggests that, in order for the SBI to operate an effective compliance procedure, its membership would have to be limited to a manageable number of representatives.[100] This approach was supported by a number of delegations during the negotiations. Some of the concerns of smaller developing countries could be assuaged by relying on traditional UN power sharing formulas and by providing for representation based on an 'equitable geographical distribution of Parties',[101] by formulating new balances and constituencies that may be better suited to this particular Convention, or to the geopolitical make up of actual Parties.[102] Further procedural safeguards, such as ensuring that the Party whose compliance is being reviewed can participate in the SBI's deliberations, would help to allay fears of exclusion from process.[103]

Equally important to the size and geopolitical balance of the institution is the quality of the participation of the individuals which serve as its members. The MPIC and the SSPIC both provide for the election of members in their capacity as representatives of Parties, and not as individuals. Such a system allows a Party that has been elected to the Committee but that is faced with limited resources or scheduling difficulties to vary the individual that attends meetings on their behalf.

The present MPIC recently signalled its concern that inconsistent attendance at its meetings was disrupting the continuity and effectiveness of its work.[104] Consistency in attendance could be made part of a procedural requirement by refining the qualifications required of representatives, or by requiring that members be elected as named individuals. The need for flexibility could be accommodated through the provision of financial assistance to eligible developing country delegates and the use of named alternates who could serve on the Committee should the principal delegate be unable to attend.

In order to limit the size and select the membership of the body that will implement Article 13, the present composition of the SBI will have to be altered significantly. Should political opposition to such a change be overcome, the present draft rules of procedure, would allow either the SBI itself or the COP to create a smaller representative Bureau or Executive Committee to carry out specific tasks assigned to it.

Existing and future powers under the Climate Change Convention

Currently the SBI is a body of very limited powers. As has been noted, not even the COP itself has the clearly stated power to review an individual Party's behaviour for conformity with its commitments under the Convention.[105]

Further powers, that have been considered necessary to the effective review of compliance in the context of other international environmental agreements, have focused on ensuring that the compliance system be transparent, and have access to as much information from as many sources as possible. To this end both the MPIC and the SSPIC will have the power to request further information from Parties;[106] to send visiting missions upon invitation by the Party concerned to conduct information gathering;[107] and to receive and assess information from accredited NGOs.[108] Certain delegates to the INC sought during the negotiations to replicate these, as well as other powers, in the Convention's compliance system.[109]

A further, enumerated function of more developed compliance systems, is the power of the subsidiary body to make specific recommendations to the COP on measures to assist or to bring about compliance by a Party.[110] This power, though it is recommendatory in nature and is filtered through the political processes of the COP, is highly significant in that it entitles the subsidiary body to form a preliminary conclusion as to whether or not a Party is in compliance, and an initial assessment of why a Party has failed to comply. The publication of a report of the SBI, detailing an impartial review that concludes that a Party is wrongfully violating the Convention, will prove a useful tool for bringing to bear public and diplomatic pressure on a Party to comply.

Process

Standing

In designing a non-compliance procedure, Parties must determine which entities will be allowed to trigger such a procedure. Article 13 anticipates a process that is 'available to Parties on their request'. This can be read as limiting standing to initiate the process in three different ways:

(1) by requiring that the process can only be initiated at the request of the Party having questions with regard to its own implementation (ie, available to a Party at its *own* request); or
(2) by limiting the right to initiate procedures to Parties to the Convention (ie, available to Parties but not the Secretariat or other subsidiary bodies); or
(3) by requiring that Parties to the Convention as a whole, through a decision of the COP, must initiate the process (ie, available on the request of the Parties).[111]

Each of these interpretations, if applied exclusively, would unnecessarily limit the potential of the Convention to promote compliance. Parties to both the MPIC and the SSPIC have found it appropriate to allow their agreements' compliance procedures to be triggered by a Party concerned about its own ability to comply, as well as by concerns expressed by other Parties, acting jointly or individually, and by the Secretariat. Allowing Parties themselves, as well as an impartial Secretariat to initiate compliance procedures, helps give such procedures a more administrative and less confrontational character, and could, in turn, help lower the political costs involved in directly challenging another Party's compliance.

Under the MPIC and the SSPIC, any Party, regardless of whether it can establish that its own rights under the agreement are being adversely affected, may raise its concerns about another Party's performance, as long as it supports its submissions with corroborating information. This helps, as well to depoliticize the process by encouraging Parties to take an interest in the implementation of the agreement per se, rather than using the Convention's mechanisms to protect individual interests.

Jurisdiction

Compliance procedures generally anticipate that only a Party's individual compliance can be brought under scrutiny.[112] A number of the Convention's commitments are, however, effectively collective. Parties as a whole, for example, undertake the implied commitment to adjust commitments in step with an improving knowledge of climate change. Although the COP has the general mandate to supervise the implementation of the Convention, there may be circumstances in which an individual Party may wish to challenge, in a forum other than the COP, whether the Parties as a whole are acting in accordance with agreed 'collective commitments'. In such a circumstance, an SBI with a limited membership may prove useful in making assessments of the Parties' collective behaviour.

The involvement of the GEF in the operation of the Convention's financial mechanism will pose an additional challenge to a compliance procedure attempting to trace whether or not an individual Party has fulfilled its commitments to provide financial resources. Although both the Convention and the GEF's new instrument provide that the GEF shall comply with the policies, programme priorities and eligibility criteria established by the COP, neither spells out a process whereby such compliance can be assessed or challenged. The GEF Council's unique decision-making structure may lead it to take decisions at variance with decisions taken by the COP. Parties may therefore wish to extend the SBI's jurisdiction to allow Parties to raise questions concerning the GEF's compliance with COP policy. This might offer one way to fulfil the Convention's requirement that the COP and the GEF agree upon arrangements that include 'modalities by which a particular funding decision may be reconsidered in light of' COP policy.[113]

Access to information

This chapter has emphasized the need for a free flow of information into and out of any process established to assess Parties' compliance with their commitments. MPIC has an open policy towards information and must receive, consider and report on 'any ... information received and forwarded by the Secretariat concerning compliance'. Although NGOs do not have standing to initiate complaints under the MPIC procedures, they may submit information to the Secretariat about 'possible non-compliance' which may, in turn, be made available to the Implementation Committee.

The COP's broad mandate to base its decisions on the best available scientific, social and technical information, and to seek and utilize information from all competent sources, should be extended to whatever subsidiary body it delegates the power to review individual Parties' compliance.

To enlist the support of the public in promoting the implementation of the Convention, as much information about Parties' compliance as possible should be made widely available. This, of course must be balanced against the need for Parties to be able to communicate to the SBI information that may be considered too sensitive to be made public. The Convention anticipates that the COP will establish criteria by which a Party may designate information as confidential as part of its normal reporting commitments, prior to its having reached the SBI.[114] This does not preclude the SBI from following the example of the MPIC and negotiating with an individual Party involved in a compliance review for access to additional information in return for guarantees of confidentiality. In this context, it is important to note that confidentiality of information has been one of the major concerns raised by Parties appearing before the MPIC.

Relationship to external institutions

Official development assistance and foreign direct investment

Under both the Montreal Protocol and the Convention the compliance of developing country Parties is linked to the provision of financial and technical resources through financial mechanisms and their implementing agencies. The experience of the MPIC has demonstrated the importance of establishing a close relationship between the SBI and the Convention's financial mechanism. Having representatives of Parties and the financial operating entity present at discussions concerning compliance will help the SBI to locate responsibility for failure to comply. This will be particularly useful in the first stages of compliance with commitments to communicate information as it will be the GEF that will provide the 'agreed full costs' of such activities. As the entity responsible for funding and coordination a significant element of developing country Parties' implementation, the GEF may know more about a particular country's state of compliance than the country's own representative.

The small amount of funds available through the GEF and the fact that it will finance only for specific projects proposed by developing country Parties, will limit the impact the GEF can have on leveraging the changes in the Parties' development paths that will be required for long-term compliance with the Convention. Should the Convention's Parties wish to promote major reforms in developing countries' climate related activities, they will have to work to bring the almost $160 billion[115] per annum in net North to South resource flows, in the form official development assistance and foreign direct investment into line with the Convention's objective. Some progress toward this end may have been made at the last meeting of the INC, when delegates opened the possibility of giving the Convention's compliance system a role in a 'permanent and feasible system for monitoring the activities of regional and multilateral financial and other institutions relevant to climate change'.[116]

Advisory opinions

The complexity of the Convention's primary commitments suggests that a number of states may come to hold good faith but conflicting interpretations of their commitments under the Convention, and may require a nonconfrontational procedure for resolving questions with regard to the meaning of some aspect of the Convention. A number of delegations, and the Co-Chairs of Working Group II suggested that the Parties may wish, in special circumstances, to seek advisory opinions from an independent, expert source. A precedent for such a procedure has already been established with the INC's request for any legal advice from the UN Office of Legal Affairs on the nature of the future relationship between the COP and the GEF.[117] Parties may wish to formalize such a procedure as yet another mechanism for avoiding disputes while maintaining the integrity of the Convention's text.

FUTURE ISSUES

Joint Implementation: A further complication

Joint implementation was conceived as a mechanism to increase the likelihood of achieving the objective of the Convention by overcoming the economic disincentives for compliance. Its proponents argue that by allowing developed country Parties to fulfil their emissions reduction commitments in countries where it is cheaper to do so, both developed and developing country Parties are encouraged to undertake activities that further the Convention's objective. Developed countries save money and political friction at home, and may prove more willing to undertake more ambitious commitments.[118] Developing countries will benefit from improved technologies and the domestic environmental and economic benefits of lessened dependence on fossil fuels. The domestic benefits of such projects carried out in developing countries may, it has been argued, encourage developing countries to take on commitments of their own.

Joint implementation thus sits comfortably within the framework of the 'facilitative' approach to compliance systems, as it encourages a non-confrontational look at Parties' abilities to comply and seeks cost-effective and politically acceptable solutions. What appears to be an economically straightforward and sensible concept, has raised serious questions in terms of its legal, procedural and institutional implications, that have yet to be resolved.[119]

The most significant of these would be revealed by a traditional dispute settlement mechanism, which is structured to assess Parties' activities against their legal commitments. Joint implementation 'for credit', even in its simplest form, would allow Parties to transfer across borders activities undertaken to fulfil their commitments. Thus while a developed country would remain responsible for financing the fulfilment of its own commitments, the responsibility for carrying them out would, in effect, be subcontracted to a developing country Party.

It is unclear how the Convention Parties, which collectively have the power to determine criteria for joint implementation, will view the legal effect of such shifts in responsibility. What began as a straightforward commitment by a single country to reduce emissions, would be bifurcated into separate commitments on the one hand to finance, and on the other to implement the proposed activity.

Parties may wish to continue to view the commitment to reduce as solely that of the developed country, and require that country to verify and ensure the compliance of the host country through bilateral channels. In this circumstance, Parties to the Convention could invoke the dispute settlement procedures for failure to achieve emissions reduction targets against the donor country only.

Alternatively, Parties may wish to retain the multilateral nature of the Convention and view the commitments of the donor and the host country as running between them and to all Parties to the Convention. Such a situation might be brought about by the more sophisticated iterations of the joint implementation schemes which envision all Parties being allocated emissions entitlements, based on formulas derived from per capita or historical emissions patterns, which could then be traded freely. Under such a system, all Parties to the Convention would have an interest, and should be entitled to enforce each Party's compliance, in order to maintain the value of their own emissions entitlements.

Adoption of a protocol[120]

As negotiations on the implementation of the Convention progress, the adoption of a protocol seems to be gaining favour as the most sensible legal mechanism for strengthening Parties' commitments to reduce net greenhouse gas emissions. Although a protocol must be adopted under the auspices of the Convention, and all Parties to it must also be Parties to the Convention, it is likely to contain a legally distinct set of relationships and commitments. Not all Parties to the Convention need become Parties to a protocol. Decisions under any protocol can be taken only by Parties to the Protocol concerned, including, presumably, decisions related to a Party's compliance with the Protocol.

The relationship between the Convention's institutions and procedures, and those that may be established by a Protocol, including a governing body, a financial mechanism and a compliance system, is as yet unclear. Should the Convention and the protocol share a compliance system, procedures could be developed within the SBI, and within the COP to vary the right to participate or vote depending on which agreement or which Parties were at issue. Given the current state of the Convention's primary commitments, Parties might, alternatively, await the outcome of protocol negotiations before deciding whether to follow the example of the ozone regime and develop a compliance procedure specific to the more developed protocol.

This would allow Parties to tailor a compliance system to the protocol's primary commitments. If, for example a protocol chooses to specify measures (such as the imposition of energy efficiency standards, minimum technological standards or carbon taxes) the emphasis of compliance assessment may shift from questions of whether a country is achieving its target within a certain timetable, to whether a party has adopted certain regulations or put in place particular technologies. This would ease some of the methodological challenges facing compliance analysis under the Convention.

CONCLUSION

The tools available for the enforcement of compliance with international environmental law are blunt and limited. Funds for the facilitating compliance are in short supply.[121] The types of sanctions contemplated for coercing compliance are unlikely to have a deterrent effect on the behaviour of wealthier or more powerful non-compliers and could not therefore be equitably applied against weaker Parties.

The political and ethical environment generated by the rhetoric of global environmental issues, such as ozone depletion, biodiversity and climate change, encourages states, regardless of their real motivations, to appear to be acting in good faith. The Convention's compliance system, in order to promote the compliance of reluctant Parties must establish both objective and normative standards whereby Parties' actions may be assessed against their commitments. Clearly articulated primary commitments and methodologies, and transparent, publicly available reports will help to expose and distinguish the inadvertent and intentional manipulation of compliance data.

A compliance procedure, strengthened institutionally and procedurally along the lines outlined above, could provide clear criteria and transparent procedures for assessing and facilitating compliance and strip away the excuses that dissenting states use to mask intentionally non-compliant behaviour. Traditional dispute settlement mechanisms must be available to step in where good faith non-compliance is exposed as a wrongful breach of commitments and to add the sanction of unlawfulness to the embarrassment of non-compliance.

The concerns of those countries reluctant to initiate compliance procedures can be addressed in part by reducing the procedural barriers, and lowering the political costs associated with non-compliance. Empowering impartial institutions, such as the Convention's Secretariat which, unlike many developing countries, will have the resources to monitor and assess compliance information, to raise questions about Parties' compliance and will help depoliticize responses to non-compliance. The Convention's compliance system must maintain an emphasis on facilitative activities, while ensuring the process sends the correct signals about the importance of the Convention's objective and its primary commitments.

The challenge that global warming shares with the degradation of the ozone layer and the depletion of biological diversity is that it operates on a strict timescale. While the precise limits of that scale have not yet been sharply defined by science, we have been told that there is some point on the horizon by which we will have to achieve a certain goal or the results may be catastrophic. Any achievements leveraged by this Convention that fall short of that critical goal, may have some worthwhile benefits, both for the environment and for human development. If the science is to believed, however, these achievements will wilt beside the large-scale misery and disruption that could be brought on by accelerated global warming. Arguments in favour of soft rules and flexible compliance systems, often grounded on rationales of cost-effectiveness and political pragmatism, must be judged against the long-term costs of doing too little too late.

The commitment to strengthen the Convention's compliance system must go hand in hand with the commitment to strengthen the Convention's commitments or risk further eroding the public's confidence in the ability of international law and global governance to deal effectively with the challenges of sustainable development.

APPENDIX 2: NON-COMPLIANCE PROCEDURES UNDER THE MONTREAL PROTOCOL

BY ALEXANDRA KEUTSCH

The Montreal Protocol has set up a relatively complex structure of non-compliance procedures with the primary aim of enabling the non-confrontational[1] and amicable resolution[2] of cases of non-compliance.

INSTITUTIONS INVOLVED IN THE NON-COMPLIANCE PROCEDURE

The Meeting of the Parties

Article 11 of the Montreal Protocol provides that the Meeting of the Parties (MOP) should meet at regular, unspecified intervals. There is no prescribed time limit, but, unless the Parties decide otherwise, the meetings are to be held in conjunction with the Conference of the Parties of the Vienna Convention.[3] In practice the MOP has met once a year, within a few days of the COP of the Vienna Convention where this also took place.

The MOP has the power under Articles 11(3)(d) and 8 to

> consider and approve procedures and institutional mechanisms for determining noncompliance . . . and for treatment of Parties found to be in non-compliance.

Under this Article the MOP set up the ad hoc Group of Legal Experts (GOLE) and the Implementation Committee (IC).

The Secretariat

The Secretariat which is set up under the Vienna Convention, has various functions under the non-compliance procedure. Article 12 of the Montreal Protocol provides that the Secretariat shall report on the compliance of Parties with their reporting requirements and with control measures, as well as

> [p]erform such other functions for the achievement of the purposes of this Protocol as may be assigned to it by the Parties.

In the non-compliance context the Secretariat assists the IC in its work, and in its second meeting the IC viewed the function of the Secretariat as being 'to take such administrative measures as [are] necessary to provide the best and the most complete information to the Committee'.

Additionally, the IC relies on the Secretariat for scientific expertise, although it has emphasized the need to '[keep] open the possibility of obtaining external scientific expertise where needed'.[4] The IC has also asked the Secretariat to organize meetings at certain times or in conjunction with other working groups or other meetings.

GOLE

The open-ended ad hoc Group of Legal Experts (GOLE) evolved out of the Legal Working Group on Non-Compliance. Because of the 'complexity of the issues', the ad hoc Working Group of Legal Experts, was convened for further discussions on 'procedures and institutional mechanisms for determining compliance . . . and for the treatment of Parties that fail to comply with its terms'.[6]

The second MOP extended GOLE's mandate 'to elaborate further procedures on non-compliance and terms of reference for the Implementation Committee'[7] with a view to adoption at the fourth MOP. In their first meeting, GOLE drafted a NCP and decided that an Implementation Committee should be set up. This was submitted to the second MOP, where the draft procedure was duly adopted as an interim measure.[8] Subsequently the GOLE acted on evidence received from reports by the IC, and revised and amended the NCP and drew up two 'indicative lists': one of possible situations of non-compliance with the Protocol and the other of measures that might be taken by a Meeting of the Parties in response to noncompliance with the Protocol. Thus, GOLE's importance can be said to have lain in the drawing up and improvement of the procedures for non-compliance.

The Implementation Committee

As already mentioned, the Implementation Committee was set up by the MOP upon the recommendation of GOLE and received its mandate from the interim non-compliance procedure contained in Annex III[9] of the Second Meeting of the Parties. Unless it decides otherwise, the IC meets twice a year directly after the GOLE meeting and directly before the MOP, with the Secretariat arranging for and servicing its meetings.[10]

The IC is not open-ended, it is now comprised of ten parties elected by the MOP for two years, based on equitable geographical distribution.[11] The first Parties elected were Japan, Norway, Trinidad and Tobago, Hungary and Uganda.[12] The work of the IC has been complicated by the fact that its members are elected on a representative, rather than on a personal basis, allowing countries to send different representatives to every meeting.

The IC's functions, as laid down in the revised NCP adopted at the Fourth MOP, are firstly to receive, consider and report on

(1) submissions of and reactions to reservations, concerns and reasons for noncompliance;
(2) any information concerning compliance or production, import and export of controlled substances received and forwarded by the Secretariat.

secondly to request further information, where it considers this necessary; thirdly to gather information in the territory of a Party where invited to do so by that Party; and fourthly

> to maintain, . . . an exchange of information with the Executive Committee of the Multilateral Fund related to the provision of financial and technical cooperation,

> including the transfer of technologies to Parties operating under Article 5, paragraph 1, of the Protocol.[13]

The basic aim of the work of the IC is to consider these 'submissions, information and observations . . . with a view to securing an amicable solution of the matter on the basis of respect for the provisions of the Protocol'.[14]

Other relevant bodies

The *ad hoc* Group of Experts on Reporting Difficulties was set up by the MOP at their second meeting

> to consider the reasons for the difficulties faced by some countries in reporting the required data and to recommend possible solutions to the Parties concerned and report on its progress to the Third Meeting of the Parties.[15]

A few other bodies might be mentioned in the context of the institutional structure of the NCP. The World Bank, UNDP and UNEP, the implementing agencies of the Multilateral Fund, are important bodies in this context as they give financial and structural help in meeting commitments. The Customs Cooperation Committee and the Harmonized System Committee set up the 'Harmonized Commodity System' which exists to facilitate reporting on imports and exports of controlled substances.

Although these bodies do not deal directly with implementation, their significance in this context lies in the fact that they attempt to make compliance easier for the Parties. This will be discussed further below.

THE NON-COMPLIANCE PROCEDURE

Under Article 7 of the Montreal Protocol each Party has the duty to report data on its production, imports and exports and consumption of controlled and transitional substances within certain time limits. If a party cannot comply with the reporting requirements, or other obligations under the Protocol, then it has to submit an explanation of the specific circumstances of the causes for non-compliance to the Secretariat.

Moreover, the NCP[16] sets up a procedure which the Secretariat has to follow when it receives a submission from a party expressing its concerns about the implementation of the Protocol by other Parties.[17] There is no provision in the NCP for any body or person other than a Party to make such a complaint. The NCP also enables the Secretariat to request a Party to provide more information where it has become aware of possible non-compliance by that Party.[18] If the matter is not resolved by the Party through administrative action or through diplomatic contacts, the Secretariat

> shall include the matter in its report to the Meeting of the Parties . . . and inform the Implementation Committee accordingly.[19]

The Secretariat also has to pass on any submissions by countries explaining the circumstances of their non-compliance to the Implementation Committee.[20]

Once the IC has received reports on data, any submissions or other evidence, it discusses and analyzes these reports and then makes recommendations and requests to the Secretariat and to the Meeting of the Parties to change procedures, talk to countries that are not complying with reporting requirements for instance, or clarify the functions of and means open to the Committee.

The Secretariat contacts the countries it has been asked to address on these issues. If these do not react, it reports this back to the IC. The Implementation Committee will again report to the MOP, which, in its function as the 'executive' body of the Montreal Protocol, can,

> taking into consideration the circumstances of the matter, decide upon and call for steps to bring about full compliance with the Protocol, including measures to assist the Parties' compliance with the Protocol, and to further the Protocol's objectives.[21]

The MOP may also make interim recommendations[22] and

> request the Implementation Committee to make recommendations to assist the Meeting's consideration of matters of possible non-compliance.[23]

More importantly, the indicative list of measures that might be taken by a MOP in respect of non-compliance with the Protocol in Annex V of the report on the fourth MOP, gives the MOP the power to

(1) give appropriate assistance, including assistance for the collection and reporting of data, technical assistance, technology transfer and financial assistance, information transfer and training;
(2) issue cautions;
(3) suspend, in accordance with the applicable rules of international law ... specific rights and privileges under the Protocol ... including those concerned with industrial rationalization, production, consumption, trade, transfer of technology, financial mechanism and institutional arrangements;

These are the main enforcement powers adopted by the MOP under the Protocol. However, there are no special procedures that give preference to recommendations by the IC.

In so far as it can be said that the MOP has ever acted under the NCP, the only instance that can be found is where the MOP 'encouraged' Hungary, Bulgaria and Poland to make every effort to make contributions in kind instead of in money to the Multilateral Fund.[24]

In its practical work until now the IC has dealt only with the compliance of Parties with the reporting requirements of the Protocol.[25] In the cases where these requirements have been met incompletely or not at all, besides instructing the Secretariat to require members to report, the IC has also tried to ascertain the reasons for this non-compliance and to reflect on what measures could be taken to help Parties which are in breach of their obligations to comply with them.

In relation to situations where reduction targets, ie substantive commitments have not been met, however, the reports of the IC have limited themselves to stating that 'according to the data reported by the Parties, there were no cases of non-compliance with the control measures of the Protocol' or to commenting on the overall position of compliance, praising the 'positive situation of many of the Parties reducing their consumption of controlled substances much beyond the extent called for by the control measures of the Protocol', and expressing 'concern ... over the trend toward increased consumption of controlled substances particularly halons, by some Parties operating under Article 5'.[26]

OTHER PROCEDURAL AND DEFINITIONAL ASPECTS

Confidentiality

A concern addressed frequently by the IC refers to confidentiality. Initially a great part of the reporting process was confidential. As early as in the second meeting of the IC, however, it was confirmed that the Meeting of the Parties had decided that only data on the production, imports and exports of controlled substances would be confidential, whereas data on consumption would not be so.[27] Although this was supposed to appease the reporting countries, concerns about the confidentiality of data were still being expressed at the seventh meeting.

The concern of countries for confidentiality of production data is understandable as a risk for competitiveness of industries exists. However, as the substances in question are to be phased out anyway, and there is a great need for openness if implementation measures are to be successful, overemphasis of confidentiality might hinder the efficient reporting of data, and the ability of the Secretariat, the IC and outside Parties to monitor and oversee the development of compliance. In the interest of transparency it would be useful if the Committee were to define more clearly what is confidential and maybe limit areas of confidentiality to areas where it is truly necessary.

Access to information

The third report of GOLE discussed[28] proposals by the European Community to include the consideration of possible irregularities, to request further information and to undertake 'examinations'.[29] The reaction to this was divided.

> Some representatives considered that the Committee needed such powers if it were to function effectively. Others, however, felt that those elements were inconsistent with the advisory and conciliatory role of the Committee. A number of them objected to consideration by the Committee of any information from non-governmental sources, such as industry, the mass media, non-governmental organizations or individuals. However, others took the view that information from such sources was important for the effective implementation of the Protocol. After consideration of the matter by a drafting group, a compromise text was approved by the Working Group as paragraph 7 of the new text in Annex I.[30]

Defining non-compliance

In its second report the IC indicated that it would like GOLE to define the meaning of non-compliance, and to prepare indicative (non-exhaustive) lists of situations of non-compliance and possible responses to non-compliance[31] for the guidance of the Committee. As a result of this GOLE drew up two draft indicative lists in relation to these issues. The first of these defined non-compliance as

i. non-compliance with provisions relating to control measures, including those covering consumption and production, industrial rationalization, exports to countries operating under Article 5(1), and relating to essential uses of Halons;
ii. non-compliance with provisions relating to control of trade with non-Parties, including the banning of import/export of controlled substances, the undertaking to discourage export of technology and refraining from providing subsidies, aid, credits, guarantees or insurance programmes;
iii. non-compliance with time schedules and non-reporting of specified data;
iv. failure to cooperate in, and to report a summary of, the activities under this Article;
[v. non-payment of contributions to the financial mechanism;]
[v. non-provision of the contributions referred to in Article 10 para. 1, for the purpose of financing on a grant or concessional basis the incremental costs agreed upon in its para. 3, as well as what is provided for in Article 10A concerning substitute substances and the transfer of technology;]
vi. failure to take 'every practicable step' consistent with the programmes supported by the financial mechanism, for transfer of technology;
[vii. non-compliance with the obligations in decisions of the Parties to the Protocols.]

However, the fourth Meeting of the Parties chose not to adopt the list and it remains unclear whether a second attempt to have it adopted will be made. The bracketed paragraphs (v) and (vii) were very controversial even within the GOLE. The difficulty here was that developing countries were trying to use a noncompliance procedure to clarify the substantive text of the Montreal Protocol, an authoritative statement that imposed duties to provide additional finance on developed countries would have been a major step forwards from the point of view of these states. However, it would seem impossible for the developed countries ever to accept such an obligation as binding and enforceable.

The list of measures 'that might be taken . . . in respect of non-compliance with the Protocol' was, as already seen, accepted by the Meeting of the Parties as Annex V of the Montreal Protocol.

No reaction to either of these developments can be seen in any of the reports by the IC following the Meeting of the Parties and no 'enforcement' action has been taken so far. The next few reports may show whether the Meeting of the Parties will make use of any of the mechanisms in the indicative list on non-compliance.

TYPES AND REASONS FOR NON-COMPLIANCE

In its first seven meetings, the IC has dealt mainly with issues of non-implementation of reporting requirements. Relying on the Secretariat's reports on data, the IC has set out in its reports the data on full or partial non-compliance with the reporting procedures, and on the compliance with control measures (substantive requirements).

Non-compliance with control measures

As has already been mentioned, the discussion on compliance with control measures has been limited to very brief statements praising countries which lowered levels of CFCs and halons more than they had to, and concern where slight increases in consumption took place. In the first few meetings not enough data had been accumulated to permit any kind of judgement on whether control measures were really being complied with. However, even in these first meetings the dearth of even such statements leads to the question whether reliance only on the reports on data submitted by the Parties themselves could in any case create a system in which a true picture of compliance with control measures could emerge.

Firstly, as will be discussed shortly, many countries have had immense problems meeting the reporting requirements and thus many reports have been filed either not at all or incompletely. This means that data on compliance with control measures are incomplete anyway. Also, the Secretariat is more likely to receive a report on time from a country which has complied with such requirements than from a country which has not and which might be more tempted to delay reporting for that reason. This means that it could well be that the rate of non-compliance with control measures is higher than can be seen from the data available at the moment.

Secondly, the developed countries are the main producers and consumers of CFCs and that makes them more likely to breach targets purely because they are major 'users' of CFCs. Many developing countries are not expected to reduce their levels, because they are so low anyway. Indeed, developing countries are allowed to increase their consumption as long as the consumption falls within a 0.3 kg per capita limit, and, as seen above, this has happened. Although such an increase is not prohibited, this could be an indication that the financial and structural mechanisms which are aimed at the virtual elimination of ozone depleting substances are not working as well as they should be.

Thirdly, relying purely on data reported by countries themselves, without any further possibilities of checking the correctness of the figures, opens up the system to abuse by parties for whom it will be easier to represent data in a way they want it seen and to 'manipulate' statistics. The Committee itself observes in its fourth meeting[32] that 'the Committee has no mandate to verify the data reported by the Parties', but it does not comment further.

In the light of these facts it seems very unlikely that non-compliance will even be discovered in many cases for some while yet. In the IC reports this area is clearly still in its infancy, which is why, unlike in the case of non-compliance with reporting requirements, the IC has not attempted to look behind the figures on reasons for and underlying factors of this non-compliance. The question of how to enforce compliance when there is a dispute is left for later discussion.

Non-compliance with reporting requirements

This takes us on to consider the non-compliance with reporting requirements. Here the IC goes much further than in the field of control measures. Firstly, it sets out exactly how many and which countries have not complied with their reporting obligations and in what way. Secondly, it asks the Secretariat to request such countries to comply. Finally, it looks into the reasons for such non-compliance by inviting the countries concerned to comment on their problems through the Secretariat, or by inviting them to the actual meetings of the IC and asking them to state their reasons there and to answer questions from Committee members. If a country does not appear at a meeting subsequent to such an invitation this is specifically mentioned in the report of the IC and thus serves as an inherent threat to countries to comply with such invitations in order not to lose face.

This procedure leads to the clear emergence of the main reasons for noncompliance. Except for Italy which has had its own bureaucratic difficulties, and which had not reported by the end of 1993, but was promising it would soon do so, the countries with most problems with reporting have been developing countries and countries with economies in transition. Another problem has been, that in some cases separate countries reported data together instead of separately, as in the case of former parts of the Soviet Union, or of the customs union Switzerland and Liechtenstein.[33] This has been treated as a violation of reporting requirements by the IC, the Secretariat and the MOP except in cases of regional economic integration organizations like the EC.[34]

As far as developing countries are concerned, the failure to report was typically caused by the lack of funds to set up or run an institutional structure for the compilation of data and drawing up of reports and for the collection of data and the monitoring of imports and exports of controlled substances, as well as by the lack of know-how as to how to go about these tasks.[35]

In the Secretariat's Third Report on the Reporting of Data the following problems are identified as the most critical:[36]

- [t]he Harmonized Commodity System is currently not adequate to ensure accurate data reporting, because it does not distinguish between individual substances;
- [d]ata based on customs statistics are not accurate or complete. Customs officers often do not have sufficient information and training to identify controlled substances . . .;
- [i]nformation from importing companies is often not available, because they treat the data as confidential;
- [i]n some cases, importing companies do not have enough knowledge to provide accurate data;
- [i]n some countries, government authorities lack the technical and financial resources to carry out data gathering.

The problems for the economies in transition have not so much been of the structural and economic kind mentioned above, but more of a political and economic nature stemming from the disintegration of the formerly centralized system of the Soviet Union and the Eastern Bloc which has made it more difficult to obtain information which was often held on a centralized or protected basis because of military uses, nuclear power generation etc. However, administrative problems are the cause of major set-backs for these countries as well.

Reactions to compliance problems

The reaction of the IC to these problems is to emphasize the need for financial and technical assistance for the countries concerned if they are to be enabled to comply with their reporting requirements. In view of the importance of this aid for the purposes of compliance with reporting and other requirements both the IC and the Montreal Protocol Multilateral Fund (MPMF) lay great emphasis on the fact that they have to work closely together and exchange information regularly. For this reason the IC has gone so far as to invite representatives of each of the implementing agencies of the MPMF (UNDP, UNEP and World Bank) to inform the Committee of the so called 'country programmes' and 'country studies' organized by them. These programmes consist of financial support including, for example, assistance for the development of institutional strengthening, technical training, demonstration and training workshops, assistance in country programme formulation, institutional strengthening for ozone layer protection,[37] as well as

> action plans for the phase-out of ozone depleting substances, facilitation of establishment of monitoring arrangements and systems for improved record keeping in order to enable monitoring of the importation and use of controlled substances ... [to] allow ... observation and evaluation of effectiveness of the country programme in reducing and phasing out the consumption of the controlled substances and compliance with Article 7 of the Montreal Protocol.[38]

All this typifies the basic approach of the IC towards the question of noncompliance: first an examination of the reasons for non-compliance and assistance in the solution of problems rather than a confrontational stance.

However, evidence supplied to the IC by the Secretariat shows that some countries have not improved their reporting or submitted data even though they have completed a country programme.[39] This is a serious drawback if facilitative system of enforcement through assistance is to work, especially as all that can be done in such a situation is for the implementing agencies 'to urge all countries to submit the required data immediately after their respective country programme has been finalized'.[40]

If, even after the extensive assistance given through a country programme, the reporting requirements of a party are still not met, this bodes ill for compliance with substantive obligations. However, the reasons for such non-compliance are not mentioned in the reports of the IC, and it is likely that some of the countries concerned would be those developing countries that hardly contribute to the depletion of the ozone layer anyway. More information on this is needed.

To strengthen further its 'amicable resolution' approach, the IC quotes the Secretariat's suggestions of other measures to help along Parties that have problems with their reporting requirements. These include:

- Legislation or regulation to complete reporting from importers and exporters.
- A customs code system for controlled substances.
- A periodic special survey of user industries to identify consumption.[41]

Some specific suggestions made by the *ad hoc* Group of Experts on Reporting Difficulties, for example that UNEP should pass on experience gained in countries where data are successfully collected, are taken up by the Secretariat for example by requesting that such data be submitted to it.

Parts of all these recommendations have been taken up in various ways, and UNEP claim that licensing systems and customs codes have led to the most reliable data in relation to country programmes.[42]

The suggestions in relation to customs code numbers have been taken up by the Customs Cooperation Council[43] and the Secretariat which have attempted to prescribe individual code numbers for each of the controlled and transitional substances as part of the Harmonized Commodity System. However, the IC Report comments that the amendment of the Harmonized Commodity System would be very laborious, and would not be able to come into force earlier than 1996, 'when most of the controlled substances have already been phased out'.[44] The result of this is that reliance is placed on the voluntary introduction of extended codes as, for example, in New Zealand and Japan. Even where a system of special code numbers for controlled substances is used, UNEP has stated that such a system will only work in relation 'to pure chemicals but [is] difficult to implement for mixtures',[45] and that on the whole the system has not been very helpful for the prompt collection of data. This seems to indicate that, again, there is an attempt at 'soft' enforcement with different regulatory measures which have not, as yet, proved to be very successful, and which might not help at all because the process of introducing a binding system takes too long.

It is interesting to note that in the report of the third meeting of the IC a short mention is made of the fact that the United States drew attention to the essential role of domestic compliance systems in enforcing the Protocol by noting it had already initiated criminal prosecutions under domestic legislation implementing Article 4 of the Montreal Protocol.[46] No further information is supplied in relation to this, but it may be an indication that effective implementation could be reached not through international but through national enforcement actions.

APPENDIX 3a: THE FRAMEWORK CONVENTION ON CLIMATE CHANGE: CONTENTS

26 July 1994
Original: ENGLISH

INTERGOVERNMENTAL NEGOTIATING COMMITTEE
FOR A FRAMEWORK CONVENTION ON CLIMATE CHANGE
Tenth session
Geneva, 22 August–2 September 1994
Item 5 (b) of the provisional agenda

CONSIDERATION OF THE ESTABLISHMENT OF A MULTILATERAL CONSULTATIVE PROCESS FOR THE RESOLUTION OF QUESTIONS REGARDING IMPLEMENTATION (ARTICLE 13)

Note by the interim secretariat

CONTENTS

APPENDIX 3b: FRAMEWORK CONVENTION ON CLIMATE CHANGE

1. INTRODUCTION

A. *Convention provisions*

1. Article 13 of the United Nations Framework Convention on Climate Change states that:

> 'The Conference of the Parties shall, at its first session, consider the establishment of a multilateral consultative process, available to Parties on their request, for the resolution of questions regarding the implementation of the Convention.'

B. *Scope of the note*

2. During the third, fourth and fifth sessions of the Intergovernmental Negotiating Committee, discussions took place in Working Group II with regard to the establishment of a procedure under the Convention whereby questions regarding implementation could be resolved amongst the Parties to the Convention. Owing to the heavy workload of the Committee and time constraints, completion of a procedure for inclusion in the Convention was not feasible. It was, therefore, decided that Article 13 would provide for the possibility of establishing such a process once the Convention entered into force.

3. Sections II - VII of the present note cover the following points:

- Section II briefly reports on the discussions that took place during the negotiations of the Committee at its third and fourth sessions;
- Section III attempts to describe the rationale behind a multilateral consultative process;
- Section IV examines the scope of application of such a process in relation to the provisions of the Convention;
- Section V looks at the relationship between a multilateral consultative process, the review of national communications within the Subsidiary Body , for Implementation (SBI), and the dispute settlement regime established pursuant to Article 14 of the Convention;

- Section VI enumerates elements that could be considered in the design of a multilateral consultative process;
- Section VII concludes by presenting possible options to the Committee for recommendation to the Conference of the Parties at its first session (COP 1), to enable it to undertake the work relating to this issue.

4. The interim secretariat has reviewed several non-compliance, dispute resolution and implementation review procedures, for example, the 1987 Montreal Protocol on Substances that Deplete the Ozone Layer, the Second Sulphur, Emissions Protocol to the United Nations Economic Commission for Europe (UN/ECE) Convention on Long-range Transboundary Air Pollution, the General Agreement on Tariffs and Trade (GATT) dispute resolution panels, and international labour and human rights conventions. The secretariat is at present preparing a review of these procedures which will be issued as an addendum to this note in due course.

5. This material is intended to serve as an initial background document for discussion by the Committee and for future discussions on this issue by the Conference of the Parties (COP).

The note does not attempt to design a multilateral consultative process.

C. *Possible action by the Committee*

6. The Committee may wish to consider commencing a discussion on this item at its tenth session. However, owing to the heavy work schedule of its eleventh session (see A/AC.237/57), it may be advisable, once an initial airing of views has been completed at the tenth session, to defer further consideration to the first session of the Conference of the Parties (COP 1) (see paras. 33–34, below).

II. BACKGROUND

7. At the third session of the Committee, Working Group II considered the drafting of a procedure whereby the resolution of questions regarding implementation under the Convention would be cooperative rather than adversarial. The views expressed at that session were that such a procedure should be based on consultation and cooperation, with the aim of assisting Parties that were, for whatever reason, failing to fulfil their commitments under the Convention. In this regard, a number of proposals were presented to the Working Group.

8. At the fourth session of the Committee, the Co-Chairs of Working Group II proposed an alternative procedure to the traditional bilateral dispute settlement regime. In presenting this proposal they informed the Committee that they had concluded that traditional approaches were insufficient in resolving questions of this kind that, owing to the global nature of the issue, may arise under the Convention. They indicated that, as all Parties would be affected by the action or inaction of all other Parties, reliance on bilateral dispute settlement procedures would not be sufficient.

9. The proposal contained, *inter alia*, the following elements:[1]

   (a) The COP would be the point of entry for any questions and the body responsible for all decisions;

(b) Questions relating to the interpretation and implementation of the Convention could be brought by Parties or by one of the subsidiary bodies;
(c) The COP would consider questions and could establish *ad hoc* panels drawn from members;
(d) In reviewing questions, the first step would be to consult the Party that was the subject of the question. The *ad hoc* panels could also consult with the subsidiary bodies under the Convention;
(e) The panels would report the results of their consultations to the COP within one year. These reports would include, if necessary, a recommendation for resolution;
(f) The COP would consider the reports and take whatever action it deemed necessary;
(g) If the Party did not comply with a decision of the COP, the latter could take any action it deemed necessary to further the objective of the Convention;
(h) If consensus were not practical, decision-making by the COP would be by a two-thirds majority;
(i) Details regarding the establishment of *ad hoc* panels would be elaborated in an annex which could be drafted by Working Group II or the COP once the Convention entered into force.

10. There was a wide range of views expressed by the Committee on the above mentioned proposal. The main points in the discussion touched upon the following questions: (a) whether a traditional dispute settlement procedure would be adequate; (b) whether the proposal was an appropriate alternative to traditional dispute settlement procedures or whether it should complement such procedures; (c) whether the COP should perform a judicial or a political role; (d) whether there was a need to undertake friendly negotiations regarding a Party's compliance; (e) whether the establishment of *ad hoc* panels would be costly and time-consuming, and (f) whether decisions by the COP under this procedure should be taken by consensus or by a two-thirds majority of the Parties.

III. RATIONALE FOR A MULTILATERAL CONSULTATIVE PROCESS

11. There are several possible rationales for having a multilateral consultative process. First, as the phenomenon of climate change is of a global character, it can be argued that the interests of all States are involved. Second, since the negative effects of non-compliance with the Convention are subtle and cumulative and may manifest themselves only after a long period of time, preventative measures and remedies could result in more effective solutions than *post hoc* dispute settlement. Third, a multilateral consultative process would emphasize cooperation among Parties in pursuit of a common goal, rather than confrontation. Although such procedures usually lack real enforcement power, their strength is manifested through peer pressure and regular accountability by Parties in an intergovernmental context. Finally, they encourage Parties to an agreement to seek consensus on issues and to strive for interpretations and decisions that will reinforce the stability and effectiveness of the regime as a whole. In this way, treaty compliance can be promoted through discussion and negotiation, rather than by adjudication of questions of law.[2]

12. Such a multilateral consultative process would be the forum for handling questions that Parties may have about the implementation of provisions by other Parties and their own implementation of the Convention. The process would be

initiated by the act of raising a question. At times it may be used frequently, if there are many questions, while at other times it may be less active.

13. Parties would, of course, remain free to resort to traditional methods of dispute settlement as a means of settling questions of interpretation or application of the Convention. However, traditional dispute settlement procedures are rarely invoked in environmental contexts. In an area where legal rules are still developing and evolving, Parties may prefer non-adversarial negotiations as a more predictable way of balancing conflicting interests in resolving problems. By interposing a multilateral consultative process between the Parties' performance of their commitments and traditional dispute settlement, the latter could acquire a largely symbolic role as a deterrent.

14. Furthermore, establishing a multilateral consultative process could lead to a more effective Convention. In response to particular questions and concerns, such a process could lead to decisions and opinions in particular cases as to whether a Party is 'in compliance' with the Convention and, where this is ambiguous, what constitutes compliance. Performing this function could lead to a more effective Convention in the following ways:[3]

(a) The process could help to build confidence in the Convention by demonstrating that implementation problems can be raised, made transparent and resolved satisfactorily;
(b) An authoritative interpretative process could set useful bounds on the diversity of legitimate interpretations;
(c) The process could offer a safety valve for considering and disposing of problem questions that might otherwise make it difficult to progress on other issues; and
(d) The process could help to point out areas where adjustment is needed and around which public opinion can be mobilized to push for policy change.

IV. SCOPE OF APPLICATION

15. A multilateral consultative process could consider any questions relating to the implementation of the Convention. The articles on commitments (Articles 4, 5, 6 and 12) would clearly fall within its purview, as would the functioning of the financial mechanism that is provided for in Article 11 of the Convention and any other article relating to implementation. This process would also apply to any amendments and annexes adopted pursuant to Articles 15 and 16.

16. If Parties were to decide to adopt protocols to the Convention, the scope of application of a multilateral consultative process established pursuant to Article 13 would need to be considered. Since protocols establish separate but related legal regimes, the Parties to the Convention and to the protocols may differ. Moreover, if more detailed commitments were elaborated in protocols, then the Parties to those protocols may consider creating additional or different review and assessment procedures, with powers that are commensurate with the additional commitments.[4]

17. Article 13 states that the process would be '*available to Parties on their request*, for the resolution of questions regarding the implementation of the Convention' (emphasis added). Parties would need to decide on the intended meaning of 'available to Parties on their request'. Further, Parties would need to decide

whether 'implementation' should include questions of interpretation as well. Questions of implementation and interpretation may be inextricably linked and may thus need to be considered in tandem. Article 14.1 makes it clear that its provisions are to be invoked 'in the event of a dispute ... concerning the interpretation or application of the Convention'. As the COP is the 'supreme body' of the Convention, it would certainly be within its purview under Article 13 to respond to questions regarding interpretation of the Convention (see Article 7.2 and 7.2(m)).

V. RELATIONSHIP TO THE REVIEW PROCESS, THE SUBSIDIARY BODY FOR IMPLEMENTATION, AND THE DISPUTE SETTLEMENT REGIME UNDER ARTICLE 14

18. The provisions of the Convention relating to implementation may be seen as a continuum consisting of the communication of information and the review process at the beginning, a multilateral consultative process in the middle and the dispute settlement regime at the end. Taken together, these provisions and procedures will constitute a collective effort to promote learning and consultation, both broadly and in response to particular questions, concerns and, perhaps, even disputes.

A. *Relationship to the review process*

19. Regular review of information related to implementation communicated pursuant to Article 12 is the foundation upon which the rest of the continuum is built. Such reviews will help promote a dynamic link between the actual experience and policies of the Parties and the evolution of the obligations under the Convention. The review process, whose details are still under design, might address some questions related to the national communication, such as methodologies and omissions, as they arise in particular communications. The interim secretariat has prepared a document for the tenth session of the Committee in this regard (see A/AC.237/63).

20. So far, the Committee, in preparing for COP 1, has favoured a review process that is facilitative, non-confrontational, open and transparent (see A/AC.237/63). Consequently, the review is not seen as a mechanism for verification or for determining whether a party is in compliance, but rather as a tool to ensure that the COP has the information necessary to carry out its mandate.

B. *Relationship to the Subsidiary Body for Implementation*

21. The Subsidiary Body for Implementation (SBI) will be the main mechanism for the review process. Consequently, there would inevitably be a close relationship between the SBI and a multilateral consultative process since both would be considering similar issues and drawing upon a similar base of information. If a question were in relation to the communication and review of information, the multilateral consultative process would only be invoked if the procedure under the review process could not resolve the question. Moreover, both the SBI and the multilateral consultative process would need similar technical support to some degree.

22. The functions of the SBI are still under review by the Committee, and consideration of its relationship to a multilateral consultative process will depend on the outcome of this review (see document A/AC.237/64). It should be noted,

however, that the Committee, at its ninth session, included the function of '[advising] on issues such as resolution of questions, dispute settlement and compliance/enforcement mechanisms' as one of the possible tasks to be carried out by the SBI (A/AC.237/55, annex I, annex to decision 9/3).

23. It is thus conceivable that the COP could request the SBI to initiate a multilateral consultative process. The SBI could carry out the work itself or it could establish a subsidiary working group to do so and report back to it. The SBI could then report to the COP. This is one design option. Another would be for the COP to establish a subsidiary body for the multilateral consultative process, to be invoked whenever needed.

24. Whatever the option chosen, the SBI may well be in a position to identify questions that should be referred to a multilateral consultative process. Therefore, it would be important for the subsidiary bodies, and in particular the SBI, to be given some level of standing to raise questions and contribute to the proceedings of a multilateral consultative process.

C. *Relationship to the dispute settlement regime pursuant to Article 14*

25. The dispute settlement regime, at the other end of the continuum, exists to ensure that genuine disputes have a legitimate means of resolution. Although, ideally, disputes should be prevented, they may arise at any point in the continuum and Parties would be free to invoke Article 14 at any time during the review or multilateral consultative processes.

26. Article 14 establishes a traditional bilateral third-party dispute settlement procedure. The presence of a separate article in the Convention on dispute resolution suggests that the multilateral consultative process envisaged by Article 13 and the dispute settlement procedure under Article 14 are not mutually exclusive. Article 14 sets out the procedure that Parties would revert to when disputes need to be resolved by an institution existing outside the Convention but whose competence is recognized by the Convention, notably, by the International Court of Justice and arbitration and conciliation commissions. On the other hand, Article 13 would provide the procedure whereby Parties to the Convention could amicably resolve their differences, thus avoiding resort to Article 14. In practice, as stated earlier, given the facilitative nature of the review process and the availability of a possible multilateral consultative process, it is unlikely that many disputes will be settled by recourse to Article 14.

27. Unlike a non-compliance regime or a multilateral consultative process that aims to resolve problems within a system without reference to external adjudicators or institutions, dispute settlement relies heavily on outsiders to the system. Moreover, it is, in essence, confrontational. Its sharp edge, however, is blunted in most environmental conventions. For example, Article 14 of the Framework Convention on Climate Change provides for consensual or voluntary jurisdiction which is determined unilaterally, prior to the dispute. However, if Parties have made no such declaration and/or if a dispute has not been resolved after twelve months, the dispute 'shall be submitted, at the request of any of the parties to the dispute, to conciliation' (see Article 14.5). A conciliation commission may be established to resolve the dispute but it may render only a recommendatory award which the Parties shall consider in good faith. (See also the Vienna Convention for the Protection of the Ozone Layer and the Convention on Biological Diversity.)

28. It is clear that, although rarely used in environmental treaties, dispute settlement procedures may serve a useful purpose as a last resort. In contrast, a multilateral consultative process would be intended for more frequent use. It would not be adversarial, as it would focus on assisting Parties in implementing their obligations under the Convention. Moreover, it would serve as a dispute prevention tool and would reflect a collective concern of the COP to ensure that all Parties fulfil their commitments under the Convention, rather than a bilateral concern as in the case of dispute settlement. The two procedures complement each other: respect for the requirements of a multilateral consultative regime would be strengthened by the knowledge that a dispute settlement procedure is always available to Parties and may be activated if necessary.

VI. POSSIBLE ELEMENTS OF A MULTILATERAL CONSULTATIVE PROCESS

29. It should be noted that the COP is not required to establish a multilateral consultative process. Article 13 of the Convention states that the 'Conference of the Parties shall, at its first session, *consider* the establishment of a multilateral consultative process, available to Parties on their request' (emphasis added). Conceivably, COP 1 could, after consideration of this issue, decide that it is not yet opportune to establish such a process. Alternatively, after considering the establishment of a multilateral consultative process, the COP could decide that a different type of process is needed to deal with questions relating to implementation.

30. Assuming that the COP does decide to explore a multilateral consultative process, the type of procedure that could be developed would depend on whether the Parties decide to establish a procedure similar to that envisaged during the third and fourth sessions of the Committee (that is, panels), or one that uses a standing committee, like the non-compliance procedures adopted by the Montreal Protocol and the Second Sulphur Emissions Protocol. The COP would need to decide whether the process would entail a conceptual framework for a flexible process consisting of various consultative forums and/or measures to resolve questions in the implementation of the Convention, or whether it would be a process that establishes a standing institutional arrangement to resolve questions.

31. Issues that would need to be considered in designing such a process include the following:[5]

(a) What types of questions could be raised?
- about the Party's own compliance
- about another Party's compliance

(b) What entities other than parties should be able to raise a question?

(c) What type of body will be required to resolve such questions?
- *ad hoc*/permanent
- relationship to the COP and/or SBI
- size and membership
- powers (fact-finding, etc.)

(d) In what ways could such questions be resolved?
- interpretations
- requests to financial mechanism for assistance
- recommendations

32. In the initial stages of developing a process, it may be best not to attempt to establish a procedure that is inflexible or that attempts to deal with all eventualities. From studies of a number of other international agreements, it appears that those which are most effective in achieving their objectives tend to incorporate processes that evolve over time, as knowledge of the issues increases and as Parties' perceptions of problems or objectives change. However, it appears to be equally important that a framework exists within which effective processes and mechanisms are able to develop.[6]

VII. OPTIONS FOR ACTION BY THE CONFERENCE OF THE PARTIES

33. The Committee may wish to recommend to COP 1 that it set up a procedure to explore further and, as needed, design a multilateral consultative process as envisaged by Article 13. This task could be assigned to:

(a) A group of technical and legal experts established by COP 1 and reporting to the COP;
(b) A group of technical and legal experts, established by and reporting to the SBI, which in turn would report to the COP.

34. The COP, at a subsequent session and in the light of the report on the subject, would decide whether to establish a multilateral consultative process.

APPENDIX 4a: FURTHER NON-COMPLIANCE PROCEDURES: CONTENTS

22 March 1995
ENGLISH ONLY

CONFERENCE OF THE PARTIES
First session, Berlin, 28 March–7 April 1995
Item 5 (e) of the provisional agenda

CONSIDERATION OF THE ESTABLISHMENT OF A MULTILATERAL CONSULTATIVE PROCESS FOR THE RESOLUTION OF QUESTIONS REGARDING IMPLEMENTATION (ARTICLE 13)

A review of selected non-compliance, dispute resolution and implementation review procedures

Note by the interim secretariat

CONTENTS

APPENDIX 4b: FURTHER NON-COMPLIANCE PROCEDURES

I. INTRODUCTION

A. *Convention provisions*

Article 13 of the United Nations Framework Convention on Climate Change states:

> 'The Conference of the Parties shall, at its first session, consider the establishment of a multilateral consultative process, available to the Parties on their request, for the resolution of questions regarding the implementation of the Convention.'

B. *Committee mandate*

2. At its tenth session, the Committee decided 'to recommend to the Conference of the Parties at its first session that it establish an *ad hoc* and open-ended working group of technical and legal experts to study all issues relating to the establishment of a multilateral consultative process and its design, and to report its findings to the Conference of the Parties at its second session' (A/AC. 237/76, para. 114).

C. *Scope of the note*

3. As indicated in the note prepared by the interim secretariat for the tenth session of the Committee (see A/AC.237/59, para. 4), the secretariat was to prepare a review of selected non-compliance, dispute resolution and implementation review procedures. Accordingly, the present note reviews the 1987 Montreal Protocol on Substances that Deplete the Ozone Layer; the Second Sulphur Emissions Protocol to the United Nations Economic Commission for Europe (UN/ECE); the Convention on Long-range Transboundary Air Pollution; the General Agreement on Tariffs and Trade (GATT) and the World Trade Organization (WTO) dispute resolution panels; the International Labour Organization (ILO); the 1982 United Nations Convention on the Law of the Sea; and the Human Rights Conventions.

4. The purpose of the following review is solely to provide background information on the above-mentioned procedures for the forthcoming discussions at the first session of the Conference of the Parties (COP 1). It does not provide a

critique of these procedures but is descriptive in its approach. Moreover, it does not attempt to design a multilateral consultative process for the United Nations Framework Convention on Climate Change.

II. THE NON-COMPLIANCE PROCEDURE OF THE MONTREAL PROTOCOL ON SUBSTANCES THAT DEPLETE THE OZONE LAYER

5. The Protocol's non-compliance procedure was adopted on an interim basis at the Second Meeting of the Parties in London in 1990. The full non-compliance procedure was only created at the Fourth Meeting of the Parties to the Montreal Protocol (hereinafter referred to as 'the Fourth Meeting'), held in Copenhagen in 1992.[1] It is based on four fundamental principles: the non-compliance regime should avoid complexity, should avoid confrontation, should be transparent, and, should leave the taking of decisions to the Meeting of the Parties.

6. The procedure may be triggered by any of the following: the Convention Secretariat; a Party regarding the implementation of the Protocol by another Party; or a Party with regard to its own implementation.

7. If one or several Parties have reservations about another Party's compliance with the Protocol, those concerns are submitted in writing to the Secretariat together with corroborating information. The Secretariat sends a copy of the submission to the Party whose implementation of a particular provision of the Protocol is at issue, and which then has a 'reasonable opportunity' to reply. The reply is sent to the complaining Parties and to the Secretariat, which forwards all information from the Parties concerned to the Implementation Committee.

8. The Implementation Committee handles questions regarding non-compliance. Its aim is to secure 'an amicable solution of the matter on the basis of respect for the provisions of the protocol.'[2] Its task is to consider the following: the annual report of the Secretariat; a reservation by one or more Parties regarding another Party's implementation of its obligations under the Protocol; and a submission by a Party with regard to its own implementation of its obligations under the Protocol.

9. The Implementation Committee is made up of ten members, who are elected by the Parties and represent their States. There is no specific provision spelling out the qualifications required for serving on the Committee. Nevertheless, it is deemed important that members of the Implementation Committee come from a multi-disciplinary background. Elected members serve a term of two years and may only be re-elected for one consecutive term. To ensure a certain level of experience among the members serving on the Committee, only half are replaced every year. Election of members is based on the principle of equitable geographic distribution. The Committee elects its own President and Vice-President, who serve a term of one year. The Committee meets at least biannually, unless it decides otherwise, and its meetings are organized by the Secretariat.

10. The Committee may request further information and also undertake further information gathering inside the territory of a Party, but only 'upon invitation of the Party concerned'.[3] While the Party under consideration has the right to participate in the consideration of its case, it is excluded from the process of elaboration and recommendation that the Committee makes to the Meeting of the Parties. Non-governmental organizations and international governmental organizations may not participate in the non-compliance procedure.

11. The non-compliance procedure is applied without prejudice to the traditional diplomatic dispute settlement procedures. Hence, in accordance with Article 11 of the Vienna Convention on the Protection of the Ozone Layer,[4] States may settle disputes through negotiations or any other peaceful means of their own choice; submission of the dispute to the International Court of Justice; arbitration; or, finally, through an ad hoc conciliation commission. It should be noted that if the Parties to the dispute decide to resort to any of the aforementioned dispute settlement procedures, they must inform the Meeting of the Parties through the Secretariat thereof.

12. The Committee reports to the Meeting of the Parties recommending the adoption of any measures it deems necessary. The Meeting of the Parties may decide upon the report and call for action to bring about full compliance with the Protocol, including measures to assist the Party's compliance with the Protocol. Annex V to the Fourth Meeting Report contains an indicative list of measures that might be taken in case of non-compliance. These are, *inter alia*: 'providing appropriate assistance', 'issuing cautions' and 'suspension of specific rights and privileges under the Protocol'.

13. The disputing Parties report back to the Meeting of the Parties on their implementation of any decision regarding non-compliance actions.

III. THE NON-COMPLIANCE PROCEDURE OF THE SECOND PROTOCOL TO THE 1979 CONVENTION ON LONG-RANGE TRANSBOUNDARY AIR POLLUTION ON FURTHER REDUCTION OF SULPHUR EMISSIONS

14. On 1 March 1993, the Bureau of the Executive Body of the UN/ECE Convention on Long-range Transboundary Air Pollution[5] held a short consultative meeting to consider ways in which supervision of compliance with the obligations contained in the various Protocols to the Convention might be strengthened. The participants at the meeting noted various precedents but focused particularly on the non-compliance procedure of the Montreal Protocol, as they saw no reason to diverge substantially from it.

15. At a special session of the Executive Body for the Convention on Long-range Transboundary Air Pollution held in Oslo on 14 June 1994, the Parties to the Convention adopted the Protocol on Further Reduction of Sulphur Emissions,[6] which aims at reducing sulphur emissions to the atmosphere beyond those levels already set in a first sulphur protocol.[7] The new Protocol establishes a much more elaborate national reporting regime than under any previous protocol under the Convention. Compliance monitoring will be based on an Implementation Committee established under Article 7 of the Oslo Sulphur Protocol. The structure and functions of this Committee are to be decided by the Parties after the entry into force of the Protocol. However, with the adoption of the Protocol, the Parties to the Convention adopted a decision setting out the envisaged structure and function of the Committee.

16. The main principles of the non-compliance regime of the Oslo Sulphur Protocol are similar to those of the Montreal Protocol, namely, to avoid complexity, to avoid confrontation, to be transparent and to leave any decision-making to the Parties. The system provides no sanctions, but rather foresees cooperative measures, such as assisting Parties to comply with the Protocol.

17. The Implementation Committee, as envisaged, will consist of eight members that will be elected. Election of members is based on the principle of equitable geographic distribution. Elected members serve a term of two years. As in the Montreal Protocol, only half the members of the Committee are replaced every year. Outgoing Parties may be re-elected for one consecutive term only. The Committee elects its own President and Vice-President both of whom serve a oneyear term. The Committee meets twice a year, unless it decides otherwise.

18. The tasks of the Implementation Committee are both compulsory and facultative. Hence, the Committee is obliged to carry out a synthesis and evaluation of the information reported by the Parties. The Committee is also obliged to evaluate progress made in the implementation of the Protocols. Additionally, it must consider any matter brought before it regarding the settlement of disputes. Finally, it is to ensure that the quality of the data provided by a Party is controlled either by the Cooperative Programme for Monitoring and Evaluation of Long-range Transmissions of Air Pollutants in Europe technical centres, or by independent experts. Conversely, the Committee may request further information, through the Secretariat, from any source it deems appropriate. It may, upon invitation of the Party concerned, gather information in its territory, and, finally, it may consider any information forwarded by the Secretariat.

19. The Implementation Committee is to consider the following inputs: a reservation that one or more Parties may have concerning the implementation of the obligations of the Protocol by another Party; a reference made by a Party with regard to its own implementation; and the report of the Secretariat. Hence, activity by the Implementation Committee may be triggered either by one or more Parties or by the Secretariat.

20. The role of the Secretariat in the Oslo Sulphur Protocol is even more marked than in the Montreal Protocol: it is not limited to the provision of information and is allowed to report on possible non-compliance, however it may have been made aware of it. Moreover, if, upon reviewing the report submitted by Parties, it becomes aware of possible non-compliance by any Party, it requests further information on the matter. If the matter is not resolved through administrative action and diplomatic contacts, the Implementation Committee is informed accordingly. Hence, although non-governmental organizations and inter-governmental organizations cannot trigger the non-compliance procedure, they may, nevertheless, provide the Secretariat with information on alleged non-compliance.

21. All complaints concerning implementation by another Party must be supported by corroborating information and submitted to the Secretariat. The Secretariat informs the Party whose behaviour is at issue and transmits all information and any eventual reply from the State concerned to the Implementation Committee. Similarly, when a Party refers itself to the Implementation Committee for consideration, it must clearly state in its submission what it considers to be the cause of its failure to comply.

22. While the Party under consideration has the right to participate in the consideration of its case, it is excluded from the process of elaboration and recommendation that the Committee makes to the Meeting of the Parties.

23. The Committee must report to the Parties on its activities at the annual session of the Executive Body. On that occasion, it makes any recommendation it deems appropriate regarding compliance with the Protocol.

24. One of the distinctions between the Oslo Sulphur Protocol and the Montreal Protocol is that in the former, reports relating to compliance are not required to be confidential. This is largely due to the fact that data on sulphur emissions do not have the same commercial implications as those concerning chlorofluorocarbons.

25. The non-compliance procedure is applied without prejudice to the provisions laid down in Article 9 of the Oslo Sulphur Protocol. Consequently, as in the Montreal Protocol, states may settle disputes through traditional diplomatic dispute settlement procedures.

IV. THE SUPERVISORY PROCEDURES OF THE INTERNATIONAL LABOUR ORGANIZATION

26. The ILO plays a pivotal role in the creation and administration of international legal instruments in the labour and social security field. It has a unique tripartite composition: governments and employers' and workers' organizations. The three main organs of the Organization are: the General Conference of Representatives of Member States (hereinafter referred to as the International Labour Conference), the Governing Body and the International Labour Office.

27. The ILO compliance monitoring machinery is uniform in that the same machinery is applied to all ILO conventions.[8] Conversely, the United Nations usually creates a different non-compliance machinery for each new convention adopted under its auspices.

28. The Constitution of the ILO[9] provides for monitoring machinery consisting of regular supervision and special procedures. This system combines a technical evaluation carried out by independent experts, with a further evaluation carried out by a tripartite organ.

29. States must periodically submit reports on the measures they have taken to implement ratified ILO Conventions (see Article 22 of the Constitution of the ILO). The frequency of reporting ranges in practice from a year to once every five years, according to the nature of the problems. The reports are examined by two bodies: the Committee of Experts on the Application of Conventions and Recommendations (hereinafter referred to as 'the Committee of Experts') and the Conference Committee on the Application of Standards (hereinafter referred to as 'the Conference Committee').

30. The Committee of Experts consists of 20 independent members, coming from all regions. These experts are of recognized competence in the field of labour, social and international law and sit in their personal capacity. Furthermore, they are appointed by the Governing Body upon the designation of the Director-General of the ILO.

31. The Committee of Experts (a quasi-judicial body) meets annually, and makes an objective and technical examination of the compliance of obligations under ratified Conventions. In addition, it examines reports by states on the implementation of non-ratified conventions and recommendations requested by the Governing Body each year.

32. The Committee of Experts is assisted by the Office's analysis of government reports and other relevant information and also considers observations from

employers' and workers' organizations pertaining to alleged non-compliance. Moreover, if States so agree, ILO representatives may gather information directly on the territory of the member concerned ('direct contacts').

33. The reports of the Committee of Experts are presented to the Conference Committee. The Conference Committee reflects the tripartite structure of the ILO. It is established by the International Labour Conference, which is the plenary conference of ILO Members, and has the task of considering the most serious cases of persistent non-compliance contained in the Committee of Experts' report. The Conference Committee calls before it government representatives of countries under examination and seeks explanation for the alleged non-compliance.

34. The findings of the Conference Committee are contained in a report which reflects the views of employers' and workers' as well as governments' representatives. The report is then submitted to, and discussed in, the International Labour Conference and subsequently published as part of the 'Proceedings of the International Labour Conference'.

35. A Party to a given convention or the Governing Body itself or a delegate to the Conference may make a complaint alleging that another Party is not securing the 'effective observance' of a convention it has ratified (Article 26 of the Constitution). To deal with the complaint, the Governing Body may establish an *ad hoc* Commission of Inquiry. A Commission of Inquiry is composed of three highly qualified individuals who serve in their personal capacity and are appointed by the Governing Body on the recommendation of the Director-General.

36. The Commission, in considering a complaint before it, may require the implicated Party to provide all information in its possession pertaining to the case. In addition to the information supplied by the Government, the Commission may hear other Parties and witnesses and even, where necessary, undertake on site visits.

37. The Commission drafts a report on the case and transmits it, via the Director-General, to the Parties and the Governing Body. The report includes recommendations on how to ensure compliance and is published in the ILO Official Bulletin.

38. Article 24 of the Constitution also provides for representations by industrial associations of employers or workers alleging failure to secure the effective observance of ratified Conventions. The Governing Body may publish such representations and any government response. It may set up a committee to examine the representation and publish its findings.

V. REVIEW AND RESOLUTION OF QUESTIONS REGARDING IMPLEMENTATION PROCEDURES IN HUMAN RIGHTS CONVENTIONS

39. In order to provide a brief outline of the review and resolution of questions regarding implementation procedures used in human rights instruments, the following section concentrates on the fundamental aspects of the process carried out under the International Covenant on Civil and Political Rights[10] (hereinafter referred to as 'the Covenant'). Other compliance control procedures under human rights conventions are essentially similar to the one reviewed below.[11]

40. The system of implementation of the Covenant centres upon the Human Rights Committee (hereinafter referred to as 'the HRC'). The HRC consists of 18 members elected from among the nationals of the Contracting Parties. One representative from each Party is allowed to serve. States elect members of the Committee in a secret ballot, with consideration given 'to equitable geographic distribution of membership and to the representation of the different forms of civilization and of the principal legal systems' (see Article 31.2 of the Covenant). The members are independent experts, mostly lawyers, and do not represent their governments. They serve for a term of four years and may be re-elected. The HRC elects its own officers and decides on its own rules of procedure.

41. The task of the HRC is limited to the review of reports submitted by states regarding their implementation of the obligations contained in the Covenant. The aim of the review procedure is to assist Parties to fulfil their obligations and, in this regard, to make available to them the experience of the Committee. The Parties to the Covenant 'undertake to submit periodic reports on the measures they have adopted which give effect to the rights recognized herein and on the progress made in the enjoyment of those rights' (see Article 40.1). Reports must be submitted every five years. They are usually considered at public hearings, to which the Party whose report is being discussed is invited to send a representative to introduce the report and to answer questions. The Committee is not a judiciary body; rather it tends to emphasize its role in encouraging a constructive dialogue instead of criticism, thus assisting in the fulfilling of the obligations under the Covenant.

42. In the light of recent or current events indicating that the enjoyment of human rights protected under the Covenant has been seriously affected in certain Party states, the Committee has resorted to the practice of requesting the states concerned to submit urgent reports on the situation (generally within three months).

43. While intergovernmental organizations and non-governmental organizations cannot participate orally in the consideration of state reports, they may submit written information or reports to be used by Committee members when considering such state reports. In addition, specialized agencies and other United Nations bodies are invited to contribute to the work of the Committee's presessional working group on Article 40, the main purpose of which is to conduct a preliminary review of periodic reports scheduled for consideration during the session.

44. At the end of the consideration of state reports, the Committee adopts concluding comments reflecting the views of the Committee as a whole on each Party state report considered during a given session. Such comments are dispatched to the Party State concerned as soon as practicable and made public at the end of the session.

45. Article 41 of the Covenant provides for an optional system of state applications whereby states may, on condition of reciprocity, accept the right of the other Parties to bring a claim to the Committee alleging a violation of the Covenant. A claim may not be brought unless a negotiation between the two Parties has been unsuccessfully completed. If satisfied that local remedies have been exhausted, the Committee 'shall make available its good offices'. The Committee must within 12 months submit a report detailing the facts and the solution reached, or, if no solution has been reached, simply indicating the facts and attaching thereto the submission of the two Parties. In such a case, the Committee 'may, with the prior consent of the States concerned', appoint an *ad hoc* conciliation commission, made up of five members acceptable to both Parties. This

commission must provide, within 12 months, a report to the Chairman of the Human Rights Committee for communication to the Parties concerned. In the event that the matter remains unresolved, the report will contain the findings of the commission on all questions of fact, the submissions of the Parties and its views on an amicable solution of the matter.

46. Within three months of receiving the report, the states concerned communicate to the Chairman of the Committee their acceptance thereof. The expenses of the *ad hoc* commission are shared equally between the two Parties concerned. The report of the commission is not binding.

47. The resolution of disputes through the 'good offices' of the HRC does not prejudice the use of any other traditional dispute settlement procedure as provided for under Article 33.1 of the Charter of the United Nations.

VI. DISPUTE SETTLEMENT PROCEDURE OF THE WORLD TRADE ORGANIZATION AND THE GENERAL AGREEMENT ON TARIFFS AND TRADE: THE PANELS SYSTEM

48. The dispute settlement procedure of the GATT, though formally based on Articles XXII and XXIII of the General Agreement on Tariffs and Trade[12] is not described therein. It has been built up over time through the evolution of customary practice, and subsequently codified.[13]

49. The Uruguay Round of the GATT[14] led to the creation of a formal international trade organization, namely, the World Trade Organization (WTO), whose institutional structure is derived from the GATT. The 'Contracting Parties', which is the supreme body of the GATT, has been renamed the 'Ministerial Conference'; it is open to all members and will meet at least once every two years. Many functions of the GATT Council have been taken over by a 'General Council' which will meet regularly, as appropriate, to decide on all issues conferred upon it by the Ministers. The Dispute Settlement Body, whose members will probably be identical to those of the Council, will be another central institution.

50. The WTO is endowed with a comprehensive dispute settlement machinery described in the 'Understanding on Rules and Procedures Governing the Settlement of Disputes' of the 1994 Uruguay Round (hereinafter referred to as 'the 1994 DSU'). The WTO will not succeed in a strict legal sense to the GATT. States which have ratified the WTO agreements without at the same time withdrawing from the GATT, will continue to apply two different sets of legal rules. Moreover, Article XVI.1 of the Final Provisions of the Agreement establishing the WTO states that '. . . the World Trade Organization shall respect the rules, decisions and customary practice of the General Agreement on Tariffs and Trade'. Similarly, Article 3 of the 1994 DSU provides that: 'the Members affirm their adherence to the principles for the management of disputes heretofore applied under Articles XXII and XXIII of the GATT 1947, and the procedures further elaborated and modified herein.' Finally, the law and the practice as developed thus far by the GATT and improved upon by the 1994 DSU, will be applied to all disputes under the GATT, the General Agreement on Trade in Services (GATS) and the Agreement on Trade Related Intellectual Property Rights (TRIPs).

51. In order to ensure the effective functioning of the WTO, the 1994 DSU, unlike the dispute settlement procedure of the GATT, sets out in great detail the procedure and the timetable to be followed in the settling of disputes. The entire procedure,

from the establishment of the panel to the implementation of the decision of the Dispute Settlement Body, must not exceed 15 months (or 18, if the decision is appealed).

52. The main feature of the WTO settlement of disputes machinery is the creation of the Dispute Settlement Body. This Body has the sole authority to establish panels, adopt panel and appellate reports, maintain surveillance of implementation of rulings and recommendations, and authorize retaliatory measures in cases of non-implementation of recommendations.

53. The purpose of both the WTO and the GATT dispute settlement procedures is not to sanction breaches of a rule under the respective agreements but to ensure predictability and maintenance of the balance of advantages in trade between the Parties. This balance is considered to be restored when the Parties to a dispute reach agreement. This principle governs the various phases of the procedure as described below.

54. The procedure commences with bilateral consultations. The member concerned must reply within ten days to a request for consultations and should enter into consultations within 30 days from the date of request. Moreover, if a WTO member, other than the consulting members, considers that it has a substantial trade interest and requests consultation, it may join therein with the consent of the Parties. If these consultations do not result in a settlement of the dispute and if both Parties so agree, the case at this stage may be brought to the WTO Director-General, who, acting *ex officio*, may offer his good offices.

55. If the Party concerned does not respond to a request for consultations within ten days, or if the consultations fail to arrive at a solution after 60 days, the Party concerned may request that a panel be set up by the Dispute Settlement Body. In support of its request a Party need only claim that a benefit accruing to it under the 'covered agreements' (basically, GATT, GATS and TRIPs) is nullified or impaired, or that the attainment of any objective of the covered agreements is impeded. Thus, it is not always necessary for a Party to the dispute to invoke the actual breach of a rule of these agreements. If the breach of a rule is invoked, the adverse effect on the balance of benefits is presumed. Conversely, if the plaintiff claims that the benefits in question have been nullified or impaired by measures that do not contravene the agreements, it has the burden of proof.

56. The establishment of a panel, though not an absolute right of the complainant, is almost automatic. A panel is to be established no later than the second meeting of the Dispute Settlement Body at which the request appears on the agenda of the Body, unless the Body itself decides (by consensus) otherwise. This means that the Party which is the subject of the complaint cannot block the establishment of a panel. The panel is to be constituted within 30 days of its establishment.

57. The panels consist of three members, unless the Parties to the dispute decide on five members. Members may not be nationals of a country whose government is a Party to the dispute. They perform their duties in their individual capacities and may not receive instructions from their government. The 1994 DSU does not give preference to governmental members (as was the case under GATT practice) and instead emphasizes the quality and independence of the members and the preference for diverse backgrounds and a wide spectrum of experience. The WTO Secretariat must suggest the names of three potential panellists to the Parties to the dispute, drawing as necessary on a list of qualified persons (previous panellists, former representatives to the GATT, scholars). If the Parties to the dispute do not

agree on the panellists within 20 days, the Director-General, in consultation with the Chairman of the Dispute Settlement Body, shall constitute the panel by appointing the panellists he considers most appropriate.

58. The panels examine the dispute, consider the various questions of fact and law involved, record their findings and recommendations, and send their report to the Dispute Settlement Body for a decision. They are required to make a report to the Body to assist it 'to discharge its responsibilities under this Understanding and the covered agreements' (see Article 11 of the 1994 DSU). In accordance with Article 11, the report of the panel must include 'an objective assessment of the matter before it and present findings and recommendations as will assist the Dispute Settlement Body in making its recommendations or rulings (see Article 7 of the 1994 DSU).

59. The panels receive written and oral submissions from the contending Parties and may receive submissions from other interested Parties. They may request members to provide any information which they deem necessary and appropriate and may also seek information and technical advice from any individual body within the jurisdiction of a member after informing the government thereof.

60. The report of the panel is structured similarly to a judgement, with an introduction, the facts of the situation, the investigation, a summary of the arguments of the Parties and, finally, its findings, conclusions and recommendations. If a bilateral settlement is reached while the dispute stands before the panel, it may confine its work to a brief description of the case and a report that an agreement has been reached.

61. In order to allow Parties to check for factual errors or omissions before drafting the final report, the panel submits to the Parties concerned the descriptive sections therein. Parties are given two weeks to comment thereon. Subsequently, the panel submits an interim report, this time including its findings and conclusions to the Parties, giving them one week to request a review. The period of review must not exceed two weeks during which the panel may hold additional meetings with the Parties. If this final attempt to reach an agreement fails, the panel must make a detailed report setting out its findings and recommending the adoption of measures it deems appropriate to the Dispute Settlement Body. The Body then circulates this report to all WTO members.

62. The panel report in and of itself has no force and is treated as an advisory opinion by the Dispute Settlement Body. The report is automatically adopted, unless otherwise decided by consensus, by the Body, which is, strictly speaking, a political body.

63. The 1994 DSU has introduced an appellate review system. Accordingly, the panel report shall not be considered for adoption by the Body until after the completion of any appeal. The appellate review is undertaken by a standing Appellate Body, which is composed of seven persons, broadly representative of the WTO membership, who are to serve a term of four years. As members of the Body, they are persons of recognized standing in the field of law and international trade and are not affiliated with any government. The appeal is limited to issues of law covered in the panel report and to legal interpretations developed by the panel. The appeal may uphold, modify or reverse the legal findings and conclusions of the panel. The appellate report is adopted by the Body, unless otherwise decided by consensus, and must be accepted unconditionally by the Parties to the dispute.

64. Prompt compliance with recommendations or rulings of the Dispute Settlement Body is essential in order to ensure effective resolution of disputes. The member concerned must inform the Body of its intentions with respect to the implementation of the ruling within 30 days after the adoption of the report of the panel. If it is not possible to immediately comply, the member concerned must be given a reasonable period of time to do so. If the 'reasonable period of time' elapses without implementation of the ruling of the Body, compensation and suspension of concessions may be resorted to. Compensation is voluntary and is the result of an agreement reached between Parties. If no satisfactory compensation has been agreed to within 20 days, the Body may authorize the plaintiff to suspend the application of concessions under the 'covered agreements'. In principle, concessions shall be suspended in the same sector as that of the issue referred to in the panel case. Nevertheless, if this is not effective or practicable, and if circumstances are considered to be of a serious nature, the complaining Party may cross-retaliate by suspending concessions under agreements other than the one in which the panel has found impairment of the balance.

VII, DISPUTE SETTLEMENT PROCEDURE UNDER THE 1982 UNITED NATIONS CONVENTION ON THE LAW OF THE SEA[15]

65. The United Nations Law of the Sea Convention (UNCLOS), adopted in Montego Bay, Jamaica, in 1982,[16] lays down a basic scheme for the settlement of disputes arising from its implementation, with exceptions laid down for certain categories of dispute. The basic structure of the dispute settlement procedure is contained in Part XV of the UNCLOS (see Articles 279–299) and Annexes V–VIII to the Convention.

66. Parties shall settle any dispute concerning the interpretation or application of the Convention by peaceful means and to this end shall seek a solution by the means indicated in Article 33, paragraph I of the Charter. Parties are free to choose peaceful means other than those prescribed in the Convention, such as regional or special arrangements or instruments in force between them outside the dispute settlement system of the UNCLOS, provided that if the Convention so requires, it should lead to the binding settlement of the dispute. A Party to the Convention which is a Party to a dispute concerning the interpretation or application of the Convention may invite the other Party to submit the dispute to the conciliation procedure. If this invitation is accepted, each Party appoints two conciliators, one of which may be its national. The four so appointed conciliators select a fifth conciliator who acts as chairman. The conciliation commission has 12 months to help the Parties to reach an amicable settlement. Within that period the commission is supposed to submit its report recording any agreement reached and, failing agreement, its conclusions and recommendations as the commission may deem appropriate for an amicable settlement. Conclusions and recommendations of the commission are not binding upon the Parties.

67. If the Parties fail to reach a settlement by peaceful means of their choice outside the framework of the Convention or through the conciliation procedure provided for in the Convention, the dispute, unless it falls under the limitations and exceptions referred to in Section 3 of Part XV of the Convention (boundary disputes, disputes concerning military activities, disputes in respect of which the Security Council is exercising the functions assigned to it by the Charter etc), shall be submitted at the request of any Party to the dispute for compulsory settlement to the court or the tribunal having jurisdiction in accordance with the Convention. On signing, ratifying or acceding to the Convention, or at any time thereafter, states

may choose by means of written declaration one or more of the following judicial bodies:

(a) The International Tribunal for the Law of the Sea;
(b) The International Court of Justice;
(c) An arbitral tribunal constituted under Annex VII of the UNCLOS; or
(d) A special *ad hoc* arbitral tribunal constituted under Annex VIII.

Such declaration does not affect the obligation of a Party to accept the jurisdiction of the Sea-Bed Disputes Chamber of the International Tribunal for the Law of the Sea with respect to the categories of disputes relating to the activities in the Area (sea-bed, ocean floor and subsoil thereof, beyond the limits of national jurisdiction) referred to in Article 187 of the Convention. If a Party does not select one of the aforementioned judicial bodies, it is deemed to have accepted arbitration under Annex VII. If both Parties to the dispute have chosen the same judicial body, their dispute may be submitted to that body only, unless the Parties otherwise agree. If the Parties have accepted different procedures, the dispute may be submitted only to arbitration under Annex VII, unless the Parties agree otherwise.

68. In accordance with the Convention, the seat of the International Tribunal for the Law of the Sea shall be in Hamburg, Germany. The Tribunal shall be composed of 21 members elected by the Parties to the Convention from among persons of recognized competence in the field of the law of the sea so as to ensure the representation of the world's principal legal systems and equitable geographical distribution. The first elections of the members of the Tribunal will be held on 1 August 1996. A quorum of 11 members is required to constitute the Tribunal. The Tribunal may also operate through special chambers composed of three or more of its members. To expedite the dispatch of business, the Tribunal shall annually form a five-member chamber which may hear and determine disputes by summary procedure.

69. In addition, the Tribunal shall establish a Sea-Bed Disputes Chamber composed of 11 members selected by a majority of the members of the Tribunal from among them. As noted above, the Sea-Bed Chamber has competence with regard to the categories of disputes relating to the activities in the Area specified in Part XI, Section 5 of the Convention, namely, *inter alia*, disputes between Parties; Parties and the Authority (the organization responsible for the organization and control of the activities in the Area, particularly with a view to administering its resources); the Authority and a prospecting contractor. The Sea-Bed Chamber, in its turn, shall establish an *ad hoc* chamber, composed of three members, for dealing with a particular dispute referred to it by its Parties in accordance with Article 188, paragraph 1(b) of the Convention. It should be noted, however, that disputes concerning the interpretation or application of a contract relating to the activities in the Area shall be submitted at the request of any Party to the dispute, to binding commercial arbitration, unless the Parties agree otherwise. In the absence of a provision on arbitration in the contract, the arbitration shall be conducted in accordance with the Arbitration Rules of the United Nations Committee on International Trade Law or such other regulations and procedures as may be prescribed in the rules, regulations and procedures of the Authority.

70. As a general rule arbitral tribunals constituted under Annex VII of the Convention shall be composed of five members. One member is appointed by each of the Parties to the dispute and the remaining three are chosen by these Parties from a list of arbitrators maintained by the Secretary-General of the United Nations to which each Party to the Convention is entitled to nominate four arbitrators. An arbitrator shall be a person experienced in maritime affairs and enjoying the

highest reputation for fairness, competence and integrity. In cases where there are several Parties having separate interests, the arbitral tribunal may be composed of more than five members. If Parties to the dispute fail to agree on the three jointly chosen arbitrators, the latter are appointed by the President of the International Tribunal for the Law of the Sea.

71. Special arbitral tribunals under Annex VIII of the Convention are constituted at the request of any Party to the dispute, subject to the limitations and exceptions referred to in Section 3 of Part XV of the Convention, relating to (1) fisheries, (2) protection and preservation of the marine environment, (3) marine scientific research, or (4) navigation, including pollution from vessels and by dumping. A list of experts is established and maintained in respect of each of the aforementioned four categories respectively by the Food and Agriculture Organization of the United Nations, by the United Nations Environment Programme, by the InterGovernmental Oceanographic Commission and by the International Maritime Organization. Every Party to the Convention may nominate two experts to each of four lists whose competence in the legal, scientific or technical aspects of a particular field is established and generally recognized. With the exception of cases where there are several Parties having separate interests, the special arbitral tribunal shall consist of five members.

The Party instituting the proceedings and the other Party to the dispute have the right to appoint two members of the tribunal, preferably from the appropriate list of experts. Only one of these two members may be a national. If the latter Party fails to make an appointment within 30 days of receipt of the notification instituting the proceedings, such appointments are made by the Secretary-General of the United Nations. The fifth member of the arbitral tribunal, who is also its President, shall be appointed by the Parties or by the Secretary-General of the United Nations if the Parties fail to agree on a candidate within 30 days of receipt of the notification instituting the proceedings.

72. The Convention also provides that the court or the tribunals referred to in paragraph 67 above, which 'considers that *prima facie* it has jurisdiction' under the Convention with regard to a particular dispute submitted to it, may prescribe, at the request of a Party to the dispute and pending its final decision, any provisional measures which it considers appropriate under the circumstances to preserve the respective rights of the Parties to the dispute or to prevent serious harm to the marine environment. Such provisional measures may be prescribed only after the Parties have been given an opportunity to be heard. If the case is to be heard by an arbitral tribunal which has not yet been constituted, and if the urgency of the situation so requires, provisional measures may be prescribed by the International Tribunal for the Law of the Sea, or, with respect to activities in the Area, by the Sea-Bed Disputes Chamber. The arbitral tribunal may subsequently either revoke or reaffirm these measures.

73. As mentioned earlier, the Convention stipulates that when signing, ratifying or acceding to the Convention or at any time thereafter, a state may declare in writing that it does not accept any one or more of the compulsory procedures under the Convention entailing binding decisions with respect of categories of disputes listed in Article 298 of the Convention. This stipulation is without prejudice to the general obligation under the Convention that Parties shall settle disputes between them by peaceful means. The categories of disputes listed in Article 298 include:

(a) Disputes concerning the interpretation or application of Articles 15, 74 and 83 of the Convention relating to sea boundary delimitations, or those involving historic bays or titles;
(b) Disputes concerning military activities, including military activities by government vessels and aircraft engaged in non-commercial service; and
(c) Disputes in respect of which the Security Council of the United Nations is exercising the functions assigned to it by the Charter of the United Nations.

Such declaration may be withdrawn by a state at any time.

74. It may be noted that the Convention also contains certain limitations on the applicability of compulsory procedures entailing binding decisions. These limitations are listed in Article 297 of the Convention which is a very complex provision. The first paragraph refers to three cases where disputes concerning the exercise of the coastal state's sovereign rights or jurisdiction shall be submitted to compulsory jurisdiction. These relate to cases where either the coastal state or other states in exercising high seas freedoms have allegedly acted in contravention of the provisions of the Convention concerning the high seas freedoms applicable to the exclusive economic zone and their reconciliation with the rights of the coastal state and acts by the coastal state, which allegedly contravene the applicable international rules and standards for the protection of the marine environment. The second and third paragraphs of that Article provide for limitations on the applicability of the compulsory procedures in cases of disputes concerning firstly, marine scientific research, whereby a state exercises its rights or discretion under Articles 246 and 253 of the Convention, and secondly, fisheries, whereby a coastal state may exercise its sovereign rights with respect to the living resources in the exclusive economic zone.

5 COMPLIANCE WITH INTERNATIONAL ENVIRONMENTAL OBLIGATIONS: A CASE STUDY OF THE INTERNATIONAL WHALING COMMISSION

Gregory Rose and George Paleokrassis

Fishermen are hunters, roaming expanses of sea seeking food, often pitted against the dangers of natural forces and, more recently, the challenges of regulators who seek to control them.

INTRODUCTION

Fishing is imbued with its own powerful symbols as mariners' tales, particularly that of Moby Dick, illustrate. It is an ancient livelihood, a cherished pastime, and has a dignity enhanced by the memories of our ancestral hunters – perhaps this is why fishermen do not tolerate bureaucratic interference or conservation lobbyists easily. Fishing is also an especially difficult economic activity to regulate. There is little reliable information concerning the nature of the resource being exploited or the rate and impact of its exploitation. It takes place far from government centres and the usual presence of society's inspectors and enforcers.

Although similarly difficult to regulate, the protection of whales has become, in the second half of the twentieth century, a deeply symbolic issue of a very different nature. Unlike most other species in the marine habitat, whales are now accorded a 'wildlife status' which recognizes their intrinsic value as species for their own sake. Fish species are popularly regarded as having little intrinsic wildlife value, rather they are simply to be managed to maintain their usefulness to human populations. For example, groups of whales are referred to in terms of their population numbers, whereas fish are referred to in terms of their stock size. These two approaches to the value of whales and fisheries have naturally resulted in differences in their management. This chapter examines some of the differences in management of whales and fish, placing the conservation of whales in the broader context of the management of fisheries, and compares the strengths and weaknesses of different regimes.

Structure

The structure adopted here is based on the analysis set out in Chapter 1. Legal regimes are analyzed according to whether they are mostly concerned with primary conservation rules, compliance monitoring, or non-compliance response systems. Those three categories are elaborated upon here, in particular, primary conservation rules – which are analyzed into rules for institutional structure, decision-making processes, primary data gathering and technical conservation obligations.

Of these rules, information gathering requires comment, as it is necessary at all points in the implementation process. Public administrators need to have adequate information to formulate primary rules (ie to identify a problem and its solution), as well as for monitoring compliance (ie monitoring activation of the solution) and to respond to non-compliance (including how to ensure that the required steps are then taken). Data from monitoring how a technical conservation obligation has/has not been implemented will loop back to inform the process of reformulating technical conservation measures. Thus, information gathering is a continual cycle, feeding data back into the implementation process at all points, beginning from rule design, and should not be considered as limited to compliance information gathering.

From an international perspective, compliance rules may be regarded as running two systems in parallel – one concerning State compliance with international law and the other concerning the behaviour of individual persons. Those primary rules dealing with conservation measures are ultimately implemented by individuals. But state compliance cannot be regarded in isolation from them – it is a reflection of the way that individuals respond to those rules as much as it is a matter of state behaviour. This is especially true in marine resources management where state control over individual activities is tenuous. Thus, the sub-text of inter-state compliance systems is concerned with individual persons, who truly determine the design of rules binding states.

BACKGROUND

Legal framework for marine resources management

Marine resources in the seas have traditionally been regarded as *res communis*, ie part of the international commons, incapable of being owned by any country. As the seas have become enclosed by national zones of jurisdiction, the size of the commons has been greatly reduced. The enclosure of the coastal waters in the territorial sea, now recognized as having a maximum seaward limit of 12 nautical miles, was the first step. It was followed by claims to exclusive national fishing zones of various widths, now recognized in the form of an 'exclusive economic zone' (EEZ) having a maximum seaward limit of 200 nautical miles. These limits were agreed during the third UN Conference on the Law of the Sea, which formulated a comprehensive package for the regulation of ocean space. Its product, the 1982 Convention on the Law of the Sea, much of which is already customary international law, came into force on 16 November 1994.[1]

Within the 200-mile zone, 90 per cent of known fisheries are enclosed. Thus, only ten per cent of fisheries are now to be found in the high seas and constitute part of the international commons. These fisheries can be subjected to ownership when captured, although not while in their natural, free state in the sea. When captured, the notion of *usu fructus* operates, ie the fruit of one's labours renders the subject of the labour one's own.[2]

The 1958 Convention on Fishing and Conservation of Living Marine Resources was the first global agreement devoted to fisheries conservation on the high seas.[3] It places an obligation on its signatories to cooperate in adopting conservation measures and introduced a compulsory dispute resolution mechanism. The next global general treaty was the 1982 Convention on the Law of the Sea, referred to above. In August 1995 states adopted a third agreement, building upon UNCLOS, on the conservation and management of straddling and highly migratory fish stocks. Some of the implications of this agreement are set out in an afterword to this chapter on page 328. All three Agreements adopt the concept of 'maximum sustainable yield'[4] in conservation of living resources. This is intended to ensure the management of those resources at a level to secure the maximum supply of foods and goods for human consumption.

Those fisheries which are located in the 200-mile zone are subject to the exclusive economic rights of the coastal state over them. They are not part of the international commons and their management is a domestic matter for the coastal state to arrange. It is a task for which the coastal state is not accountable beyond its own domestic political processes.[5] Unfortunately, coastal states in both developed and developing countries share a record of failure in domestic fisheries management and international efforts to set standards are now being rallied to improve the situation.[6] At this stage, it is unlikely that such standards will become binding for coastal state fisheries management. However, a voluntary 'Code of Conduct for Responsible Fishing' is being elaborated which may in future become binding.[7]

Many marine species are highly mobile and a single population (or 'stock') may migrate over long ocean distances, or straddle the high seas and an exclusive fishing zone, or overlap two or more exclusive fishing zones. In relation to these 'shared' species, which include most of the great whales, states are required by UNCLOS to seek to cooperate in their management. Article 63 of the 1982 Convention requires states to form regional and sub-regional organizations in order to foster cooperation between them in the conservation of marine living resources. In the case of marine mammals[8] and highly migratory species (such as tuna),[9] in particular, states are required to cooperate through international organizations.

Thus, by 1982, shared management through a system of institutional regimes was conceived as the most practical approach to maintaining the economic or intrinsic value of marine species which are located under the jurisdiction of more than one state, in the high seas, or under a mixture of both.

General legal framework for whale management

As whales are highly migratory, and are often to be found in the coastal waters of several countries or in the high seas, they are sometimes suggested to be part of the international commons without ever being subject to national jurisdiction.[10] However, this suggestion should be seen as being of symbolic value intended to stress the importance of international cooperation in the proper management of whales.

An international agreement for cooperative management of whaling was first established in 1931. It was soon replaced by the International Convention for the Regulation of Whaling (ICRW). The ICRW was signed by 15 states in 1946 as a voluntary arrangement adopted, initially, only by whaling states. The objective was to protect the whaling industry from the effects of over-whaling rather than to protect whales as a species. This is evident in the Preamble to the Convention which, despite providing that the 'history of whaling has seen overfishing of one area after another and of one species of whale after another' to near extinction, making it 'essential to protect all species of whales from further overfishing'[11], continues by stating that the Convention's aim is

> to establish a system of international regulation for the whale fisheries to ensure proper and effective conservation and development of whale stocks . . . and thus make possible the orderly development of the whaling industry.[12]

The intention was that the ICRW should provide a means of controlling the exploitation of whale stocks thereby fulfilling a similar function to that under international fisheries agreements. The ICRW treated whaling as a form of fishing; for example, the Preamble refers to 'whale fisheries'. Thus, whales were regarded as a part of the international commons on the high seas, just as fish were. The doctrine of the freedom of fishing of common resources on the high seas applied to whaling activities, except as otherwise explicitly agreed by the Parties to the ICRW. However, since the enclosure of resources within the 200-mile zone as state property, whales found within these zones are considered subject to the exclusive control of the coastal State. On the high seas and in cases where they travel across zones, states are to seek to cooperate in their management.

Due to their special wildlife status, marine mammals are given particular mention in Article 65 of the UNCLOS, which provides that they are exempt from the general obligation to utilize fishery resources optimally within the 200-mile fishery zone:

> Nothing in this Part restricts the right of a coastal State or the competence of an international organization, as appropriate, to prohibit, limit or regulate the exploitation of marine mammals more strictly than provided for in this Part. States shall cooperate with a view to the conservation of marine mammals and in the case of cetaceans shall in particular work through the appropriate international organizations for their conservation. management and study.

It should be noted that the 1995 Fish Stocks Agreement is not intended to apply to marine mammals.

Historic Mismanagement of Marine Resources

The definition of marine resources as common property is merely one type of management strategy. It is a passive approach to fisheries management, simply making resources freely available as of right to those that can make use of them. A less passive strategy may involve more central intervention to regulate access to and rational use of resources. Yet other strategies may involve assignment of the resources into private hands for them to manage conservatively so as to maintain the economic value of the asset. These strategies may be adopted among the community of states at the international level for shared fisheries, or between individuals at the domestic levels for national fish stocks.

The pattern that normally follows the common property strategy is that production drawn from the resource is increased until a 'tragedy point' is reached, whereupon a decline in production occurs.[13] This happens because the economic imperative of a common property regime is often to harvest the resource before someone else does. The usual effect is a severe depletion of the resource, since harvesting efforts increase beyond the capacity of the resource to regenerate itself.[14] This creates acute problems for species which reproduce slowly and whose offspring require nursing, such as whales, thus making them a species very sensitive to over-harvesting.

The over-exploitation of common property has occurred both in whaling and fisheries. In 1938 the world fish catch was 15 million tonnes; by 1958 it had risen to 28m; by 1978 to 64m; by 1986 to 80m; and it is expected to reach 100m by the year 2000, at which stage it is projected to level off.[15] This continued increase in the tonnage of fisheries caught has led to a significant depletion of fisheries stock throughout the world, in particular there has been a large decline in stocks of herring and mackerel in the north-east Atlantic, yellow-fin tuna in the eastern Pacific and blue-fin tuna in the south-west Pacific.[16] In relation to whales, it is estimated that before intensive whaling began there were over 3,050,000 great whales. Due to such whaling, by 1977 there were only 1,953,000[17] and this figure has undoubtedly declined significantly since then.

Overfishing was first identified as a problem in relation to a few shared stocks in the North Sea in the late nineteenth century, but cooperative management regimes developed only gradually in the 20th century. These regimes deal with particular species, populations or regions where fish stocks are located. For example, several regional conventions were concluded for the Atlantic, Baltic and Black Seas.[18] The history of fisheries management has shown, by and large, that smaller fisheries management bodies established by the participating states themselves have had actual management powers, while broader international fisheries bodies have tended to limit themselves to narrow and inoffensive mandates, such as the gathering and dissemination of fish stocks, information and fisheries technologies.

As noted above, fishing is an intrinsically difficult activity to regulate. Wider diffusion of high technology fishing methods and increasing demands from growing human populations are further pressures against conservative management. The traditional distinction between legislative jurisdiction and enforcement jurisdiction in the law of the sea also accentuates difficulties in ensuring compliance with international law. Enforcement powers over vessels on the high seas usually rest with the flag state alone, or may in some cases be shared with the coastal state in its zones of maritime jurisdiction. As modern fishing vessels often move between zones, enforcement can involve several states and thus be problematic. Therefore, attention needs to be devoted to ensuring that the norms are designed so as to be simple to implement and that enforcement can be easily coordinated or shared.

These are among the many reasons for the pattern of failure among fishing commissions. The following study of the operation of the ICRW examines the legal and institutional reasons for these failings in relation to whale management and draws comparisons and lessons from other fishery management regimes. Those which are compared are the European Union (EU) Common Fisheries Policy, North East Atlantic Fisheries Commission (NEAFC), North Atlantic Fisheries Organization (NAFO), South Pacific Forum Fisheries Agency (FFA) and Convention for the Conservation of Antarctic Marine Living Resources (CCAMLR).

PRIMARY RULES – CONSTITUTIONAL AND PROCEDURAL

The ICRW applies to factory ships, land stations and whale catchers (Article II), and to 'all waters in which whaling is prosecuted by them' (Article I). Thus, the Convention has global application, which is extremely important given the extent of whale migrations. It deals with whales in both the international commons and areas under national jurisdiction.

Constitutional structure

IWC membership

The ICRW creates a framework for the formulation of conservation norms by way of creating and empowering an international organization. The International Whaling Commission (IWC) is established under the Convention and is made up of a commissioner from each of the 39 member nations. There are no membership criteria for joining the IWC – nations can become Parties to the ICRW even if they do not take part in any whaling activities (eg Switzerland is currently a member). It convenes once a year and each member nation has one vote in decisions it takes. Both IWC members and non-governmental organizations (NGOs), who act as observers and do not vote, attend the meetings. Members can withdraw from the ICRW on six months' notice[19] and have in the past withdrawn or threatened to withdraw as a means of exerting pressure on the IWC to protect their individual commercial interests.

This should be contrasted with other organizations which have a regionally determined membership, such as the EU or NAFO. The North Atlantic Marine Mammals Conservation Organization (NAMMCO) has adopted into its constitutive rules an unusual right to veto prospective members, so as to filter out nations with whaling concerns which do not coincide with those of the founding members.

There are three IWC committees responsible for inter-sessional matters (since the full commission convenes only once a year) – these are the Technical, Scientific, and Finance and Administration Committees. This structure is unremarkable and is reflected in fisheries commissions. Under Article V of the ICRW, the Commission can adopt regulations to save whale resources, but such amendments have to be based on 'scientific findings'. Therefore, the Scientific Committee reviews catch data and research programmes and make recommendations to the IWC on such matters as research areas, quotas, and rate of stock depletion.[20] The Technical Committee does not have to restrict itself to scientific criteria only, and drafts amendments for consideration by the IWC and has a Sub-Committee which reviews infractions of IWC rules.[21] The Finance and Administration Committee deals with personnel matters, expenditure, and the budget.[22] The latter Committee consists of five representatives, while the member nations may have any number of representatives on the two other committees although each nation is restricted to only one vote. The IWC also has a small permanent Secretariat based in Cambridge, Britain.

Decision-making Process

Under its constitutive rules, the IWC can formulate conservation norms. These are the 'primary rules' for whale management and are the regulations found in the Schedule to the ICRW, a document separate but fundamentally linked to the Convention. Although amendments to the Convention require the unanimous agreement and subsequent ratification of all member nations, Article III of the ICRW provides that a three-quarters majority is required to amend the regulations in the Schedule. The regulations are binding on all Commission members, even those that do not vote in favour of them. However, there is the option of objecting to a regulation thus becoming exempt from its terms and delaying its implementation in all member nations.[23] Finally, the IWC can pass a resolution by means of a simple majority, although such resolutions are not binding on Commission members.

Ability of objectors to opt out

Article V(3) of the ICRW provides that even where a proposed regulation has achieved the three-quarters majority it only comes into force as a binding regulation 90 days after the notification of this fact to the governments of the member nations by the IWC. If any government lodges an objection to the regulation within this 90-day period the amendment shall not become effective with respect to any of the governments for an additional 90 days;[24] thereupon any other government can also object at any time during this additional 90-day period, or before the expiration of 30 days after receipt of the last objection received during that (the additional 90-day) period, whichever is later.[25] It is only at the end of this period that the regulation comes into force and it only binds those governments that have not objected to it.[26] Therefore, a member is not bound except to what it has specifically agreed to. Professor Birnie has stated that 'resort to this procedure by whaling states has delayed many conservationist proposals during the past 30 years'.[27] For instance, in 1958, when the British commissioner attempted to introduce a conservation-oriented proposal, Norway and the Netherlands withdrew from the IWC and other countries refused to continue in their absence.[28] Further, when a five-year moratorium on blue and humpback whaling was passed in 1959, objections were filed by almost every whaling nation.[29] The first IWC harvest rate was not reduced for 18 years,[30] despite recommendations and findings by the Scientific Committee.

The belief that sufficient consensus had been reached to achieve a moratorium on commercial whaling was shattered at the IWC's 44th Meeting held in Glasgow in June–July 1992 when Norway announced its decision to resume commercial whaling for 296 minke whales in the northern summer of 1993. Political pressure to shore up consensus and pull Norway back into the ranks involved the decision being internationally condemned and boycotts of Norwegian goods. It has been estimated that as a result of these boycotts, lobbied for by international non-governmental organizations, Norway has lost export contracts up to US$30m.[31]

The US entered the fray in August 1993 when it threatened Norway with trade sanctions if Norway continued to engage in commercial whaling in violation of the moratorium. The European Parliament adopted a Resolution on 27 May 1993 condemning Norway's decision.[32] Six EU members at the IWC meeting in Glasgow signed a statement expressing their 'deep disappointment' at Norway's action. Since Norway was seeking EU membership it seemed inconceivable, given this condemnation, that the EU would accept an application unless Norway showed that it conformed to information conservation standards. In fact, the EU has now softened its line and Norway has appealed to the EU for the same concessions for whaling as the Swedes managed to extract in the recent enlargement talks with the EU in relation to bear and beaver hunting in Sweden.[33] The US has also softened its tone, perhaps due to Norway's outstanding diplomatic achievement in 1993 in the Middle East peace process. These events demonstrate the vagaries affecting application of political pressure directed to holding consensus when a recalcitrant state uses an opt-out provision in a common resource convention to which it is Party.

The existence of the opt-out provision is by no means unique to the ICRW, it can be found in the constitutions of other international fisheries organizations. The North East Atlantic Fisheries Commission (NEAFC) came into being in 1963. Until 1977 it provided the framework for the regulation of fisheries in parts of the Arctic and Atlantic Oceans, which were high seas fishing commons until the introduction of EEZs brought them under national jurisdiction. The NEAFC's principal task was to recommend conservation measures to ensure rational exploitation of various stocks. However, as is the case with IWC Regulations, the Recommendations are only binding on states that do not object to them and the application and enforcement of these was left to each member nation. The objection procedure had the effect of leading to the adoption of the least ambitious management programme, so as to ensure that all would participate. The establishment of a fisheries catch limit required the consent of all member nations *and* the approval of two-thirds of the delegations. Despite the fact that some stocks were being over-fished in the region the requisite consent to establish a limit was never obtained until 1974. Even when they were set, they were not adequately enforced. Furthermore, as a result of bargaining between members the limits were set too high and in many cases exceeded the highest limit proposed by any Party.[34] This occurred as a result of the members' inability to resolve arguments over individual allocations which were often resolved by simply raising the limit. The allowed catch was distributed between the NEAFC members by means of a system of quotas. The distribution of quotas, just as the catch limits themselves, became highly politicized issues. Consequently, 86 per cent of proponents' scheme gave proponents a higher proportion of the catch than did any other proposal.[35] In many cases the catch limit adopted by the NEAFC exceeded the highest limit proposed by any Party as a result of the members' inability to agree on individual quotas, which were often resolved by simply raising the limit.

It has been suggested that by 1976 many NEAFC stocks were further from a state of 'rational exploitation' than they were in 1959 when the NEAFC treaty was signed.[36] The NEAFC measures were too little, too late, the necessary enforcement measures were not taken, and the ability of objectors to opt out was a significant flaw in its design. The criticisms outlined above together with the establishment of the 200nm EEZs led to the reconstitution of the NEAFC in 1980 in a form simply to facilitate information exchange and consultation concerning the management of fish stocks. No common fisheries management system has resulted in areas now under national jurisdiction.[37]

A similar problem arises in the North West Atlantic Fisheries Organization. The effect of the existence of the opt-out provision is most clearly illustrated by Spain's action in utilizing it to exempt itself from a number of NAFO's conservation measures and setting itself a quota in 1989 more than ten times that allotted to it by NAFO.

In contrast, the EU's Common Fisheries Policy (CFP) allows no opt-out. The CFP evolved in the 1970s as a means of ensuring EU member states equal access to each other's fishing grounds, especially when those fishing grounds were extended through the adoption of EEZs. The CFP applies to EU common waters, which are those on the north east coasts of the member states, ie the Atlantic Ocean and North Sea Coasts but not the Mediterranean or Baltic Sea coastal waters. As to the common waters, member states' abilities unilaterally to set fisheries exploitation limits are severely limited. They can impose their own conservation measures only in relation to strictly local fisheries affecting their own citizens. There are a large number of other constraints on states imposing unilateral measures, therefore fisheries policy within the EU is largely centrally determined by EU bodies. Decisions are taken on the basis of a weighted voting procedure by the Fisheries Council, made up of the Fisheries Ministers of each member state. It acts as the legislative organ, and the Commission Directorate-General for Fisheries as the executive organ, although the latter also enacts delegated legislation.[38]

The CFP does not permit a member state to opt out of a decision to conserve fisheries in EU waters. Although negotiations may be bitter and protracted, the weighted voting system compels recalcitrant member states to abide by a majority vote decision and enables the development of a coherent common resource management strategy. This is clearly preferable to a looser decision-making structure which permits a dissatisfied regime participant to go its own way.

One must conclude that an opt-out provision is an undesirable feature in a multilateral natural resources management agreement. It undermines the fundamental principle of a common commitment for protection of a common resource. Whereas it might have been necessary to countries to opt out when the ICRW was adopted in 1946, due to the contemporary emphasis on absolute sovereign independence and the lack of awareness of the dire situation of shared resources, the situation is different today. A common theme of international relations is interdependence and this is nowhere more evident than in the case of depleted shared natural resources.

It remains necessary to protect minority interests in a multilateral natural resources management agreement, as in any constitutional agreement. The EU system of weighted voting is one example of how to balance minority and majority interests, and the use of counter-balancing influences by other decision-making organs, such as scientific and economic committees is another. Decisions might be required to be exposed to public scrutiny in order to ensure that a broader political accountability is factored into the decision-making process. These constitutional aspects of the primary rules framework will vary with the resource situation for which they are designed. For example, the greater political cohesion present in an economic integration organization is likely to mean that more sophisticated, compelling and complex decision-making arrangements can apply.

Scientific whaling

Article VIII of the ICRW allows a contracting government to issue permits authorizing the killing, taking and treating of whales for purposes of scientific research 'notwithstanding anything contained in this Convention' subject only to 'such restrictions as to number and subject to such other conditions as the Contracting Government thinks fit'. Therefore, the taking of whales under this article is not subject to the commercial quotas fixed by the IWC. It is immediately apparent that this leaves a government with a high degree of discretion in deciding how many, and what type of whales it will authorize to be taken for scientific purposes, but like all discretions it is open to abuse. Accusations have been levelled against a number of nations suggesting that they have issued scientific permits in order to mask the killing of whales for commercial purposes.[39]

To regulate scientific whaling better, the IWC adopted a resolution amending the Scientific Committee's Rules of Procedure to require that proposed permits for scientific whaling be submitted to the Scientific Committee for prior review so that it could make recommendations upon them. At its 38th Meeting the Commission adopted a resolution outlining the criteria to be applied by the Committee in evaluating the scientific value of a proposed permit, including that the proposed research should contribute relevant information that should answer significant whale management questions and that the proposed take would materially facilitate the conduct of the comprehensive assessment of the commercial whaling moratorium. A further resolution adopted at the Commission's 39th Meeting provided a mechanism whereby the IWC could review the Scientific Committee's report on the proposed permits and make its own recommendations to member governments under Article VI as to whether the proposed research was consistent with the IWC's conservation policy.[40] Where the Commission, based on the Scientific Committee's comments, deemed that the proposed permits did not satisfy each criterion or meet its conservation policy it could recommend to the relevant member government to refrain from issuing permits. The Commission's resolutions, however, are non-binding and it is open to a contracting government to ignore a recommendation from the Commission and proceed with the issue of its proposed permits.

The scientific permits provision is a clear loophole in the decision-making structure of the IWC which subsequent non-binding resolutions have not fully resolved. In the broader context of fisheries management, this loophole in collective decision-making procedures is peculiar to the IWC. In effect it is a second opt-out provision in the ICRW with the potential to undermine cohesive and coherent management of whale populations. However, it is slightly more limited than the opt-out provision, in that resolutions require that a scientific programme be scrutinized and recommended and that whales captured should be used only for local consumption. Like the opt-out provision, it might be described as a 'safety valve' for those states who would not otherwise participate in the work of the IWC but, to ensure it is not abused, it requires tighter definition of compulsory scientific standards to be observed.

Scientific basis and Precautionary Principle

A lack of primary information plagues the effective management of common resources in general and fisheries in particular. Despite the significant research which concerns whales, the case is no different for them. Article V of the ICRW requires amendments to whale catch quotas to be based on scientific findings.[41] Since the 1950s the Scientific Committee has made repeated demands for more research because it felt that the scientific methods it was using were unable to assess population trends, so to set quotas, with any degree of accuracy. These demands generally did not result in political commitments to fund or conduct such research sufficiently. During the same period the predominant recurrent objection made by whaling nations to the Scientific Committee's recommendations to reduce quotas, season lengths and size limits related to the weakness of scientific data. Therefore, the requirement for scientific data had two-fold effect on the IWC's ability to restrict the catch quotas:

> it made the Commission reluctant to impose constraints, and it gave those states which favoured continued whaling a ready (and almost continually utilized) ground for objecting to those constraints which did emerge.[42]

This absence of scientific certainty concerning whale population sizes and trends is a long-term problem and is likely to continue. Rather than wait until a perfect set of scientific information is available, a management paradigm which permits conservative action despite imperfect or inadequate data is needed for current use. The 'Precautionary Principle' may well be that paradigm. Denmark's IWC Commissioner in his opening statement at the 1993 IWC Meeting supported 'precautionary approaches to the utilization of whales'.[43]

The Precautionary Principle has been adopted in a wide range of international instruments, such as the Rio Declaration on Environment and Development, Principle 15 of which states that

> Where there are threats of serious or irreversible damage, lack of full scientific certainty shall not be used as a reason for postponing cost-effective measures to prevent environmental degradation.[44]

Other international instruments in which it is articulated deal with the fields of marine pollution, protection of the ozone layer, reduction of greenhouse gases, and the conservation of nature. Recently its introduction into the field of fisheries management has been debated by the international fisheries community.[45] See the Afterword to this chapter on page 328 for a brief discussion of the 1995 Fish Stocks Agreement.

Although there is no universally accepted standard definition of the Precautionary Principle, a variety of common elements can be recognized in definitions of the principle:

1. The vulnerability of the environment and the scarcity of resources necessitates their protection and conservation.
2. Science has a limited ability to predict accurately threats to the environment. This element is important in fisheries management, where it is especially difficult to determine the relationship between an observed effect in the marine environment and a particular fishing activity suspected of causing the effect. It has been argued that '... experience in fisheries has indicated that delaying regulation in order to accumulate data may lead to undesirable

changes in stocks, such as stock collapse. Indeed there may be cases where perfect or better information will not greatly enhance the management process'.[47]

3. There is a need to set conservative evidentiary thresholds for taking action. Two terms have most often been used to define the threshold, ie 'threats of serious or irreversible harm' (in the Rio Declaration), and 'unacceptable impacts' (in UN General Assembly Resolution 44/225).[48] These set the level of risk or harm which triggers a determination that the proposed fishing or whaling activities are not compatible with precautionary management.
4. There is a requirement to remove the burden of proof from those opposing a potentially destructive activity and to place it onto those seeking to promote such an activity. In this context it is interesting to note that John Gummer, who made the UK's opening statement at the IWC's 44th Meeting in Glasgow (1992) said that 'the burden of proof for lifting the moratorium . . . must rest with those who say they want to continue to exploit [whale stocks]'.[49]
5. Impact assessments should be conducted prior to undertaking a proposed activity. It has been suggested that in the fisheries context this would involve an evaluation of the environmental effects of a fishing activity as well as an evaluation of the socio-economic effects.[50]

Naturally, the extension of this principle to fisheries and to whaling has been opposed by major distant water fishing nations (and the FAO) who cite as their main reasons the absence of agreement as to what constitutes an acceptable threshold at which to apply the principle and the shift of the burden of proof. In fact, Japan, Korea, Norway and the Russian Federation have 'expressed grave reservations over the use of the precautionary [principle] as a tool of fisheries management'.[51] The inclusion of the precautionary approach in the 1995 Fish Stocks Agreement may provide an exciting precedent for wider application of the principle to marine living resources, and it has proved right those who had predicted that, since Rio, it was 'no longer a question of whether the principle should be applied to the high seas management, but how it should be applied.'[52]

At the IWC's 44th Meeting in 1992, a catch limit algorithm (CLA) was adopted as a central feature of the proposed revised whale management scheme. This is a mathematical formula designed to account for all variables, including lack of reliable information, concerning whale population sizes and for setting catch limits which would ensure that populations are not depleted. If it proves as well designed as anticipated, it will contain safeguards against poor information and, thus, represent a partial implementation of the Precautionary Principle in whale management.

As the required data sets for management of extensively utilized natural resources are inadequate, and will remain so as management needs become increasingly extensive and complex and the limits of what is scientifically certain become increasingly evident, one can confidently predict that the Precautionary Principle will become a predominant resources management paradigm. The actual threshold levels for application, management strategies and harvest formulae will need to be redefined for each different resource utilization application, however, the principle is likely to stand as a pillar in the making of conservation measures for common resource management.

PRIMARY RULES – INFORMATION GATHERING

Gathering of information in relation to marine ecosystems poses difficulties which the ICRW does not attempt to deal with. It lacks provisions for regular, on-going or periodic assessments of whale populations. The member nations conduct their own national research programmes and make information available to the IWC through their voluntary participation in the Scientific Committee.

A one-off assessment requirement was introduced into the ICRW Schedule in 1982, together with the moratorium on commercial whaling introduced in that year.[53] It required a comprehensive assessment of whale populations prior to the lifting of the ban. It is not clear that the provision requires a comprehensive assessment of all population groups prior to the recommencement of commercial whaling for that species, and the Commission seems to have accepted that each group can be comprehensively assessed individually and at different times in order to permit the recommencement of commercial whaling for that population.

In 1992 the IWC resolved that a 'fully effective' inspection and observation scheme would be needed as part of the management regime adopted when the moratorium is lifted. This would consist of two elements: population assessment and monitoring; and an international inspection and observer scheme. It has been suggested that population assessments would need to be conducted at least every five years and that monitoring would need to be linked with the proposed observer scheme.[54] However, as of the time of writing, no regular assessment procedure is in place.

The lack of a formal primary information gathering mechanism in the IWC is a characteristic it holds in common with fisheries organizations. For example, the European Union itself does not conduct primary research but may provide funding for national programmes. Primary information gathering conducted under the auspices of the EU is based on voluntary reporting. Fishermen must keep logbooks and make fish landing and transhipment declarations.[55] Unfortunately, however, the data is not fully reliable as fishermen are reluctant to make records and declarations which will ultimately lead to restrictions being placed on their activities. Therefore, information gathered through voluntary reporting needs to be verified against independent research. Primary fisheries research for the formulation of conservation rules under the EU Common Fisheries Policy is conducted independently by the Advisory Committee on Fisheries Management of the International Council for Exploration of the Seas, which advises the EU Fisheries Council.

Structural deficiency in the gathering of information for primary rule-making is a common problem in marine resources management. The financial, technical and human resources needed have led to short cuts and best guesses. This is not a problem that is easily remediable in the foreseeable future. Therefore compensatory safeguards are needed. In this respect, the Precautionary Principle must be referred to again as providing a conceptual framework within which such safeguards can be designed.

PRIMARY RULES – CONSERVATION MEASURES

Schedule to ICRW

Total catch – Blue Whale Unit

The ICRW entered into force in 1949 with a Schedule which contained several restrictions, the most important of which was a ban on the killing of grey, humpback and right whales.[56] The Schedule also provided for the adoption of the blue whale unit (BWU), which was used in the 1930s as a standard measurement for oil production from different whale species. Under this scientifically inaccurate system, one blue whale was equal to three humpbacks or five sei whales and the IWC set quotas in BWUs.

The result of the initial restrictions was greatly to increase, rather than decrease, competition time in the whaling industry and whale takes. Seasonal time limits and quotas only encouraged whaling nations to create increasingly advanced ships and killing techniques in order to capture as much of their respective quotas as possible. The consequence was a period of intense international competition categorized by whalers as 'the Whaling Olympics'.[57]

The IWC was unable to halt the decimation of whales throughout the 1950s and 1960s because it set harvest rates too high and it did not have any control over its members. This led to a severe depletion in whale populations and blue whales in particular. In 1973, in the face of strong opposition from Japan and the former USSR, the IWC took steps to reduce sperm and minke whale quotas and phase out the killing of Antarctic fin whales.

New management procedure

The 1974 IWC Meeting saw the adoption of an Australian proposal for selective moratoria under a New Management Procedure (NMP) which outlined the management of whales pursuant to the concept of a 'maximum sustainable yield' (MSY). The proposal called for each species to be placed in one of three categories, according to recommendations given by the Scientific Committee.[58] Those whale species whose populations fell below the MSY level were categorized as 'Protection Stocks' and were to be protected from any hunting until they reached a sustained management level. Whale populations 'at or near' MSY levels were categorized 'Sustained Management Stocks' and were required to be maintained at those levels. Finally, populations above the MSY level were categorized 'Initial Management Stocks' and could be reduced to MSY. The NMP was put into effect in 1975 and throughout the mid to late 1970s and early 1980s the IWC consistently reduced its quotas. However, the biological data required to make the NMP work effectively were always unavailable and whale populations continued to diminish.[59] This led the Commission to impose a moratorium on commercial whaling and undertake work to develop Revised Management Procedures (RMP).

On 23 July 1982 the IWC adopted a regulation instituting a five-year moratorium on commercial whaling beginning in 1986. There was a 25 to 7 vote in favour of the moratorium;[60] however, several nations opposing the ban threatened to file objections and continue whaling in spite of the moratorium.

As noted above, in 1992 the Commission adopted a Catch Limit Algorithm (CLA) under its proposed RMP. This gives higher catches than the NMP for populations close to their unexploited levels, but becomes more conservative as the population size drops. Another advantage of the CLA is that it is entirely mechanical and, as it is already fully agreed, it limits the opportunity for political manipulation for excessive quotas. The catch limits set by the IWC should be contrasted with the much wider range of technical conservation tools used to manage fisheries under the EU Common Fisheries Policy.

Common Fisheries Policy

Fishing fleet capacity limits

A major problem in EU fisheries management is caused by the over-capacity of EU member states' fleets. It is calculated that the fleet capacity to fish is currently 40 per cent in excess of available fishing opportunities.[61] This problem is being unsuccessfully dealt with by a ten-year scheme of Multi-Annual Guidance Programmes (MAGPs) to restructure the EU fleet. Under this scheme each member state must present to the EU Commission for its approval two five-year programmes to adjust national fleet capacity, and must report back annually on implementation of the programmes. The MAGPs provide, *inter alia*, for aid for member states for the temporary or permanent withdrawal of vessels from service and for the development of new markets for available fish species which are currently not considered commercially attractive.[62]

Unfortunately, the MAGPs have not proven to be particularly effective in terms of capacity reduction as they are not tightly regulated by the member states responsible for their implementation. The EU Commission promotes implementation of the MAGPs by a combination of incentives and penalties. Financial support for restructuring the EU fleet can be regarded as a form of implementation assistance, providing an incentive. However, it is rare in international fisheries management and is possible in the EU only because substantial funds are available for general economic integration. On the other hand, in recognition of member state failings, the EU Commission froze MAGPs grants in October 1990 for construction of new vessels in Greece, Ireland, the Netherlands, and the UK.

To improve implementation of the CFP, a central register of fishing vessels has recently been created. The use of this register could facilitate the introduction of a scheme of vessel licences, entailing capacity limits and better enforcement systems. At present, capacity limits are only in place in relation to Portuguese and Spanish fishermen and their waters. The EU also operates a licensing system to limit access to areas which contain species of special importance and requires special licensing for some vessel activities, such as trawling the sea floor. While the IWC also maintains a register of whaling vessels it lacks the opportunity to use it in ways which can restrict whaling efforts.

Fishing effort limits

Technical conservation measures include setting limits on catches of particular species, restrictions on the use of certain gear, restrictions on catching certain fish species during specified seasons and in specified areas, and restrictions on the allowable end use of some fish species. The cornerstone of these restrictions is the total allowable catch (TAC) fixed for species by the EU Fisheries Council each year, with quotas being allocated to individual member states. This system has often been criticized for its inefficiency, in that, like the 'Whaling Olympics', it encourages fishermen to use up the quota before their competitors do and requires close surveillance to enforce the limit. TACs in the EU are adopted following much political bargaining amongst the member states and the result has been that over the years TACs have been set too high. The influence of politics is moderated in the allocation of quotas to each member state according to the principle of 'relative stability', which is made up of a number of factors including past catches and the needs of certain regions particularly dependent on fishing. The proportions into which the TACs were originally divided in 1982 have been used when adopting quotas for later years[63] and member states have shown a great reluctance to upset this status quo, despite the alterations in fishing patterns brought about by the entry of Spain and Portugal into the EC in 1986.

TACs can be supplemented by season and duration restrictions, for instance, vessels engaged in certain fisheries may be required to lay up in port for ten consecutive days each month. These are ways of reducing fishing effort without reducing the fleet capacity. However, this means that the fleet is always fishing at a level below its capacity and it is inherently economically inefficient. The EU does also impose fishing gear restrictions, such as prohibiting the use of guns or explosives. More effective and enforceable technical conservation measures control fishing capacity or techniques rather than impose catch limits on fishing effort.[64] Ultimately, though, the CFP has been unable to meet its conservation aims. Three-quarters of the fish stock within EU waters are exploited at unsustainably high levels.[65] A major problem has been the continuing moves by member states to block the Commission's management efforts due to the political importance in appeasing their own fishing communities.

In conclusion, it is more effective to control fishing capacity and techniques than catch quantities. Conservation measures need to be designed so as to be efficient and simple to apply and easy to enforce. The setting of total allowable catches generally fails to meet these needs and its effects have often been arbitrary and undesirable. The fact that fishermen at sea are largely beyond the physical control of an administrative authority needs to be borne in mind. Other approaches being applied in the European Union, such as gear, area, season, and duration restrictions, are easier to enforce in port, rather than at sea, and are therefore less expensive and stand a greater chance of success. However, tackling the problem of overfishing at its root source, that is the over-capacity of fleets to fish, is the most simple, efficient and logical approach to adopt where the economic interdependence or integration of the states concerned permits fleet restructuring. A centrally administered system of vessel licences, such as that proposed in the EU, may achieve fleet capacity control for other common multilateral marine resource management organizations (although without socio-economic cushioning provided by the EU). Such licensing also lends itself to easier compliance monitoring through surveillance and monitoring using up-to-date technologies.

COMPLIANCE MONITORING

The ICRW leaves responsibility for implementation of the Convention entirely to its member nations, who are to 'take appropriate measures to ensure the application of the provisions of this Convention and the punishment of infractions against said provisions . . .'.[66]

Infractions reporting system

Under Article IX(4) member nations are required to submit to the IWC full details of infractions by persons or vessels under its jurisdiction together with a statement of the measures taken for dealing with the infractions and the penalties imposed. The reports are then reviewed annually by the Infractions Committee, a sub-committee of the Technical Committee. Finally, under paragraph 31 of the Schedule each government is required to send the IWC copies of all its laws and regulations relating to whales and whaling and to changes in such laws and regulations.

Serious problems have emerged within this system, one of which was that until 1976 (when penalties were reported uniformly in US dollars) there was no requirement for penalties to be reported in a common currency, thus blocking effective comparison of penalties and their harmonization. A more serious problem was that many governments failed to send infraction reports or copies of their laws and regulations on time or at all. However, most serious of all were the recurring allegations of governments submitting false infraction reports and inaccurate catch data after collusion between the national inspectors and whaling vessel owners. These suspicions were seemingly confirmed by a number of factors, one of which was the undisputed evidence of a continuing decline in almost all whale stocks.

National inspectors' system

The gathering of information on compliance by individual nations is facilitated by national inspectors, at least two of whom have to be maintained on each factory ship for the purpose of maintaining a 24-hour inspection. The ICRW Schedule also requires 'adequate inspection' to be maintained at each land station. The inspectors are appointed and paid for by their governments, to whom they are ultimately accountable.[67] The potential for abuse of a national inspector system is apparent. Recent revelations concerning the massive whaling operations of the fleet of the former USSR, conducted in flagrant contravention of the ICRW, are strong testimony to such abuse.[68]

In the EU, similar problems arise within the national inspector system. Member states are principally responsible for monitoring and are required to report annually to the Commission on their inspections at sea and in port of vessels under their jurisdiction, including as well inspections of vessel logbooks and landing declarations, and on the warnings, prosecutions and penalties which resulted. Nevertheless, national authorities fail to ensure that conservation measures are implemented. This is partly due to the inadequacy of their staff and facilities for monitoring, inspectors' collaboration with fishermen, and partly to the physical difficulty of obtaining evidence which is so easily dropped overboard.[69]

International Observer Scheme

The suspicion that certain whaling nations were not complying with their obligations under the Convention led to the adoption of the International Observers Scheme (IOS) in 1972. The scheme consisted of a series of bilateral and trilateral agreements between the major whaling nations for the mutual exchange of observers in the four main whaling regions (Southern Hemisphere, North Pacific, North Atlantic and Antarctic).[70] The observers were appointed by and responsible to the IWC but were paid by the member nation nominating them.

The observers' role was to inform the Commission as soon as possible of any serious infractions and to submit reports to the Commission when the operation returned at the end of the season 'noting compliance or non-compliance with each regulation'.[71] One shortcoming was that the observers were not provided with criteria to determine which infractions were 'serious'.

The observers' reports were first reviewed in 1973 by the Technical Committee which concluded there had been 'encouraging progress' in the scheme's first year. In the subsequent years progress was made with the number of reported infractions declining.[72] However, at the IWC's 28th Meeting in 1976 the Infractions Sub-Committee recommended the expansion of the scope of the IOS, both in terms of the species of whales and the geographical area being covered at that time.[73] In 1979 a Technical Committee Working Group recommended a broader expansion in the scope of the IOS and these recommendations were adopted in full as a Resolution at the IWC's 31st Meeting.[74]

However, little progress was made in negotiating new bilateral IOS agreements during the early 1980s with only a few agreements being successfully implemented before the moratorium on commercial whaling came into force in 1986. The last observers appointed by the IWC were appointed at its 38th Meeting in 1986 two were appointed for the Japanese and Soviet factory ships operating during the last Southern Hemisphere pelagic season in 1986/87 and one for the Japanese coastal whaling operation. All the remaining bilateral agreements lapsed in 1986.[75]

Despite the progress made in transforming an ineffective system of national enforcement, which was undoubtedly abused by many whaling nations, into a system of international observation of whaling activities, a number of problems still remain in relation to achieving the effective enforcement of the IWC's regulations. The most important consequence of a reciprocal observer scheme is that, as the IOS operated by means of arrangements between states whaling in the same region, it naturally led to an exchange of inspectors from states that have a mutual interest in whaling operations. Non-whaling nations were not represented although the regulations to be enforced reflected in part the views of non-whaling nations. If non-whaling nations wish to participate in any future observer scheme, they may have to be willing to incur expenses, for instance payment of the inspectors they appoint, and it may be that this will act as a deterrent to them. It has been suggested that this problem could be met through increased IWC membership dues or a state levy based upon the value of the whale products.[76] The fact that no observer scheme is yet in place to monitor Norway's commercial whaling operations, which resumed in the 1992/93 season, is further testimony to the shortcomings of a reciprocal observer scheme. The IOS was not centrally administered. Only in the last few years before the scheme lapsed in 1986 was it expanded to cover whaling for smaller minke whales and more regions; a centrally administered scheme arguably would have been interested to respond more quickly to scrutinize whaling operations and expand the scheme in this way.

New monitoring proposals

Time will tell what form of arrangement will be instituted by the IWC in light of its decision at its 44th Meeting to create a 'fully effective' inspection and observation scheme in the revised management procedures. There is, as yet, no indication of whether this will result in a centrally administered scheme and it appears as if little has yet been decided concerning alteration of the international observer scheme.[77] A Resolution for the adoption of a Revised Management Scheme was proposed by Japan and Norway at the 45th Meeting in Kyoto in May 1993 but it failed to receive the requisite number of votes to be adopted.[78] At the IWC's 45th Meeting, Norway submitted a draft proposal for an observer scheme.[79] However, the proposal was not presented before the IWC and thus was not voted upon.

Norway proposed that national inspectors should be maintained at each land station and whaling vessel and that IWC observers should be maintained on each vessel that could accommodate them or at each land station. The national inspectors were to be appointed and paid by the nation having jurisdiction over the vessel or land station in question. The proposal also provided, *inter alia*, that national inspectors would have the authority to instruct a vessel's master to correct catching operations in case of infractions and to have access to the vessel's log books and the right to use communications equipment. IWC observers, however, would have no authority to interfere with whaling operations and could only report infractions to the IWC in writing, with a copy to the contracting government whose whaling operations were being observed. Further, the IWC observers would not have the right to use a vessel's communications equipment. This proposal may fall short of the need for a fully effective observer scheme.

Ideally, any new scheme should consist of a centrally administered international inspectorate. The inspectors would also need to have experience in whaling management and speak the language of the state whose vessel is being monitored or have an interpreter available. The scheme would also ideally be run in conjunction with a monitoring and surveillance scheme such as that in the South Pacific Region (see below).

The ICRW's lack of central monitoring powers is found in other fisheries conventions. For instance, the NAFO operates a Joint Inspection Scheme which allows Parties reciprocal rights to board and inspect vessels. The Commission for the Conservation of Antarctic Marine Living Resources operates a system of inspection[80] and a Scheme of International Scientific Observation[81] which are slightly more centralized. The inspection system allows inspectors designated by the state on whose vessel they are present to board and inspect listed vessels of other states in the Commission, without a reciprocal arrangement being necessary. A major disadvantage of this system is that the high cost of inspections is voluntarily incurred by inspecting states. It is not surprising that the number of inspections conducted each year has already tapered off since the system was introduced in 1991. A possible solution to this problem may be to require that fishing vessels be required to pay a 'resource rent' to cover the costs of inspections. Such rents could be levied by the country having jurisdiction over the activities of the company operating the fishing enterprise and reimbursed to the inspecting state through a central fund. The CCAMLR scheme of scientific observation involves member states designating research work assigned by the

CCAMLR. However, the observers themselves are assigned only voluntarily in bilateral arrangements as between CCAMLR members.

Central monitoring

The EU Commission Directorate-General for Fisheries has very few independent, central monitoring powers. It has a small inspectorate and can report incidents to member states for attention. Vessels which repeatedly offend can be required at each port where they land fish to produce a certificate validated by their previous port of landing, in order to subject them to closer official scrutiny. In 1993 the EU Fisheries Council agreed to monitor pilot schemes to assess the effectiveness of satellite monitoring of fishing vessels. Ideally, all licensed vessels could be fitted with satellite transponders which would enable automatic monitoring and electronic recording of their movements and activities. It is noteworthy that the CCAMLR, which established an inspection scheme only in 1992, agreed in 1993 to examine the installation of transponders to facilitate location of vessels in Antarctic waters so as to discourage illegal fishing.

Cooperative surveillance

The Forum Fisheries Agency (FFA) presents an exceptional case as it has taken a lead in establishing a comprehensive system of surveillance to inform a cooperative monitoring process. The FFA was established in 1979 and comprises 16 states from the South Pacific region (mainly small-island states). The region contains vast stocks of tuna which are much sought after by distant water fishing nations (such as Japan, Korea, Russia and Taiwan) but the South Pacific states do not individually have the resources to enforce their sovereign rights over the resources in their EEZs.[82]

The FFA functions as a consultative and advisory body whose primary objective is to enhance the abilities of its member nations to exercise their sovereign rights of management of living marine resources in their EEZs. It does this by pursing policies of cooperation amongst its members. Such cooperation has included the harmonization of fisheries regimes and policies towards distant water fishing nations, the exchange of information, and the development of cooperative management arrangements.[83] To achieve this end, it standardizes licensing procedures, terms and conditions of access to its fishing zones, and coordinates surveillance and enforcement functions. The harmonization of the minimum terms and conditions of access for foreign vessels are adopted and implemented by all FFA member nations through legislation or administrative arrangements having the force of law.

In relation to cooperative monitoring activities, the South Pacific states entered into the Niue Treaty on Cooperation in Fisheries Surveillance in the South Pacific Region in 1992. The Treaty's main objective is to enhance the effectiveness of regional or sub-regional surveillance and enforcement through cooperation on a reciprocal or joint basis.[84] The FFA provides coordinating assistance to two regional fisheries surveillance programmes – the Pacific Patrol Boat Programme and aerial surveillance patrols provided by the Australian and New Zealand armed forces. A satellite-based regional maritime surveillance and communications network has also been established which will allow each member nation to be connected to a central database at the FFA through an Inmarsat A terminal.[85] It is proposed that by mid-1994 there will be in force a vessel position and data acquisition system whereby any vessel intending to operate in the region will have to carry integrated Inmarsat C and Global Positioning System equipment that will be linked to a computer which will transfer their position and catch data to a central database at the FFA. The accuracy of the data will be guaranteed through an observer programme and periodic inspections either at sea or in port.[86]

The FFA and EU examples show that successful compliance monitoring is largely a matter of application of resources – human, technical and financial. The physical environment to which these resources are applied is a paramount concern in the design of the compliance information gathering system. This blue planet's vast expanse of oceans cannot be efficiently monitored by uncoordinated coastguard patrol boats or aeroplanes. Therefore the coordinated use of electronic communications and automated satellite technologies assisted by a computerized central information system is necessary for shared management of marine resources. This system can be implemented by states individually for vessels under their flag or in their waters but might itself need to be monitored by central cross-checking of national compliance information gathering. In addition, to ensure that a monitoring system's gaps in surveillance capability are covered, it may be necessary to operate more than one type of surveillance system. For example, the use of transponders might need to be supplemented by aerial inspections, so as to identify the presence and cover the activities of vessels which are not fitted with or have tampered with transponders. The costs of such monitoring need to be recovered from the enterprise benefiting from the use of the resource. National levies on such enterprises could be contributed to an international fund and reimbursed to those states carrying out agreed monitoring activities.

NON-COMPLIANCE RESPONSES

Centralized responses

ICRW deficit

Article IX(1) of the ICRW calls on member nations to apply the provisions of the Convention and to punish infractions carried out by persons or vessels under their jurisdiction. Article IX(3) makes it clear that prosecution of these infractions can only be 'instituted by the Government having jurisdiction over the offence'. The introduction of EEZs in the mid-1970s have meant that coastal states have a greater jurisdictional role to play in prosecuting infractions. Each nation also is required to submit to the IWC copies of all national laws relating to whaling and annual reports of breaches of the ICRW and sanctions taken to attend to those breaches.[87]

Due to the lack of a central non-compliance response mechanism, central enforcement of IWC regulations can take place only indirectly, by way of political pressure within IWC meetings. Such pressure is generated by adverse publicity and condemnatory resolutions adopted by the Commission concerning illegal activities.

EU Sanctions and Incentives

In contrast, the EU has sanctions penalizing the over-fishing of quotas, but they are ineffectively utilized. These sanctions comprise a declaratory judgement by the ECJ that a quota has been exceeded; the withdrawal by the EU of money for supporting the export price of fish (which has hardly ever happened); or a reduction in an offending state's quotas for the following year.[88] The EU, by virtue of its financial resources as an economic integration organization, also offers incentives for compliance, such as the grants offered under the Multiannual Guidance Programmes for the reduction of fleet capacity, referred to above.

The FFA common register

Another approach to common enforcement of the conservation laws of member countries, is that of the Forum Fisheries Agency. It maintains a common register kept of foreign vessels that may wish to apply for licences to fish. A vessel must be in good standing on the register before it may be licensed to fish in the region. Good standing status is automatically conferred on a licensed vessel but may be withdrawn in certain circumstances, such as where the vessel has committed a serious fisheries offence. The removal of good standing ('black listing') has never yet taken place, but its threat has been used successfully on a number of occasions.

The FFA system of vessel control through licensing lends itself to effective compliance responses more than the quantitative limit (TAC) approach to regulation. This can be combined with other national measures such as gear, area, season and duration restrictions, which are more capable of enforcement through a licensing and satellite surveillance system than by inspections alone. The FFA therefore offers a centrally coordinated approach to management under national jurisdiction of resources which are migratory and shared. Due to the convergence of interests of coastal states in the region in fisheries management matters, the approach appears to be successful. It may provide some insight on how to manage resources which are traditionally regarded as in the international commons.

MEMBERS' UNILATERAL ECONOMIC SANCTIONS

US Sanctions

As noted above, the IWC has no central non-compliance response mechanisms, such as the provision of assistance and incentives, or sanctions such as withdrawal of licences. Therefore, enforcement of IWC regulations has proceeded by way of unilateral action taken by some member states against offending member states. The adoption by the US Congress of the Pelly Amendment[89] in 1971, under which the US could ban all fisheries imports from a country whose fishing operations 'diminished the effectiveness of an international fishery conservation program' meant that by the mid-1970s, 'cavalier flouting of the IWC had become a luxury of the past'.[90] In addition, in 1979 the Packwood-Magnuson Amendment was adopted. This gives the US authority to reduce as appropriate an offending state's allowance of fish from the American Exclusive Economic Zone against nations that ignore the

Commission's recommendations.[91] The US' threat of applying the above certification procedures led the Republic of Korea to abandon its proposals in 1986 and 1987 for scientific research whaling which had been rejected by resolution of the IWC.[92] These provisions were also used to force some whaling countries to join the IWC, for example, Chile and Peru.

Nevertheless, there are other more recent examples of the US' increasing reluctance to use or threaten these measures against nations who breach IWC regulations or whose proposals for research whaling have been rejected by the IWC. For example, in 1984, following Japan's objection to the IWC's ban on sperm whale harvest, the US threatened sanctions but eventually negotiated an agreement with Japan.[93] The agreement was controversial because it restricted Japan to 'catch limits acceptable to the United States'[94] and made no mention of the IWC. In 1988 the IWC rejected Norway's research harvest proposal, however Norway ignored the IWC's recommendations and continued to plan for the harvest. The US subsequently decided that Norway's proposals were acceptable in spite of the views of the IWC and therefore took no action against Norway.[95] The US threatened sanctions against Iceland in 1986, 1987 and 1988 because it sold 4000 tons of whale meat to Japan annually in contravention of an IWC proviso requiring local consumption of the produce of scientific whaling.[96] The US never actually applied the sanctions 'probably because Iceland responded by halting the construction of a NATO base in Keflavik, Iceland'.[97] What has tended to occur is that sanctions are threatened but subsequent negotiations result either in reduced action or none at all. For example,

> [I]n light of the military allegiance between the nations reflecting their shared strategic interests, the United States is increasingly reluctant to threaten sanctions against Japan for violation of non-binding IWC resolutions.[98]

Similarly, on the occasions when sanctions have been applied, their effect has often been negligible. For example, when Japan proceeded with its research whaling proposals after they had been rejected by the IWC in 1987 the US imposed sanctions that prevented Japanese fishing in the US EEZ 'but did not impose a more damaging ban on selected imports'. In fact, Japan did not have a quota within the US zone. Further, it is important to bear in mind that the US exports $1.5 billion worth of fish to Japan, an amount Japan has twice threatened to reduce.[99]

Despite the successes the US has achieved in promoting adherence to and compliance with the ICRW through threatening economic sanctions, it is apparent that, even in a state which is the world's major economic and military power, there is wariness against taking action which might damage national interests. There are limitations to what an individual state can or is willing to try to achieve for the promotion of a common good. It follows that, if multilateral environmental agreements would contain adequate centralized enforcement provisions there would be less need for unilateral action by individual countries to enforce them. Concerted collective enforcement action would also be less damaging for the states imposing sanctions and would be far more effective.

Central authorization of sanctions

It has been suggested, therefore, that an appropriate non-compliance response in multilateral environment agreements could involve a mechanism which utilizes multilateral decision-making and authorizes imposition of economic sanctions as a matter of national discretion. An international decision-making organ, such as the IWC, needs to have the authority to authorize its members to impose sanctions.

> Without effective enforcement provisions, [multilateral environmental agreements] will increasingly cease to have any practical utility...[100]

Such an authority would not infringe on member nations' sovereignty because members would not be required to impose sanctions but would be authorized and urged to do so if it chooses.[101]

As most breaches are perpetrated for economic gain, often by countries in economically vulnerable positions, and as economic sanctions have proved effective in the past, (eg where the US has chosen to apply them to enforce IWC scientific whaling resolutions) it is logical to conclude that economic sanctions are an appropriate non-compliance response. Whereas the imposition of unilateral economic sanctions might be regarded as trade restrictions in conflict with trade liberalization principles under the GATT, the authorization of such trade restrictions under a widely subscribed to international agreement might ensure the legitimation of those restrictions.

Non-members' unilateral actions

Non-members of the IWC, such as non-governmental organizations, have attempted to reduce the level of or halt whaling activities, often with surprising effect. The most dramatic example of such action has been the 'terrorism of the high seas'[102] conducted by the Sea Shepherd Society. This organization has used unlawful acts, such as the sabotage and bombing of whaling vessels. Another example was the 1974 economic boycott against Soviet and Japanese goods which was mobilized by 21 national and international environmental groups and was supported by over five million group members worldwide.[103] The boycott attracted a substantial amount of media attention and proved to be very successful in that it led to both the USSR and Japan reducing their quota demands and opposition to conservationist proposals. Greenpeace was also central to the 1993 boycott of Norwegian fisheries products in response to Norway's resumption of commercial whaling that year.

It is clear that sanctions have been central as non-compliance responses in regimes for the cooperative management of common marine resources. The sanctions applied have been trade restrictions and fisheries access restrictions. The use of incentives to deter non-compliance is rarer and is in evidence in relation to conservation of shared marine living resources only in the EU. This need not be the case. The Montreal Protocol Fund for protection of the ozone layer demonstrates that international funds to assist compliance with multilateral environmental agreements are politically possible.

Restricting fisheries access is possible only in circumstances where states responding to breach of the management regime are in a position physically to control the access of another state's vessels to the responding state's fishing waters. As the case of the US restrictions on Japanese access indicated, this is determined by circumstance and may leave the sanctioning state itself in a vulnerable situation. The coordinated use of trade restrictions, on the other hand, is a far more flexible, collectively applicable and powerful sanction_ One might expect that, as common resources become increasingly scarce, the use of such trade sanctions is going to increase and that mechanism to ensure that they are fair, measured and legitimate restrictions on liberalized trade regimes will be developed.

REINING IN FREE-RIDERS

Although almost all the major whaling nations are now members of the IWC, there remain a few nations actively engaged in commercial whaling that are not signatories to the Convention, such as Iceland (which withdrew from the IWC in June 1992) and, possibly, Taiwan.[104] Most non-IWC whaling is conducted from shore stations with minke whale being the primary species taken.

Whaling by non-IWC members is referred to as 'pirate whaling' because those nations that take part in it knowingly interfere with the conservation policies of the principal international organization for the regulation of the industry. 'Pirate' whaling was most prevalent in the 1960s and 1970s. Naturally IWC regulations do not apply to non-members and some IWC members, in particular Japan, have in the past taken advantage of this by registering their vessels under the flag of a non-IWC member[105] and by establishing joint ventures with nonmember nations.[106]

Trade restrictions

The continued refusal of nations such as Spain, Portugal, Taiwan and Korea to join the IWC in the late 1970s led the Commission to introduce specific measures. Between 1976 and 1981 the IWC adopted a series of resolutions to stop pirate whaling. These resolutions drew to the attention of non-members their overexploitation of certain whale stocks. Other resolutions urged member nations to prevent both the 'import into their countries of whale products from nonmember nations' and also 'the transfer of factory ships, whale catchers, or gear, apparatus or appliances used in the conduct of whaling operations, and to discourage the dissemination by its citizens of expertise and assistance necessary to the conduct of whaling operations in any form'.[107] These Resolutions were non-binding but were given significant force by the fact that they were mostly adopted unanimously by the major IWC nations, such as the US, the former USSR and Japan. The US went further when, on 14 December 1978, the US Secretary of Commerce certified Peru, Chile and the Republic of Korea under the US Pelly Amendment for whaling in conflict with the goals of the Convention. It is acknowledged that this threat of economic sanctions encouraged these nations to join the IWC by the following year.[108]

Adverse publicity

A further measure to aid in the identification of 'pirate' whalers, in particular those controlled by IWC member states, was the Commission's compilation, beginning in 1979, of a 'Register of Whaling Vessels' subject to IWC quotas and regulations.[109] This gave publicity to some pirate whaling operations and led to their cessation. Since 1987 Norway, Iceland and Japan have refused to provide the requisite information following 'acts of terrorism' by non-governmental organizations against their ships. In spite of this, the Register is still in existence and is compiled from official shipping registers that are readily available (eg The Lloyds' Register).[110]

Inter-organizational networking

Attempts to prevent 'free riders' such as pirate whalers from enjoying the benefits of a multilateral conservation regime while not participating in it and so undermining its effectiveness, have to reach beyond the participants in that regime. The IWC has cooperated with the UN Environment Programme[111] and the UN Food and Agriculture Organization[112] to encourage non-members to become signatories to the ICRW. Non-governmental organizations have also played a role. For example, Japan's practice of buying significant amounts of whale meat from non-IWC states ceased only when Greenpeace internationally publicized the fact.[113]

The experience of the IWC in dealing with free riders indicates again the primacy of economic sanctions in the form of trade restrictions. These have been authorized multilaterally, by resolution of the IWC, and unilaterally, in the case of the US Pelly Amendment. Political pressure has also been relatively effective against pirate whalers. As free riders are not part of the organization implementing the particular conservation regime, political pressure has been applied through other organizations with political influence, such as relevant UN agencies and international NGOs. Clearly, it is essential for the organization responsible for implementing the particular conservation regime to build alliances with other organizations in order to ensure broad participation in its own regime.

CONCLUSION

In international law, whales and fish found on the high seas form part of the global commons and states should cooperate in their management and conservation. Where states share jurisdiction over whales and fish, as is the case for highly migratory species and straddling stocks, again they should cooperate in their management and conservation.

The management and conservation of whales poses similar challenges to the management and conservation of fish. The IWC's record in implementation and enforcement of international law for the whale conservation has been mixed. Attempts to regulate the whaling industry up to 1970 were poor at best and, since then, steps have been taken to halt the severe depletion of whale populations but with limited success, due in part to substantial illegal whaling. In the case of fisheries, stock collapses due to over-harvesting continue at present.

The constitutional structures and powers of organizations entrusted with conservation of these marine resources have a great deal to do with their ability effectively to formulate, implement, monitor and enforce conservation rules. There is a need to ensure that constitutive and decision-making rules promote rather than hinder effective conservation rules. Unfortunately, for many marine resources conservation organizations, the opt-out clause often thwarts the search for agreed common conservation measures. In current times, when there is great consensus for responsible conservation, more cohesive and binding decision-making rules are probably possible and are certainly desirable.

Resources for information gathering provisions are weak throughout agreements for the management of marine living resources and data bases are often inadequate. The ICRW requirement that IWC decisions have a scientific basis has therefore presented another kind of constitutional weakness – in the form of opportunity to manipulate decision-making processes. However, as fisheries science comes to terms with the endemic problem of scientific uncertainty, it may well be that the very uncertainty itself comes to present a conservation imperative. Efforts to formulate the Precautionary Principle hold a great deal of promise in this regard.

The range of conservation measures which can be imposed on fishing activities are varied and sophisticated. They include limitation of fishing fleet capacity through the use of common licensing and a common register, and the limitation of fishing effort by means of restrictions on duration and season of fishing activities, restrictions on quantity, species and sizes of fish which may be caught, and on the fishing gear which may be used. Of these measures, the limitations on fleet capacity and restrictions on duration, season and fishing gear are the most efficient and effective to implement. This has a great deal to do with the economic inefficiencies and disincentives built into restrictions on quantities, species and sizes (which may promote captured fish being discarded at sea or sold illegally), as well as the practical difficulties of monitoring the catch of a vessel at sea. Unfortunately, the IWC relies heavily on quantity and species limitations as its principal conservation measures. This is perhaps due to the culture of that organization, brought about by a lack of cohesion in the members' interests and their lack of economic integration, which has not hindered effective conservation rule-making.

The physical characteristics of a common natural resource sought to be conserved, the intensity of its utilization, the availability of adequate human, technical and financial resources for monitoring, together with the kind of conservation measures sought to be imposed, determine the suitability of proposed compliance monitoring regimes. For example, monitoring of emissions to the atmosphere or to the seas, and of protection of migratory terrestrial species, of birds and of marine living resources, each present profoundly different physical challenges. In the case of harvesting of marine living resources by industrialized fishing vessels, the use of modern electronic technologies presents itself as essential. Surveillance flights and port or sea inspections are likely to be more practicable over intensely fished European Common Waters rather than over expanses of the Pacific Ocean. Primary conservation rules need to be designed to be effective within the limits of the available resources for monitoring. All monitoring techniques entail substantial costs which need to be recoverable as resource rents.

For any international compliance monitoring regime concerned with marine living resources, the lessons of the IWC and of the EU indicate that a centrally coordinated and controlled monitoring regime is more reliable than national self-monitoring or simply reciprocal schemes. As the FFA cooperative approach indicates, a range of internationally coordinated variants are available between the extremes of purely national self-monitoring and independent central inspectorates.

International non-compliance response mechanism for protection of shared whales and fisheries are generally weak. The IWC has no response mechanism at its disposal at all and even a cohesive economic integration organization such as the European Union has relatively poorly developed non-compliance response mechanisms. In the case of the IWC, this has meant that political pressure and unilateral economic sanctions have been the main responses adopted. These are *ad hoc* and unsatisfactory. Economic incentives and sanctions are the most flexible and appropriate tools and, of these, sanctions are the more easily applied. Therefore, there is a need to ensure that these are collectively available and can be applied fairly through a central authorization process. Development of such collective non-compliance responses require rapid elaboration of practical understandings of the relationship between trade and environmental protection.

An agreement to manage an international commons is usually susceptible to the raids of 'free riders'. In the case of shared marine living resources in modern times of economic independence, some of these operations are politically and economically vulnerable. Therefore, adverse publicity, inter-organizational political networking and use of centrally authorized economic sanctions may be effective tools to curb such 'piracy'.

The enforceability of international environmental law is evolving gradually. As in an emerging social science, we discover that the parts of international environmental regimes are inter-connected. Primary conservation rules need to be designed so that they can be enforced. This requires that the international organization designing rules have an effective constitutional and decision-making structure. In particular, it must build cohesion and creatively address deficiencies in scientific data. Enforceable rules also require a compliance information system which is centrally coordinated and verified. Finally, noncompliance and free-riding require enforcing responses. These will involve trade and economic sanctions which are centrally authorized and coordinated. Information on the effectiveness of primary rules, compliance and noncompliance responses needs to be fed back into the organization's decision-making processes. Thus, an international environmental organization incrementally develops effective rules and enforcement regimes for the conservation of common resources.

PART 3

The Implementation of International Agreements

6 THE ROLE OF THE EC IN IMPLEMENTING INTERNATIONAL ENVIRONMENTAL LAW

*Martin Hession**

INTRODUCTION

The European Community (now, since the coming into force of the Maastricht Treaty, the European Union) has signed all the most recent multilateral environmental agreements.[1] Yet the actual value of its contribution to dealing with global environmental problems is difficult to assess. From a legal perspective, at the heart of the problem is the failure of EU member states to agree on the extent of EU power. The general constitutional rules of the EU on division of powers are a matter of some complexity and confusion even in the internal sphere – as the current debate on subsidiarity demonstrates.

In relation to external matters the heightened sensitivities of states leads to a still more spirited defence of their independence of action. It has been argued that the participation of the EU only raises further difficulties in the process of negotiation of international agreements. The confused operation of a division of powers in the external sphere can lead to internal wrangles becoming the subject of international scrutiny and to inaction as the member states direct themselves to question the legalities of various EU competencies rather than to deal with the substantive international issue in hand.[2] While the European Court of Justice (ECJ) has expressed the view that the precise division of powers between the EU institutions and the member states need not concern third states,[3] in practice this problem is precisely what has concerned them.

Another view is that the current legal uncertainty over external competences, far from inhibiting international action by the EU, actually facilitates it by allowing 'practical' solutions which respect the realities of what the

* The full text of this chapter previously appeared as an article in the *Review of European Community and International Environmental Law (RECIEL)*, Vol. 2, Issue 4, FIELD, London 1993.

international community and member states find acceptable. Thus, a degree of discretion is left both to the European Commission and member states in concluding their arrangements for international cooperation and both are reluctant to refer matters to the ECJ prior to using political levers to preserve or obtain legal responsibility.

In the international trade and marine fisheries conservation area a balance has been struck in the favour of central EU institutional control, as these policy areas are exclusive to it. In other areas, including environmental policy, the rules derived from the *ERTA* Case[4] remain the basis of EU international action and the system so created leaves ample room for conflicting interpretations.

PARTICIPATION IN MIXED AGREEMENTS

Exclusive competence

In the absence of specific treatment of international competences in the Treaty of Rome, the ECJ has delineated a scheme of EU competences based on general principles. The consequence of *effet utile*, supremacy, and Article 5 of the Treaty, has been to define two classes of EU competence, one which is exclusive, and one which is concurrent.

The Treaty of Rome as originally adopted contemplated only two express external competences, ie under the Common Commercial Policy (CCP)[5] and Association Agreements.[6] In respect of the CCP the Court consistently maintains that all measures internal and external which fall within the scope of that policy are reserved to the EU.[7] This is because Article 113, which describes that policy, admits only of a unitary system of regulation and pre-empts member state action irrespective of EU measures.[8] Aspects of the Common Fisheries Policy (CFP) also became exclusive (in the CCP sense) in 1979 by reason of Article 102 of the Act of Accession 1972, which required that the European Económic Community have a policy on fisheries conservation by that date.[9]

Pre-emptive exclusive competence

Until 1971 it was generally assumed that the Community was limited to participation in the CCP, CFP and Association Agreements only. In other policy areas the Community was authorized to act internally, but the Treaty of Rome required neither a unitary system in internal and external matters nor provided an obligation for the Community to act in related external matters.

In a grand departure, the ECJ, dealing with transport policy in the *ERTA* Case, found that internal legislation creates implied external competence where external agreement is 'necessary' to achieve the objectives of the policy.[10] *ERTA* created a new model of external competence based on the pre-emptive effect of EU law. The implied external power is exclusive as the assumption of individual member state obligations likely to affect common rules or alter their scope would jeopardize the internal attainment of EU purposes and would be incompatible with the uniform application of EU law.[11]

Some difficulty has arisen in the interpretation of the words 'likely to affect or alter their scope'. On the narrowest interpretation, only laws which are in conflict with an EU law are pre-empted. On the broadest interpretation, all measures which fall within the scope of existing EU measures then will be preempted.

Concurrent competence

The *Kramer* Case[12] and the *Rhine* Case[13] confirmed what was inherent in *ERTA* – that *implied external power extends to what is necessary to attain the objectives of the Treaty*.[14] The Treaty is the origin of competence in all cases, though competence is exclusive only in some. Outside the CCP and CFP, member states retain power to adopt legislation in the absence of existing EU provisions and so EU powers are not exclusive. Nonetheless the EU has the 'potential' to adopt measures and the *Rhine* Case confirms that these measures may take the form of international agreement.

Preserving institutional balance

The *Rhine* Case goes further however, and the *EEA* Cases[15] seem to confirm, that the duty on member states as expressed in *ERTA* – not to interfere in the operation of EU legislation – is only part of the story. The legislative autonomy and the institutional balance of the EU may require that member states do not accede to a convention which would prejudice these matters, even where there is as yet no legislation in place.

The *Rhine* Case raises questions which have later been ignored by the EU institutions. In an area of legislative activity which was not subject to a Community proposal until just some months prior to the ECJ becoming apprised of the matter, the Court ruled that the member states could participate in an international treaty, called the Laying-Up Fund Agreement, only insofar as it was necessary to secure the Community's accession. The repeal of earlier treaties was necessary for the new treaty to come into force and the Court allowed the member states to participate only insofar as it was necessary for them to effect the repeal.

This suggests that the EU now has exclusive competence to conclude international agreements, not only where EU internal legislation already exists, but where member state accession to the international agreement would prejudice the institutional balance peculiar to the Treaty of Rome. Despite the difficulties inherent in such an approach, the *Rhine* case appears to lay down a balance of participation which is at odds with the position of member states and in the absence of a conclusion by the EU Council of Ministers on the matter. Without clarifying its reasons for doing so, the Court appears to have ruled that the fact and extent of participation by the EU in an international agreement is only a political matter within the Council's discretion where it falls within concurrent EU and member state competence and the agreement does not prejudice the institutional balance and autonomy of the EU legal order broadly defined.l6

Subsidiarity and international participation

Where the Council of Ministers has adopted measures by unanimity, action challenging the competence of the measures are unlikely. However, the Single European Act introduced the possibility of qualified majority voting for certain environmental measures and the Maastricht Treaty has extended the possibility of majority voting on environmental matters considerably, thus greatly intensifying questions of the binding nature of measures and therefore the issue of *ultra vires*. The ECJ, following a general policy in favour of European integration, has never found an act of the EU to be *ultra vires* on grounds of lack of competence per se. The concepts of necessity and institutional balance have supported the ECJ approach. Yet the concept of subsidiarity,[17] also introduced in the Single European Act and extended by the Maastricht Treaty, is a countervailing principle relevant at least to the assessment of necessity of action. It seems likely that member states finding themselves in a minority vote will soon test the justifiability of subsidiarity and it relationship to the other principles relevant to the exercise of competence.

Subsidiarity ordinarily arises in the context of local and sub-regional action supposed unsuitable for EU action. The United Kingdom in particular has raised the argument that certain international measures dealing with global, rather than European, issues also fall foul of the subsidiarity principle. This argument, however, ignores the addition of a fourth objective to the EU environment policy by the Maastricht Treaty, ie promoting measures at an international level to deal with global environmental problems. In any event, the definition of subsidiarity in Article 3b of the Treaty lies uncomfortably with the broader considerations relevant to a decision to become involved in international environmental action. Where member states or some of them conclude that they alone cannot deal with an international problem and they therefore wish to coordinate its management through an international agreement, it is difficult to conclude that the EU is not the more appropriate level of action as between themselves and therefore externally as well.

ENVIRONMENTAL COMPETENCE IN EXTERNAL AFFAIRS

Article 130r of the Treaty of Rome was recently extended by the Maastricht Treaty to delineate a very wide statement of EU potential environmental competence. Declarations attached to the Single European Act 1987 and the Maastricht Treaty 1993 confirm that the ERTA Case principles continue to apply to the concurrent external relations power provided for in Article 130r(4).[18]

The superiority of and pre-emptive effect of EU law applies to EU legislation under concurrent EU and member state competence. However, two other factors of particular relevance to the environment must also be mentioned:

(1) The Treaty also prescribes three forms of EU measures with different binding effect, ie regulations, directives and decisions.[19] As environment policy has evolved as a directive-driven area of legislative activity, the constraints of directives are important for it.[20]

(2) In the area of environment, Article 130t of the Treaty of Rome authorizes member states to adopt more stringent standards not otherwise incompatible with the Treaty.[21]

Directives

Of particular relevance to the implementation of directives is the recent *International Labour Organization (ILO)* Case[22] which examined the Community Social Policy in the context of external obligations. The *ILO* Case has implications for environment policy as social policy too is based on directives establishing minimum standards. The decision confirms that the *ERTA* Case position as to the pre-emptive position of EU legislation is applicable to directives, even though states can exercise discretion in their implementation.

Adopting stricter standards

In a refinement of the *ERTA* decision, the ILO case confirms that member states are precluded from entering into international agreements where the operation or scope of EU directives would be affected, but that for this preclusion to apply there is need for actual or possible conflict between the directive and the agreement to be adopted.[23] The judgement brings some comfort to member states as, insofar as a directive authorizes them to undertake stricter environmental standards, the judgement confirms that such directives do not pre-empt member states from also concluding international agreements setting stricter standards.[24] On this point and in response to a European Commission argument to the contrary, the ECJ ruled that 'difficulties' in establishing what is in fact a stricter standard and what arises from the operation of multiple systems of law were not sufficient to preclude independent international agreements by member states.[25] A point not raised in the no Case, however, is that the exercise of such independent member state authority may still breach other aspects of the Treaty of Rome (see Article 130t).

Negotiating accession to mixed agreements

While the EU has acceded to certain agreements alone, where exclusive competence over the whole subject matter has been established, this phenomenon is broadly limited to the Common Fisheries Policy area.[26] As a result of the division and sharing of competences in the internal and external spheres in other policy areas, the EU and member states resort to concluding mixed agreements, ie to which both are party. The mixed agreement has survived in the CCP despite a broad interpretation of the scope of the CCP, as member states are usually successful in arguing some residual competence which remains with them.[27] For example, this argument has on occasion extended to those member state responsibilities in respect of protectorates and overseas territories not subject to EU discipline.[28]

The procedural provisions of Article 228 of the Treaty of Rome give the European Commission the role of negotiating international agreements with the EU.[29] In practice the Commission has sought a mandate from the Council of Ministers to negotiate binding agreements, although until Maastricht this has been an explicit requirement only in respect of agreements under the CCP.[30] Mandates have tended to limit the Commission to consistency with existing legislation and the final power to conclude EU agreements resides with the Council in any event.[31] Too restrictive mandates have caused delays in the negotiation.[32]

Through regular coordination meetings during negotiations, the member states and the Commission attempt to coordinate their positions on competence and the substantive issues. In practice the Commission speaks and negotiates where there is exclusive competence. Where competences are mixed or there is no clear division the Commission may speak by agreement but the Presidency of the Council ordinarily takes the lead.[33] In the absence of a common position the member states are subject to general duties of cooperation and unity which may require their abstention in the negotiations.[34] Only in the now rare instances where the EU has no competence, whether exclusive or potentially concurrent, are the member states entirely free to pursue their own policy.[35] Where the EU has some exclusive competence, the member states are under an obligation to make every effort to facilitate its accession to the agreement.[36]

IMPLEMENTATION AND ENFORCEMENT

The novelty of the EU as an international treaty regime lies in its methods of implementation and enforcement. It is a framework agreement covering a wide range of matters with a unitary decision-making structure, a single court for the interpretation of the law, and a system which is directly effective in national law by express requirement of the Treaty of Rome.

EU legal instruments, including the Treaty of Rome itself, which are sufficiently clear and precise and unconditional and which are applicable to individuals, have direct effect in the national legal systems.[37] Direct effect enables individuals to rely upon EU obligations against the member state and, in some circumstances, against other individuals. EU law also imposes interpretative obligations[38] and may suspend the operation of national, constitutional[39] and procedural[40] rules which lie in the way of a provisions enforcement.

Effect of international agreement[41]

Article 228 of the Treaty of Rome confirms that international agreements entered into by the EU are binding on the member states. At least to the extent that it is an EU agreement, the conclusion of a mixed agreement by the Council puts it in the category of EU acts which are 'an integral part of Community law'.[42] Though the conclusion of the agreement is by decision (a category of internal measures which has never been found to give rise to direct effect), it appears clear that the agreement itself, quite independently of the method and modalities of the conclusion,[43] once concluded is a category of act which may have direct effect,[44] and may be the subject of an Article 177 reference.[45] The *International Fruit* judgement[46] suggests that direct effect may be conditional upon reciprocal enforcement by third states. The *Kupferburg* Case indicates that while other institutions are free to determine the effect of an agreement in the legal order, in the final analysis the interpretation and effect of an agreement are for the ECJ to decide.[47]

As Article 228 effectively bans the EU from adopting agreements which conflict with the Treaty, it suggests that international law is not generally superior to EU law.[48] However, international law may well be superior to EU secondary legislation, ie regulations and directives, though there is little in the way of authority on the point.[49]

Enforcing mixed agreements

Even international agreements which are not of a character which may create direct effects remain EU obligations and require implementation. The European Commission may take action against recalcitrant member states under Article 169 of the Treaty of Rome for breach of EU agreements.[50] The extent to which mixed agreements are EU agreements under Article 228 returns us to the problem of division of competence. The Commission has considered broaching the point[51] in relation to the Irish governmental policy on badger slaughter for tuberculosis eradication. That policy raised questions as to whether there was a national breach of the Berne Convention on the Conservation of European Wildlife and Natural Habitats.[52] However, EU implementation of the Berne Convention is limited to the protection of birds under the Wild Birds Directive.[53] The dominant legal view was that EU enforcement action in relation to species other than wild birds was not permissible.

This raises the question of which portion of a mixed agreement is binding under EU law. While the published text of Council decisions to conclude an agreement often remains silent on the matter, the extent of EU participation is discussed and is recorded in the minutes of the meetings authorizing conclusion.[54] Ordinarily these minutes are merely to the effect that the division of competences remains unchanged by adoption of the agreement.

In practice it seems accepted that where an agreement covers areas within its competence, the EU participates only to the extent of its exclusive or internally legislated competence.[55] If the EU is party to other areas of the agreement this is not in substance but in form only.[56] Nevertheless, as a matter of law, it is possible to argue that the ECJ has the authority to look behind decisions to conclude agreements and that these formal documents are not the final word on the extent of participation or the effects of an agreement on the member states and individuals.

FUTURE DEVELOPMENTS

The number of cases brought to the ECJ concerning the division of powers has been relatively small with a long intermission in the 1980s. The interests of the member states and Commission alike in preserving room for political manoeuvre, the dominance of consensus in the Council's decision-making processes, and the reluctance of the ECJ to intervene where inter-institutional agreement is possible, have maintained this state of affairs. Two factors suggest that this is set to change and that the issues of competence and enforcement will soon become the subject of greater judicial scrutiny.

First, the proliferation, increasing complexity and greater domestic impact of environmental agreements suggest that new agreements are likely to create rights more appropriate to direct enforcement or more likely to prejudice individuals. As a result, and despite political controversy, the Commission may well be encouraged to take enforcement action in respect of international obligations. Even in the absence of a will to enforce, there is room for individuals to refer questions to the ECJ concerning international agreements and the issues of EU participation and responsibility for them.[57]

Second, in the aftermath of the coming into force of the Maastricht Treaty, the profusion of legal bases for internal and external action under Articles 130s and

228 of the Treaty of Rome, each encapsulating a different political balance, legislative procedure and voting mechanism, will encourage increased recourse to the ECJ by member states and EU institutions alike.[58] Delays in authorization and ratification of international environmental agreements will continue as a result of the confusing definitions of EU voting mechanisms in the environmental area. The vague drafting of Article 130s gives ample ground to argue for the retention of unanimous rather than majority voting in the Council in many cases. However, the Commission and the European Parliament, whatever disagreements they may have over the ill-defined dividing line between the new Cooperation Procedures and Codecision procedures, will have a common interest in the adoption of majority voting.

The enforcement mechanisms laid out in the Treaty of Rome have severe limitations. EU law is enforced by the ECJ through a series of procedures designed to ensure its application by national courts and administrations, rather than by any central EU administrative system. Direct enforcement by the EU has so far occurred only in the area of competition policy, where there are direct investigations and the Commission may impose fines. In most other policy areas the EU must rely on member state enforcement mechanisms and the Commission's limited powers under Article 155 of the Treaty of Rome. The lack of direct enforcement powers undermines the effectiveness of EU environmental law.[59] Common environmental legislation currently provides at best the impetus to rationalism in enforcement. Equal application of EU law, however, requires more, including a common or minimum standard in respect of procedural and evidential rules.[60]

The continuing complexities caused by shared competencies, the proliferation of different legal bases within the Treaty for the conclusion of international agreements, and the increasing interrelationship of trade and environmental issues, has been confirmed by the recent decision of the European Court concerning the Uruguay Round Agreements. In the Uruguay Round Treaties,[61] the Court, while acknowledging that the Community had exclusive competence to conclude the GATT 95 agreement, held that only certain elements of the GATS and TRIPs agreements fell within the exclusivity described by Article 113. The Decision suggests that, despite the concern expressed in some quarters that environmental agreements with trade implications may undermine the external unity of the Community if adopted pursuant to another basis, it cannot be automatically assumed that such agreements fall within an expansive legal interpretation of this policy.[62] The Court has sent a clear signal that the early tendency towards an expansive definition of exclusive competencies is at an end, and that it cannot be expected to resolve all the inherent contradictions now implicit in the present structure of the Treaty.

External policy and its relationship to the internal division of powers is not high on the EU agenda perhaps, but the forthcoming review of the Treaty of Rome in 1996 presents an opportunity to the member states to simplify and clarify it without recourse to the ECJ. If the EU is truly dedicated to the rule of law and a constitutional system of governance, this clarification is essential. Even if only on grounds of efficiency, the system requires some clear thought and clear expression. The paradox of EU participation in external relations is that it can at times hamper rather than promote a strong and unified line on many matters.

7 A CASE STUDY OF A REGIONAL APPROACH TO COMPLIANCE WITH CITES IN SOUTHERN AFRICA

Farhana Yamin and Annabella L Gualdoni

INTRODUCTION

To a great extent our countries depend on natural resources of which wildlife is a main element. In turn, our wildlife ultimately depends on our ability to secure its future through effective law enforcement. Only then will we be able to achieve the sustainable development vital to raise our countries from poverty.

Moses Okua, Uganda's Commissioner for Wildlife and Chairman of the Lusaka Agreement Expert Group meeting.[1]

The Lusaka Agreement emerged from the 1992 African Wildlife Enforcement Cooperation Conference convened by the Zambian Ministry of Tourism with the support of a number of non-governmental organizations (NGOs) interested in promoting increased compliance of the Convention on International Trade in Endangered Species of Wild Fauna and Flora (CITES).[2] At the Conference, law enforcement officials from eight southern African countries expressed their grave concern that existing international and national legal mechanisms were inadequate to halt the exploitation of fauna and flora in their region.[3] Accordingly, they recommended the establishment of new arrangements to supplement, and support, increased compliance with CITES.[4] This chapter examines one of their key recommendations – the negotiation of a regional agreement (the Lusaka Agreement) which aims to establish a regional Task Force to investigate criminal networks operating across African national borders – and the potential impact this Agreement might have in securing increased compliance with CITES.

By way of background, this chapter examines the overall structure of CITES and the compliance responses by different southern African countries. The chapter then reviews some of the specific impediments to increased compliance with CITES and the resulting need for new legal mechanisms to promote compliance. The third part of the chapter describes the negotiating history of the Lusaka Agreement as this negotiating process itself makes an important contribution to increased compliance. The important roles NGOs and international institutions play in developing new mechanisms and international agreements to facilitate compliance is highlighted. The current draft provisions of the Lusaka Agreement are discussed in the light of their potential contribution to increasing compliance with CITES.[5] See Chapter 8 of this volume for Xinxia Wang's discussion of the challenges associated with implementing CITES in China. The conclusion assesses the merits of the Lusaka Agreement to increasing compliance with CITES as well as the contribution regional approaches might make to increasing compliance with other environmental conventions.

THE CITES BACKGROUND

This section provides an overview of the main elements of CITES' compliance system in terms of its primary rules, compliance information systems and noncompliance response systems.[6] It highlights some of the strengths and weaknesses of CITES compliance system in the light of actual CITES implementation by southern African countries and their efforts to improve compliance.

CITES primary rules

A treaty's primary rule system consist of the actors, rules and processes related to the behaviour targeted by the treaty.[7] CITES seeks to protect biodiversity through the regulation of international trade in endangered animals and plants or their products.[8] Its primary rules address the activities of actors engaged in such trade rather than focusing on processes which, if regulated, could also have a positive impact on wildlife conservation, such as sustainable management, habitat destruction or the establishment of protected areas.[9]

The main primary rules of CITES provide for the listing of species in different annexes according to the extent to which they are threatened.[10] Once listed under CITES annexes, trade in regulated species becomes subject to the CITES' permit system which is under the control of the national Management and Scientific Authorities which CITES requires its Parties to establish.[11] It should be noted however, that while CITES provisions specify the functions these Authorities must undertake, CITES does not provide details as to their administrative and institutional form. Finally, the Convention contains a general provision requiring Parties to take appropriate measures to enforce its provisions, including measures 'to penalize trade in, or possession of, CITES regulated specimens'.[12] This could include the use of trade sanctions and the use of criminal proceedings.

CITES compliance information system

Compliance information systems consist of the actors, rules and processes that collect, analyze and disseminate information on violation and compliance.[13] CITES was one of the first environmental treaties to provide for sophisticated information gathering, reporting and international monitoring provisions.[14] Parties are required to submit annual reports to the CITES Secretariat on the amounts of trade conducted in listed species and their overall implementation of CITES. These reports provide valuable information to help identify sources of illegal trade and monitor compliance levels.[15] CITES' monitoring and reporting requirements make Parties' actions more transparent and are useful because a Party may prefer to comply than to have to report that it has done nothing, therefore risking negative public opinion.[16] Although it represents the stick, rather than the carrot, approach to compliance, the threat of negative public opinion can induce a Party to comply.[17] Monitoring can also reduce the fears of complying states that other countries will become free-riders.[18]

In addition to Parties' reports, CITES involves a range of actors in information gathering and monitoring. For example, the CITES Secretariat in Geneva is charged with monitoring implementation and compliance with the Convention and overseeing the permit system on an international level.[19] It also acts as an intermediary between exporting and importing states, for example, to verify the authenticity of trade documents and provides Parties to the Convention with information on persons suspected of being involved in illegal wildlife trade. The Secretariat also conducts implementation training seminars throughout the world and sends Parties updated information on national legislation.[20]

NGOs have also played an important role in improving compliance of CITES provisions.[21] For example, by allowing NGOs to attend the Conference of the Parties and informally present information about CITES implementation, CITES has been very successful in eliciting higher degrees of compliance than might otherwise have been the case.[22]

CITES non-compliance response system

Non-compliance response systems describe the actors, rules and processes governing the formal and informal responses available to induce non-complyers to comply. They determine the type, likelihood, magnitude and appropriateness of responses to non-compliance which can consist of positive inducements (eg financial), sanctions and preventative measures.[23]

Regular meetings of the Parties advance compliance with a treaty because they constantly remind the signatories of their treaty obligations and enable them to take appropriate action as circumstances change.[24] CITES Conferences of the Parties are held every two years in order to review implementation of CITES and to make recommendations for improving its effectiveness. In order to ensure responsiveness to the changing conditions of wildlife, each party has the right to propose amendments to Appendix I or II. Passage requires a two-thirds majority vote of parties present at a meeting of the Conference of Parties. Amendment of Appendix III can take place unilaterally simply by notifying the Secretariat.[25]

The Conferences have played a critical role in addressing some of CITES' shortcomings and promoting increased compliance. For example, at the 1979 Conference in San José, Costa Rica, delegates from developing countries argued that CITES failed to recognize the perspectives of developing countries by not taking into account the need to secure economic benefit to developing countries to justify the high costs of habitat protection. These concerns gave way to adoption of Conference Resolution 3.15 at the New Delhi Conference in 1981. That resolution provides for the downlisting of certain Appendix I populations for the purpose of sustainable resource management.[26]

More recently, the 28th and 29th CITES Standing Committee Meetings in June 1992 and March 1993 called for the destruction of rhino horn stockpiles and urged all Parties to CITES to implement previous CITES resolutions in this respect.[27] The government of China was specifically urged to take action to stop trade in rhino horn or face trade sanctions on wildlife products. After examining actions undertaken by various governments and deciding that measures taken by China and Taiwan were not adequate and had failed to comply with previous CITES resolutions, the 30th Meeting of the Standing Committee in September 1993 decided to recommend that Parties to CITES should consider banning all trade in wildlife species with China and Taiwan.[28] This decision was taken despite the fact that CITES does not expressly mention enforcement provisions in the form of trade sanctions. The Standing Committee's actions illustrate the dynamic, evolutionary nature of CITES and in particular the important role its institutions now play in promoting increased enforcement and compliance.[29]

Compliance with CITES in Southern Africa

Treaties may codify existing behaviour or else require new action.[30] The implementation of CITES in Africa has often been a combination of both. The implementation of CITES provisions, through amendments to pre-existing legislation or in some cases new legislation, illustrates this.[31]

Malawi, for instance, did not expressly include CITES regulations in its national legislation until the passage of the National Parks and Wildlife Act of 1992, which repealed its 1954 Game Act.[32] However, the present Act, through its institution of progressive wildlife impact assessments, actually goes farther than CITES requirements in seeking to balance international trade with domestic management.[33] Swaziland has also amended its domestic laws since its acceptance of CITES through the 1991 Amendment to the Game Act.[34] Uganda did not accede to CITES until 1991, and it did not simultaneously enact new national legislation to reflect its accession to the international treaty.[35] Zimbabwe, on the other hand, timed its accession to CITES in 1981 with the enactment of its Control of Goods (Import and Export) (Wild Life) Regulations. In 1990 other regulations relating specifically to the registration of ivory and horn were included in the Parks and Wildlife (General) Regulations.[36]

Although the above southern African countries have each responded differently to CITES, by placing restrictions on international trade in endangered species, all of these countries can be said to have complied with the majority of substantive primary rules contained in CITES. The overall effectiveness of their compliance efforts depends, however, on the way in which they have implemented the specific structural elements called for by CITES, such as the establishment of administrative institutions to oversee permit systems and legal mechanisms to enforce CITES' relevant national legislation.

It also depends on the extent to which Parties have complied with subsequent resolutions adopted by the Conference of the Parties. The differences in approach to complying with further CITES resolutions as well as differences in the way in which administrative and legal mechanisms operate has hampered more effective compliance with CITES. These differences illustrate some of the weaknesses CITES suffers from in eliciting more effective compliance and explain why some southern African countries consider further cooperative efforts a priority.

Factors impeding increased compliance

Lack of specific primary rules

Permit systems are CITES' basic means to control international trade. The countries related to the Lusaka Agreement each have their own permit systems, but these are not comprehensive and at times are inconsistent with CITES requirements.[37] These inconsistencies and loopholes reveal a weakness in CITES primary rules in that these do not provide sufficient details for the operation of the permit system. The failure to be more specific has meant Parties have a wider discretion to interpret and implement their own permit systems.

Kenya, for example, has a problematic permit system for goods in transit through its territory, which allows a seller to detain a shipment in Kenya if that shipment originated in another country. Permission for re-export is not required, which creates a situation with much potential for abuse.[38] Zambia's 1982 National Parks and Wildlife Act (Elephant and Rhinoceros) Regulations prohibit trade or hunting of these species, cancel all licences issued for their hunting, and prohibit the issuance of new trophy permits. While the regulations are consistent with CITES, a department of the government may still obtain authorization to export raw ivory: this is a gaping loophole.[39] South African law fails to state whether CITES criteria for issuing import permits should apply. Domestic law requires permits to hunt wild animals, and it specifically prohibits the export of CITES Appendix II animals. However, the law also allows any landowner who is granted a certificate of 'adequate enclosure' to hunt, at any time, a specified number of protected species within the area. The owner may also permit others to hunt on his land.[40]

Lack of administrative capacity and technical resources

CITES administrative mechanisms are important because they facilitate communication between Parties and assist in the systematic development of wildlife policy and law. However, lack of administrative capacity and technical resources have seriously hampered effective compliance in southern Africa.[41]

The sheer size and fluidity of the borders between many African countries makes cross-border smuggling an attractive route for poached animal trophies. Tanzania's Selous Game Reserve alone is the size of Scotland.[42] Its large, open sea-board on its eastern boundary is guarded by only a few, ill-equipped wildlife technicians, thereby facilitating illegal border crossings.[43] Law enforcement agencies require more helicopters to conduct surveillance and field patrols more efficiently, and technicians need training in special undercover intelligence operations.[44]

In addition to technical resources, many southern African countries lack administrative capacity to respond effectively to sophisticated, well resourced cross-border smugglers. For example, even the collection and collation of information about known smugglers presents problems because of a continued lack of equipment such as computers.[45] Often proper coordination between relevant CITES management authorities and enforcement officials is lacking. A member of the Kenya Wildlife Service notes that his country, and others like it, lack cooperation between different local law enforcement agencies, eg police, customs, and wildlife services. The various departments treat each other with suspicion, which makes the flow of information between them difficult.[46]

The failure of domestic entities to cooperate effectively on a national level is duplicated at interstate level where there is a lack of cross-border relationships with law enforcement agencies in neighbouring countries.[47] Insufficient cooperation between domestic law enforcement officers and their colleagues in neighbouring countries to prevent illegal trade must also be seen against the background of abundant cooperation between international crime syndicates. Often these syndicates receive considerable support from local communities of common tribes on both sides of the borders, who give sanctuary to each other after committing acts of poaching and smuggling. For example, the people of the Saboat/Sebei, Masai and Somalis tribes in Kenya are assisted by their fellow tribesmen in Uganda, Tanzania and Somalia, and vice-versa.[48]

Unfortunately, unlike more recent conventions such as the UNEP's 1992 Convention on Biological Diversity, CITES does not provide for a financial mechanism to assist Parties to invest in technical resources or capacity building to address some of these problems and thus increase compliance.

Legal impediments

Colonel O B Tiroyamodimo of the Botswana Defence Force describes how some of the largest elephant herds are found within his country's international borders in areas which have little or no human presence which means that criminals' movements cannot be detected.[49] Rhinos face similar problems, and both animals are often shot from across the border during the dry season when they come to the river for water. These simple geographical facts present a number of additional legal challenges to the successful apprehension and conviction of those involved in illegal CITES trade.

Zambia's National Parks and Wildlife Service notes that most of its violations involve aliens.[50] It is legally difficult, however, to cross into a neighbouring country while in hot pursuit without risking infringement of sovereignty.[51] Since the enforcement powers of officers are restricted to their own jurisdiction, they are effectively powerless abroad – again making interstate cooperation critical for all actions concerning apprehension of suspects.

It is difficult to institute legal proceedings against known poachers once they return to their home countries, due to the absence of binding extradition agreements in poaching and smuggling cases. Where extradition is successful, rules of evidence concerning the gathering and presentation of information differ from country to country thus assisting defendants to avoid prosecution on technical grounds.[52] To counter-balance this, Swaziland now allows a shift of the legal burden of proof onto those caught in possession of any elephant or rhinoceros trophies.[53] This does not, however, catch behind-the-scenes financiers who may never handle trophies but whose participation is critical to sophisticated international crime syndicates.

Successful prosecution often appears to be a waste of resources in view of the weakness of the penalties sometimes imposed. A game warden can earn more from the sale of contraband tusks than from one year's honest work,[54] and a tusk sold on the underground market can feed a poacher's family for several months.[55] Low criminal penalties obviously do not discourage or prevent someone from engaging in such a lucrative business. Although CITES provides that Parties should penalize unlawful trade, it gives no guidance as to what level of punishment should be imposed on those convicted of illegal trade or possession. The result is a wide range of varying penalties from one state to another which is unhelpful so far as controlling international trade is concerned.[56]

The lack of uniform levels of penalties is particularly relevant in the context of a CITES Appendix I listing. One perverse effect of this is that because some consumer demand remains, illegal trade becomes an extremely lucrative economic activity. Credible and effective deterrence involves increasing the severity of criminal penalties.[57] The CITES ban on ivory and rhino tusks has necessitated an almost constant revision of African countries' criminal laws thus adding to existing administrative strains, and social pressures.

For example, Swaziland has already increased its maximum penalties to what its own Royal Adviser on Nature Conservation calls 'draconian anti-poaching measures'. The mandatory prison sentence in Swaziland is five to 15 years, with no option of a fine.[58] Those penalties were enacted in response to continual court failure to handle poaching cases responsibly. The government emphasizes that it wants its measures to be preventative rather than curative, and so far there has indeed been a marked decrease in the poaching rate since the enactment of the new law and a publicity campaign.[59] Botswana's Parliament is reviewing bills which would create tougher laws by increasing jail sentences and fines for killing elephants and rhinos to 10–15 years and US$25,000–50,000 respectively.[60] In Uganda, on the other hand, the maximum penalty for unlawful possession or trading in ivory or rhino horn is only a maximum one year prison sentence and/or a fine.[61]

Despite these increased fines and penalties, the economic incentive for illegal trade remains so high that some countries have considered that other, even more draconian, measures are justified. For example, Dr Richard Leakey, the controversial former director of the Kenya Wildlife Services, instituted a drastic, but effective, 'shoot-to-kill' anti-poaching policy in that country's game parks. Leakey's efforts were praised internationally by many and increased Kenya's elephant and rhino populations, and its earnings from tourism and the amount of aid from international donors, but were not always domestically popular.[62]

Understandably, the lack of hostility from local communities has made it impossible to use such measures successfully on a long-term basis. Similarly, intensified military wildlife operation has brought a great decrease in poaching since its introduction in Tanzania in 1989–1990.[63] The military has also been used to curb smuggling in certain border areas in Zimbabwe and Botswana. However, the use of the military requires huge political and financial commitment. Again it cannot provide a lasting basis for increased domestic law enforcement to serve international conservation purposes.[64]

Political instability and armed conflict

Sometimes a Party may fail to comply with a treaty despite sincere intentions, the availability of funding and genuine efforts to achieve compliance.[65] Political instability can, for example, undermine the ruling government's efforts and have unexpected effects on wildlife conservation.

Dr Madope from Mozambique has described how the guerilla war in his country has devastated natural resources and facilitated cross-border incursions by poachers into game reserves and other areas.[66] Weapons from the war in Mozambique have made their way into Swaziland, where poachers have used them to decrease that country's rhino population seriously.[67] Poaching has also provided a source of revenue for guerilla movements. Jonas Savimbi's UNITA, which is supported by the US, has reportedly killed 100,000 elephants to finance its war against the government of Angola.[68] Likewise, after their battles with UN troops, Somalian gangs have been reported to cross Kenya's lightly-guarded borders to hunt elephant in Kenya. The ivory is brought back to Somalia for sale to international smugglers and to UN troops keen on purchasing ivory jewellery and trinkets![69]

The impacts of economic insecurity and military conflicts on a country's compliance efforts are enormous. The importance of increasing long-term political stability and economic prosperity should not therefore be overlooked in designing new mechanisms for increased compliance for existing or new environmental conventions.

Lack of financial resources

The preceding discussion serves to highlight two key shortcomings in CITES. First, its lack of a financial mechanism to assist Parties, particularly developing country Parties, to improve compliance, and second, its failure to provide a comprehensive framework which gives financial incentives to Parties, and individuals, to engage positively in long-term wildlife conservation.

The lack of financial resources is critical. As discussed above, some countries simply do not have the resources to meet the costs of law enforcement and increased CITES compliance. Southern African countries are barely able to meet payment of salaries and wages, let alone equipment, materials, transport, and other essentials.[70] Increased budgets for wildlife preservation are limited, especially in the face of other, more pressing development needs. Furthermore, the full economic cost of maintaining biodiversity is high. President Ali Hassan Mwinyi of Tanzania summed up the feelings of many in suggesting:

> that [Tanzania] has a rich wildlife resource is an accident of geography. It belongs to all mankind. The international community should therefore contribute to its survival.

It could take an estimated US$100 million or more a year in aid to compensate for lost revenue from trade in endangered species.[71] CITES does not provide funds of this kind. For these reasons, support amongst government officials and the public for additional resources to allow greater compliance with CITES is low.[72]

African countries would be more likely to comply with measures that consider their economic interests and where costs do not outweigh benefits. Sustainable trade in wildlife products and tourism are some of the possible activities that could raise funds and resolve some of the tensions between developmental needs and conservation goals that CITES currently faces. These activities could provide a source of revenue for conservation programmes and act as an incentive to avoid converting a habitat that has proved to be otherwise economically valuable.[73]

Specific suggestions have come from a number of countries, including Zimbabwe and South Africa, who want to have a legal trade in the rhino horns which they cut from live rhinos to save them from the poachers.[74] Another suggestion is that elephant products should again be traded along the guidelines of CITES' Appendix II, rather than its current status under Appendix I, in a managed trade. This would permit the sales of confiscated ivory, ivory from elephants which die a 'natural death,' and from culling operations for herd control, and the proceeds could be used for conservation projects.[75] For example, Zimbabwe used to acquire wildlife funds from the sale of elephant tusks, hides, and meat taken from culling operations. Since the ivory ban the National Parks and Wildlife Service has lost that source of income, and it has not been replaced by any additional funds.

Disagreements about the merits of the 'sustainable management' approach *vis à vis* the merits of maintaining trade bans for endangered species have been discussed by the CITES Conference of the Parties.[76] These discussions parallel those taking place in the context of the International Whaling Commission and the merits of continuing the ban on commercial whaling.[77] At present those in favour of continuing complete trade bans in ivory and rhino horn appear to have sufficient support at the CITES Conference of Parties.

To the extent that these particular trade bans are successful in supporting conservation, they will increase long-term pressure for trade to occur or else reopen discussions on the need to provide a comprehensive financial mechanism within CITES, to assist compliance efforts and to compensate countries compelled to forego economic opportunities.

AFRICA'S NEED FOR MORE COOPERATION: THE LUSAKA AGREEMENT

> 'Is cooperation among poachers and smugglers better in breaking the law than cooperation among law enforcement agencies in keeping it?'
>
> Lt General C S Tembo, Zambia's Minister of Tourism.[78]

Lieutenant General Tembo's opening remarks to the First African Wildlife Enforcement Cooperation Conference make clear that unilateral compliance efforts by southern African countries have met with limited success in eliminating illegal wildlife trade. Strengthening CITES requires greater cooperation amongst Parties' law enforcement agencies.[79] Increased cooperation, and increased compliance require an improved legal framework and additional financial and technical resource flows. It is the recognition that the adoption of a regional agreement might facilitate greater cooperation and increase financial and technical resource flows that has led to the negotiation of the Lusaka Agreement.

The following section describes the Lusaka Agreement's negotiating history, highlighting the important role that NGOs and international organizations have played in developing new mechanisms to increase compliance with international agreements. The provisions of the current negotiating text of the Lusaka Agreement, attached as Appendix I, are discussed in the light of their potential contribution to increasing compliance with CITES. The general merits of a regional approach in relation to strengthening compliance in the context of other environmental treaties are also touched upon.

Negotiating history

First African Wildlife Law Enforcement Cooperation Conference

The Lusaka Agreement originated from the recommendations of senior wildlife law enforcement officers from eight African countries at the first African Wildlife

Law Enforcement Cooperation Conference on 9–11 December 1992 in Lusaka, Zambia. This Conference, held under the auspices of the Zambian Ministry of Tourism, was sponsored by two UK-based NGOs – Tusk Force and the Environmental Investigation Agency (EIA) – with additional financial assistance from David Shepherd Conservation Foundation. All three organizations have considerable expertise of CITES illegal trade, gained in some instances through their own extensive undercover investigative work funded by members.

Zambia's Ministry of Tourism recognized that its own wildlife service needed support and additional resources to make its operations more effective and to rehabilitate Zambia's wildlife parks and game management areas.[80] It was aware, however, that it did not exist in a vacuum from its neighbouring countries and it would require a group effort to stop poaching and smuggling within its own borders. Conscious of the important and positive role that NGOs, such as Tusk Force and the EIA, have played in facilitating compliance, the Ministry requested their assistance when the new Zambian government came into power. The subsequent role these NGOs played in supporting the Conference illustrates the powerful role NGOs can play in eliciting compliance with international agreements.[81]

The Conference was attended by law enforcement officials from the national parks, police, customs and army departments of eight east and southern African countries (Botswana, Kenya, Mozambique, Tanzania, South Africa, Swaziland, Zambia and Uganda), as well as representatives from CITES, INTERPOL, the US Fish and Wildlife Service (US FWS), the UK Overseas Development Agency (ODA) and the Foundation for International Environmental Law and Development (FIELD).[82]

Situation reports were given by officers from each country at the outset outlining the many problems they faced in their anti-poaching and smuggling activities, and some of the steps they have already taken to combat crime.[83] Three specialist working groups considered problems relating to investigations, cross-border poaching and customs and made specific recommendations in respect of these.[84] Presentations were made by the CITES Secretariat and Interpol providing useful information about how their international organizations might assist national law enforcement officers.[85] In addition, a presentation from FIELD outlined some of the legal loopholes and shortcomings of these countries' legislation concerning CITES implementation.[86]

Conference recommendations

Participants agreed improving detection of CITES violations was a high priority in the short term to deter CITES infractions and thereby increase compliance.[87] It was further agreed unanimously that law enforcement officers would be powerless to act against international crime networks until there was a legal framework enabling cross-border liaison and investigations.

The central feature of such a legal framework should be the establishment of a small, permanent organization ('the Task Force') whose function would be to collect, coordinate and disseminate information to assist investigation and prosecution of cross-border networks engaged in illegal trade.[88] A draft text of an international agreement incorporating these suggestions was drawn up to assist follow-up consultations.[89]

In January 1993, Lt Gen Tembo on behalf of the Zambian Ministry of Tourism approved the concept of the Lusaka Agreement. Working closely with the support of the Ministry, the sponsoring NGOs continued to support the Agreement by providing financial and administrative assistance. The CITES Secretariat also provided assistance by refining the Initial Negotiating Text and, perhaps more importantly, by bringing the Draft Agreement to the attention of the CITES Standing Committee which endorsed the agreement in principle.[90]

Intergovernmental negotiations

Another meeting of the Lusaka Conference participants was held immediately prior to the United Nations Environment Programme (UNEP) Conference on Financing Conservation of the Rhinoceros in Nairobi, Kenya in July 1993. At the request of the Zambian government UNEP's legal department was invited to attend the meeting to provide its legal and negotiating expertise to develop the text. The July meeting resulted in a much improved text which was widely circulated to participants at the UNEP Rhinoceros Conference.[91]

Following the July meeting, UNEP accepted Zambia's invitation to facilitate further development of the Agreement by providing not only legal expertise but also an interim Secretariat and financial resources to organize official intergovernmental negotiations.[92] Until this point in time, the sponsoring NGOs, the Zambian government and individual participants had borne the organizational and financial burden of previous meetings.[93]

UNEP's legal, administrative and financial support made an important contribution to the development of the Lusaka Agreement and illustrates the critical role international institutions can play in fostering greater compliance. For example, as a result of UNEP's official invitation to the eight governments initially concerned with the Lusaka Agreement to submit comments on the Second Draft at the end of 1993, senior officials from the foreign ministries and legal departments of each of these countries became involved in the Lusaka Agreement.[94] Until then attendance had been largely limited to law enforcement officers. Thus the negotiation process itself encouraged cooperation and information sharing between different government departments – one of the objectives of the Agreement!

UNEP's status as an intergovernmental and expert environmental organ encouraged greater participation in the Lusaka Agreement negotiation process in at least two important respects. First, Lesotho, Malawi, Namibia, and Zimbabwe, who had not participated in earlier meetings, partly due to political differences and partly due to their apprehension about the involvement of NGOs in the process, were formally invited by UNEP to attend UNEP's First Expert Group Meeting on the Lusaka Agreement held at UNEP headquarters in March 1994.[95] The fact that the invitations were sent by a neutral, 'official' UN body, rather than a particular government or supported by 'meddlesome' NGOs, may have played an important role in overcoming reservations by Lesotho, Malawi and Zimbabwe as all attended UNEP's First Expert Group Meeting on the Lusaka Agreement.[96]

The wider participation of countries within southern Africa was supplemented by the presence of the international donor community. UNEP invitations to the donor community has encouraged participation from this important constituency at an early stage.[97] Donor interest and financial support will be critical to the long-term success of the Lusaka Agreement.

Donor presence and support, as well as the anticipation of the CITES Conference of the Parties in November 1994, may even have been one of the reasons which motivated southern African countries to bring the negotiations to a successful conclusion by adopting the Lusaka Final Act.[98]

Main provisions of the Lusaka Agreement

The objective of the Revised Initial Negotiating Text of the Lusaka Agreement, set out in Article 3, is 'to reduce and ultimately eliminate illegal trade in wild fauna and flora and to establish a permanent Task Force for this purpose'.[99] The Revised Initial Negotiating Text of Lusaka Agreement provides the legal basis to set up a centrally located, multinational Task Force of African wildlife law enforcement officers.[100] The following sections provide an explanation of some of the key features of the Agreement.

The Preamble and definitions

The Preamble deliberately refers to the provisions of the 1968 African Convention on the Conservation of Nature and Natural Resources, CITES, and the 1992 Convention on Biological Diversity.[101] This provision is intended to make clear that the Lusaka Agreement is to be seen in the context of these existing conventions and not as a replacement.

References in the Preamble to poaching remain bracketed because it is not yet clear whether the Lusaka Agreement is intended to cover poaching as well as illegal trade. Article 2 (g) defines illegal trade as 'any cross-border transaction, or any action in furtherance thereof in violation of national laws of a Party to this Agreement for the protection of wild fauna and flora'. Poaching does not always have a cross-border or a trade-related element. Some countries fear that in the event of a dispute about the Task Force's legal competence, the inclusion of the words 'poaching' in the Preamble could strengthen the case for allowing the Task Force to investigate essentially domestic and non-trade related infractions of a Party's national legislation.

Geographical scope

Article 1 makes clear that the Agreement will only apply to areas under the national jurisdiction of its Parties. This reflects a concern to keep the Agreement a regional one. Parties' obligations cover those activities under their direct control, rather than, for example, focusing on activities that might reduce demand for illegal wildlife products in countries such as China or Taiwan.

The Task Force

Functions

The establishment of a Task Force to investigate international smuggling and cross-border wildlife and plant poaching lies at the heart of the Lusaka Agreement. This Task Force's functions are defined in Article 5. The main purpose of the Task Force is to facilitate cooperative activities between national law enforcement offices to carry out investigations. The Task Force may also investigate violations of Parties' national laws for the protection of wildlife and flora and present evidence gathered during such investigations to the proper national authorities for prosecution.[102] It also will assist the relevant national authorities to carry out investigations and help return confiscated wild fauna and flora to the state of origin. To this end, Parties are required to designate an existing national wildlife law enforcement agency, or 'National Bureau,' to be responsible for liaison with the Task Force.[103]

To fulfil these functions the Task Force is intended to establish and maintain centralized databases containing information on activities that pertain to illegal trade.[104] The Task Force would investigate people and organizations involved in illegal trade throughout the territories of the Parties, notably syndicates and networks now in operation which sustain poaching to supply such trade.[105] The main objective should be to apprehend entire networks, rather than just individuals.

Parties are also obliged to cooperate with each other and the Task Force, to provide it with relevant information, technical assistance and scientific data relating to illegal trade.[106] Parties are obliged, however, to maintain the confidentiality of any classified information and to use such information only for the purposes of implementing the Agreement.[107] This provision is intended to ensure that information is not misused for political or other unrelated purposes. Parties may also utilize suitable intergovernmental, nongovernmental, international or national agencies and bodies in information collection or other tasks.[108] Some countries have expressed concerns about the role NGOs might play in this regard and as a result this portion of the Negotiating Text remains in brackets.

Composition

The Task Force is intended to be a permanent, independent entity possessing international legal personality.[109] Within its territory, each Party is obliged to recognize the legal capacity of the Task Force and to grant it and its Officials such privileges and immunities as are necessary to perform its functions and to meet the goals of the Agreement.[110]

It is to be made up of a Director, Field Officers and an Intelligence Officer.[111] A 'Field Officer' means a member of a government organization, department or institution, who is employed as a law enforcement officer with national law enforcement jurisdiction and is seconded to the Task Force. The Director is intended to be chosen from among the Field Officers to act as the Chief Executive Officer of the Task Force.[112] The role of the intelligence officer has not been defined in the current text.

Accountability

During negotiations one of the most important issues about the Task Force concerned is how an independent, international organization with legal capacity to investigate violations of national laws could remain accountable to its Parties whilst at the same time maintaining its integrity. Notwithstanding their desire to cooperate to enhance compliance with CITES, southern African countries negotiating the Lusaka Agreement were concerned about sovereignty and the risk of an 'outside', international body investigating and prosecuting their nationals.

The existing negotiating text strives to balance the Task Force's independence with accountability in a number of ways. For example, the Task Force is ultimately accountable to the governing council, established by Article 6, which is responsible for deciding the general policies of the Task Force and for approving the appointment of its officer.[113] In addition, to protect their individual independence, in particular from political interference, all officers are to be given fixed terms approved by the governing council. Finally, each Party will send at least one Officer from its national bureau to serve with the Task Force. This seconded structure of the Task Force is intended not only to facilitate closer cooperation between National Bureaux and the Task Force but also to ensure that each Party has a means of keeping check on the Task Force's activities.[114]

Funding

The funding provisions for the Task Force are set out in Article 8. The governing council is given powers to 'determine the payment and currencies of contributions by the Parties to the budget of the Task Force'.[115] Parties are obliged to pay annually their agreed contributions to the budget in accordance with the schedule determined by the governing council.[116]

The financial provisions state that '[o]ther resources of the Task Force may include such extra budgetary resources as grants, donations, funds for projects and programmes and technical assistance'.[117] These would, however, be subject to the overall decision-making of the governing council which is composed only of Parties to the Agreement.

Legally, and at the level of political representation, donor interests do not appear to have decision-making powers over the expenditure of funds. This can be contrasted with the financial provisions of the 1992 UN Framework Convention on Climate Change and the Convention on Biological Diversity. These Conventions provide that financial priorities, programmes and eligibility criteria must be determined by their respective Conference of the Parties which obviously includes donor Parties. Convention-related funding decisions must be executed by the Global Environment Facility (GEF) providing an additional layer of complication in terms of donor control.[118] By keeping decision-making powers in the hands of the governing council, the present negotiating text of the Lusaka Agreement appears to avoid the risk of donor interference or donor-led conservation projects. The simplicity of these arrangements is clearly attractive for future Parties to the Lusaka Agreement. It remains to be seen, however, whether the lack of a formal decision-making role will deter donors from supporting the Lusaka Agreement.[119]

THE MERITS OF A REGIONAL APPROACH

Mitchell argues that regional agreements are one type of non-compliance response system, a mechanism which tries to respond to and correct previous non-compliance with a treaty.[120] Regional agreements focusing on how enforcement, like the Lusaka Agreement, may be particularly well-suited to increasing compliance for the following reasons.

Common interests

Similarities in a region increase the number of common interests. This facilitates compliance because states are more likely to comply themselves when they know others are complying as well.[121] A regional approach, with only limited numbers of players, allows each state to assess clearly the effect of noncompliance by its regional partners on its own compliance efforts. In the case of conservation involving extensive cross-border migration of wildlife, each state becomes aware very quickly of the effects a neighbouring state's action (or lack of action) has on its own wildlife.

Specific cooperation

Knowledge of neighbouring states' common interests and of the consequences of their actions allows detailed discussion about the nature of future joint actions. The background papers for the Lusaka Agreement are full of specific, practical suggestions for improved cooperation. These include local cooperation at the warden and ranger levels,[122] as well as between various law enforcement agencies in respect of joint operations at airports, border checks, and other areas.[123] A regional approach is more conducive to the development of detailed recommendations which can be seen as primary rules. This can be contrasted with the rather vague recommendations developed in other global instruments such as Agenda 21 or the recently adopted UN Programme of Action for Small Islands Developing states.

Existing cooperation processes within a region assist the development of trust and allow Parties to test, on a pilot basis, the success of a particular approach. Current examples of regional cooperation in the area of wildlife conservation have greatly facilitated the negotiations of the Lusaka Agreement. For example, Mozambique tries to train its game scouts in cooperation with the Kangwane Formation Centre in South Africa.[124] The Botswana Defence Force Anti-poaching team notes that its success has been facilitated by its relationship with the Namibia Nature Conservation and its recent friendship with the South African Police Endangered Species Protection Unit. Botswana is trying to establish a similar relationship with Zambian agencies.[125] The Zambian National Parks and Wildlife Service (NPWS) in fact has cooperated with law enforcement organizations in Zimbabwe, Botswana, and South Africa since 1990. This cooperation has led to increased monitoring and some successful arrests and convictions.[126] A regional agreement can build upon, and activate, further interaction between Parties, a factor which in itself generates increased cooperation and improves compliance over the long term.[127]

Increased enforcement

Mitchell rightly points out that Parties are often far more comfortable with allowing increased enforcement actions against their own nationals, than in allowing other Parties to take formal or informal enforcement proceedings against them.[128] This is particularly likely to be the case where a Party considers it has already come a substantial way in terms of implementing an international agreement into its own national legislation. Countries supporting the Lusaka Agreement have, to a large extent, implemented CITES into their national context. They consider the next most urgent step is to work together to remove international legal and financial barriers which otherwise constrain the enforcement capabilities of their national agencies.[129] In one sense, the entire Agreement can be seen as a non-compliance response system which seeks to reflect current wildlife conservation needs in Africa that have not been met by other international environmental agreements.

Increased funding

International funding for environmental purposes remains pitifully inadequate in the light of increasing environmental degradation and pollution.[130] Existing overseas development assistance (ODA) budgets are dwindling as developed countries are hit by economic recession, whilst competition for these funds remains intense as developmental pressures encourage developing countries to liquidate their environmental assets to meet short-term needs.

Lack of funding was cited as just one reason that efforts to establish coordination with neighbouring countries have faltered. In coming together to negotiate the Lusaka Agreement, law enforcement agencies were obviously hopeful to solicit funds from donor agencies and government to increase funding for enforcement efforts.[131] They were hopeful that a coordinated, regional approach to seeking funds, facilitated by the adoption of a legally binding agreement, might be more successful in securing funding than increased use of bilateral approaches.

One advantage of a regional agreement is that its objectives can be highly focused and its budgetary implications easily identified and quantified. Negotiators of the Lusaka Agreement talk to donors about increased funding to buy radios, patrol boats, or pay for charges for landing at air strips. They talk about the cost of attending wildlife enforcement courses for customs officials to teach identification of wildlife species, products, and by-products and procedures for participating in undercover operations.[132]

This avoids the kind of complex, circular and at times unnecessary acrimonious 'dialogue' taking place between developed and developing countries in the context of the GEF and how this will operate to meet developing countries funding needs under the Biodiversity and Climate Change Conventions.[133] Not only have these discussions divided countries, and NGOs, into opposing camps in complex international negotiations on how to interpret concepts such as 'incremental costs' or 'global environmental benefits'.[134] They have also resulted in literally millions of dollars of being spent on trying to find the 'right' approach to the identification and quantification of the costs and benefits of conservation measures as well as how to involve local communities in these decisions.[135]

One virtue of the Lusaka Agreement is that it avoids this highly-politicized and at times sterile international debate and focuses both donors and developing countries to adopt a pragmatic, flexible approach to funding needs. A regional approach to follow up specific aspects of the Biodiversity or the Climate Change Convention could draw upon the lessons of the Lusaka Agreement.

Increased participation

One of the biggest challenges for international law and international institutions is how to operationalize the environmental maxim 'think global, act local'.[136] There is widespread acceptance of the fact that citizens' involvement and local decision-making by those engaged in conservation (or in causing environmental pollution) is critical to the long-term success of any conservation strategy. Yet traditionally, international law and decision-making have been dominated by central government officials, especially from foreign ministries, who may have little specific knowledge about an environmental problem and may not articulate the concerns of local communities.[137]

The experience of the Lusaka Agreement illustrates that regional agreements may be more successful in increasing participation from a broader national constituency than global agreements. Although international bodies such as UNEP and the CITES Secretariat as well as 'northern' NGOs such as EIA and Tusk Force, played an important role in supporting the negotiations of the Agreement, the real impetus for the Agreement came from those involved in frontline conservation efforts in the developing countries – law enforcement officers from within Africa. Even the foreign ministries' involvement has come at a relatively late stage thus allowing technicians and the 'people involved on the ground' from the region to develop consensus recommendations without having to think continually about the wider political difficulties and repercussions.

This is far less likely to happen in the case of global agreements as international initiative usually comes from international institutions or developed countries. Moreover, because the initiatives are taken straight to the foreign ministries, much more time and effort has to be spent devising consultation procedures to involve the people themselves than would be needed if the initiative came from them in the first place.

CONCLUSION

African countries need to develop further legal norms and create new or existing institutional structures to overcome their identified problems. Allan Thornton of the Environmental Investigation Agency has expressed that the type of mutual cooperation and enforcement envisioned by the Lusaka Agreement is vital to the protection of endangered species.[138] The Lusaka Agreement is designed to overcome some of the legal and law enforcement problems which hinder increased compliance with CITES and thus assist more effective wildlife conservation and management.

However, if demand for wildlife products in both developing and developed countries were curbed, poachers and smugglers would no longer have a reason to violate CITES. It is difficult to put the burden of CITES compliance continually on poor, African farmers who have few economic options and certainly have no incentive to put global biodiversity concerns above their immediate subsistence needs. One limitation of the Lusaka Agreement is that it does not address the consumer 'demand side' of the conservation equation. The Lusaka Agreement illustrates that southern African countries are willing, to the extent that this is under their control, to improve compliance with their international obligations to safeguard their share of the world's heritage of wildlife and flora. It remains to be seen what efforts – global, regional or unilateral – donors or consumer states will take to educate consumer demand and thus support southern Africa's initiative.

8 THE IMPLEMENTATION OF CITES IN CHINA

*Wang Xinxia**

INTRODUCTION

The Convention of International Trade in Endangered Species of Wild Fauna and Flora (CITES) was adopted in March 1973 and entered into force in July 1975. Today, with 118 Parties, CITES has been recognized as one of the most important international conventions for the conservation of wildlife. Developments within the last few years concerning CITES have brought China – a Party to CITES since 1981 – to the centre of international attention. Controversy has arisen over China's use of animal parts for making handicrafts and as medicine. The old, long-kept cultural traditions on one hand, and China's commitments under CITES on the other, have been severely tested. This chapter addresses some aspects of implementation of CITES in China and touches upon some issues of wide discussion within CITES.

OBJECTIVES AND DECISION-MAKING MECHANISMS OF CITES

Objectives

Though not explicitly stipulated in the text of CITES, its principal objective is believed to be to ensure better conservation of endangered species of wildlife through regulating trade in them to prevent actual or threatened extinction.[1] The Convention contains three Appendices, which list endangered species of wild fauna and flora that may be affected by trade, and places different degrees of regulation on their trade. Appendix 1 includes species threatened with extinction and for which trade must be subject to particularly strict regulation

* The full text of this chapter previously appeared as an article in *RECIEL*, Vol. 2, Issue 4, FIELD, London 1993, and has not been updated by the author due to time constraints.

and only authorized in exceptional circumstances.[2] Appendix 2 lists species not necessarily now threatened with extinction, but which may become so unless trade is strictly regulated. It further contains so-called look-alike species which are controlled because of their similarity in appearance to the other regulated species, thereby facilitating more effective control.[3] Appendix 3 includes 'all species which any Party identifies as being subject to regulation within its jurisdiction for the purpose of preventing or restricting exploitation, and as needing the cooperation of other Parties in the control of trade'.[4]

Implementation mechanisms

The Conference of the Parties (COP), established pursuant to Article 11 of the Convention, is the highest decision-making body concerned with the implementation of CITES. It meets every two years to review the implementation of the Convention. As part of its review, the COP may consider the adoption of amendments to Appendices 1 and 2, review progress made towards the restoration and conservation of the species contained in those Appendices, and make recommendations to improve the effectiveness of the Convention.[5]

Another important implementing mechanism is the Standing Committee set up by Resolution 2.2 (1977). It is composed of six regional representatives, the depository government, the past host Party and the next host Party. According to the mandate described in the Resolution Conference 6.1 (1987), the Standing Committee provides general policy and general operational direction to the Secretariat concerning the implementation of CITES, carries out such interim activities on behalf of the COP as may be necessary, and acts as Bureau at meetings of the COP until the rule of procedures are adopted at the start of each meeting of the COP.[6] Although the Standing Committee is not legally described as a decision-making body, its wide and powerful mandate, given by the COP, means that the Standing Committee may, to a certain degree and within the scope of its competence, play the role of an interim COP.

Facilitator for China's wildlife protection law

Opening up to the outside world

Although the undertaking to protect wild animals in China started as early as the 1960s, it did not achieve development of any magnitude or significance until the 1980s. The accession by China to CITES – one of the earliest international legal instruments concerning wildlife that China has acceded to, has opened up and strengthened contacts and cooperation between Chinese wildlife conservation agencies and groups, and international conservation groups. The subsequent increasing involvement of China in CITES activities and the strong message sent by the international conservation movement to the Chinese as to how other people felt about conservation of wildlife, led the government to become more aware of domestic problems related to wildlife conservation and management, both in the CITES-regulated sphere and outside it. The necessity of a national conservation law to provide a legal basis and guidelines for the protection and management of wildlife, and to deter illegal overexploitation of natural resources, became apparent to decision-makers and law makers. These considerations led to the enactment of the Law of PRC for the Protection of Wild

Animals in 1988 (1988 Law). A few months later the Inventory of Key Wild Animals for State Protection (National Inventory) was adopted and published. This Inventory is similar to CITES Appendices, except that the National Inventory contains only those CITES-listed species native to China and has some differences in grades.

Effectiveness of the 1988 law in relation to CITES

The 1988 Law provides for two grades of protection and management of key, rare or endangered animals contained in the inventory. The law prohibits the hunting of wild animals of first and second grade without a special hunting permit, issued by the competent administrative department under the state council for first grade species and by the provincial governments for second grade species. There are no specific provisions in the law concerning CITES-listed species introduced or brought into the country and not, therefore, included in the national inventory. As a result domestic law is not applicable to those 'non-inventory' CITES species.

Consequence of non compliance under Chinese law

The 1988 Law provides for severe penalties for violation. Anyone who illegally catches or kills wild animals under state protection shall be prosecuted for criminal responsibility in accordance with the 1988 Amendment to the Criminal Code of China and may expect sentences of imprisonment for up to seven years.[7] For those found guilty of illegal trade, profiteering, and smuggling of state protected animals and products thereof, the sentences may range from ten years to the death penalty.[8] In 1988 two individuals responsible for killing, illegal selling and profiteering in giant panda were prosecuted and sentenced to death.

As mentioned earlier, however, the domestic law provided little help to those CITES-listed species which are missing from the inventory.

BRIDGING THE GAP BETWEEN CITES AND DOMESTIC LAW

In order to enforce CITES provisions better and narrow the gap between the international Convention and the relevant national law, the Regulation for the Protection of Terrestrial Wild Animals was adopted in 1992 (hereafter referred to as 1992 Law). For the first time in China this law stipulates that rare and endangered species of wildlife introduced or brought into the country from outside can be treated as key animals under state protection, subject to approval by the competent administrative department of forestry under the states council.[9] The Law thus establishes a link between CITES-regulated species and the species contained in the national inventory. In April 1993, the African Elephant, African Rhinoceros and several other kinds of animals (including any identifiable parts and derivatives) were approved by the Ministry of Forestry to be the key animals under state protection. Therefore these species now enjoy the same status of protection as those contained in the inventory of key wild animals for state protection. Those responsible for killing or profiteering in these species can expect penalties in accordance with the Criminal Code of China.

Challenges to old Asian traditions

Endangered species v. endangered culture

China has a long history of using ivory to make artware and animal parts such as rhino horn, tiger bone and bear gall bladder as medicine. However, since all those species are on CITES Appendix 1, trade in the animals and their products is prohibited. The trade ban has direct bearings on both the medicine manufacturers and the handicraft workers. It endangers the very existence of all these cultural traditions both in terms of unpredictable raw material supply and anticipated drastic decline in demand; and in view of strong sentiment of some of the range states, animal right advocates throughout the world as well as the opinion which currently prevails within CITES against use of animal parts for consumptive purpose.

The African elephant issue

The African elephant was on CITES Appendix 2 in 1975. When the population dropped dramatically in the 1980s because of poaching and the failure of CITES to control illegal trade in ivory, African elephant was uplisted to CITES Appendix 1. Trade in ivory was banned at the Seventh Conference of the Parties in 1989.

China had been importing 50 tons of ivory per annum since 1980 and re-exporting handicrafts made of ivory mainly to Europe, Japan and the US. This trade had brought China tens of millions of dollars each year. This was the main reason why China entered a reservation on the uplisting of the African elephant. One result of the trade ban was that China has lost most of its international markets – which dealt a heavy blow to its ivory handicraft industry and put thousands of handicraft workers out of work. Political and economic pressures were put on China to accept the trade ban. After assessing the overall situation that it was facing, China decided to withdraw its reservation to the listing of the African elephant on Appendix I, and stopped all trade in ivory and its products in 1991.

Controversy over bear and tiger products

The gall bladders of bear and tiger bone have been used as medicine in some of the Asian countries, including China, for a long time. Although for those people who turn their back on animal products it may be debatable and questionable whether it is necessary to use animal parts to cure human illness, the medicinal properties of gall bladder and tiger bone are beyond any doubt. Nevertheless, the international concerns over the current threat posed to the animals in question by the medicinal trade have not been ignored in China. Alternatives are being considered, both to meet the concerns of the international community over the possibility of the animals being further endangered, and at the same time to seek ways to preserve the ancient oriental traditions, with the endorsement of the member states of CITES. Captive breeding centres for bears and tigers in Sichuan and Liaonin provinces are among measures to be considered.[10] Research on artificial tiger bone is also underway and has given its first encouraging result. Finally, consideration is being given to negotiating a kind of regional arrangement with neighbouring countries aimed at strengthening cooperation in combating smuggling and illegal trade in tigers.

The recent lesson from rhino horn

Rhino horn was first mentioned in *Shennong Bencao Jing* ('Dictionary of Herbs') compiled as early as 2000 years ago (15 BC–174 AD). Its value has been proved by clinical application as having blood-cooling, fever-reducing and detoxificating effects. Rhino horn has been considered by Chinese doctors as a 'magic remedy'[11] and a precious heritage left over by ancestors from the treasure house of traditional Chinese medicine.

In the past 200 years rhinoceros became a rare species due both to excessive hunting for trade, and to habitat destruction. CITES Appendix 1 listing of rhino in 1977 did not help to prevent the rhino population from being threatened by highly profitable and speculative illegal trade in rhino horn. The 28th CITES Standing Committee meeting in June 1992 and its 29th Meeting in March 1993 called for destruction of rhino horn stockpile and urged all Parties to CITES to implement CITES Resolution 6.10 of 1987.[12] China was specifically mentioned and was urged to take action to stop trade in rhino horn or face sanctions on wildlife products from all Parties to CITES.

Like the decision made by China in 1991 to drop its reservation on the listing of the African elephant, China's decision to prohibit all trade, internal and external, in rhino horn and products made from it has been taken after fierce debate within China and despite the strong opposition from public health sectors and the internal trade department. The overwhelming view expressed at the time when the decision was made was that unless something really convincing is done to comply with the relevant resolutions of CITES, neither diplomatic persuasion efforts nor reiteration, however firm, of the great importance attached by the government to this issue would help relieve pressure. This led to the promulgation by the state council of the 'Notice on the Prohibition of Trade in Rhinoceros Horn' on 29 May 1993. 'Notice' is a form of administrative regulation in China and is binding on all relevant administrative agencies and individuals throughout the country. This notice is considered to be the first legally binding instrument ever adopted by a Party to CITES specifically on rhino horn. For those Chinese who are proud of famous traditional Chinese medicine this decision is a great sacrifice, made for the effectiveness of CITES and in order to make a significant contribution to the global rhino conservation strategy.

The whole matter is far from ended, however. People are still waiting to see how the Notice is going to be implemented. The trade in rhino horn and its products is apparently out of the control of the government according to the investigations made by some of the international organizations. Serious efforts may be necessary on the part of the government to enhance law enforcement capability by training law enforcers and allocating more financial resources. It is expected that the standing committee of CITES meeting in September 1995 in Brussels will consider the report to be submitted by the CITES Secretariat on measures taken by the countries concerned, and take decisions thereon.

SOME ISSUES OF WIDE DEBATE WITHIN CITES

Role of trade in the wildlife conservation

Trade in wildlife species must be regulated so as not to threaten the survival of wildlife. Some people argue that if this trade goes out of control, it should be prohibited. But things are not that simple. There is a view which holds that it is actually the trade that helps to conserve endangered species. The arguments are, *inter alia*: trade could be the most reliable fund-generating method, in the long term, for the conservation of endangered species, especially in view of the fact the most CITES-listed species are located in developing countries where shortage of funds has always been a major problem in financing conservation plans. Instead of banning trade, efforts should be made to control it, and properly controlled trade could stand in the way of illegal trade, which increases after a trade ban and in places where there is considerable demand. This concept found some support at the 8th COP of CITES in March 1992. Resolution 8.3 states: 'Commercial trade may be beneficial to the conservation of species and ecosystems and/or to the development of local people when carried out at the levels that are not detrimental to the survival of the species in question.' It was agreed at the UNEP meeting between the rhinoceros range states, consumer states and donors on financing the conservation of the rhinoceros held in June 1993 in Nairobi that studies be carried out on the probable impacts of a resumption in a legal international trade in rhinoceros products.

Efforts also have been made to tighten conditions for trade with non-Parties to avoid the risk of using non-Parties to CITES as routes for illegal trade to CITES and thus jeopardizing the effectiveness of CITES. Non-Parties are called to meet certain requirements including presenting proper documentation for trade with Parties to CITES.[13] CITES has been quite successful in urging non-Parties to join. Recently the Republic of Korea has indicated its willingness to accede to CITES.

Trade sanctions may be used to enforce CITES against non-complying Parties. This measure has been proved effective in forcing governments to be fully alert to their problems and take corresponding measures to repair the situation. Thailand and Italy have experienced the general trade ban for their failure to control trade in CITES species and have enacted relevant legislation. Another recent example is China, which is facing the possibility of such trade sanctions and has decided to implement the relevant CITES resolutions seriously.

Confrontation of two schools of thought

The problem of world wildlife conservation and rational utilization has provoked many different opinions. It is also true that within CITES there are arguments with regard to which direction to be heading and what attitude to take: protectionist (absolute ban on trade in endangered wildlife) or conservationist (proper management of human use of ecosystem to ensure the sustainability of exploitation of natural resources). The 8th COP of CITES witnessed the acrimonious struggle between these two groups. It is anticipated that the debate will carry on until countries arrive at a common understanding and acceptable solutions as to what serves the best interests of wildlife conservation and development, and benefits human beings.

CONCLUSION

The cultural backgrounds and traditions unique to some Asian countries have imposed some difficulties in the implementation of CITES. In such cases political will, consciousness of international commitments and obligations of states, and enforceable and effective domestic measures are essential to compliance. While states are aware of their duties under international law, different cultural traditions and customs should be understood in order to appreciate the difficulties and problems of the countries concerned. The goal should be to find a solution acceptable to all. The question whether the prohibition of trade in endangered species is in the best interest of wildlife conservation should be thoroughly explored with minds open to all options. If an acceptable solution cannot be agreed, trade sanctions as punishment for non-complying Parties should be used as a last resort.

9 INTERNATIONAL AGREEMENTS AND ENVIRONMENTAL MANAGEMENT FOLLOW-UP IN BANGLADESH

*Chowdhury R Abrar**

INTRODUCTION

Bangladesh is located at the confluence of the Ganges, the Brahmaputra and the Meghna rivers. The country is prone to floods, cyclones and other types of natural disasters. The severity and frequency of natural calamities during the last decade have caused Bangladesh to look at the global and regional factors causing environmental degradation in the context of its own experiences and to seek to mitigate them through international action.

BANGLADESH'S ENVIRONMENTAL PROFILE

Bangladesh is the tenth most populated country in the world (114.7 million people in 1990). Population density (1169 per square kilometre of cultivable land) surpasses all other countries, save that of Singapore.[1] Such a huge population exerts a tremendous pressure on the country's natural resources, further weakening its already fragile ecosystems. This is manifested in, for example, decreases in soil fertility and organic matter; massive reductions in forest land and the decimation of rainforests and mangrove forests; the degradation and steady loss of wetland habitats; increased threats to rare and endangered species, plants, animals, fishes, birds and their habitats; increased incidences of water and air pollution; enhanced levels of salinity in coastal areas; and the lowering of water tables due to the uncertainty of aquifer recharge.

---

* An earlier version of this chapter previously appeared as an article in *RECIEL*, Vol. 2, Issue 4, FIELD, London 1993.

People's response

It is under these conditions that awareness about environment related issues has increased at a very significant rate at all levels recently. The increased interest in academic circles is evidenced by the number of seminars and workshops taking place and the publication of reports of a specialized nature. Environmental research institutes such as the Bangladesh Centre for Advanced Studies (BCAS), the Research Advisory Services and the Bangladesh Unnoyon Parishad have undertaken many diverse projects, including a study of the greenhouse effect on the coastal belt; a critical appraisal of the multi-million dollar Flood Action Study; a project on freshwater wetlands management; and a study on the use of ozone depleting substances in Bangladesh.

The period is also marked by the rise of a new genre of activist NGOs with a range of interest areas. The National Conservation Movement (NACOM), the Coastal Area Resource Development and Management Association (CARDMA), and the Policy Research Development Alternatives (UBINIG), to name a few of the organizations, are involved in activities ranging from the monitoring of waterfowl and the preservation of biodiversity, to the organization of protests against the dumping in Bangladesh of hazardous wastes imported from developed countries. The various development-oriented NGOs, such as the Bangladesh Rural Advancement Committee (BRAC), the Proshika Human Resource Development Centre and Caritas, have incorporated a social forestry programme into their overall ambit of work.

Donors' response

The donor community has been performing a supporting role to such NGO initiatives. Most of the multilateral donors have conducted their own studies on the status of the environment of Bangladesh. The donors have been engaged in a host of environment-related activities providing financial and technical resources.[2] Most donors require the government to undertake environmental impact assessment studies for projects funded by them. An Environmental Management Action Plan is under formulation, with financial assistance provided by the United Nations Development Programme.

Government's response

At the governmental level, a number of initiatives were undertaken leading to the formulation of new policies and the formation of institutions. The severe floods of 1987 and 1988 had a considerable impact on the government's approach to the environment issue. By 1989 a separate Ministry of Environment and Forests had been created. Within the Ministry, the Department of the Environment[3] (DOE) has been entrusted with a greater role in environmental impact assessment (EIA) and in formulating the policies of various agencies involved in activities affecting soil and water conservation, afforestation, wildlife, critical habitats, fisheries and other natural resource issues. The Ministry has been granted status as a permanent member in the Executive Committee of the National Economic Council. The Fourth Five Year Plan, the principal instrument of national economic planning, includes, for the first time, a separate chapter on environment and sustainable development, emphasizing the environmental policy objectives of the government for the 1991–95 period.[4] The Planning Commission has also established an 'environmental section' to ensure intersectoral linkages. A National Environment Committee, comprising academics, experts, resource persons, government representatives and NGOs has also been set up and will be chaired by the Prime Minister.

Apart from these institutional initiatives, several sectoral and multi-sectoral strategies relating to the environment have been drawn up. The National Conservation Strategy and the National Environmental Policy Paper are being finalized. In 1992 the government prepared the National Environment Policy and Action Plan. An Environmental Preservation Act is currently under consideration. It would provide the DOE with more clearly defined regulatory authority, enabling it to formulate codes, guidelines, EIA provisions and standards for environmental quality. Apart from these, various sectoral plans such as the National Water Plan, the Flood Action Plan, the Coastal Environment Management Plan and the Forestry Master Plan have either already been finalized or are currently being prepared.

The government has also taken up certain other activities with vigour. In order to support tree plantation activities, it has initiated a 'food for plantation' programme, under which food is provided in return for public participation in the planting and nursing of trees on government land. In the same spirit, 1990 was declared the Year of the Environment; and the 1990s, the Decade of the Environment.

NGO-government collaboration

In the environmental field there has been increased collaboration between the NGOs and the government. NACOM is providing expertise to conduct a census of migratory birds in close cooperation with the DOE. At a more general level there is a shared feeling that the government is increasingly receptive to NGO ideas and is more willing to involve NGOs in its environment related programmes. In the second phase of the forestry programme funded by the Asian Development Bank, the NGOs are collaborating with the government to plant saplings on government lands. NGOs are also assisting the government with EIAs and the government has received NGO support in its public awareness campaign against the reptile-skin trade. The government is also drawing upon the expertise of the private research bodies.[5]

INTERNATIONAL AGREEMENTS

In the context of the heightened awareness about the environment and the country's sensitivity to global and regional environmental conditions, Bangladesh has signed and ratified a number of important international agreements, treaties, conventions and protocols. It is understood that a number of other agreements are under active consideration as regards accession and ratification, and specific implementation strategies are also envisaged. Some of the important international agreements to which Bangladesh has become a party are discussed below, together with a brief description about the country's position on the issues concerned. Each section also includes a set of recommendations dealing with the way in which enforcement could be improved.

TRADE IN ENDANGERED SPECIES: CITES

Illegal trade in wildlife threatens many endangered species with extinction. The Convention on International Trade in Endangered Species of Wild Flora and Fauna (CITES) aims to protect endangered species from over exploitation by animal and plant trades, by a system of import-export permits. Bangladesh ratified the instrument in February 1982. The Wildlife Preservation Act of 1973 prohibits hunting, killing and the capture of game animals without a permit. It also forbids trade in such animals and the subsequent processing or manufacturing of related goods, without a valid permit. A major limitation of this legislation is that it lacks the back-up of a strong regulatory authority to ensure enforcement and its punitive provisions are also weak.

Frogs' legs and goods made using lizard skin were considered to be particularly lucrative export items of Bangladesh. The Wildlife Act and subsequent ratification of CITES have put a stop to official import and export of endangered species or goods produced using their bones and skins.[6] Due to the small number of people involved in such trade, the legislation did not meet any effective resistance.

Although not yet a signatory to the 1979 Convention on the Protection of Migratory Species of Wild Animals, Bangladesh is reportedly completing the preparations to accede to this instrument. The wetlands of the country host a variety of seasonal migratory birds, especially Siberian waterfowl. Public campaigns have been organized to treat these birds as 'guests' but, nevertheless, they often fall prey to local hunters.

CITES also forbids trade in endangered flora. Illegal logging is rampant but there is no cross-boundary trade in logs.

Three recommendations have been made in order to protect Bangladesh's wildlife.

(1) a national centre on endangered species should be formed comprising academics, governmental experts and representatives, and environmental research and activitist groups, which would coordinate and initiate research, monitor progress on the implementation of policies and recommend policy actions and legislative measures;
(2) legislative action should be taken to impose stricter penalties on those breaching the Wildlife Act, and the responsibility of the institutions to enforce them should be clearly defined; and
(3) public awareness campaigns focusing on endangered species, including migratory birds, should be conducted.

Protection of wetlands

Ramsar Convention 1971

In 1971 the Convention on Wetlands of International Importance, Especially as Waterfowl Habitat, commonly known as the Ramsar Convention, was adopted and required the Contracting Parties to use wisely all wetlands (inland, coastal and marine) under their jurisdiction. Under the Convention each Contracting Party agreed to designate at least one wetland of international relevance for conservation. Bangladesh acceded to the Ramsar Convention in May 1992 and designated 59,600 hectares of the Sunderbans as the conserved area.

Bangladesh is rich in wetlands. One study shows that by applying the definition used by the Ramsar Convention, two-thirds of the country may be classified as wetlands.[7] The wetlands encompass a number of ecosystems including mangrove forests, natural lakes, fresh water marshes, ponds, estuaries and manmade reservoirs. Increased human encroachment in the form of flood control mechanisms such as embankments, drainage systems, conversion of wetlands into farmland, road and railroad building, increased salinity, pollution, hunting and trapping have done considerable damage to the wetlands. There is no existing 'policy package' in Bangladesh which supports environmentally sustainable goals in wetlands management.[8]

There is a host of problems relating to wetlands management. Public ownership is divided among a large number of agencies governed by various sectoral organizations, most of which are geared towards the exploitation of wetland resources, rather than their protection, improvement and sustainable use. Lack of coordination of sectoral activities, compatible and complementary resource use patterns, knowledge, technology and resources are the principal impediments to wetlands development.[9]

The following measures are necessary to protect wetlands in Bangladesh:

(1) specific legislation dealing with the management and preservation of wetlands and including clear enforcement guidelines should be formulated;

(2) a national inventory encompassing all types of wetlands should be drawn up which would identify priorities for future survey, research, management and protection and which would also provide a sound basis for monitoring; and,

(3) a National Wetlands Committee should be established, comprising experts and representatives from government agencies, NGOs and environmental activist groups, to provide overall guidance to wetlands management activities and to recommend a National Wetlands Policy.

Ozone layer depletion

The Vienna Convention 1985 and the Montreal Protocol 1987

The Vienna Convention for the Protection of the Ozone Layer 1985, provides a framework for international cooperation for the monitoring of ozone layer depletion, research, exchange of information and transfer of technology. The Montreal Protocol on Substances that Deplete the Ozone Layer 1987 provides for a freeze on the production of chloroflurocarbons (CFCs) and calls on countries to cut their production. In August 1990 Bangladesh ratified the Vienna Convention and the Montreal Protocol.

Bangladesh does not produce CFCs or any other ozone depleting substances (ODS). In the absence of any systematic information, a study on the use of ozone depleting substances was carried out in 1992.[10] The study found that on average 230.3 metric tonnes of ODS were imported and 206.3 metric tonnes were consumed annually over the 1986–91 period. The per capita consumption of ODS is extremely low in Bangladesh – two grammes per year. It has further been estimated that even with a high growth scenario (ie the total consumption rising to 1408 metric tonnes by 2010) the per capita consumption would only rise to eight grammes per year.

In spite of this favourable situation with respect to consumption of ODS, the government, as a signatory to the Montreal Protocol, must discourage any future increase in ODS use. Investors from Japan and Korea have recently shown an interest in setting up assembly and production plants in Bangladesh, for refrigerators and air conditioners for example. Owing to its international obligations, the government has not yet responded to these proposals.[11] The Industrial Policy of 1991 spells out the need for maintaining a balance between industrialization and environmental concerns.

The following measures will further foster implementation by Bangladesh of the Vienna Convention and the Montreal Protocol:

(1) options should be explored and inducements provided to substitute CFCs with ammonia in refrigeration and freezing plants;
(2) the aerosol plants should be encouraged to substitute ODS by mechanical devices or other ozone friendly propellants; and
(3) for the maintenance of an accurate inventory, ODS import goods should be labelled clearly, stating the name and the quantity of ODS contained therein.

Biodiversity

Biodiversity Convention 1992

The Convention on Biological Diversity was another important achievement of the Rio Earth Summit. It provides a framework which will enable each government to decide how best to conserve its own biodiversity. Although a state's sovereign rights over its biological resources were reaffirmed, the Convention requires states to take account of the importance of maintaining biodiversity and to use such resources in a sustainable manner. Bangladesh is a signatory to the Convention.

Bangladesh's location in the tropical zone has been conducive to it harbouring a rich variety of flora and fauna. Bangladesh contributes most to the international biodiversity pool in two ways: firstly, by its extremely rich genetic pool of rice varieties; and secondly, as the site of a significant tiger population. Five thousand species of flowering plants, 500 species of fish, 750 species of birds, 119 species of mammals and 124 species of reptiles indicate the large reservoir of floral and faunal resources. However, poor wildlife management and ignorance of bionomics have led to the loss of ten per cent of mammalian fauna and four per cent of reptiles over the past 150 years.[12]

Unplanned and insensitive development practices have resulted in the encroachment of forest lands; the creation of water control structures and embankments; the destruction of mangrove forests for shrimp cultivation; *jhum* cultivation by the national ethnic minorities; over-exploitation of some reserves such as bamboo, canes and medicinal herbs; and saline intrusion, which have done an enormous amount of damage to the biological diversity of the country. It is under these circumstances that Bangladesh's signing of the Biodiversity Convention is of particular significance.

Bangladesh should follow these recommended measures if it is to preserve its biodiversity effectively:

(1) steps should be taken for the preparation of an inventory of the country's floral and faunal biological resources, and for the monitoring of changes in those resources over time;
(2) *in situ* conservation in the form of wildlife sanctuaries, national parks, game reserves and coral reef parks, and *ex situ* conservation measures such as gene banks and zoos should be established;
(3) coordination, collaboration and integrated action among different agencies in the development and maintenance of forests and wetlands should be ensured;
(4) measures should be taken for the dissemination of information about the importance of biodiversity preservation, amongst both decision-makers and the general public; and
(5) public participation in the enforcement of various protective regulations should be ensured.

Greenhouse effect

Convention on Climate Change 1992

Signed at Rio, the UN Framework Convention was aimed at the stabilization of greenhouse gas concentrations in the atmosphere at a level which would prevent dangerous anthropogenic interference with the climate. The Convention commits the Parties to develop and update national inventories of anthropogenic emissions and their removal by sinks; to cooperate in preparations for adaptation to the impacts of climate change; to take climate change considerations into account in their relevant economic, environmental policies and actions; and to employ appropriate methods to mitigate the adverse effects of climate change. Bangladesh is a signatory to the Convention.

Bangladesh has been identified by the United Nations Environment Fund as one of the ten countries most vulnerable to any rise in sea level associated with global warming. One estimate suggests that sea level rise due to global warming may be about 20 centimetres by the year 2030 and could reach 1 metre by the turn of the next century.[13] It has also been estimated that such a rise in sea level will inundate 5608 million acres of existing coastal land, which is 15 per cent of the total land area; 13.74 per cent of net cropped land; and 401,600 hectares of mangrove forests, including most of the Sunderbans. This would also mean displacement of over 11 per cent of the population, (ie 13 million refugees). It would also cause irreversible damage to coastland flora and fauna. Other predicted consequences of global warming include increased monsoon rainfall,[14] with estimates ranging from 5–100 per cent, which would have significant implications for agriculture, flooding, river sediment loads and flood protection works; increased frequency and severity of flooding and tropical cyclones; and increased severity of droughts in drought-prone areas.[15] Global warming, therefore, poses a serious threat to Bangladesh but there is very little that it can do to offset the impact. The problem is further compounded because uncertainty in the predictions concerning the timing and the magnitude of changes makes it very difficult to design counter-measures.

Although measures to control global warming which are within the power of Bangladesh are limited, these are some possible steps:

(1) emphasis should be given to a better understanding of the likely effects of sea level rise and climate change by the establishment and sustained monitoring of a number of impact indicator sites;
(2) meteorological, hydrological and oceanographic data should be properly coordinated and analyzed in order that trends in temperature, precipitation, calamity, sea level and cyclone frequency and intensity can be followed;
(3) a sustained campaign appealing to the world to share the cost of helping Bangladesh redress the relevant problems should be mounted at the international level.

Conclusion

The effective implementation and follow-up of these agreements is being impeded by a lack of funds, expertise, manpower and appropriate scientific information (at both the pre- and post-signing stages), an absence of coordination between the governmental agencies and ineffective legal instruments which need to be updated.

In spite of these shortcomings, one may conclude that Bangladesh has addressed environmental issues with a fair degree of emphasis. With limited resources it has attempted to take effective measures to set the legal and policy context for country implementation of the international agreements. However, there is clear evidence that implementation is not strong, owing to resource constraints. These constraints could be eased if funds were to be made available to Bangladesh from the GEF – the only channel available for the transfer of international assistance to address global environmental degradation.

PART 4

Enforcement Measures: the Use of Economic Instruments and Financial Resources

10 TRADE SANCTIONS: EFFECTIVE ENFORCEMENT TOOLS

*Leesteffy Jenkins**

INTRODUCTION

The proposition that trade sanctions are a legitimate means of achieving international environmental objectives is controversial. The legal and policy dilemmas it poses are probably best highlighted by a 1991 decision of a dispute resolution panel (tuna dolphin 1) convened under the General Agreement on Tariffs and Trade (GATT). It held that the United States could not, consistent with GATT, prohibit the importation of tuna products for environmental reasons based solely on the production method used to harvest such tuna, nor could the United States use trade measures to protect natural resources outside of its own territorial jurisdiction.[1]

Despite this restrictive ruling, the GATT panel suggested that trade actions taken in accordance with 'international cooperative arrangements' may be justified under the exceptions provisions of GATT.[2] This paper explores that suggestion, ie the use of trade sanctions as a means of enforcing international environmental agreements (IEAs). Four IEAs that currently utilize, or are considered to present opportunities for the use of, trade provisions as an enforcement mechanism are reviewed. Consequently, recommendations regarding the most effective use of trade sanctions as a means of enforcing IEAs generally can be made.

CONSENSUS IS NOT EFFECTIVE

The Western concept of international law is based on the Roman concept of *gentili ius gentium,* law upon which all nations agree. This is the principle of

---

* An earlier version of this chapter previously appeared as an article in *RECIEL,* Vol. 2, Issue 4, FIELD, London 1993.

consensus. The community of nations, or at least a majority of those concerned, establishes principles of conduct, through direct agreement or by State practice, and these principles thereby become international law. Theoretically, if countries agree to establish principles or standards, they will abide by them. Hence, consensus has been equivalent to enforcement because it has, in theory, eliminated the need for coercive measures.

Yet even in theory the consensus principle is dubious, as politically powerful nations have often predominated international 'consensus'. A consensus agreement may often consist of no more than a policy not to disagree, rather than the many Parties' positive affirmation of mutually agreed substantive rules. Hence, there may be little motivation on the part of some Parties to act positively upon the consensus agreement. On a practical level, consensus is no longer the principal mode of international rule-making. Increasingly, majority voting is being used in the international community.

Vague compromises

Further, reliance upon consensus has recently resulted in agreements that have little utility or are unenforceable because they are vague compromises. Agenda 21, the action agenda developed and signed during the UN Conference on Environment and Development (UNCED) is a good example of an IEA which was agreed upon by consensus but which is unenforceable in practice.[3] The oceans chapter of Agenda 21[4] contains arguably conflicting provisions.[5] Having participated in Prepcom IV, the last preparatory meeting prior to the signing of Agenda 21 in Rio, I can attest to the fact that this was not accidental. After five weeks of negotiations, the countries participating in the negotiating process could not reach consensus on several provisions. As a result, in order to conclude the negotiations, language was agreed upon that was so vague that it would satisfy all concerned Parties and their various interpretations. Agenda 21 can now be cited by both environmental conservationists and their opponents alike in support for their conflicting views. 'Consensus' decision-making resulted in a document that means something different to everyone. This type of agreement on words rather than principles, will not result in enforceable agreements.[6]

In an age of conflicting interests between an ever increasing number of nation states, unanimous agreement on universal principles is becoming increasingly rare. Not all countries are going to adopt the same provisions, or vote or even participate in the same negotiations. If such countries are free to avoid the international obligations undertaken by others, without suffering adverse consequences, the goals of agreements will be undermined. In the case of environmental agreements, in particular, this is unacceptable. Many environmental resources are shared of necessity and a maverick nation abusing them can negatively impact on all others. Therefore, a system of enforcement for IEAs must be developed.

CURRENT IEAs LACK ADEQUATE ENFORCEMENT

Although few IEAs today rely exclusively upon consensus for rule-making, fewer still have recognized that a lack of real consensus necessitates adequate enforcement mechanisms. As a result, decisions of institutions established under some IEAs[7] are ignored by member countries that do not agree with the policy decisions of the IEA institution. Consequently, IEA institutions such as the IWC, the Inter-American Tropical Tuna Commission (IATTC) and CITES have little capacity to ensure protection for the resources for which they have responsibility.

Granting IEA organizations enforcement powers may be difficult. Historically, enforcement powers have been inextricably tied to the concept of sovereignty: only states have had the sovereign right to enforce laws within their own jurisdiction.[8] With some exceptions the concept of enforcement jurisdiction is territorially based.[9] Theoretically, no international juridical body may interfere with that right and granting an IEA organization enforcement powers may result in its infringing upon the sovereignty of its member countries. Nevertheless, IEAs cannot continue to function effectively without such enforcement provisions.

CITES

CITES regulates commercial trade in endangered and threatened animal and plant species through the use of a trade permitting system.[10] Parties to CITES agree that they will not grant import or export permits for plants and animals specifically regulated under CITES unless certain criteria set forth in the Agreement are met.[11] As long as these criteria are met, Parties to the Agreement may allow the importation or exportation of listed species to and from member and non-member countries alike.

Although known as a wildlife 'trade' treaty, CITES does not actually contain enforcement provisions. The permit system is basically an honour system. Members agree to abide by their obligations in good faith. If Parties do not abide by their obligations there is little the treaty organization can do to enforce compliance.

The problems inherent in this type of system are typified by the current CITES controversy over the continued trade in and popular use of rhinoceros horn and tiger parts by the Peoples Republic of China and Taiwan.[12] Both animals are listed in CITES Appendix I, which bans commercial trade in these species. After reviewing evidence that both China and Taiwan are currently violating their CITES obligations, the Standing Committee, the CITES juridical body which has authority over such matters, issued a decision which provides:

> that the measures taken by the Peoples Republic of China and the competent authorities in Taipei are not adequate to sufficiently control illegal trade in rhinoceros horn and tiger parts, including failure to comply with measures outlined in Resolution Conf. 6.10. Parties should consider implementing stricter domestic measures up to and including prohibition in trade in wildlife species now.[13]

The decision further requests that both China and Taiwan implement specified protection measures by the end of November 1993 if they are to be in compliance with their CITES obligations. If China and Taiwan do not comply with these recommendations, however, neither the Standing Committee nor the Plenary, has any means other than moral suasion to encourage compliance. On April 4 1994, the United States sanctioned Taiwan using the Pelly Amendment by 'partially' suspending the importation of wildlife products. China was certified under Pelly, but not sanctioned. The sanctions against Taiwan were lifted on June 30 1995.

International Whaling Convention

Like CITES, the International Convention for the Regulation of Whaling (ICRW)[14] contains no enforcement provisions. As a result, the International Whaling Commission (IWC), the organization responsible for implementing the provisions of the ICRW, has no means by which to encourage effectively compliance with its decisions.[15]

For example, in 1982 the IWC voted to implement a ban on commercial whaling beginning with the 1985–86 whaling season.[16] Accordingly, the ICRW Schedule was amended to provide for zero quotas on both pelagic and coastal whaling[17] until the IWC completed a 'Comprehensive Assessment' of the effects of the moratorium and until such time as the IWC determined that a resumption of commercial whaling was appropriate.[18] To date, the IWC has not amended the treaty to provide for quotas on commercial whaling. Despite this, Norway, a treaty member, resumed commercial whaling in 1993.[19] Because the IWC has no enforcement powers, it has been unable to stop Norway's commercial whaling. As a result, other whaling countries may soon resume commercial whaling as well, despite the continued IWC ban. Without enforcement powers, the IWC is powerless to implement its desired policy effectively. It is significant that the environmental community has chosen trade boycotts as its method of pressuring Norway to comply with the IWC ban.

Inter-America Tropical Tuna Commission

Like the IWC and CITES, the IATTC[20] currently has no mechanism by which to enforce its provisions, although it is currently considering adopting enforcement provisions.[21]

The IATTC was set up as a regional management body to regulate and maintain the populations of yellowfin and skipjack tuna and other types of fish taken by tuna fishing vessels in the Eastern Pacific Ocean. In addition to its jurisdiction over tuna stocks, the IATTC in recent years has become more involved in regulating the methods by which tuna fisherman harvest tuna in the Eastern Tropical Pacific (ETP). Specifically, the IATTC currently restricts the number of dolphins that may be killed by its member countries in a given year.[22]

The IATTC relies upon consensus for all its decision-making. Despite the Commission's reliance on consensus, however members of the IATTC have in the past disregarded its decisions.[23] As a result, the IATTC in the past has discussed the implementation of enforcement mechanisms, including the use of trade sanctions.

Montreal protocol

The Montreal Protocol on Substances that Deplete the Ozone Layer (the 'Protocol')[24] regulates international trade in CFCs, carbon tetrachloride, and trichloromethane.[25] Although the Protocol contains trade provisions, those provisions are not used as a means of enforcing the Agreement. Instead, like CITES, the Parties to the Protocol agree to restrict trade in certain specified substances. In order to enhance its effectiveness, the Protocol contains provisions banning trade in certain ozone depleting substances with non-member countries.[26]

Pursuant to the Protocol, member countries are required to limit and reduce their production and consumption of specified substances within a set period of time. If, however, individual Parties do not meet the requirements set forth in the Protocol, there is currently no effective mechanism by which member countries may enforce compliance by the non-performing Party.[27]

UNILATERAL ENFORCEMENT

US unilateral action

In recent years, the United States has unilaterally employed the threat of trade sanctions as a means of encouraging individual countries to comply with their international obligations under both CITES and the IWC.[28] The primary law that permits the United States to impose trade sanctions under such circumstances is the Pelly Amendment to the Fisherman's Protective Act of 1967 ('Pelly').[29] Under Pelly, the US President may impose trade sanctions on any country that 'diminishes the effectiveness of any international programme for endangered or threatened species'.[30] In addition to Pelly, the United States has, in the past few years, passed four additional laws that restrict imports from countries engaging in practices which harm marine mammals and other marine species,[31] sea turtles,[32] birds[33] and dolphins.[34]

Although the United States has been criticized for engaging in unilateral action to protect wildlife, it has only once actually imposed trade sanctions on any country for violating an IEA.[35] To date, the threat of trade sanctions has been sufficient to encourage intransigent countries to comply with their international obligations.[36] Furthermore, it appears that the loudest expression of criticism of US action comes from foreign trade officials rather than foreign environmental officials.[37] Similarly, the US Trade Representatives Office (USTR) has also been opposed to the adoption and implementation of these US laws![38] The opponents of these laws claim that they violate GATT, rather than that they are an ineffective means of protecting the global environment and wildlife resources.

IEA enforcement provisions would reduce unilateral action

The development of strong enforcement provisions, including trade sanctions, by IEA organizations would reduce the necessity for unilateral action in most of those circumstances in which the United States has threatened trade sanctions. Despite what critics of US policy may think, the United States Executive Branch has never enthusiastically embraced US laws that utilize trade sanctions to achieve environmental and conservation goals.[39] The development of strong multilateral enforcement mechanisms would greatly diminish, though not necessarily eliminate, the necessity for unilateral action to protect environmental and wildlife resources.

Avoiding sovereignty issues

Effective enforcement cannot be accomplished unless an IEA contains inducements for encouraging behaviour modification by intransigent countries. States use their police powers to induce citizens to obey the law. Similarly, if IEAs are to be enforced effectively, treaty organizations must be able to rely upon more than moral suasion.

One means of implementing enforcement powers in IEAs is to grant IEA organizations some form of police powers, for instance, the right to arrest citizens who engage in activities which violate IEAs. This, however, would result in direct infringement of countries' sovereign rights.

A better means of granting enforcement powers to IEA institutions is through the use of an enforcement mechanism which utilizes multilateral decision-making without invasive enforcement, such as through the use of trade sanctions. Ideally, an IEA organization would have the power to authorize its members to impose trade sanctions against intransigent Parties, as well as against non-member countries that engage in activities which reduce the effectiveness of the IEA. Sovereign rights would not be infringed upon if member countries were not required to impose trade sanctions, but rather, authorized and urged to do so if they so chose. Such a scheme would have the added advantage of permitting member countries to vote in favour of trade sanctions, even if for political or other reasons actual imposition of trade sanctions was not feasible for the voting country.

TRADE RULES MUST BE REFORMED

The inevitable question that arises when one speaks of utilizing trade sanctions is do they violate the GATT? As the 1991 Panel Decision indicated, the GATT does not recognize that trade measures may constitute a legitimate means of enforcing international environmental objectives. If trade sanctions are to develop as a viable enforcement mechanism in the context of IEAs, the technical legal rules in the GATT will need to be reformed.

How a product is produced is important

Currently, the GATT does not permit contracting states to regulate trade in goods by reference to the process by which the goods are produced. Such types of regulations are considered to be 'process standards', and process standards under the GATT are presumptively not allowed.[40] A country may set standards that regulate the intrinsic qualities of the product, but not how the product or good was produced.

If, however, the international community is to protect both global and domestic environments effectively, trade rules must explicitly recognize that many environmental and conservation objectives cannot be achieved unless countries are able to regulate the process by which natural resources are utilized or made into products. From an environmental perspective, it is not only important that the physical characteristics of a finished product are environmentally sound (ie it is free from contaminants), the process or methods used to produce such products must also be ecologically sound. For instance, concerns over threatened loss of habitat, or species, or increased levels of pollutants in local and global environments, are raised by certain production processes. It is imperative that countries be permitted to distinguish between products that are physically 'alike' but that were produced in drastically different manners, and to adopt trade regulations that take into account those differences.[41]

Yet, in the tuna dolphin 1 case, the GATT dispute resolution panel held that the United States could not distinguish between Mexican cans of tuna whose physical characteristics are identical to other imports (called 'like products' in trade terminology) but which were produced in drastically different manners. Thus, the fact that the Mexican tuna was harvested using a technique called encirclement netting – which kills large numbers of dolphins – was considered irrelevant.[42]

This dilemma applies to other IEAs as well. For example, CITES authorizes its Parties to allow the importation of certain (Appendix II) species if the Management Authority of the importing state is satisfied that the species to be imported will be handled so as to minimize the risk of injury, damage to health or cruel treatment of such species.[43] If in accordance with CITES, country A permits the importation of macaws, for example, from country Y, but not from country Z because country Z has not met the CITES requirements, country Z would have grounds for challenging country X's restriction under the GATT. The macaws are, after all, 'like products' and the production process would be considered irrelevant.[44] If country Z was not a member of CITES it would have a strong claim that country A had impaired its rights under GATT.[45]

Advised domestic trade sanctions

IEA organizations have no means of accomplishing their goals independently of state action. Trade measures are a relatively acceptable means of state action to accomplish such goals. At present, however, no IEAs specifically authorize the use of trade sanctions as a means of enforcing their provisions. Until this happens, countries at a minimum should be able to use domestic trade measures upon the 'advice'[46] of an IEA in order to enforce the policy decisions of the IEA.

Current GATT jurisprudence, however, may not recognize a state's right to use trade measures to protect resources outside of its territorial jurisdiction.[47] Although the GATT panel in the tuna dolphin 1 case suggested in dicta that trade restrictions taken in accordance with an international cooperative arrangement may be permissible under the exception provisions of GATT, it is not clear that would in fact prove true when an actual dispute arose. Further, unilateral actions not specifically authorized by an IEA organization would remain illegitimate.

Either all IEAs would need to be amended to permit specifically the imposition of trade sanctions or a few key technical rules in the GATT would need to be changed. It would be more effective and efficient to change a few GATT rules than to wait until the Parties to the numerous IEAs negotiate enforcement provisions. Yet, even if all IEAs were amended, trade sanctions could not be imposed against non-member countries without violating the GATT as currently formulated.

IEA non-member countries

Although the GATT contains provisions under which countries may waive certain GATT rights when they join in other international agreements,[48] the waiver rules would not be applicable to situations in which an IEA organization institutes action against a non-member country. The anomaly of this situation is that the GATT can be used to protect countries that show the least interest in international institutions, ie countries that both refuse to join the IEA or to acknowledge its standards. Thus, for instance, if the IWC tried to authorize trade sanctions against Iceland for violating the IWC ban on commercial whaling, Iceland (a non-member country) could challenge any trade action taken in accordance with the IWC decision at the GATT.

Until the GATT is modified to recognize the common resource base upon which international trade is built, it will continue to work against the use of trade mechanisms as a means of enforcing implementation in IEAs. IEA organizations will not be able to prohibit effectively non-member countries from engaging in the very activity that the international organization is meant to regulate and such countries will continue to have an incentive not even to join IEAs which may adopt trade sanctions as an enforcement mechanism.

CONCLUSION

A distinction can be drawn between IEAs which employ trade provisions as part of their method of operation (such as under CITES or the Montreal Protocol), and the use of trade sanctions as a means of enforcing these IEAs. Trade sanctions are punitive and extend beyond the range of operation of the trade provisions of the IEA. As yet, IEAs do not use trade sanctions against either Parties or non-Parties. However, such sanctions have been threatened by the US unilaterally in relation to breaches of IWC decisions by IWC member and non-member states, and have been used in one instance to punish Taiwan for acting in contravention of CITES.

Given that economic disincentives will undoubtedly continue to play a role in the failure of particular countries to abide by the decisions of IEAs, it only makes sense that economic incentives also be part of the solution. The use of trade sanctions is a viable form of enforcement that does not infringe upon traditional notions of national sovereignty. Unfortunately, no IEAs specifically authorize formal international trade sanctions and the use of trade sanctions to enforce IEAs is largely blocked by the free trade provisions of the GATT. Rather than amend all the relevant IEAs in order to avoid conflict with the GATT, and even then only among IEA Parties rather than non-Parties, it would be simpler and more effective to amend the GATT. This would allow IEA organizations to advise their members to introduce trade sanctions, as voluntarily domestic trade measures, in order to enforce the IEA against Parties and non-Parties. This may be the most effective and rational means of encouraging countries to abide by the decisions of the international community in a world where diminishing natural resources render the manner of their use an economic and ethical concern for all.

11 THE USE OF JOINT IMPLEMENTATION TO INCREASE COMPLIANCE WITH THE CLIMATE CHANGE CONVENTION*

Farhana Yamin

INTRODUCTION

The concept of joint implementation is relatively new to international law.[1] In the area of climate change, joint implementation was introduced and considered during sessions of the Intergovernmental Negotiating Committee for a Framework Convention on Climate Change (INC) in the context of two different, but related, concerns expressed principally by certain OECD member states and the European Community (EC).[2] Briefly these concerns were (1) that the Convention should be flexible and permit joint implementation to allow groups of countries to join together to undertake and fulfil commitments collectively; and (2) that in order to secure global environmental benefits at the lowest global cost and to transfer financial resources, the Convention should allow a joint implementation system based on the notion of a tradable emission permits or 'credits' scheme.

The final text of the 1992 UN Framework Convention on Climate Change ('Convention') allows the possibility of joint implementation between Parties in both of these senses.[3] However, the precise circumstances of how joint implementation should take place under the Convention, the way in which this should occur, and the legal and institutional modalities required to establish and operate joint implementation activities remained to be decided as negotiations drew to a close. Accordingly, the Convention's negotiators agreed that these matters should be considered further at the first meeting of the Conference of the Parties (COP I) which should 'take decisions regarding criteria for joint implementation'. In March 1995, at COP 1, Parties adopted a number of general

* An earlier version of this chapter previously appeared as an article in *RECIEL*, Vol. 2, Issue 4, FIELD, London 1993.

criteria to govern a pilot phase of 'activities implemented jointly' under the Convention.[4] The purpose of this pilot phase is to allow the Parties to experiment with approaches to the joint implementation of commitments, in order that they may answer some of the very complex questions reflected in this chapter. During the pilot phase, which is anticipated to last until 2000, no credit will be available for reductions in emissions gained by activities implemented jointly.

This chapter is structured as follows. Some of the basic background questions are set out and a number of significant international legal, institutional and procedural issues raised by the concept of joint implementation are examined, including tradable emission permits or 'credit' schemes. These issues must be addressed by the international community *before* the COP adopts substantive criteria on joint implementation under the Climate Change Convention. This is followed by an analysis of the legal implications of the Convention's provisions on joint implementation and the scope of substantive and procedural decisions which the COP will have to consider in order to sanction and regulate Parties' joint implementation activities.

JOINT IMPLEMENTATION AND INTERNATIONAL LAW: BASIC QUESTIONS AND BACKGROUND ISSUES

The concept of joint implementation

The most important economic feature of the concept of joint implementation is that a state with quantitatively defined commitments to reduce its emissions is allowed to 'buy' reductions in emissions from another state or states (hereinafter referred to as 'host states') which are able to reduce their emissions (or enhance and protect their sinks and reservoirs) more cheaply than the first state. In addition to receiving an economic reward for this, the host state may also benefit from joint implementation by acquiring more efficient technology and perhaps reduced local environmental impacts.

The defining legal feature of joint implementation is that substantive, binding commitments taken on by a state in its individual and sovereign capacity can be fulfilled either in cooperation with another state and/or by measures taken in the territory of another state. The specific legal mechanism for establishing a joint implementation system involves two substantive steps: first, establishing a system of entitlements to emission rights[5] and second, imposing obligations which can be fulfilled in exchange for either

(1) a transfer of a tradable emissions *permit*, issued as part of a global tradable permit system, or
(2) the implementation of a particular *project* in a host state through the provision of financial or other assistance by the state in return for a 'credit' from the host state, or regulating agency, which counts towards the achievement of the former's commitments.

In addition, joint implementation cannot take place without a minimum of administrative and related legal and institutional arrangements.

The essential legal feature, which is common to both the permit or the project system of joint implementation, is that they allow *transfers* and *assignments* of emissions reductions between states. In this sense the project-based-joint implementation system is simply a type of tradable permit system, albeit a less sophisticated one. In this chapter the term 'transfer' will be used to refer to both trade in emissions permits or to arrangements which have the effect of assigning or crediting emissions reduction from a project in a host state or states to the account of another state.

One significant difference between a permit system and a project system, which has legal implications for the role joint implementation can play in the Climate Change Convention, arises from the fact that a permit system is a 'closed' system while a project system is an 'open' one. In a 'closed' permit system, a global limit on greenhouse gas emissions is established on the basis of relevant scientific data and the remaining emission budget apportioned between every state via the permit. Every state has quantitative limits on what it can or cannot emit. Every state may then sell its permits to the extent that its own limit has not been exceeded. By contrast, an 'open' project system of joint implementation does not establish a global limit on greenhouse gas emissions. Thus whilst some states' emissions may be quantitatively limited, others may have no limit. An important shortcoming of the 'open' project system of joint implementation is that, in principle, overall global emissions can continue to increase indefinitely, at any rate, no matter how many successful joint implementation projects are undertaken. This calls into question how the COP can, if at all, assess the effectiveness of this kind of joint implementation in contributing to the objectives of the Convention given the specific requirement of Article 7 (2) (e).[6]

The economic advantages of joint implementation

Joint implementation has been advocated by a number of economists and environmentalists keen to extend the use of market mechanisms and economic incentives to achieve environmental goals.[7] It is argued that joint implementation gives individuals or states greater flexibility to decide how to achieve environmental goals than traditional command and control techniques. This flexibility ensures compliance with environmental goals at lower costs and enables such goals to be reached quicker than might otherwise be the case.

In addition to reducing costs, it is also argued that at the international level, joint implementation can promote sustainable development by increasing the flow of financial aid and resources to developing countries because these can offer emission abatement opportunities which are cheaper than domestic opportunities available to developed countries.[8]

Significant international legal issues

A fully-fledged form of joint implementation, which would allow transfers of permits or credits arising from projects between all states, has never been used to control pollution activities on a large scale in an international context.[9] The only notable international environmental precedent is the Montreal Protocol, which permits a limited form of joint implementation by allowing member states of the European Community to reduce their emission or consumption of controlled substances as a group.[10]

Joint implementation, through a tradable permit or a credit system, raises new and complex issues in international law. These issues need to be addressed by the COP when designing the pilot phase for activities implemented jointly and, in due course, when adopting criteria on joint implementation. As these issues also have legal implications which go beyond the climate change context, this chapter suggests that they are of relevance to, and deserve consideration by, the wider international community. This chapter discusses three issues which raise important legal questions:

(1) How can transfers of permits or credits be reconciled with existing principles of public international law, in particular, the principle of permanent sovereignty over natural resources?
(2) Which law would govern such transfers and the regulation of disputes?
(3) What institutional mechanisms are needed for an international joint implementation system to function, and what should the relationship between such institutions be?

A system of joint implementation established pursuant to the Climate Change Convention would be governed by the rules of public international law. Accordingly, it is necessary to determine whether international law, and international institutions, created by the Convention or otherwise, are capable of accommodating the development of a joint implementation system.

Permanent sovereignty over natural resources

Anthropogenic greenhouse gas emissions are by-products of the development and exploitation of natural resources. Although degrading and undesirable, it can be argued that these emissions constitute an exploitation of natural resources. Accordingly, limiting the use of natural resources which produce greenhouse gases, and limiting greenhouse gas emissions, would restrict the exploitation and development of natural resources.

The exploitation and development of natural resources within a state is clearly recognized as being within the state's permanent sovereignty.[11] Under international law, states may enter into international agreements in which they

- accept limitations or restrictions on their sovereign right to exploit natural resources or
- dispose or transfer their natural resources.[12]

Joint implementation poses a number of fundamental questions regarding the nature of a state's right to transfer emissions reductions to another state or to a private person:

- Can a state which has transferred its emission permit or credited emissions from a project to another entity seek to revoke the transfer?
- If so, in what circumstances, and on what basis, can it require such permits or credits to be retransferred?
- What guarantees, if any, does a state or other entity who has bought such permits or provided investment to produce the 'credits' have against future nationalization, expropriation, or confiscation, and what is the nature and quantum of any compensation to which this state or entity might become entitled?

- In these circumstances, what rights and obligations flow to states who may not be party to the original transfer transaction from the fact that changes in the Earth's climate and its adverse effects are a common concern of humankind?

The main point about these questions for joint implementation is that they raise questions about legal certainty. Without such certainty no-one would dispute that joint implementation would be fundamentally flawed and inoperable. Similar questions have been raised by many developing countries and a number of international arbitral awards, in the context of the interpretation of the principle of permanent sovereignty over natural resources as set out in various UN General Assembly Resolutions. The international legal status and effect of these Resolutions has been the subject of arbitral interpretations following the expropriation in the 1960s and 1970s by Libya, Iran and Kuwait of a number of oil concessions granted by them to certain British and American oil corporations. In each case, the arbitral tribunal held that the principle of permanent sovereignty over natural resources meant that a state which granted a concession to a foreign private person for a certain period could take back that concession before its term expired by nationalization, confiscation or expropriation, provided that certain conditions, including the payment of 'appropriate compensation,' were fulfilled.[13]

The principle of permanent sovereignty over natural resources, and these arbitral decisions, makes clear that if governed by international law, transfers in joint implementation emission reductions between states and private persons in another country could, in principle, be subject to *revocation* in accordance with the principle of, and conditions attached to the exercise of, permanent sovereignty over natural resources.

A state which bought a permit or credit would have to accept that it could not be guaranteed that these would be protected against expropriation. Similar uncertainty would attach to a traded permit between two states which was governed by international law. A further uncertainty arises in the specific context of the Climate Change Convention from which Parties are free to withdraw at any time after three years from the date on which the Convention entered into force for that Party.[14] Any joint implementation under the Convention would have to anticipate the possibility of such withdrawal and what effect this would have on the continuing legal obligations of Parties involved in the transfer.

Should a state choose to reappropriate, or otherwise alter the terms of a transfer, it is unclear how the International Court of Justice or an arbitration body would approach the issue of appropriate compensation with regard to tradable emission permits or credit. The body of arbitral decisions resulting from the oil cases in the 1960s and 1970s provides some useful general guidance on the determination of compensation.[15] However, tradable emissions permit or credit transactions may involve novel aspects, concerning the nature of the loss to the state deprived of a credit and the methodology for calculating the economic value of permits or credits. Parties to the Convention may further have to face whether, or to what extent, non-Parties to the original permit or credits transactions may intervene in such a dispute in view of their potential roles as 'guardians' and considering that emissions may cause irreparable, adverse changes to the Earth's climate, which is a common concern of humankind.

Questions such as these are difficult, if not impossible, to resolve on the basis of existing substantive rules of public international law. This does *not* make the establishment of joint implementation impossible per se. It does indicate, however, that resolution of some of the legal uncertainties which joint implementation involves may require the consideration and possible adoption of *new* rules of public international law. The adoption of criteria for joint implementation (under the pilot phase and beyond) by the COP would contribute to the development of new rules of international law but the complexity of this task must not be underestimated.

The development and adoption of such new rules may transform the legal relationships between Parties that engage in collaborative activities pursuant to the Climate Change Convention. Due to the nature of international law, adoption of such rules could also have significant legal implications outside the context of the Climate Change Convention. All states, developed or developing, therefore need to reflect and consider fully the legal implications of adopting criteria on joint implementation.

General institutional and procedural issues

The above discussion has focused on one of the legal implications of the substantive rules of public international law on joint implementation. The possible development of additional rules, as well as interpretation of existing ones, also requires consideration of the general institutional and procedural aspects of joint implementation. In view of the range, complexity and interrelatedness of these aspects, it is the intention of this chapter to highlight some of the salient legal considerations.[16]

State sovereignty and choice of law

Transfers of emission permits or credits under the Climate Change Convention could be undertaken by states, international organizations or private persons (companies). The question which arises is this: which legal system governs or should govern such transfers and the regulation of any disputes arising from this?

As between states, it is clear that the law governing transfers would have to be agreed between the Parties. The possibilities include public international law or some other law chosen by mutual agreement between the states involved. As states are reluctant to accept submission to each other's municipal law, it is likely to be public international law. However, it is uncertain which law would govern transfers between states and private Parties and trade between private Parties should such transfers be sanctioned by the COP as joint implementation under the Convention. In respect of transfers involving private entities, the pertinent legal question is whether disputes arising, for example, from the expropriation of previously transferred credits from a joint implementation demonstration project should be subject to the municipal law of the host state, or should such disputes be 'internationalized' and placed within the realm of public international law?

It is important to bear in mind that the choice of law governing the determination of the legal standard for the amount of compensation appropriate in the case of expropriation has been the subject of controversy in the international community for some time. Many developing countries have taken the position that international investment contracts between states and private Parties are not international agreements, in that they are not governed by public international law.[17] This view is disputed by many developed countries which have consistently refused to accept this aspect of the Charter of Economic Rights and Duties of States and have stressed that principles of public international law are relevant in the determination of compensation for expropriation of international investment contracts.[18]

The question of which law should govern the transfer of permits or trade has important legal consequences in relation to the exercise of state sovereignty over natural resources in general. The question of sovereignty is not merely a point of academic interest but is highly relevant in the current circumstances for two reason:

(1) Several Parties to the Convention are preparing or have prepared demonstration projects involving private entities from foreign countries and are considering future arrangements relating to the transfer or sharing of credits for which it will be relevant to decide if municipal or public international law applies,[19] and

(2) The Global Environment Facility (GEF), the entity entrusted on an interim basis with the operation of the financial mechanism of the Convention, is engaged in discussions about its role in stimulating the early development of a tradable emissions market and ways to encourage private sector investment in joint implementation projects which may have implications for the exercise of the rights of state sovereignty.[20]

The GEF is examining, in particular, the development of financial and nonfinancial strategies to

> alleviate risk in high risk investments in natural resource development and management to catalyze additional private sector investment in the developing countries which would reduce greenhouse gases at an acceptable cost and in an environmentally sustainable manner.[21]

The GEF Draft Document specifically identifies 'currency and foreign exchange repatriation risks; and country or political risks: embodying convertibility and repatriation as a specific case but including all forms of unwelcome political interference, including nationalization'.[22] The GEF Draft Document further states that:

> Each of these risks can be alleviated by financial remedies of one kind or another, ranging from injection of risk capital or non-recourse debt to investment guarantees-services for which the World Bank Group can act as intermediaries.[23]

While it may be the case that such risks can be alleviated through financial incentives, countries may also wish to consider whether, and if so to what extent, their sovereign rights to determine which law should apply to transactions arising from joint implementation projects may be adversely affected.

Issues relating to institutional competence

In terms of institutions, an international system of joint implementation would, at a minimum, appear to require:

- the adoption of a set of rules to define the rights and obligations involved in transfers of permits or credits, ie the creation of a market,[24]

- the establishment of an institution, or institutions, with competence to regulate and oversee the effective observance and performance of the market's rules; and
- an extensive and effective monitoring, compliance and verification process.

The extent to which this market can then effectively regulate itself depends, of course, on the initial rules which are decided for it and the extent to which the institutions and entities involved in its establishment maintain their powers and competence to intervene and regulate.

Before establishing a system of joint implementation Parties to the Convention should clarify:

- the role which each of the bodies set up by the Climate Change Convention[25] or to be set up by the COP[26] is to play in either the adoption of rules establishing joint implementation or its subsequent operation; and
- lines of accountability and transparency of decision-making within and between these bodies.

It is relevant to note that whilst the COP is the 'supreme body of the Convention' and is responsible for overseeing the effective implementation of the Convention, including the effective functioning of all the other institutions, it is not clear how any of the other bodies will function and how broadly or narrowly they will interpret the mandate defined for them by the Convention. For example, Article 9 allows the Subsidiary Body for Scientific and Technological Advice (SBSTA) to 'identify innovative, efficient and state-of-the-art technologies and know-how and *advise on the ways and means of promoting development and/or transferring such technologies*' (emphasis added). This could be interpreted broadly to cover not only scientific and technical advice but also advice concerning the wider social and economic aspects of joint implementation projects which aim to transfer state-of-the-art technology.

Similarly, the Subsidiary Body for Implementation (SBI) may consider its role 'to assist the Conference of the Parties in the assessment and review of the *effective implementation* of the Convention' (emphasis added), to cover the monitoring, compliance and verification aspects of joint implementation projects as a whole.[27] The fact that it is required to 'assess the overall aggregated effect of steps taken by Parties in the light of the latest scientific assessments concerning climate change' suggests that whilst it is not intended to assess the effects of particular projects, it may nevertheless play an important role in decision-making concerning joint implementation. This is particularly so because in order to assist COP 1 with the reviews required by Article 4 (2) (d), it may have to consider the *effectiveness* of an 'open' joint implementation system (which permits a host state to collaborate in joint implementation projects whilst its own emissions increase without limits). The SBI could, after assessment, report to the COP that this kind of joint implementation is not the most effective way for Parties to implement the Convention.

Finally, in view of the important and potentially catalytic role the Convention's Financial Mechanism may play in the process of encouraging the establishment and operation of a market for joint implementation projects, it is particularly important to clarify legal uncertainties concerning the basis and extent of the GEF's competence *vis-à-vis* the COP, bearing in mind its designation as the interim operator of the Convention's Financial Mechanism.[28]

COP 1's decision to establish a pilot phase for activities implemented jointly did little to clarify the roles of these bodies, as it merely provides that SBSTA 'will, in coordination with the SBI, establish a framework for reporting' these activities to the COP.

Dispute settlement

To ensure that disputes between states, or other entities, are settled on a consistent basis, and to promote the legal certainty which is necessary to underpin the kind of long-term investments required for joint implementation projects, the establishment of a binding and mandatory form of dispute resolution would appear to be indispensable. The Convention does not contain provisions on dispute resolution that meet these requirements.[29]

Compulsory, adversarial, and backward-looking dispute resolution procedures were considered by some delegations to be out of place in the Convention.[30] This was due, in part, to a perception that in terms of achieving the Convention's *environmental* objective, it was unnecessary, and perhaps unhelpful, to focus on mechanisms to determine violations and compensation or impose punitive measures against Parties unable to fulfil their commitments. Article 13 of the Convention therefore requires COP 1 to consider the establishment of 'a multilateral consultative process,' to assist Parties' compliance with the Convention. However, if joint implementation results in large flows of public or private investment to host states, as its proponents intend, states with important economic, financial or commercial stakes in joint implementation projects, whether as buyers or sellers of permits or credits, may consider the 'multilateral consultative process' an inadequate and inappropriate forum in which to pursue claims.

The development of annexes with detailed rules of procedure to enable the conciliation and arbitration mechanisms established by the Convention to come into effective operation becomes an even more important task.[31] In view of the numbers of joint implementation projects being planned, it would appear prudent and sensible to develop such annexes before a system of joint implementation is adopted.

JOINT IMPLEMENTATION UNDER THE CLIMATE CHANGE CONVENTION

Significant legal issues

The concept of joint implementation appears, or is implicit, in the Convention in a number of different places. To assist exposition of the significant legal issues concerning joint implementation, the most important provisions relating to joint implementation in the Convention are set out in the Annex to this chapter.

The textual legal analysis offered in this chapter discusses the relevant provisions of the Convention to illuminate discussions about the nature and permissibility of joint implementation activities by Parties to the Convention. Specifically, the chapter addresses the following legal issues or questions:

- which Parties can collaborate in joint implementation activities;

- which commitments can joint implementation relate to or support;
- in what circumstances can joint implementation count towards implementation of a Party's commitments; and
- when, if at all, can the COP 1 take decisions to adopt criteria for-joint implementation and what is the nature of the decision-making process required for such an adoption.

Legal interpretation

The text of the Convention reflects the consensus which emerged on many of these issues. However, it leaves open other issues which could not be adequately addressed in the time available or on which no consensus could be reached. Accordingly, the final text of the Convention reflects a delicate balance of interest between different states on the role joint implementation can play in the Convention as currently *adopted*, as well as how joint implementation can be further developed through review and consideration by the Conference of the Parties at a later stage.

In accordance with common legal practice, the analysis that follows is based on the international legal principle that:

> A treaty shall be interpreted in good faith in accordance with the ordinary meaning to be given to the terms of the treaty in their context and in the light of its object and purpose.[32]

For the purposes of interpretation, the context includes the Preamble and any annexes.[33] In addition, the Convention expressly states that '[i]n actions to achieve the objective of the Convention and to implement its provisions, the Parties shall be guided, *inter alia'*, by the Principles set out in Article 3.

The scope for joint implementation between Annex I Parties and non-Annex I Parties under the Convention

Article 4 (2), which sets out commitments, only applies to the EC and developed country Parties listed in Annex I. The third sentence of Article 4 (2) (a) of the Convention contains a permissive provision relating to joint implementation which states that '[t]hese Parties [ie Annex I Parties] may implement such policies and measures jointly with other Parties and may assist other Parties in contributing to the achievement of the objective of the Convention and, in particular, that of this subparagraph'. However, Article 4 (2) (d) establishes limits to the operation of this provision by stating that 'the Conference of the Parties, at its first session, shall also take decisions regarding criteria for joint implementation as indicated in subparagraph (a)'.

Taken together, Article 4 (2) (a) and (d) make clear that joint implementation under the Climate Change Convention can only take place after the COP has adopted criteria for joint implementation. Any benefits of joint implementation activity can only be applied towards a Party's obligations under Article 4 (2) (a) to the extent that such criteria have been adopted and entered into force, and to the degree that the activity complies fully with such criteria. In the absence of such criteria, joint implementation under the Convention cannot and should not take place.

Article 4 (2) (a) thus draws a distinction between:

- joint implementation with other Parties with regard to policies and measures which Annex I Parties are taking pursuant to subparagraph (a); and
- the provision of assistance by Annex I Parties to other Parties to achieve the objectives of the Convention, including, in particular, subparagraph (a).

The text therefore envisages 'joint implementation' and 'assistance' as two separate, but related, matters.[34] This chapter only addresses joint implementation.

Annex I Parties may collaborate in joint implementation activities in respect of their specific commitments under Article 4 (2) (a) and (b). The most pertinent legal question here is whether the reference to 'other Parties' in the last sentence of subparagraph 4 (2) (a) allows joint implementation only between Parties listed in Annex I, or whether Annex I Parties can collaborate in joint implementation activities with developing country Parties.

As adopted, the text of the Convention appears to support the conclusion that, taking account of its ultimate objective and the applicable principles, as well as the specific commitments, joint implementation is permitted only among Annex I Parties and in respect of policies and measures located within the limits of their collective national jurisdiction or control. This is supported by the following legal considerations.

In order to determine the circumstances under which joint implementation is permitted under the Convention, one must look at the specific provisions of the text. The Convention does not contain a general permissive provision which endorses or allows joint implementation between all of its Parties in respect of any of their commitments.[35] Significantly, there are no provisions on joint implementation in relation to the commitments all Parties have under Article 4 (1). It appears, therefore, that the activities and circumstances in relation to which joint implementation can occur are carefully defined, and delimited, by the context of Annex I Parties' specific commitments contained in Article 4 (2) (a).

Article 4 (2) (a) is unambiguous in requiring each Annex I Party to undertake national policies and measures to limit its anthropogenic emissions of greenhouse gases and protect and enhance its sinks and reservoirs. The words in the last sentence of subparagraph (a) which permit joint implementation are in effect a permissive proviso which qualifies this otherwise unambiguous obligation to undertake *national* policies and measures in respect of emissions which arise or are located within the jurisdiction or control of the Annex I Party.

As adopted, the text of this permissive proviso does not appear to allow Annex I Parties to undertake joint implementation activities which deal with sources of anthropogenic emissions, or sinks and reservoirs that lie beyond the limits of these Parties' jurisdiction or control, ruling out, in effect, joint implementation with developing country Parties as part of their measures to achieve the commitments in Article 4 (2) (a).

This is because the proviso confines the scope of Annex I Parties' joint implementation activities to such policies and measures as required by Article 4 (2) (a). The reference to 'such policies and measures' appears to be a clear reference to the specific 'policies and . . . corresponding measures' described in the previous two sentences of Article 4 (2) (a) which only Annex I Parties are obliged to adopt and implement. It is *not* a reference to the general commitment to formulate and implement 'programmes containing measures' to mitigate climate change which all Parties are required to undertake pursuant to Article 4 (1) (b).[36]

The nature of the 'policies and measures' referred to in Article 4 (2) (b) differs from the nature of the 'measures' required under Article 4 (1) (b) in one important legal respect which circumscribes the ability of Annex I countries to collaborate in joint implementation projects with non-Annex I countries. This is due to the fact that the 'policies and measures' which an Annex I Party is required to adopt pursuant to Article 4 (2) (a) and (b) must relate to 'limiting its anthropogenic emissions of greenhouse gases and protecting and enhancing *its* greenhouse gas sinks and reservoirs' (emphasis added).[37]

Article 1 (4) of the Convention states that '[e]missions means the release of greenhouse gases and/or their precursors into the atmosphere *over a specified area* and period of time' (emphasis added). As there is no contrary indication in Article 4 (2) that the emissions being addressed are global anthropogenic emissions', the reference to 'its anthropogenic emissions' must in order to be consistent with the specific commitments set out in Articles 4 (2) (a) and (b), refer to emissions released by a Party over its own territorial area.

It is relevant to note, by contrast, that the general commitment of wording in Article 4 (1) (b) makes no distinction between, on the one hand, emission sources and sinks reservoirs under the jurisdiction or control of a Party, and on the other hand, those which lie outside this jurisdiction or control. This provision clearly allows an Annex I Party to undertake collaborative projects with developing country Parties to limit emissions or enhance and protect sinks and reservoirs. However, these collaborative measures would not appear to form part of the specific commitments a Party can have under Article 4 (2) (a).

Thus joint implementation would only appear to cover actions which deal with Annex I Parties' own aggregate anthropogenic emissions and the total sinks and reservoirs that lie within the limits of their collective national jurisdiction or control, or in the case of a Party which is a regional economic integration organization, such as the EC, within the competence of that regional economic integration organization.[39]

Against the above, it could be argued that, notwithstanding that measures and policies required in Article 4 (2) (a) refer to anthropogenic emissions sources, sinks and reservoirs physically located within a Party's jurisdiction, an Annex I Party might 'match up' or 'twin' anthropogenic emissions arising from sources located within its jurisdiction with a sink or a reservoir that lies outside its jurisdiction. A Party could thus argue that it was limiting its own emissions sources through the enhancement of a developing country Party's sinks. On this basis, an Annex I Party could therefore adopt a national programme which stated that its only limitation measure was that all emissions from its power stations would be 'limited' through the financial support and technical assistance for an afforestation project in a developing country Party.

This argument is certainly not inconsistent with the wording of Article 4 (2) (a), and if accepted, would allow an Annex I Party to undertake joint implementation with a developing country Party as part of its Article 4 (2) commitments. However, accepting this view requires giving the term 'its' an unusual and rather special meaning in this context. Under international law, a special meaning can be given to a term if it is established that the Parties so intended.[40] The Parties to the Convention may wish to consider whether the term 'its' was intended to have a special meaning which would commit Annex I

Parties to enacting *national* measures that have the effect of enhancing sinks and reservoirs located *beyond* the limits of their own jurisdiction. In this regard it should be noted that one consequence of accepting a special meaning for the term 'its' would be to blur the distinction between the Parties' general commitments and the specific commitments of Annex I Parties, which perhaps lies at the heart of the Convention.

In considering these matters, it is also necessary to bear in mind that the Convention states that principles contained in, *inter alia*, Article 3 should guide Parties' actions to achieve the objective of the Convention and to implement its provisions. Article 3, together with the negotiating history of the Convention, and taking into account the ultimate objective of the Convention, is therefore relevant in considering whether joint implementation between Annex I Parties and developing country Parties is permissable. They may also suggest that there are strongly arguable grounds of law and policy to deny joint implementation between Annex I and developing country Parties under the Convention – at least until the latter are subject to specific commitments under an amended Article 4 (2) (a) and (b). The most relevant principles include, but are not limited to:

- equity;[41]
- developed countries should take the lead in combating climate change and the adverse effects thereof;[42]
- developed countries need to take immediate action in a flexible manner on the basis of clear priorities, as a first step towards comprehensive response strategies at the global, national and, where agreed, regional levels;[43]
- common but differentiated responsibilities and respective capabilities;[44]
- the specific needs and special circumstances of developing country Parties;[45] and
- policies and measures to deal with climate change should be cost-effective so as to ensure global benefits at the lowest possible cost.[46]

As discussed above, the COP may find it difficult, if not impossible, to assess the overall effectiveness (and hence cost-effectiveness) of joint implementation in contributing to the ultimate objective of the Convention.[47] This is because in a project-based joint implementation system, where developing country Parties have no commitments to limit greenhouse gases, global emissions can continue to increase indefinitely in both the Annex I Party *and* the developing country Party. This kind of joint implementation thus not only undermines the specific commitments of the Annex I Parties, but also the ultimate objective of the Convention.

Should the Parties consider that joint implementation between Annex I Parties and developing country Parties could be allowed under the Convention, and consider criteria for joint implementation, it may be useful to consider and reflect further on the nature of additional commitments, if any, which joint implementation might entail, particularly for developing country Parties. For example, paragraph 27 of the INC Secretariat's Note on Joint Implementation suggests that, for completeness and to avoid double counting of emissions, 'each Party involved in a joint implementation project may have to describe the results of the [joint implementation] project' and that this would mean that a 'developing country Party that was not yet required to communicate information under Article 12.5 would do so on this respect alone'.

A relevant legal consideration for non-Annex I Parties to bear in mind here is that Article 7 (2) (2) of the Convention specifically requires the COP to assess the effectiveness implementation in achieving the objectives of the Convention.[48] The overall success or effectiveness of joint implementation projects under the Convention will therefore be a matter which is reviewable by the COP, as well as by the Parties involved in joint implementation. As a practical matter, where joint implementation projects take place in developing country Parties (which have no quantified commitments to reduce emissions), an assessment of the effectiveness of joint implementation would appear to require not only effective monitoring and verification, but also a determination as to the projected emissions of such countries with, and in the absence of, joint implementation projects.

The provision of relevant information about the projected emissions by developing country Parties cannot, in a legal sense, be considered as amounting to a commitment to maintain emissions at a particular level. A determination as to the projected emissions of a country, considered by the COP or another agency, such as the GEF, as part of their assessment of the effectiveness of joint implementation, and accepted as valid by the Party providing the information, could constitute evidence of state practice which has important legal consequences in international law. It may be useful to reflect upon and consider the adverse legal implications, if any, of offering information with respect to joint implementation activities as part of the decisions they may wish to take about more detailed criteria for joint implementation beyond the pilot phase.

CONCLUSION

The COP will have to consider not only the legal issues raised by joint implementation but also the practicality of putting joint implementation into effect. The experience of the 12 member states of the European Community, which is committed as a developed country Party to achieving its commitments jointly, may prove instructive in this regard. The 12, relatively homogenous, member states of the Community have, so far, failed in their related efforts to agree on joint implementation amongst themselves to reduce sulphur and nitrogen dioxides under the 1988 Large Combustion Directive.[49] In drawing conclusions as to its relevance to the Parties of the Climate Change Convention it will be necessary to understand and balance the environmental, ethical, economic and social, as well as the legal, aspects of joint implementation.

This chapter has touched upon a number of legal issues raised by the establishment and operation of an international system of joint implementation under the Climate Change Convention. Many of these issues are complex and require further reflection and consideration by delegates. In and of themselves, complexity and the need for reflection alone should not impede the adoption of joint implementation if it is the view, and the will, of the international community that an international system of joint implementation is indeed the best way to put into effect their determination to protect the climate system for the benefit of present and future generations of humankind. Complexity, and the need to ensure that whatever is ultimately agreed can stand the test of time, call for the further consideration of all the relevant issues raised by joint implementation.

APPENDIX 5: EXTRACTS OF RELEVANT CONVENTION PROVISIONS ON JOINT IMPLEMENTATION

Article 3 (3), Principles

Efforts to address climate change may be carried out cooperatively by interested Parties.

Article 4 (2) (a) and (b), Commitments

The developed country Parties and other Parties included in Annex I commit themselves specifically as provided for in the following:

(a) Each of these Parties shall adopt national[50] policies and take corresponding measures on the mitigation of climate change, by limiting its anthropogenic emissions of greenhouse gases and protecting and enhancing its greenhouse gas sinks and reservoirs. These policies and measures will demonstrate that developed countries are taking the lead in modifying longer-term trends in anthropogenic emissions consistent with the objective of the Convention, recognizing that the return by the end of the present decade to earlier levels of anthropogenic emissions of carbon dioxide and other greenhouse gases not controlled by the Montreal Protocol would contribute to such modification, and taking into account the differences in these Parties' starting points and approaches, economic structures and resource bases, the need to maintain strong and sustainable economic growth, available technologies and other individual circumstances, as well as the need for equitable and appropriate contributions by each of these Parties to the global effort regarding that objective. These Parties may implement such policies and measures jointly with other Parties and may assist other Parties in contributing to the achievement of the objective of the Convention and, in particular, that of this subparagraph.

(b) In order to promote progress to this end, each of these Parties shall communicate, within six months of the entry into force of the Convention for it and periodically thereafter, and in accordance with Article 12, detailed information on its policies and measures referred to in subparagraph (a) above, as well as on its resulting projected anthropogenic emissions by sources and removals by sinks of greenhouse gases not controlled by the

Montreal Protocol for the period referred to in subparagraph (a), with the aim of returning individually or jointly to their 1990 levels these anthropogenic emissions of carbon dioxide and other greenhouse gases not controlled by the Montreal Protocol. This information will be reviewed by the Conference of the Parties, at its first session and periodically thereafter, in accordance with Article 7.

Article 4 (2) (d), Commitments

The Conference of the Parties shall, at its first session, review the adequacy of subparagraphs (a) and (b) above. Such review shall be carried out in the light of the best available scientific information and assessment on climate change and its impacts, as well as relevant technical, social and economic information. Based on this review, the Conference of the Parties shall take appropriate action, which may include the adoption of amendments to the commitments in subparagraphs (a) and (b) above. The Conference of the Parties, at its first session, shall also take decisions regarding criteria for joint implementation as indicated in subparagraph (a) above. A second review of subparagraphs (a) and (b) shall take place not later than 31 December 1998, and thereafter at regular intervals determined by the Conference of the Parties, until the objective of the Convention is met.

Article 7 (2) (c), Conference of the Parties

[The COP may] [f]acilitate, at the request of two or more Parties, the coordination of measures adopted by them to address climate change and its effects, taking into account the differing circumstances, responsibilities and capabilities of the Parties and their respective commitments under the Convention.

Article 11 (5), Financial mechanisms

The developed country Parties may also provide, and developing country Parties avail themselves of, financial resources related to the implementation of the Convention through bilateral, regional and other multilateral channels.

Article 12 (8), Communication of information related to implementation

Any group of Parties may, subject to guidelines adopted by the Conference of the Parties, and to prior notification to the Conference of the Parties, make a joint communication in fulfilment of their obligations under this Article, provided that such a communication includes information on the fulfilment by each of these Parties of its individual obligations under the Convention.

COP 1 DECISION 5/CP.L

Activities implemented jointly under the pilot phase

The Conference of the Parties,

Recalling that, in accordance with Article 4.2(d) of the United Nations Framework Convention on Climate Change, the Conference is required to take decisions regarding criteria for joint implementation as indicated in Article 4.2(a).,

Noting that the largest share of historical and current global emissions of greenhouse gases has originated in developed countries, that per capita emissions developing countries are still relatively low and that the share of global emissions originating in developing countries will grow to meet their social and development needs,

Acknowledging that the global nature of climate change calls for the widest possible cooperation by all countries and their participation in an effective and appropriate international response, in accordance with their common but differentiated responsibilities and respective capabilities and their social and economic conditions,

Recognizing that,

(a) According to the provisions of the Convention, the commitments under Article 4.2(a) to adopt national policies and to take corresponding measures on the mitigation of climate change apply only to Parties included in Annex I to the Convention (Annex I Parties), and that Parties not included in Annex I to the Convention (non-Annex I Parties) have no such commitments,

(b) Activities implemented jointly between Annex I Parties and non-Annex I Parties will not be seen as fulfilment of current commitments of Annex I Parties under Article 4.2(b) of the Convention; but they could contribute to the achievement of the objective of the Convention and to the fulfilment of commitments of Annex 11 Parties under Article 4.5 of the Convention,

(c) Activities implemented jointly under the Convention are supplemental, and should only be treated as a subsidiary means of achieving the objective of the Convention,

(d) Activities implemented jointly in no way modify the commitments of each Party under the Convention.

1. Decides:

(a) To establish a pilot phase for activities implemented jointly among Annex I Parties and, on a voluntary basis, with non-Annex I Parties that so request;

(b) That activities implemented jointly should be compatible with and supportive of national environment and development priorities and strategies, contribute to cost-effectiveness in achieving global benefits and could be conducted in a comprehensive manner covering all relevant sources, sinks and reservoirs of greenhouse gases;

(c) That all activities implemented jointly under this pilot phase require prior acceptance, approval or endorsement by the Governments of the Parties participating in these activities;

(d) That activities implemented jointly should bring about real, measurable and long-term environmental benefits related to the mitigation of climate change that would not have occurred in the absence of such activities;

(e) That the financing of activities implemented jointly shall be additional to the financial obligations of Parties included in Annex 11 to the Convention within the framework of the financial mechanism as well as to current official development assistance (ODA) flows;

(f) That no credits shall accrue to any Party as a result of greenhouse gas emissions reduced or sequestered during the pilot phase from activities implemented jointly;

2. Further decides that during the pilot phase:

(a) The Subsidiary Body for Scientific and Technological Advice will, in coordination with the Subsidiary Body for Implementation, establish a framework for reporting, in a transparent, well-defined and credible fashion, on the possible global benefits and the national economic, social and environmental impacts as well as any practical experience gained or technical difficulties encountered in activities implemented jointly under the pilot phase;

(b) The Parties involved are encourage to report to the Conference of the Parties through the secretariat using the framework thus established. This reporting shall be distinct from the national communications of Parties;

(c) The Subsidiary Body for Scientific and Technological Advice and the Subsidiary Body for Implementation, with the assistance of the secretariat are requested to prepare a synthesis report for consideration by the Conference of the Parties,

3. Further decides:

(a) That the Conference of the Parties shall, at its annual session, review the progress of the pilot phase on the basis of the synthesis report with a view to taking appropriate decisions on the continuation of the pilot phase;

(b) In so doing, the Conference of the Parties shall take into consideration the need for a comprehensive review of the pilot phase in order to take a conclusive decision on the pilot phase and the progression beyond that, no later than the end of the present decade.

10th plenary meeting
7 April 1995

12 FINANCING GLOBAL ENVIRONMENTAL PROTECTION

*Andrew Jordan and Jacob Werksman**

UNCED AND THE DEBATE ON FINANCE

One of the most contentious issues raised at the June 1992 United Nations Conference on Environment and Development (UNCED) was whether, and to what extent, the developed countries would meet the additional cost of measures undertaken by the developing countries to protect the global climate system and preserve biodiversity. It was generally recognized that sufficient financial incentives would need to be built into the agreements then under negotiation to encourage greater developing country support, but little discussion took place as to how these incentives would actually function in practice. After protracted negotiations, a compromise of sorts was reached. Developing countries pledged to implement certain measures to address global environmental problems in return for new and additional finance provided by the industrialized states. The total amount of 'additionality' was not specified.[1] However, the additional money was earmarked for the *incremental costs* incurred by developing country Parties in implementing the terms of any agreements they entered into.

Over the last five years, the terms 'additionality' and 'incrementality' have appeared with increasing regularity in international negotiations and agreements. Broad conceptual agreement on additional financing contributed to the successful re-negotiation of the Montreal Protocol in 1990[2] and to the adoption of the Conventions on Climate Change and Biodiversity.[3] The successful use of financial bargains between North and South in these issue areas appears to have had an important precedent. An expectation has developed that financial transfer packages or other 'selective inducements'[4] will be needed to accelerate and strengthen the process of negotiating international

* An earlier version of this chapter previously appeared as an article in *RECIEL*, Vol. 3, Issue 2/3, FIELD, London 1994.

environmental regimes in other areas of global concern such as desertification and deforestation.

In practice, however, the two concepts have proved elusive and little agreement exists over how much money should be transferred and how it should be used. This is partly because additionality and incrementality touch the heart of deeper political debates over which countries should shoulder the responsibility for human-induced global environmental change, and on how the costs of responding to such change should be apportioned between countries. Historical grievances and the temptation to link finance to other disputed issues in international politics, serve only to complicate the debate even further. However, some measure of agreement must be sought or the implementation of agreements signed at Rio may be jeopardized.

This chapter reviews the emergence of the terms 'new and additional' and 'incremental cost' in international environmental politics. It focuses on the theoretical and practical difficulties that have arisen during initial stages of implementing the Climate Change Convention and in the operation of the Convention's financing institution, the Global Environment Facility (GEF).

ADDITIONALITY AND INCREMENTALITY

Additionality describes the origins of the financial resources needed to solve global environmental problems, while incrementality determines the total *size* of those resources needed to address a particular area of concern (eg biodiversity, marine pollution). The concepts, thus, interlock: the greater the incremental costs, the more additional resources will be required; the more additionality that is provided, the greater the 'total' incremental cost that can be met.

The concepts have tended to take on different meanings in different contexts. The first context is that of *regime formation* (ie international negotiations), where bargains are struck between countries to produce international law and policy. Finance can help to lubricate the process of international diplomacy. The second context is the more drawn out process of *operational decision-making* (ie the implementation of international accords), where implementation programmes are drawn up, individual projects are identified and ranked, and finance begins to flow. The rapid entry into force of both the Rio Conventions has forced differences of opinion, which were subsumed during the process of negotiation, to the surface.

'New and additional' financial resources

At the core of the concept of additionality is a general understanding that resources should be provided by the industrialized world over and above existing flows of international finance for measures taken by developing countries to address global environmental challenges.[5] Additionality can be viewed as the price which the South demands for its participation in international attempts to solve global environmental problems, and a small contribution to offset the North's general ecological debt. The word 'new' is generally understood to describe either the sources of funding or the financial mechanisms used to provide them.[6] The term 'additional' suggests that the assistance supplements rather than diminishes existing flows of finance.[7]

The additionality debate

The principle of additionality could now be said to form one of the central planks of the Group of 77 (G-77) developing countries' negotiating strategy in international discussions on environment and development.[8] On a very general level, the industrialized states have been sympathetic to the South's plea for extra financial assistance but they have carefully avoided making specific commitments. Some donor states have sought to put promises into action, and have pledged their support for the new and additional funding mechanisms of the Montreal Protocol Multilateral Fund (MPMF) and the recently restructured Global Environment Facility (GEF).[9] Neither fund, however, has sought to define, or even clarify, the additionality of its contributions.

The rationale for additionality

The concept of additionality has an intellectual coherence and is politically attractive to both North and South. The developing countries' calls for additionality are symptomatic of a number of underlying concerns, some essentially practical others with a moral and ethical dimension. First, developing countries claim that their attempts to industrialize should not be hindered by the costs of measures designed to ameliorate problems not of their making. Additionality would provide them with the inducement to leapfrog the polluting and wasteful stages of industrialization. Second, capital constraints and an overwhelming need to address domestic concerns such as poverty and food security do not allow for tackling environmental problems with the same vigour as the industrialized world. During the 1980s, flows of finance from the North (aid, private flows and export credits) declined sharply (largely as a result of reductions in private flows) and even reversed as the debt problem reached its peak in the mid to late 1980s.[10] Calls for additionality are thus one attempt to address much deeper inequalities and economic imbalances in the world economy. During international negotiations for the Conventions and the GEF, the developing countries insisted that contributions be additional and disbursements concessional (ie in the form of grants or very low interest loans). They were particularly concerned that contributions to the GEF would not diminish the funds available for development assistance.[11]

The notion of providing an extra quantum of finance specifically for the global environment holds a certain appeal for the North as well. First, allocating a certain amount of money for sustainable development or the global environment makes for good and publicly visible 'gesture politics'. Second, separating out a distinct portion of money for global warming or ozone depletion raises the hope that it will be used more 'efficiently' (in the sense that it specifically funds global environmental projects rather than development related activities), while also helping to parry criticism that existing flows of aid fail to reflect global environmental concerns.

Additionality baselines

Additionality is a relative term, which predicates the need for some form of bench mark or baseline, above which an 'additional' increment can be discerned. The most common interpretation of additionality sets this baseline at the level of existing development assistance. Total net resource flows to the South in 1991 amounted to US$ 131bn (at 1990 prices) (World Resources Institute, 1994)[12] of which US$ 73bn (56 per cent) was in the form of Official Development Assistance (ODA).[13] Although global aid volume has grown markedly in gross terms in the last 20 years, as a percentage of OECD GNP it has hardly changed and remains lodged at around 0.33 per cent. Additionality, so measured, would thus constitute any increase in ODA over and above 0.33 per cent.

Developing countries have pressed for a higher, aspirational baseline of 0.7 per cent of GNP, which has been the UN's official target for ODA since 1970.[14] At present only five developed countries could be said to be meeting or exceeding this target.[15] Not surprisingly, individual OECD donors support definitions of additionality that place their practices in the best light. Sweden, a country which nets its contributions to the GEF and the MPMF from a general multilateral aid budget (thereby failing on a narrow construction of an additionality test applied specifically to Sweden itself)[16] that is around 0.92 per cent of its domestic GNP, would clearly have a strong incentive to push for the acceptance of a 0.7 per cent baseline and indeed has made representations to that effect.[17]

The US government, in the context of ozone protection, describes additionality as 'the allocation of *more funds* specifically to ozone protection, but not necessarily the allocation of funds in addition to overall resource flows' (emphasis added).[18] On this interpretation, any extra money which is diverted to environmental protection is judged to be additional regardless of its origins.[19] In the context of GEF's pilot phase the US announced that it was not prepared to contribute 'additional' funds to the GEF's core fund. Instead, the US negotiated a co-financing agreement with the GEF, contributions to which are re-directed from the regular US Agency for International Development (USAID) budget.

Finally, some countries have argued that additionality should be measured over and above the level of *total* net resource flows, including resources in the form of private flows of money.[20] The US Government has implied that increased flows of North–South private investment might also be considered as releasing further additionality, even when levels of publicly financed ODA remain constant.[21] If net financial transfers are taken as the unit of account (ie total flows minus interest and dividends on loans) the bench mark in 1990 would have been just US$ 34bn. The concept of additionality could then be stretched to include such things as debt forgiveness or 'debt-for-nature' swaps. The adequacy of money allotted to the GEF and MPMF could be judged to be either very large or relatively small, depending on the baseline adopted.

Additionality post-Rio

The texts of the Climate Change and Biodiversity Conventions do not clarify the meaning of additionality, and merely use the umbrella term 'new and additional finance'. If 'existing flows' is to be the baseline, then what is 'additional' can only be calculated on the basis of what a donor would have done had they not entered into an international agreement or pledged to support an international fund. The absence of a definition opens up an enormous opportunity for conflicting interpretations and expectations.

An accurate calculation or indeed enforcement of additionality will be difficult to achieve not least because it would transform a general commitment to a specific obligation. But, as the demand for regular flows of development assistance continues to increase and finance becomes more closely linked with the future prospects for global environmental governance, greater scrutiny may need to be applied to the measurement and enforcement of additionality. Arguably, this may help to engender trust between Parties and may improve the quality of the overall cooperative effort.

INCREMENTAL COST FINANCING

The term 'incremental cost' is important because it quantifies the size of the payment to developing countries will receive from developed countries as compensation[22] for acceding to, and implementing the terms of, international environmental agreements. Just as with the term 'additionality', recipient Parties clearly have an incentive to try and maximize the size and scope of the total side payment; providers, the converse.

Incrementality can be traced to the text of the revised (1990) Montreal Protocol. During the negotiations, countries of the South expressed concern that measures to address ozone depletion, a problem they repeatedly stressed was not of their making, would 'add new burdens to their economies and adversely affect their standard of living'.[23] What were termed 'incremental burdens' by negotiators were eventually incorporated into the text of the revised Protocol as 'incremental costs'.

In the Montreal Protocol the sources and technical solutions for ozone depletion are relatively easy to identify. Defining and implementing the term 'incremental cost' has proved comparatively straightforward and Parties have agreed on a broad list (an 'indicative list') of costs judged to be eligible for 'incremental' cost financing.[24] In terms of climate change, a problem more complex and uncertain to predict and alleviate, the task will be far more challenging.

Much of the controversy surrounding the concept of incrementality has arisen because of expectations attached to the concept when it was expressed as a broad principle. Thus far, the work of developing a specific definition for incrementality in the Climate Change Convention has been carried forward by two separate but related institutions: the Convention's Conference of Parties, and the GEF, which is to serve as the interim[25] 'operating entity' of the Convention's financial mechanism. The future of the incremental financing issue will probably be determined by the continuing interplay between these two institutions.

Incremental costs and the Climate Convention

All Parties to the Convention, developed and developing countries alike, have committed themselves to undertake a wide range of measures to address the threat of climate change. These 'general commitments' are designed to develop, collect and disseminate information on climate change and possible responses, to implement programmes containing measures to reduce net emissions of greenhouse gases and to facilitate adequate adaptation to climate change. Developed country Parties further commit themselves to provide *new and additional resources* to meet the *agreed full incremental costs* of developing country

Parties. The term 'agreed full incremental cost' was, in itself, a compromise. Throughout negotiations, developed countries had advocated the use of the single qualification 'agreed', whereas developing countries preferred the term 'full'.[26] As a last minute compromise, the two qualifiers, 'full' and 'agreed', were combined to produce the seemingly contradictory term 'agreed full incremental costs'.[27]

Incremental costs and the GEF

During the GEF's pilot phase (which began almost a year before the Convention was signed at Rio), donor country Participants defined incremental cost as that segment of an eligible project's total cost which directly benefits the global environment, but which would not normally be in the interest of a host nation to finance itself. Only those projects which generated global benefits, but which required extra concessional financing to be viable to the host nation (ie national costs exceeded national benefits), were judged to be eligible for GEF support in the pilot phase. 'Domestically beneficial' projects were to be excluded.

In the context of the GEF, then, incremental cost is the difference between the national costs and national benefits of a project designed to generate global environmental benefits. So, for example, the GEF could meet the incremental cost of re-designing a proposed coal-fired power station project to utilize a local supply of natural gas, thereby realizing the global benefit of reduced CO_2 emissions. In this example, the GEF would pay for the incremental cost of the conversion; the 'baseline' cost of the coal-fired station would have been financed by the host nation (either from its own resources or from international lending or the private sector).

Since Rio, discussions on developing an operational definition for incremental costs in the climate change context has been proceeding within the INC and the GEF on parallel tracks. The INC, a large and loosely structured intergovernmental body with limited administrative and research capacity but a wide-ranging agenda, has thus far failed to resolve the issue beyond renewing its requests to its Secretariat for further clarification of the issues. As this vacuum developed, the GEF administration launched its own multi-million dollar research Programme for Measuring Incremental Costs for the Environment (PRINCE).[28]

Certain commentators expressed surprise over PRINCE's approach to measuring incrementality because it appeared both to erode significantly the level of financial resources that would be available under the Conventiorr and prejudge the outcome of discussions which are scheduled to begin at the first meeting of the Convention's Conference of the Parties (COP) in 1995.[29] The Convention provides specifically that the COP (and not the GEF) will 'decide on ... policies, programme priorities and eligibility criteria' for the financial mechanism.

It is easy to imagine that the bulk of the measures to be undertaken by developing countries under the Convention will have national as well as global benefits. Because of this, GEF conceded early on that 'only a limited number of projects are likely to be ... eligible for full funding from GEF'. The GEF suggests that the rest of the increment, to cover that portion of the costs seen to have 'national' benefits, should come from 'other sources of domestic and foreign funding sources'.[30] In a later statement the GEF claimed that: 'in typical cases, the incremental cost will be a relatively small proportion of the total cost of the re-designed or alternate activity...'.[31]

'Gross' and 'net' incremental costs

As policy-makers begin to struggle with the implications of these early attempts to apply incremental cost principles, two competing interpretations can be said to have emerged: *gross* and *net* incremental costs.[32] Gross incremental costs can be defined as the difference between the total costs of implementing a proposed project and that course of action which the developing country would have pursued had it not undertaken commitments under the Convention. Supporters of this interpretation rely on a direct reading of the text of the Convention and tend to lay stress upon the word *full* in 'agreed full incremental cost'.[33] Net incremental costs, on the other hand, can be viewed as the additional cost of complying with the Convention *minus* the value of any domestic benefits thereby generated. Generally, this has been the approach taken by the GEF, and justified on the grounds that it is more 'cost-effective' than funding the full cost of projects (ie by funding only those aspects of a project that specifically yield global environmental benefits, more funds will be available to fund the globally beneficial aspects of further projects). The significant difference between the two approaches is that on the gross cost interpretation, developing countries are left better off than they would have been without Convention funding, whereas on the net cost interpretation developing countries are left no better off (except for their share of the global environmental benefit) than had the Convention not been adopted.[34]

The G-77 coalition and China have signalled that they expect the costs of *all* the commitments mentioned in the Climate Change Convention to be met including those measures with primarily domestic benefits such as adaption, research and training.[35] They have expressed concern that some developed countries are attempting to reduce the scale of transfers by disallowing projects which are domestically beneficial from being eligible for funding (ie the net cost approach).[36]

If the net approach is followed, developing countries may be asked to look outside the GEF for funding. To implement the Convention, developing countries may be forced to fend for themselves in financial channels ungoverned by the principles of the Convention. This may, in turn, lead to an unsystematic and uneven distribution of resources. No system would be in place to ensure funding from other sources is new and additional, and at the same time on the concessional terms agreed to under the Convention. Ironically, the net approach, if adopted, would render those countries least capable of fulfilling their obligations (and thus most likely to benefit nationally from enhanced capacity) which are least eligible for extra funding. Least developed countries would be saddled with an inequitable share of the global burden of climate change (for which they have relatively less responsibility) under a Convention in which developed country Parties have committed themselves to 'take full account of the specific needs and special situations of the least developed countries in their actions with regard to funding and transfer of technology'.

Negotiated incremental costs

On closer analysis, the line dividing the two interpretations is more blurred than the simple 'net' and 'gross' typology suggests. There are, for example, measures which could be taken to reduce global warming at a negligible incremental cost (correcting subsidies for example) or even a negative incremental cost (eg energy efficiency measures). Meanwhile, it is likely that for certain types of projects (eg game parks to protect biodiversity and institutional strengthening) the incremental cost might approach 100 per cent (ie because nothing would have been done in the absence of the respective Convention). Indeed, the GEF suggests that 'there are cases when the incremental cost will be equal to the full cost of the activity'.[37]

In practice, a balance between the gross and net interpretations will probably emerge out of a process of *negotiation*,[38] a view now reflected in statements from the GEF.[39] Negotiations could proceed on two levels: at a sectoral level to determine the eligibility of certain classes of activity through the preparation of indicative lists; and at the project level to determine the scale of assistance to individual interventions. What remains to be agreed on are a set of guidelines to structure and inform these negotiations. These should be agreed by the COPs and may draw upon the research emerging from the PRINCE programme.

Incrementality baselines

As with additionality, incremental costs can only be defined against some kind of hypothetical baseline which measures what a host nation would have done in the absence of an international agreement. Incremental cost baselines are as difficult to establish as additionality baselines, not least because if a proposed project is financed then the baseline situation will never occur. The baseline is intrinsically hypothetical, since it can be premised upon a number of very different scenarios and may adopt many different forms, and hence is open to manipulation. King[40] suggests that the baseline could be based on a number of factors, including economic efficiency, equity, and existing trends. In the case of the power station example (above), the costs and benefits of a hypothetical coalfired power station project over the next 10 to 20 years would need to be calculated. This would not be easy. The interim Secretariat to the Climate Convention notes that rules of 'economic, environmental, technical, and financial *reasonableness*' may need to be applied, but these have yet to be formulated and agreed upon.[41]

Conclusions

As implementation of the Rio Conventions proceeds, the importance of measuring, verifying and perhaps enforcing additionality and incrementality will increase. Yet, both are relatively elastic terms and the potential for conflict and confusion remains high. For example, the foregoing underscores the importance of having proper baselines, calculated according to what a donor or recipient would have done had they not entered into the respective global environmental agreement. Clearly, there are enormous difficulties in estimating and, more importantly, verifying this 'counterfactual'. Further, both donors and recipient Parties have an incentive, and the latitude allowed them by the vagueness of international agreements, to push the rules of assessment in their favour, leaving plenty of room for discord and conflict in the future.

A vital need has arisen for some form of mutually acceptable calculus or set of criteria for measuring both terms. As the process of implementation begins to roll forward, the policy debate may now turn to fundamental questions about the types of institutions and decision-making structures appropriate to developing and applying these criteria. Issues such as additionality and incrementality involve sophisticated social, economic, moral, scientific and political judgements. Policy-makers must decide if such complex issues can be handled by rambling debates in large intergovernmental bodies such as the Conventions' COPs or the UN's Commission on Sustainable Development. The alternative is that responsibility and a degree of decision-making power be delegated to more powerful organizations such as the World Bank which have a great deal of experience in international finance, or programmes such as PRINCE. However, the involvement of these and other similar institutions will probably raise hackles within the green lobby and in the Third World.

The foregoing discussion challenges the simple idea that the Rio Summit resolved the issue of how to finance the transition to sustainable development. One suspects that there are very profound discrepancies in the manner that North and South perceive the need for, likely role and scope of additional financial transfers. The developed states tend towards a *minimal* interpretation; transfers being a price (to be minimized wherever possible) to be paid for enlisting the support of the South in tackling common problems. Meanwhile the developing states seek perpetually to advance a *maximal* interpretation of additionality and incrementality, arguing that 'new' environmentally related transfers are a rightful and legitimate means to address the inequities inherent in the operation of the world economy. These represent very different standpoints and do not appear to be easily reconcilable. In the short term, the task of balancing these has been delegated to the COPs and the GEF. The pathways through which these two bodies evolve in the coming years will come to represent a fascinating test case of how well international institutions can adapt to the challenge of sustainable development.

13 THE UN FRAMEWORK CONVENTION ON CLIMATE CHANGE: THE EUROPEAN CARBON/ENERGY TAX AND ITS INTERNATIONAL TRADE LAW IMPLICATIONS

James Cameron and Zen Makuch

INTRODUCTION

This chapter points to potential conflicts between a global environmental agreement and the rules of international trade law with particular emphasis on the European Community (EC) CO_2/energy tax. It is, by necessity and design, speculative. It is to be hoped that the potential differences, which would be an impediment to the successful resolution of the accelerated climate change problem, be removed by constructive consultation and negotiation. There is a great deal at stake for trade interests and the environment. Trade and economic activities concerning the maximization of competitive advantage, with its associated rises in the standard of living and employment, must be sustainable, facilitating ecosystem protection and food production.[1] The search for balance between these considerations is admirably summed up in Article 3(5) of the UN Framework Convention on Climate Change:

> The Parties should cooperate to promote a supportive and open international economic system that would lead to sustainable economic growth and development in all Parties, particularly developing country Parties, thus enabling them better to address the problems of climate change. Measures taken to combat climate change, including unilateral ones, should not constitute a means of arbitrary or unjustifiable discrimination or a disguised restriction on international trade.[2]

EUROPEAN COMMUNITY POLICY

Since 1973,[3] the EC has formulated a policy on the reduction and prevention of air pollution. This is reflected in its 1973, 1977, 1983, 1987 and 1992 Action

Programmes for the Environment. In particular, the 1987 and 1992 action programmes stress the importance of concentrating community action on the priority area of reducing air pollution at source. The European Council, in June 1990, called for the adoption, at the earliest possible time, of targets and strategies for limiting emissions of greenhouse gases.

As a major player in the negotiations for the conclusion of the Climate Change Convention, the European Community has added its voice to the need for universal action to combat the greenhouse effect.[4] At the time, the Community pledged its cooperation in the negotiations and accepted both the scientific statement of the Intergovernmental Panel on Climate Change (IPCC) and the conclusion that action should be taken immediately, on an international scale, even in the absence of scientific certainty as to the precise implications of the greenhouse effect. The Community further affirmed its intention to play a full part in the 'definition and implementation of a global response' to the threat of world climate change, and committed itself to take urgent action to stabilize or reduce emissions of greenhouse gases within the EC.

As part of its commitment to this reduction, the European Community has introduced a three-part Community-wide strategy. The components of that strategy are:

(1) Fiscal measures;
(2) Specific non-fiscal measures; and
(3) Complementary national programmes.

The latter two non-fiscal measures include conventional measures and instruments such as research and development programmes to stimulate adoption of clean technologies, promote the use of renewable sources of energy, and increase energy efficiency. Such programmes would include the creation of 'carbon sinks' to absorb carbon dioxide, eg the planting of forests, and greater education on consumer efficiency. They would also envisage the redesigning of the European transportation infrastructure to make it more energy efficient.[5]

THE CO_2 ENERGY TAX

The main fiscal instrument was going to be the proposed tax on both carbon dioxide emissions and non-carbon dioxide emitting sources of energy.[6] However, on 15 December 1993, EC Environment Ministers decided to ratify the Climate Change Convention in the absence of the CO_2/energy tax despite the fact that the tax was originally seen as a key instrument for cutting back greenhouse gas emissions. The six member states which originally linked adoption of the Convention to the tax (Germany, the Netherlands, France, Belgium, Denmark, and Italy) adopted a Declaration stating that they would have preferred a tax and the member states made a commitment to conclude the work on the tax by the end of 1994.[7] More recently, the Commission's redraft of the proposal indicated that a CO_2/energy tax is still a key policy goal.[8]

The precise workings of the tax are yet to be finalized. The tax as currently proposed would be split 50/50 between the carbon and energy content of fossil fuels and other energy sources (except renewables). Energy based on the burning of fossil fuels, such as oil, gas and coal, would be taxed both on the carbon emissions and on the energy content. The tax would be levied on all solid, viscous or gaseous fossil fuels, either in their crude state where they are used as motor or heating fuel or in their final form where the motor or heating fuel is obtained by processing the crude product. Thus, raw materials are not taxed,[9] but nuclear energy and hydroelectric power, though emitting no carbon dioxide, are taxed on the basis of the energy they use. The tax becomes chargeable at the time of extraction of the crude products, production of their derivatives, or importation,[10] ie when the products are released for consumption. The tax basis would be a $10 surcharge per barrel of oil, with the equivalent amount of energy, applied progressively, with the rate rising from $3 per barrel in 1993 to $10 per barrel in the year 2000.[11]

In the case of electricity and heat generated as secondary sources of energy, where the carbon dioxide emissions component of the tax is concerned, the heat and electricity produced from primary fossil sources of energy are not taxed as such, but on the basis of the fossil inputs used. For the purposes of transparency, there is a requirement to indicate on invoices relating to supplies of electricity or heat the amount of tax included in the price.[12]

The debate surrounding the EC carbon/energy tax contributes to the development of issues in the trade/environment context, such as the use of unilateral measures in tackling global environmental problems, the use of economic instruments to achieve environmental objectives, green subsidies, the internalization of external environmental costs, green product discrimination, the eligibility of taxes to be adjusted at the border, like products, and technology transfer.

Before the carbon/energy tax will be brought into force, the EC has stipulated that other members of the OECD group must adopt similar measures,[13] (the 'conditionality' clause). Some countries have shown a willingness to impose domestic taxes on their own emissions of greenhouse gases (primarily carbon dioxide). Denmark and the Netherlands already have such legislation in place, and others are considering similar action. The EC's position on harmonization outwards, is that it will monitor events in other countries such as the USA and Japan, which have not yet implemented fiscal measures as a way of stabilizing carbon dioxide emissions.[14]

If this situation remains then EC member states will be further dissuaded from implementing an added cost of doing business when foreign competitors are not similarly burdened. Equally, there are good environmental policy grounds for a concerted approach to the solution of a global problem. Accelerated climate change appears to be one of those problems where cooperation renders higher returns than competition. This is a serious, but not wholly unfamiliar challenge for the thoughtful policy-maker - how do you cooperate and compete successfully, where there is tremendous uncertainty, great complexity, contradictory ideologies, a desire for harmonization and unilateral higher standards, an argument for integration and special pleading (for environment or free(er) trade depending on where one stands)?

The Montreal Protocol,[15] in our view is gradually working its way towards earning the status of a model system in this regard. Unfortunately its subject matter is so much simpler and more precise than climate change that it cannot simply be transposed. The Montreal Protocol provides for specific international measures, including regulation of trade in specified substances between Parties and a complete ban on trade in controlled substances between Parties and non-Parties. It has set, and revised through intergovernmental meetings, phase-out timetables for ozone-depleting substances. These phase out timetables are then passed on to the regional and national implementing powers. The EC is considering further amendments of its own implementing regulations to deal with the problems associated with CFC substitutes at its Environment Council Meeting on 28 June 1993. While greenhouse gases present more complex problems in terms of targets, and indeed the mechanics of implementation, nonetheless the Montreal Protocol is useful as a guide to future global cooperative action to forward the aims of the Convention.[16]

Certainly, OECD studies suggest that in the context of global climate change, the most efficient type of international abatement agreement would combine: simultaneous abatement commitments by all major emitting countries; economic incentives (global carbon taxes or tradable-permit systems) being used to achieve abatement objectives; and the reduction of subsidies for existing energy sources (excluding renewables).

UNILATERAL ACTION

The importance of multilateral international agreements should not, however, obscure the value of unilateral or bilateral action. It is important for countries not only to adjust their own policies but also to pursue bilateral agreements and technical assistance programmes that promote greater energy efficiency and change in consumption patterns. Indeed the Climate Change Convention does envisage unilateral action being taken to address the global climate change problem provided that it is transparent and does not unjustifiably discriminate against exports. Witness the inclusion of the words '... including unilateral ones ...' in the last sentence of Article 3 (5), referring to measures taken to combat climate change.

The argument would therefore run that if a measure, including a unilateral measure, is not motivated by commercial protectionism and its effects on trade are proportionate to its protection of the global environment (climate) then the measure will be consistent with the principles of the Convention. These arguments are presented further below.

This may seem unproblematic, but consider the use of the word 'unjustifiable' in front of 'discrimination'. It may well be argued that environmentally justifiable discrimination is, implicit in that coupling of words in the closed context of the objective and principles of the Convention. Accelerated global warming is a problem of considerable scale affecting the life-support systems of the planet and the interests of future generations. Therefore, environmental measures which would cause some discrimination in trade relations might still be justified. Whether the disciplines of the GATT would permit this conclusion is discussed below.[17]

In Article 4 (2) (a), the national policies to be adopted by developed country Parties, envisages policies and measures adopted by regional economic integration organizations. Thus, it may comfortably be argued that the EC as a regional organization,[18] having signed the Convention, can point to the carbon/energy tax as one element of such action.

GATT AND CO_2/ENERGY TAX

Border tax adjustment

As an instrument which will affect international trade, the EC CO_2/energy tax, if implemented, could face opposition over its ability to comply with the rules of GATT, which tend to be construed strictly. In particular, the carbon/energy tax will be examined carefully in the context of the rules for adjustment at the border.[19] Such adjustment would include remission of taxes for exports, export subsidies to compensate firms for the increased cost imposed by the tax, and, enforcement of the tax on imported products. As proposed, the EC Directive envisages that there will be remission of the tax on exports of fuel and the imposition of tax on imports.[20] Articles II, III, VI and XVI of the GATT[21] prescribe related rules in this area.

Whether the EC carbon/energy tax is the kind of tax which is eligible for adjustment is itself an issue. Energy taxes have been termed as 'taxes occultes' for the purposes of border tax adjustment rules under the GATT.[22] The Working Party which dealt with the subject felt that such taxes could not be said with certainty to be eligible for adjustment, and that adjustment for such taxes was not 'normally made'.[23] However, the fact that the carbon/energy tax is to be taxed on both the product and the process, puts it in a unique category of its own. Its application is clear where the tax is directly levied on products such as motor or heating fuels rather than their production methods. But, EC regulatory problems would arise with respect to the tax treatment of secondary sources of energy such as electricity. And, it is not exactly clear whether these tax components could be labelled 'indirect taxes' for the purpose of adjustment. This is an area which will require further clarification, particularly taking into account the dual nature of energy as a product in itself and as a fundamental part of production processes.

Most favoured nation treatment

Imports

Under GATT rules the EC is allowed to impose taxes at the border on foreign products which have not been the subject of similar measures in the country of origin, provided such taxation does not result in effective discrimination in favour of EC products.[24] Article III(1) of the GATT gives this permission thus:

> internal taxes ... affecting the internal sale, purchase ... or use of products, and internal quantitative regulations requiring the mixture, processing or use of products in specified amounts or proportions, should not be applied to imported or domestic products so as to afford protection to domestic production.

Article III(1) goes on to further prescribe in section 2:

> The products of the territory of any contracting Party imported into the territory of any other contracting Party shall not be subject, directly or indirectly, to internal taxes or other internal charges of any kind in excess of those applied, directly or indirectly to like domestic products.

GATT panels have consistently upheld the non-discrimination principle which underlies this provision. For instance, in the *Superfund* decision,[25] a small tax differential of 3.5 cents per barrel in favour of domestic versus foreign petroleum was found to be in violation of Article III (2).

However, in another part of the decision the panel was asked to determine the GATT compatibility of a second provision[26] of the same legislation which imposed a charge on chemical derivatives equal to that charged for 'like' taxable chemicals which were sold in the United States.[27] The GATT panel determined that since that tax was directly imposed upon the products it was eligible for border tax adjustment. It also found that since the tax rate on the imported substances was equivalent to the tax for like domestic substances this provision did meet the national treatment requirement of Article III(2) (first sentence).[28]

Like this US measure, the EC CO_2/energy tax does not appear to differentiate on the basis of the origin of energy products though the provisions of the draft Directive are flexible enough to allow this to occur. If there is no differentiation then the rationale used in determining the outcome of the two *Superfund* measures, *vis-à-vis* GATT Article III (2), would yield the conclusion that the EC CO_2/energy tax would not be in breach of the discrimination rule inherent in this provision. In particular, Articles II and III are structured to permit the use of taxes to be applied to final products as long as they are equally applied. Similarly, if an EC country imposes the CO_2/energy tax in an even manner, without the use of exemptions or rebates on a domestic preferential basis, then there would be no inconsistency with the non-discrimination articles (Article I, II and III) of GATT.

Alternatively, those who wish to challenge the legality of the tax may seek to establish that such a consumption tax is a disguised import duty. If the EC state observes the transparency provisions of GATT by giving proper public notice of the regulation and its underlying rationale then it will not likely be seen as a disguised import duty. (It is presumed that the tax is being implemented in good faith pursuant to the aims of the Climate Change Convention and environmental and human health protection in general rather than as a disguised restriction on trade.)

If an EC state imposed the tax on imports from a state which already taxed energy production in a manner similar to that of the EC state, then a clear case for discrimination under Article III(1) could be made on the basis that the imported product is being taxed twice while the domestic product is only being taxed once. This would not be the case if the 'conditionality' clause of the Convention is properly observed, with both states offering remission of the tax on exported products.

There may also be situations under Article III(1) of GATT in which a party which may otherwise be an exporter of petroleum to a state which is primarily a producer of nuclear power, and whose firms provide most of the domestic supply of energy, may be attempting to break into that party's domestic energy market where the two energy sources have some similar or identical uses. In this circumstance, differential tax treatment under the draft Directive which favours the domestic nuclear industry may be seen as 'affording protection to domestic production' in violation of Article III (1). Alternatively, it can be argued that price discrimination against fossil fuel products whose CO_2 production levels are high compared to nuclear energy production is a quantitative restriction on trade according to Article XI (1) and is therefore GATT-prohibitive. This would give rise to a valid action for 'nullification and impairment' along the lines discussed below.[29]

Exemptions

If the CO_2/energy tax is to be a successful inducement towards CO_2 reduction it must offer exemptions to firms which minimize their contribution to global warming by decreasing their energy use in their production activities. These exemptions are evident in Article 11 of the draft EC Directive establishing the CO_2/energy tax. As proposed, Article 10 offers another partial or full exemption to domestic firms. It provides that the Commission may authorize member states to grant tax reductions or exemptions to firms that are seriously disadvantaged by an increase in imports from third parties which are not subject to a similar tax.[30] Keeping in mind the most favoured nation treatment requirement of Article III (2), one must ask whether such exemption must also be given to all energy imports.

While there are exceptions to most favoured nation treatment in the GATT, there is no GATT decision which would except the CO_2/energy tax from the application of this principle. The obligation created by GATT Article I's most favoured nation principle requires that any advantage accorded to a product from one country must be given to all other countries. Therefore, a literal interpretation of Article I would render the conclusion that any exemption must be applied to all imports in the same manner as domestic energy products. This does not appear to be what the framers of the EC CO_2/energy tax had in mind.

Like products

On the issue of 'like products', an area which still requires development in the context of the interaction of international trade and environmental law, the picture is even cloudier than that of border tax adjustment. One can foresee problems arising from the definition of 'like product'. The time has not yet arrived when distinctions are made in the type of product, based on the process by which it was made (ie energy-intensive or non-energy-intensive product, level of CO_2 emissions), but perhaps by the arrival of consensus on the issue of the carbon/energy tax, some formulas for definition might have been conceived.

GATT Article III contains the relevant requirements which apply to situations involving 'like products'. The problem here is that the CO_2/energy tax applies to a range of energy types including coal, electricity, nuclear power and renewable energy resources. Both GATT and its surrounding jurisprudence are unclear about the definition of 'like product' and yet this definition is critical in determining the GATT legality of the CO_2/energy tax. In practice, GATT has given a broad interpretation to Article III (2) in order to block discriminatory treatment in favour of domestic industries.

The panel decision in the GATT *Superfund Case*[31] is illustrative of this point. This 1987 GATT panel report, adopted by the contracting Parties, provided that the section of the Superfund Amendments and Reauthorization Act of 1986 establishing an 11.7 cents per barrel tax on imported petroleum, and an 8.2 cents per barrel tax for domestically produced petroleum, in order to fund the Superfund Program for the clean-up of hazardous waste sites violated the national treatment obligation (specifically Article III (2) of the General Agreement).

The case also refers to a Report of the Working Party on Border Tax Adjustments, adopted by GATT Parties in 1970, which suggests that one of the ways for identifying 'like products' is by reference to their end uses in the market.[32] This test, when applied to the energy products subject to the CO_2/ energy tax, yields the conclusion that oil, coal, electricity, nuclear power, and renewable energy resources are not 'like products' pursuant to Article III (2). The Working Party also specified that like products evaluations are to be based upon a product's properties, nature and quality.[33] The physical characteristics of the energy sources that are subject to the CO_2/energy tax are as different as their end uses.

Problems also arise in the context of 'like products' which are secondary sources of energy (eg electricity). Under the proposals the tax will already have been levied on the primary fossil inputs.[34] It will therefore not be possible to remit the tax on an export of electricity, nor, it would appear, to impose tax on electricity imports. The EC is still considering how electricity imports can best be regulated.

The above discussion yields the conclusion that separate categorization of energy products according to their sources will serve as the basis for GATT-based 'like product' comparisons under Article III (2).

Subsidization

Unfortunately, the GATT, despite the addition of the SCM agreement, does not contain provisions which adequately address the trade distortions posed by domestic subsidies schemes. Production subsidies will tend to reduce market share for imports thereby diminishing or removing any comparative advantage possessed by importing firms that are not similarly assisted, resulting in trade distortions. However, Article XVI (4) does limit the use of export subsidies that are given to firms on the basis of their export performance.[35] A list of these subsidies is attached to the GATT Subsidies Code. This Article also curtails the use of export subsidies on primary products where they result in greater market share for the subsidising nation. Domestic subsidies which cause material injury to industry may be countervailed according to Article VI.[36]

Exemptions

Some confusion is likely to arise with regard to the qualification of firms for the above-mentioned exemptions, and the extent of the exemptions. The granting of exemptions, from payment of the CO_2/energy tax, to industry may be seen as a subsidy, especially when that exemption only operates on export. This is likely to make the price of the product more expensive in the domestic market than it is on export, action expressly prohibited under GATT Article XVI (4). Such subsidies may be the subject of countervailing duties, according to Article VI (2).[37] However, where the internal tax rebates are not unreasonable, countervailing duties do not apply.[38]

Remission, reduction, credits

In addition to tax exemptions, tax reductions, refunds and credits could feature prominently under the EC CO_2/energy tax regime.[39] The issue raised by these provisions concerns the use of production or export subsidies to offset the competitive disadvantage for EC firms *vis-à-vis* foreign firms which are not subject to a similar tax.

On the matter of tax remission it is not an infringement of GATT rules to allow remission of the CO_2/energy tax on exports even if it means that exports will be sold for less than they are in the producer nation. This is the case as long as the rebate or exemption does not exceed the amount of the tax and is not unreasonable in the circumstances. However, as we shall see in our analysis of Article 11 of the draft Directive establishing the CO_2/energy tax, the rebate may exceed the amount of taxation giving rise to a potential breach of GATT provisions.

As well as possessing the features of a consumption tax, the EC CO_2/energy tax is also a production tax since it is based on the amount of energy used and CO_2 released in the production process. The tax is structured so as to incline producers and consumers to favour energy production which is efficient and reduces the release of CO_2 emissions. As such, a significant question arises over whether the instrument used to effect environmental cost internalization with reference to production processes is a direct tax. The legitimacy of export rebates for production process improvements would likely be treated in the same fashion as import charges. If they are based on a direct tax (eg they have a direct effect on prices) an exemption from Article XVI is permitted. As a direct tax, the CO_2/energy tax is likely to have an effect on prices. If this is true, the direct production subsidy provided by an export rebate would be compatible with GATT Article XVI (4).

The problem arises where, according to GATT Article XVI, a 'contracting Party grants or maintains a subsidy ... which operates directly or indirectly to increase exports of any product from, or to reduce imports of any products into, its territory.'[40] The Article further provides that if there is 'serious prejudice' to the interests of any other contracting Party, consultations may be commenced with a view to 'limiting the subsidization'.[41]

To evaluate whether a subsidy runs afoul of Article XVI (1) the test to be applied is based on comparing the levels of exports or imports that would exist in the absence of the subsidy.[42] In the absence of countervailing measures will there be an increase in exports or a decrease in imports? This will depend on the specific applications of the EC CO_2/energy tax to Article 10 and especially Article 11. For instance, Article 11 contemplates situations in which new investment expenditures by (presumably only) domestic firms on energy efficiency or limiting carbon dioxide emissions receive tax reductions or *equivalent* refunds for their investment expenditures.

Tax neutrality

If tax neutrality is implemented, as prescribed by Article 15 of the EC CO_2/energy tax proposal, and firms receive refunds for investment measures without a corresponding adjustment in their other tax responsibilities, this could serve as a subsidy to production for domestic and export markets. Article 15 does not provide for this corresponding adjustment when firms receive benefits under Articles 10 and 11 of the tax proposal. If Articles 10 and 11 are operationalized without an adjustment or their use leads to an increase in market share for domestic firms versus importers through preferential tax treatment then they will give rise to review under GATT Article XVI (1) as potentially countervailable subsidies and will likely be in violation of GATT Article III as discriminatory measures. If, on the other hand, Articles 10 and 11 apply equally to domestic and foreign firms, there will be no incompatibility with GATT provisions.

In summary, the use of countervail measures to equalize the losses in comparative advantage which attach to CO_2/energy tax related subsidies is consistent with GATT Article VI (3). In order to apply such measures a nation must show material injury to a domestic industry pursuant to Article VI (6).[43] Accordingly, countervail measures may be introduced which are equal to or less than the amount of the subsidies provided by the exporting nation. This is subject to the rule identified in Article VI (4) which disallows countervail measures against refunds of taxes on exports.[44] Once the Article VI (6) 'material injury' requirement is met there is no need to establish a violation of Article XVI in order to implement a countervailing measure against an export subsidy so long as the relevant protocol for the nation implementing the measure is observed. For the reasons mentioned in this section countervailable actions may well take place depending on the implementation measures undertaken by EC states concerning the CO_2/energy tax.

Nullification and impairment

Articles XXII and XXIII provide a framework for dispute resolution under GATT. Article XXII calls for consultations between disputing Parties. In situations concerning the nullification or impairment of GATT benefits Article XXIII allows for representations to be made by Parties and, if no satisfactory solution has been reached, the matter may be referred to the contracting Parties. Among the possible steps in the dispute resolution process are: consultation, conciliation, actions based on the recommendations of contracting Parties and, sometimes, GATT legal retaliation.

We have highlighted situations, involving import controls and export subsidies, where the proposed CO_2/energy tax may collide with GATT rules and disciplines. Indeed some Parties have argued that 'nullification and impairment' of GATT benefits takes place the moment that a domestic subsidy is introduced concerning GATT-bound products.

When no violation of a GATT provision can be easily made out 'material injury' may be taken as the basis for satisfying the nullification or impairment requirement. This standard has yet to be properly defined by the contracting Parties though it would not likely be based on a strict test of quantifiable damages. If, *prima facie*, it appears that a GATT benefit may be nullified or impaired or that profit levels may have risen for firms competing with EC firms were it not for the implementation of the CO_2/energy tax then the basis for a complaint will have been established. This position reflects the finding of the contracting Parties with respect to Article XVI applications to production subsidy notification and consultation rules.[45]

Unfortunately, disputes based on allegations of GATT incompatible subsidies hardly further the cause of trade liberalization since the applicable remedy is the use of a countervailing measure. As a further step, suspension of GATT obligations over non-compliance with GATT disciplines only occurs in the rarest of circumstances. Disputes over the implementation of the CO_2/energy tax proposal are unlikely to go this far due to the broad range of industries affected, the considerable financial losses which might be suffered in a protracted trade war and the need to protect the national trade balance and export led growth strategies in these recessionary times. Still Article XXIII retaliation is a distinct possibility when nullification or impairment of GATT benefits can be established.

GATT Article XX exceptions

Introduction

If the EC CO_2/energy tax were implemented in a manner which constituted a quantitative restriction on trade, an illegal subsidy or a breach of the nondiscrimination articles then there would have to be some consideration of whether the tax might be protected or made non-countervailable through the use of a GATT exception. The most helpful exception in this regard is Article XX. The relevant provisions of Article XX are reproduced below:

> Subject to the requirement that such measures are not applied in a manner which would constitute a means of arbitrary or unjustifiable discrimination between countries where the same conditions prevail, or a disguised restriction on international trade, nothing in this Agreement shall be construed to prevent the adoption or enforcement by any contracting party of measures:
>
> ....
>
> (b) necessary to protect human, animal or plant life or health;
>
> ....
>
> (g) relating to the conservation of exhaustible natural resources if such measures are made effective in conjunction with restrictions on domestic production or consumption

Article XX provides limited exceptions to the contracting Parties' general GATT obligations for measures based on national policy considerations.[46] Such exemptions do not include measures that constitute arbitrary or unjustifiable discrimination between countries or that are disguised restrictions on international trade. In considering the applicability of the Article XX exception to any offending measures in connection with the implementation of the CO_2/energy tax it is important to note that there has never been an instance where an environmental measure was judged to have met these tests.

In practice, it is difficult to judge whether the EC CO_2/energy tax meets the requirements of the Article XX exceptions. There is a good deal of flexibility concerning the means by which it will be interpreted and implemented by member states. As well, GATT jurisprudence concerning the interpretation of Article XX is still embryonic in form giving rise to uncertainty about the breadth of its scope. For instance, an international environmental convention which permits the use of Trade Related Environmental Measures (TREMs) has never been the subject of a GATT panel ruling.[47] Nevertheless, a discussion of the issues which the above-mentioned cases raise allows some tentative conclusions to be reached.

Article XX(b): Human, animal or plant life or health

Recently, GATT panels have imposed significant limitations on the Article XX(b) health and safety exception. If upheld in subsequent rulings, these limitations will be quite invasive for environmental policy-makers at all levels of governance. As stated, Article XX(b) is designed to allow exceptions from GATT regulations in order to allow contracting Parties to maintain or implement laws which they feel are necessary to preserve the lives of people, flora and fauna. For this purpose, a strong argument can be made that a regulation that limits the use of a product which is demonstrably harmful to the environment or to health can be protected from GATT-based penalties by invoking the Article XX(b) exception.[48]

In a GATT dispute it is customary for the Party wishing to employ Article XX(b), as a means of protecting an environmental regulation from GATT's general obligations, to meet the burden of establishing that the regulation: 1) was justified and not arbitrarily applied; and 2) was proportional in scope (ie necessary) to the concern giving rise to the action so as to meet the objectives of the GATT exception.[49] Although Article XX(b) still allows a safe haven for many important environmental initiatives, limiting the application of the exceptions to a domestic restriction by placing added requirements on the term 'necessary,' recent panel decisions have diminished the ability of Article XX(b) to reconcile environmental and international trade policies and laws.

The *Tuna/Dolphin* panel limited the application of this exception by holding that Article XX(b) is available only for health, safety, and preservation regulations within a contracting Party's jurisdiction, and not anywhere within the global commons (or within the jurisdiction of a third Party state).[50] It is not clear from the panel's report whether this jurisdictional limitation applies to the scope of the Party's action, or to the actual location of the individual or species to be protected. The panel based its finding that Article XX(b) did not extend 'extrajurisdictionally' upon a somewhat erroneous understanding of the negotiating history and underlying rationale for the Article.[51] Most importantly, this jurisdictional limitation constrains a contracting Party from unilaterally protecting the at-risk resources of the global commons, such as the ozone layer, climate, ocean water quality, and at-risk species inhabiting common areas such as the high seas.

Article XX(b) was also interpreted by a GATT panel in the *Thailand Cigarettes* Case, a decision related to restrictions on imports and exports of cigarettes.[52] It found that while the restrictions supported a valid health measure, they were not necessary to achieve this goal since alternative, less trade restrictive measures were also available. In the *Thailand Cigarettes* Case the panel interpreted the Article XX(b) 'necessity' test as requiring that: no reasonably available alternative measure consistent with the GATT existed, and the measure taken was the least trade restrictive measure of all available alternatives.[53] The *Tuna-Dolphin* panel report expanded the scope of these requirements in noting that the United States had not proven that it had previously attempted all options available to it in carrying out its dolphin protection objectives using GATT sanctioned measures. Possible measures would have included – but not been limited to – multilateral solutions such as the negotiation of international arrangements (ie an international environmental convention on dolphin protection).[54]

This approach is highly restrictive for environmental policy purposes since it limits the capacity of the contracting Parties to engage in legitimate unilateral actions, actions which frequently serve an important role in the evolution of environmental protection mechanisms gained from both domestic regulations and international agreements.[55] Proving a negative and that no other alternative way of achieving a policy goal is better than the one selected is an unenviable task when the GATT goal is to minimize trade restrictions with little regard-for the environmental consequences. Furthermore, deliberations at the diplomatic level concerning the achievement of consensus in the international community necessary to respond to an environmental issue, is at times a cumbersome and time consuming though valuable process. By design, it is not a panacea for all environmental issues since several issues have a more local character, without a significant transboundary dimension. For this reason, the polities of nations often differ in their demands for environmental protection as does their prioritization of these issues. In general, national environmental regimes are best suited to developing regulatory responses where these differences among nations are not in some sense shared. As well, international negotiations lack the capacity to respond to environmental threats quickly. Even if it is accepted that, rather than an international environmental response, a unilateral import restriction was the only measure available, the panel took the view that the United States regulation was not 'necessary' according to the Article XX(b) test on the grounds of its unpredictable application.[56]

On the issue of alternative measures, the CO_2/energy tax can be favourably distinguished from the regulation under scrutiny in the *Tuna-Dolphin* Case which was based on the most restrictive type of trade mechanism (a complete ban on products). Moreover, less trade-restrictive alternatives would require some level of voluntariness from industry. There is little evidence to suggest that energy products would be priced higher on a voluntary basis simply for environmental reasons. Similarly, it has not been the case that reduced energy use or reduced CO_2 emissions have featured in any industry sectors policies despite knowledge of the negative environmental impacts which accompany energy consumption.

The *Tuna-Dolphin* panel raises another important question about the criteria which collectively satisfy the 'necessity' requirement. Implicit in the decision is the view that in setting an identifiable, clear standard of environmental protection concerning the preservation of a particular species there must be scientific evidence which establishes that such a standard is justified or necessary. If this interpretation is granted, then several potentially damaging environmental activities which have not yet had their causes scientifically proven may be questioned by GATT panellists, causing considerable consternation among environmental policy-makers.[57] Given the embryonic nature of environmental science, scientific uncertainty abounds. This limitation should not serve as a justification for ignoring several pressing environmental problems for in doing so one may be foregoing any opportunity for remedying present and future environmental harm while allowing it to become more ubiquitous and potentially irreversible. Failure to act in the absence of scientific certainty would also represent a violation of the internationally recognized Precautionary Principle that has developed in the field of international environmental law.[58]

It is a plausible interpretation of the panel ruling that the 'necessity' standard is to be measured primarily upon the existence of an acceptable level of certainty in regulatory application rather than the legitimacy of the environmental protection objective at hand.[59] Hence, if it is shown that the environmental protection regulation is evenly applied and is not arbitrary or unpredictable then the scientific underpinnings for the regulation are irrelevant to a panel.

In defending the use of the Article XX(b) exception one might begin by arguing that the CO_2/energy tax is a necessary measure for combating global warming. This argument would be buttressed by reference to the quantity and quality of negative environmental impacts posed by energy use, particularly those uses which cause CO_2 emissions. The link must then be established between these activities and the phenomenon of global warming with its associated threats to human, plant, and animal life.

While there is considerable agreement about the relationship between CO_2 emissions and planetary temperature rises a Party opposing the tax may, nevertheless, argue that there is considerable scientific uncertainty about direct impacts on animal, plant and human health. In establishing its case the EC would have to minimize the breadth of scientific dissent, in part, by offering the Climate Change Convention as evidence of scientific consensus and a desire by many nations to act upon such consensus.

Following the ratio decidendi of the *Canada-United States Tuna* Case,[60] the two tests, contained in the Preamble of Article XX related to 'unjustifiable discrimination' and 'disguised (trade) restrictions', are met as long as the CO_2/energy tax is evenly implied to the products of all importing countries and there is public notice given of the purpose of the tax and the nature of its application. The 'discrimination' element would also depend in part upon a finding of discrimination under GATT Articles I to III.

In meeting the 'justification' and 'proportionality' requirements it would be of assistance to the EC to provide evidence that the effect of the measure was to reduce dependence on energy sources with the highest CO_2 emissions or that the revenue collected from the tax was used in some way to combat global warming rather than as a means of bolstering general state revenues. If, on the contrary, it is established that the demand for energy with a high CO_2 release factor is inelastic *vis-à-vis* the CO_2/energy tax it will be more difficult to support it upon a GATT challenge.

The CO_2/energy tax would automatically satisfy one branch of the *Tuna-Dolphin* Case test of 'necessity' by accepting that unilateral acts must follow efforts to forge a multilateral response to the environmental objective at hand. The Climate Change Convention serves as the multilateral response to global warming and the introduction of the tax represents a unilateral act of the kind referred to in Article 3 (5) of the Convention.

One of the aims of the EC carbon/energy tax is to encourage consumers and industry to reduce their levels of carbon dioxide emissions and use energy more efficiently. In this sense the tax seeks the alteration or modification of consumer/producer behaviour.[61] But this modification of behaviour can only be achieved or targeted at consumers and producers within the EC. According to the GATT rules, such policies cannot be extended so as to influence other countries, since that would involve 'extrajurisdictionality': a phrase coined by the GATT *Tuna-Dolphin* panel. This sentiment is also expressed by a United Nations General Assembly Resolution: States should 'refrain from exercising political coercion through the application of economic instruments with the purpose of inducing changes in the economic or social systems . . . of other countries.'[62]

On the issue of extraterritoriality, it must be recognized that the climate change phenomenon is a global one, giving rise to the argument that domestic legislation is justified since the domestic environment is affected by CO_2 emissions. This is completely acceptable from a GATT perspective. However, there are GATT difficulties when a regulation is designed to protect ecosystems or their components beyond national borders or *de facto* requires other national jurisdictions whose goods are subject to the tax to implement the same regulation in their own jurisdictions so as to neutralize the effects of the regulation.

The EC CO_2/energy tax may not have this influence on OECD member nations due to the 'conditionality' principle inherent in section 1(2) of the Climate Change Convention. As stated previously, this provision makes OECD member group implementation of similar CO_2/energy tax schemes in their states a condition precedent to the implementation of the EC CO_2/energy tax. This may only be true if the principle is strictly observed and this is done by all OECD Parties. For non-OECD nations whose goods are produced through energy intensive production processes and compete with EC goods are strongly encouraged to implement a similar tax so as to avoid favourable treatment for their EC competitors pursuant to Articles 10 and 11 of the Convention. Those opposing the tax would argue that, when applied in this way, in particular, Article 10 constitutes a form of *de facto* extraterritorial regulation. If the competing nation does not implement a CO_2/energy tax regulation then the EC tax regulation could be applied in a way which favours EC firms.

It would also be argued that the EC CO_2/energy tax contains another element of extraterritoriality. If the tax is to be applied to energy imports then its objective of reducing energy use and CO_2 emissions for environmental protection purposes will also be extended extraterritorially for the purpose of discouraging exporting nations from developing energy products whose use harms the environment of the exporting nation and other areas of the planet beyond the EC. This is especially difficult in circumstances where the extraterritorial effects of regulation unfairly burden developing countries that are not in a position to develop similar environmental protection measures (the EC CO_2/energy tax may very well do so). Once sovereignty over natural resources enters the equation, the extraterritorial portion of the tax also comes dangerously close to violating Principle 21 of the Stockholm Declaration and Article 12 of the Rio Declaration both of which discourage extrajurisdictional environmental regulation.

In order to meet the extrajurisdictional concern the EC would argue that the tax on imports affects energy products whose consumption will take place in the EC after they are exported, with the polluting event taking place directly within EC jurisdiction. It would also be pointed out that climate change is a transboundary phenomenon, and as such, the energy sector activities of exporting nations subject to the tax does have an environmental effect on EC nations since all nations contribute to global warming. In this sense, the limited extraterritorial effect of the tax would be argued to fall within the scope of the GATT Article XX(b) exception.

It could be further provided that, in the absence of the tax, the economic reasons against regulation are so overwhelming that a limited form of extraterritorialism is a 'necessary' component of the overall health protection package. This would only likely be the case if there are exemptions for imports which are already subject to a similar regulation (ie the non-discrimination principle is observed).

Article XX(g): Conservation of exhaustible natural resources

Article XX(g) exempts a Party defending a regulation from observing its regular GATT obligations for measures, 'relating to the conservation of exhaustible natural resources if such measures are made effective in conjunction with restrictions on domestic production or consumption.'[63] In the *Canada-United*

States Tuna Case[64] the GATT panel explained the application of Article XX to import bans. Pursuant to its Fishery Conservation and Management Act the United States imposed a ban on Canadian tuna imports for conservation purposes in a dispute over territorial waters. The United States embargo was put in place shortly after the seizure of United States fishing boats in the Canadian exclusive economic zone (EEZ) by the Canadian government.

While Canada did not dispute that tuna was an exhaustible resource under Article XX(g) it did take the view that the United States embargo was in violation of Article XI, which prohibits quantitative trade restrictions, and Articles I and III, which require that quantitative import restrictions be consistent with the most favoured nation treatment principle. The GATT panel found that the import ban was inconsistent with Article XI(l). Since the restriction applied to species for which the catch had not thus far been restricted in the United States and had been maintained when restriction catches were no longer in force the measure could not be protected by the Article XX(g) exception. The panel did not give an opinion on the relationship between the offending measure and conservation goals.

This issue was addressed in the GATT dispute panel in its report on Canada Measures Affecting Exports of Unprocessed Herring and Salmon (Salmon-Herring). The report stated that any trade measure taken under Article XX(g) must be 'primarily aimed at' conserving the resource.[65] According to this requirement, trade related environmental measures with the aim of preserving a resources do not have to be proven to be necessary to preserve the resource. They simply have to be:

(1) primarily aimed at preserving the resource;
(2) taken in conjunction with domestic restrictions on the use of the resource; and
(3) primarily aimed at rendering the domestic restriction effective.[66]

Before the *Tuna-Dolphin* ruling, Article XX(g) was viewed as a safe haven from GATT-based challenges to natural resource conservation measures. Unfortunately, the *Tuna-Dolphin* panel report, interpreted Article XX(g) very narrowly, in part, by finding that Article XX(g), like Article XX(b), does not extend to measures which are beyond a Party's geographical jurisdiction.[67]

The panel limited the application of Article XX(g) even further by interpreting Article XX(g)'s 'primarily aimed at' test in a way which takes on board the features of the Article XX(b) 'necessity' test. The combination of these requirements further constrains the ability of the contracting Parties to use the Article XX(g) exception for its intended purpose, thus denying the achievement of greater flexibility for GATT disciplines in coping with widely supported environmental protection objectives.

The effect of the Article XX(g) jurisprudence is to set out five tests which a regulation must pass in order to be protected by the exemption. Two of the tests, which are evident in the *Tuna-Dolphin* decision – 'necessity' and 'extra-territoriality' – have been discussed above. The other three, taken from the *Salmon-Herring* decision, are discussed below. First, it may be difficult to establish that the CO_2/energy tax is primarily aimed at the preservation of natural resources.

Surprisingly, the Preamble of the draft CO_2/energy tax Directive mentions a number of purposes but resource conservation is not mentioned among them.

One of the indirect benefits of the tax is that it may encourage greater energy efficiency, but one can imagine several other instruments for the protection of energy resources which would promote their conservation in a more effective fashion (eg rationing, quotas, and other direct restrictions on use). As well, the tax was developed in response to the Climate Change Convention ratification process. The main purpose of this Convention is to reduce greenhouse gas emissions, not to conserve natural resources although the two have a cause effect relationship. In addition, some forms of energy production (ie hydroelectricity, nuclear energy) do not give rise to concerns of natural resource exhaustion. However, the argument can be made that various natural resources which are harvested for energy production (eg coal, oil, natural gas, and peat) are more likely to be conserved under the CO_2/energy tax regime and, therefore, that the tax qualifies for Article XX(g) treatment.

The remaining two tests would *prima facie* appear to be met if the CO_2/energy tax is applied in a non-discriminatory manner. The application of the tax to imports applies in conjunction with similar domestic restrictions and is designed to make the domestic restriction effective. If the tax were not applied to imports then firms may seek to lower their energy costs by purchasing energy from foreign sources which would be cheaper (other factors being equal). The absence of a tax on imports would also be a factor that influences a small number of energy intensive firms to relocate in countries with brown rather than green environmental regimes. Finally, the application of the tax on a differential price basis tied to CO_2 emissions discourages energy production generally and especially with respect to energy sources that are greater contributors to climate change.

CONCLUSION

The EC has strongly declared its support for measures to combat global warming. As already discussed, the EC was at the forefront of the negotiations towards the Framework Convention on Climate Change, and has expressed its intention to introduce fiscal and non-fiscal measures to reduce CO_2 emissions and improve energy efficiency. However, since the problem requires not only unilateral but also multilateral global solutions, the strength of the EC's response must be assessed not only in the light of unilateral measures adopted at the EC level (and national measures adopted by member states), but also in terms of the EC's response to measures adopted by other Parties, and indeed non-Parties, to the Convention which are aimed at or which have the effect of combating the greenhouse effect. In this regard *all* areas of EC policy will be relevant, including those in relation to trade and external affairs. Once again, the Community will be required to strike a balance between two objectives: economic development and environmental protection.

In this regard, it is interesting to note the EC's response to certain controversial taxes on fuel consumption introduced in the US. The US taxes are: the gas guzzler, which taxes cars having fuel economy ratings below a given level (22.5 miles per gallon); the luxury car tax; and the Corporate Average Fuel Economy standard (CAFE), which sets a fleet average standard of 27.5 miles per gallon and taxes cars which achieve worse gas mileage. The EC has initiated formal GATT proceedings challenging the compatibility of these laws with the GATT, and a dispute panel has been set up. This challenge comes in addition to the EC's existing GATT challenge to the US Marine Mammal Protection Act.[68]

The EC alleges that the US fuel taxes discriminate against EC luxury car manufacturers, such as BMW, Mercedes, Jaguar and Porsche, in favour of American ones. The argument appears to be that since the US taxes are assessed on average fuel consumption across the range of cars produced, there is *de facto* discrimination against European luxury car makers which tend to manufacture (and sell into the American market) large, high fuel consumption vehicles, whereas American companies tend to produce a wider range of both high consumption and fuel-efficient cars, thus lowering their exposure to the effects of the tax.

In challenging the US taxes the EC may expose its own proposals for a CO_2/energy tax to closer US examination, and could be considered at odds with the EC's environmental protection objectives, as stated in the Treaty and in secondary legislation. The US taxes, whether or not, as the EC might argue, they are essentially revenue-raising and not environmental measures, are measures which would seem to encourage energy efficiency. In this sense they are environmentally beneficial. Moreover, the EC challenge comes despite the European Parliament's own calls for a two-year moratorium on GATT panel judgements concerning the environment pending the strengthening of GATT articles and practices following the *Tuna-Dolphin* decision.[69]

If the EC is to proceed with the CO_2/energy tax and wishes to avoid legal retaliation from the US (in part as a response to the EC challenge of US taxes) then it must re-evaluate the GATT compatibility of its own proposal. This chapter has raised several concerns in this regard. Among the most central are those dealing with most favoured nation and tariff concession obligations, subsidization and countervails, production and process method regulation and dispute settlement fora. Many of these areas can be satisfactorily remedied without amendments to the draft Directive provided that implementation decisions are sensitive to GATT rules. If EC members fail to consider GATT disciplines further at the implementation stage then there is little reason to expect that the CO_2/energy tax will be saved by GATT Article XX(b) or (g) exceptions in the event of a challenge.

In the end, either non-implementation of the tax or its successful challenge at GATT are two environmentally unacceptable prospects. Without the CO_2/energy tax EC member states will almost certainly fail, jointly or separately, to meet their commitment to stabilizing CO_2 emissions at 1990 levels by the year 2000. One would suspect that the same will be true for EC members' major trading partners. In the absence of reciprocal implementation of a CO_2/energy tax by OECD states on the basis of the 'conditionality' principle there is little hope that the environmental objective of stabilizing greenhouse gas emissions will be met in a timely fashion. At the very least, the many unresolved and problematic trade and environment issues raised by the Convention demand immediate analysis and negotiation so that developed countries will fulfil their leadership responsibilities in securing the successful implementation of the Convention.

NOTES AND REFERENCES

1 COMPLIANCE THEORY: AN OVERVIEW

1 This chapter builds on the second chapter of Mitchell, R B *Intentional Oil Pollution at Sea: Environmental Policy and Treaty Compliance*, Cambridge, MA: The MIT Press 1994 ('Mitchell').

2 Brierly J L (1944) *The Outlook for International Law*, The Clarendon Press, Oxford 1993, 1–2 as cited in Morgenthau, H J *Politics among nations: the struggle for power and peace* (Brief ed.), revised by Thompson, K W, McGraw-Hill Inc., New York, NY, p 253. ('Morgenthau').

3 Donoghue, J E (February 1993) 'On learning not to think like a lawyer: improving the effectiveness of international environmental law'; Washington, DC (unpublished manuscript), p 6, ('Donoghue').

4 For the major works on realism, see Morgenthau, supra note 2; and Waltz, K (1979) *Theory of International Politics*, Addison-Wesley Publishing, Reading, MA ('Waltz').

5 See Morgenthau supra note 2 at p 268.

6 Waltz, K 'Anarchic orders and balances of power', in Keohane, Robert (ed), (1986) *Neorealism and its critics*, Columbia University Press, New York, NY, p 328.

7 Morgenthau, supra note 2 at p 267. See, for example, Henkin, L (1979) *How Nations Behave: Law and Foreign Policy*, Columbia University Press, New York, NY, p 47; Young, O (1989) *International Cooperation: Building Regimes for Natural Resources and the Environment*, Cornell University Press, Ithaca, NY, p 62 ('Young'); and Chayes, A and Chayes, A (July 1991) 'Compliance Without Enforcement: State Behavior Under Regulatory Treaties', *Negotiation Journal* 7, p 31 ('Chayes and Chayes'). For an introduction to institutionalist views, especially regime theory, see Krasner, S (ed) (1983) *International Regimes*, Cornell University Press, Ithaca, NY ('Krasner'); and for its application to international environmental problems see Haas, P, Keohane, R O and Levy, M (1993) *Institutions for the Earth: Sources of Effective International Environmental Protection*, The MIT Press, Cambridge, MA ('Haas, Keohane and Levy').

8 Young supra note 7 at p 61.

9 Krasner supra note 7.

10 For the seminal work in this area, see Keohane, R O and Nye, J S Jr. (eds) *Transnational Relations and World Politics*, Harvard University Press, Cambridge, MA.

11 Fisher, R (1981) *Improving Compliance with International Law*, University Press of Virginia, Charlottesville, VA ('Fisher'), p 20. Young, O (1979) *Compliance and Public Authority: A Theory with International Applications*, Johns Hopkins University Press, Baltimore, MD, p 104, ('Young, *Compliance and Authority*').

12 See, for example, Downs, G W and Rocke D M (1990) *Tacit bargaining, arms races, and arms control*, University Michigan Press, Ann Arbor, MI; and Lipson, C (Autumn 1991) 'Why are some international agreements informal?', *International Organization* 45:4 ('Lipson'). On ambiguity in treaty rules, see Chayes, A and Chayes, A, Spring 1993 'On compliance'; *International Organization* 47:2 pp. 188–192 ('Chayes A and Chayes A').

13 Chayes and Chayes supra note 7 at p 318.

14 On this point, see Young, O (1991) 'The effectiveness of international institutions: hard cases and critical variables', in Rosenau, J N and Czempiel, O (eds) *Governance Without Government: Change and Order in World Politics*, Cambridge University Press, New York, NY, p 183, ('Young, "The effectiveness of international institutions"'), Chayes, A and Chayes, A supra note 12, pp 188–192; and Levy, M A 'The Effectiveness of International Environmental Institutions: What We Think We Know, and How We Might Learn More,' Paper prepared for presentation at the Annual Convention of the International Studies Association, Acapulco, Mexico, pp 23–27, March 1993.

15 Morgenthau supra note 2 at p 259.

16 Keohane, R O (1984) *After hegemony: cooperation and discord in the world political economy*, Princeton University Press, Shelf, Princeton, NJ, p 116 ('Keohane').

17 Peterson, M J (1988) *Managing thefrozen south: the creation and evolution of the Antarctic treaty system*, University,of California Press, Berkeley, CA.

18 Morgenthau supra p 260; Strange S 'Cave! hic dragones: a critique of regime analysis', in Krasner supra note 7 at p 350 ('Strange').

19 Martin, L L (Autumn 992) 'Interests, power, and multilateralism', *International Organization* 46:4; Waltz supra note 4 in Chapter 9.

20 Keohane supra note 16 at p 99.

21 Stein, A A 'Coordination and collaboration; regimes in an anarchic world' in Krasner supra note 7 at pp 138–139; Keohane supra note 16 at pp 120–124.

22 See Keohane, supra note 16 at p 105; and Puchala, D and Hopkins, R 'International regimes: lessons from inductive analysis' in Krasner supra note 7 at p 90.

23 Franck, T M (1990) *The power of legitimacy among nations*, Oxford University Press, New York, NY; Puchala and Hopkins supra note 22 at p 66.

24 Ruggie, J G 'International regimes, transactions, and change: embedded liberalism in the postwar economic order', in Krasner supra note 7 at p 200.

25 Allison, G T (1971) *Essence of decision: explaining the Cuban missile crisis*, Little Brown, Boston, MA; Janis, I L (1982) *Groupthink: psychological studies of policy decisions and fiascoes*, (2nd ed), Houghton Mifflin, Boston, MA; Steinbruner J D (1974) *The cybernetic theory of decision: new dimensions of political analysis*, Princeton University Press, Princeton, NJ.

26 Abram Chayes develops a clear argument regarding how these factors lead to compliance in arms control agreements in his excellent article, 'An Inquiry into the Workings of Arms Control Agreements', *Harvard Law Review* 85. See also, Young, *Compliance and Authority*, supra note at pp 25 and 178; Young supra note 7 at pp 78–79.

27 Waltz supra note at p 208; Stein supra note 2l at p l37.

28 Kratochwil, F V (1989) *Rules, norms, and decisions: on the conditions of practical and legal reasoning in international relations and domestic affairs*, Cambridge University Press, Cambridge, England, p 14.

29 Strange supra note 18 at p 348; Gilpin, R (1981) *War and Change in World Politics*, Cambridge University Press, Cambridge, MA, Chapter 2 ('Gilpin').

30 Montreal Protocol on Substances that Deplete the Ozone Layer, 16 September 1987, reprinted in 26 ILM 1541 (1987) ('Montreal Protocol').

31 Realists, however, tend to assume that such changes work against compliance: regimes are only too easily upset when either the balance of bargaining power or the

perception of national interest (or both together) change among those states who negotiate them. (Strange supra note 18 at p 345).

32 Gilpin supra note 29 at pp 51–2; Gilpin, R (1975) *US Power and the Multinational Corporation: The Political Economy of Foreign Direct Investment*, Basic Books, Inc., New York, NY; and Haas, P M (1990) *Saving the Mediterranean: the politics of international environmental cooperation*, Columbia University Press, New York, NY ('Haas').

33 Haas supra note 32.

34 Finlayson, J A and Zacher, M W, 'The GATT and the regulation of trade barriers: regime dynamics and functions', ('Finlayson and Zacher') in Krasner supra note 7 at p 312.

35 Oye, K (1986) 'Explaining cooperation under anarchy: hypotheses and strategies', in *Cooperation under anarchy*, Princeton University Press, Princeton, NJ ('Oye').

36 Krasner, S D (1985) *Structural Conflict: The Third World Against Global Liberalism*, University of California Press, Berkeley, CA, p 29; Rosenau, J (Autumn 1986) 'Before Cooperation: Hegemons, Regimes and Habit-driven Behavior in World Politics'; *International Organization* 4; and Jervis, R (April 1988) 'Realism, Game Theory, and Cooperation'; *World Politics* 40.

37 Stein supra note 21 at p 117.

38 Morgenthau supra note 2 at p 267.

39 Schelling, T (1978) *Micromotives and Macrobehavior*, Norton, New York, NY.

40 Stein, A A (1990) *Why Nations Cooperate: Circumstance and Choice in International Relations*, Cornell University Press, Ithaca, NY ('Stein, *Why Nations Cooperate*').

41 Axelrod, R and Keohane, R O 'Achieving Cooperation Under Anarchy: Strategies and Institutions' ('Axelrod and Keohane') in Oye supra note 35 at p 235.

42 Stein supra note 21 at p 130.

43 Krasner, S (April 1991) 'Global communications and national power: life on the Pareto frontier', *World Politics* 43.

44 Snidal, D (Autumn 1985) 'The Limits of Hegemonic Stability Theory', *International Organization* 39. See also Olson, M (1965) *The Logic of Collective Action: Public Goods and the Theory of Groups*, Harvard University Press, Cambridge, MA, Chapters 1 and 2 ('Olson'); and Hardin, R (1982) Collective Action, Johns Hopkins University Press, Baltimore, MD ('Hardin').

45 See, for example, Olson supra note 44; Hardin supra note 44; and Axelrod, R (1984) *The Evolution of Cooperation*, Basic Books, New York, NY ('Axelrod').

46 Waltz supra note 4 at pp 196–197.

47 Waltz supra note 4 at p 70.

48 Stein supra note 21 at pp 128–130.

49 Morgenthau supra note 2 at p 298.

50 Indeed, since states that violate a treaty are unlikely to enforce it, unsuccessful enforcement efforts only increase the relative gains of non-compliant states. As with compliance, models of limited rationality or habit-driven behaviour may best explain the variance between those who enforce and those who do not.

51 Young, O 'Regime Dynamics: The Rise and Fall of International Regimes' in Krasner supra note 7 at p 100.

52 Waltz supra note 4 at p 209.

53 Keohane supra note 16 at pp 105–106; Axelrod and Keohane supra note 41 at p 250; and Young supra note 7 at pp 75–76.

54 Keohane supra note 16 at p 105; and Morgenthau supra note 2 at p 267.

55 Stein, *Why nations cooperate* supra note 40 at p 187; and Axelrod and Keohane supra note 41 at p 227.

56 Axelrod and Keohane supra note 41 at p 247.

57 It remains an empirical question whether this is common or 'exceptional' international behaviour (Chayes and Chayes supra note 7 at p 311).

58 Convention on Long-Range Transboundary Air Pollution, 13 November 1979, reprinted in 18 ILM 1442 (1979) ('LRTAP Convention'); Protocol to the 1979

Convention on Long-Range Transboundary Air Pollution on the Reduction of Sulphur Emissions or their Transboundary Fluxes by at Least 30 Per cent, 9 July 1985, *UN Doc ECE/EB.AIR/12* reprinted in 27 ILM 707 (1988), ('LRTAP Sulphur Protocol').

59 Young 'The effectiveness of international institutions' supra note 14 at pp 183–185; Haas, Keohane, and Levy supra note 7.

60 Article 10 of London Amendments to the Montreal Protocol on Substances that Deplete the Ozone Layer, 29 June 1990, reprinted in 30 ILM 539 (1991), ('London Amendments'); Article 4(3) and Article 11, Framework Convention on Climate Change, *UN Doc A/AC.237/18 (Part II)/Add.1* (15 May 1992).

61 See the introduction and conclusion of Haas, Keohane, and Levy supra note 7.

62 For example, two governments could be equally committed to reducing population growth but one with a predominantly Catholic population might prove significantly less successful at complying.

63 Examples include the Montreal Protocol and the LRTAP Convention.

64 For a discussion of the inherent uncertainties surrounding actual emission reductions for a given tax level, see Epstein, J M and Gupta, R (1990) *Controlling the Greenhouse Effect: Five Global Regimes Compared*, The Brookings Institution, Washington, DC, pp 15–17.

65 A seminal study on these issues is Pressman, J L and Wildavsky, A (1973) *Implementation: How Great Expectations in Washington are Dashed in Oakland, or, Why It's Amazing that Federal Programs Work at All, This Being a Saga of the Economic Development Administration as Told by Two Sympathetic Observers Who Seek to Build Morals on a Foundation of Ruined Hopes*, University of California Press, Berkeley, CA.

66 See Hamlin, T B (1989) 'Debt-for-nature Swaps: A New Strategy for Protecting Environmental Interests in Developing Nations', *Ecology Law Quarterly* 16; Blum, E (1993) 'Making Biodiversity Conservation Profitable: A Case Study of the Merck/INBio Agreement', *Environment* 35:4; Anonymous, (10 October 1990) 'Soviet Union Gives Finnish Metal Company Go-ahead to Modernize Two Nickel Smelters' *International Environment Reporter*, p 421.

67 Chayes and Chayes supra note 7 at p 318.

68 Keohane supra note 16 at p 159.

69 For example, individual traders may be convicted and punished for trades in endangered species prohibited by the Convention on International Trade in Endangered Species of Wild Fauna and Flora, 3 March 1973, TIAS No 8249, 27 UST 1087, 983 UNTS 243 reprinted in 12 ILM 1085 (1973) ('CITES'). For an analysis of the CITES agreement, see Trexler, M C (1989) 'The Convention on International Trade in Endangered Species of Wild Fauna and Flora: Political or Conservation Success?' (unpublished thesis), Berkeley CA ('Trexler').

70 Young, *Compliance and Authority* supra note 11 at pp 22 and 44.

71 Chayes, A and Chayes, A (1991) 'Adjustment and Compliance Processes in International Regulatory Regimes' in Tuchman Mathews, J (ed), *Preserving the Global Environment: The Challenge of Shared Leadership*, W W Norton and Co, New York, NY, p 290 ('Chayes and Chayes, "Adjustment and Compliance"').

72 Lemonick, M D (2 August 1993) 'The hunt, the furor,' *Time*.

73 Morgenthau supra note 2 at p 265; Chayes and Chayes supra note 2 at p 324.

74 See Waltz supra note 4 at p 208; Gilpin supra note 29 at p 169; and Olson, M (1965) *The Logic of Collective Action*, Harvard University Press, Cambridge, MA, p 35.

75 See Gilpin supra note 29 at p 30; Waltz supra note 4 at pp 136 and 157; and Krasner, 'Structural Causes and Regime Consequences: Regimes as Intervening Variables' in *International Regimes* supra note 7 at pp 13–15.

76 Gilpin supra note 29 at p 36. Strange suggests that compliance with multilateral treaty rules, eg, GATT, is best explained by parallel bilateral deals that allow more efficacious and direct application of power (Strange supra note 18 at p 352).

77 Gilpin supra note 29 at p 31.

78 Morgenthau argues that attempts by weak states to violate, by strong states to enforce, and the success of both, depend on 'political considerations and the actual distribution of power' (supra note 2 at p 266).
79 Young defines 'obedience as a response to a command from an identifiable authority figure in a specific situation' (*Compliance and Authority* supra note 11 at p 5).
80 Waltz supra note 4 at pp 177–8. See also Gilpin supra note 29 at pp 173–4.
81 Gilpin supra note 29 at p 156.
82 Lipson, C 'The Transformation of Trade: The Sources and Effects of Regime Change', in Krasner supra note 7 at pp 254–5.
83 Young, 'The Effectiveness of International Institutions' supra note 14 at p 187.
84 Keohane supra note 16 at p 99. For extended discussions of reciprocity, see Keohane, R O (Winter 1986) 'Reciprocity in International Relations', *International Organization* 40:1 ('Keohane, 'Reciprocity' ') and Axelrod supra note 45.
85 Axelrod and Keohane supra note 41 at p 232. See also Axelrod supra note 45; Keohane, R O 'The Demand for International Regimes', in Krasner supra note 7; and Jervis, R 'Security Regimes', in Krasner supra note 7.
86 Young, *Compliance and Authority* supra note 11 at p 58; and Wittman, D (September 1989) 'Arms Control Verification and Other Games Involving Imperfect Detection', *American Political Science Review* 83.
87 Keohane, 'Reciprocity' supra note 84 at p 12.
88 Id.
89 Conybeare J, 'Trade Wars: A Comparative Study of Anglo-hanse, Franco-italian, and Hawley-Smoot Conflicts' in Oye supra note 35 at p 151.
90 For a more extended discussion of compliance system design, see Mitchell, R B and Chayes, A 'Improving Compliance with the Climate Change Treaty' in Lee, H (ed) *Shaping National Responses to Climate Change: A Post-Rio Policy Guide*, Island Press, 1995.
91 Young, however, cautions against attributing too much power to institutions (*Compliance and Authority* supra note 11 at p 44), as do Finlayson and Zacher supra note 34 at pp 311–312, and Puchala and Hopkins supra note 22.
92 Young, *Compliance and Authority* supra note 11 at p 3.
93 Stein supra note 21.
94 Axelrod and Keohane supra note 41 at pp 228–232.
95 As a student of Jervis noted, 'what . . . are we to cooperate *about*?' (Jervis, R (April 1988) 'Realism, Game Theory, and Cooperation', *World Politics* 40, p 331).
96 Axelrod supra note 45.
97 Fisher supra note 11; Kennedy, D (1976) 'Form and Substance in Private Law Adjudication', *Harvard Law Review* 89; and Donoghue, J E supra note 3.
98 Chayes, A (Spring 1991) 'Managing the Transition to a Global Warming Regime or What to Do Till the Treaty Comes', *Foreign Policy* 82, p 16.
99 Considerable debate exists over whether formal treaties provide greater or lesser likelihood of behavioural change. Puchala and Hopkins conclude that the degree of formalization of a regime and its rules 'have relatively little to do with the probabilities of participant's compliance' (supra note 22 at p 88). Charles Lipson has recently written an excellent article on the value of informal agreements (supra note 12). In contrast, Abram Chayes and Antonia Chayes argue that 'it seems clear that an international regulatory regime will stand a better chance of achieving its objectives if its based on a formal treaty' (1992) 'Non-proliferation Regimes in the Aftermath of the Gulf War', in Nye, J and Smith, R (eds), *After the storm: lessons from the Gulf War*, Madison Books and the Aspen Strategy Group of the Aspen Institute, Lanham, MD, 50.
100 Kaplow, L (Spring 1990) 'Optimal Deterrence, Uninformed Individuals, and Acquiring Information About Whether Acts are Subject to Sanctions', *Journal of Law, Economics & Organization* 6 pp 93–128; and Kaplow, L (March 1992) 'The Optimal

Probability and Magnitude of Fines for Acts that Definitely are Undesirable', *International Review of Law and Economics* 12 pp 3–11.

101 See, for example, Young, 'The Effectiveness of International Institutions' supra note 14 and Chayes and Chayes, 'Adjustment and Compliance Processes' supra note 71.

102 Jervis, R 'From Balance to Concert: A Study of International Security Cooperation', in Oye supra note 35 at p 74. See also Downs, G W, Rocke D M and Siverson, R M 'Arms Races and Cooperation', in Oye supra note 35.

103 The term 'zone of possible agreement' comes from Howard Raiffa's excellent (1982) *The art and science of negotiation*, Harvard University Press, Cambridge, MA.

104 For a detailed account of the negotiation of the Montreal Protocol, see Benedick, R (1991) *Ozone Diplomacy: new directions in safeguarding the planet*, Harvard University Press, Cambridge, MA.

105 Levy, M 'European Acid Rain: The Power of Tote-board Diplomacy' ('Levy') in Haas, Keohane, and Levy supra note 7.

106 United States General Accounting Office (1992) *International environment: international agreements are not well monitored, GAO/RCED-92-43* GPO, Washington, DC.

107 Sessions, K (1992) *Institutionalizing the Earth Summit: The United Nations Commission on Sustainable Development*, United Nations Association of the USA, New York, NY; and Glass, J A (March 1993) 'Selective Service: Non-Governmental Organization's Influence in Enforcing International Environmental Agreements', (unpublished undergraduate thesis), Harvard College, Cambridge, MA, ('Glass').

108 Convention on Wetlands of International Importance Especially as Waterfowl Habitat, 2 February 1971, 996 UNTS 245 reprinted in 11 ILM 969 (1972), 5 IPE 2161, ('Ramsar Convention').

109 Finlayson and Zacher supra note 34 at p 313. This has been an especially important contribution of the Standing Consultative Commission in the arms control arena (Earle, R (1988) 'SALT II Compliance Controversies', in Krepon, M and Umberger, M *Verification and Compliance*, Ballinger Publishing Co, Cambridge, MA.)

110 See, for example, Jervis, R 'From Balance to Concert', supra note 102 at p 73; Finlayson and Zacher supra note 34 at p 298; and Krasner, S D 'Regimes and the Limits of Realism: Regimes as Autonomous Variables' supra note 75 at p 362.

111 See Jervis supra note 102 at p 73, Oye supra note 35 at p 15, and Fisher supra note 11 at p 317.

112 Montreal Protocol, Article 5(5).

113 Schelling, T (1960/1980) *The Strategy of Conflict*, Harvard University Press, Cambridge, MA.

114 Young supra note 11 at p 20.

115 See Fisher supra note 11 for an excellent discussion of some of these limitations. The most extensive empirical study of international sanctions is Hufbauer, G C and Schott, J J (1985) *Economic sanctions reconsidered: history and current policy*, Institute for International Economics, Washington, DC. Hawkins, K describes the limits of such strategies in the domestic realm in (1984) *Environment and enforcement: regulation and the social definition of pollution*, Clarendon Press, Oxford, England.

116 Brundtland, G H (April 1993) 'The road from Rio', *Technology Review* 96:3, p 63.

117 Axelrod supra note 45 at p 132; Chayes and Chayes, 'Adjustment and Compliance' supra note 71.

118 Chayes and Chayes supra note 7 at p 323.

119 See, for example, Day, D (1987) *The Whale War*, Sierra Club Books, San Francisco, CA.

120 Young, 'The Effectiveness of International Institutions' supra note 14 at pp 176–178; and Chayes and Chayes supra note 7 at p 8.

121 Axelrod and Keohane supra note 41 at pp 234–237.

122 Morgenthau supra note 2 at p 266.

123 Rules similar to those banning trade with non-Parties to the Montreal Protocol

could be applied to non-compliant Parties (Article 4).

124 Oye, K 'The Sterling-dollar-franc Triangle: Monetary Diplomacy 1929–1937' in Oye supra note 35.

125 Lyster, S (1985) *International wildlife law an analysis of international treaties concerned with the conservation of wildlife*, Grotius Publications, Cambridge, England, pp 4041.

126 Convention on International Trade in Endangered Species of Wild Fauna and Flora, supra note 69.

127 Chayes and Chayes supra note 7 at p 318.

128 Reiss, A J Jr. (Fall 1994) 'Consequences of compliance and deterrence models of law enforcement for the exercise of police discretion', *Law and Contemporary Problems* 47, 4, pp 83–122 and 300.

129 Mitchell, R B *From Paper to Practice: Intentional Oil Pollution and Treaty Compliance*, Cambridge, MA: The MIT Press (forthcoming).

130 See, for example, Keohane, R O (1984) *After Hegemony: Cooperation and Discord in the World Political Economy*, Princeton University Press, Princeton, NJ, Haas supra note 32; and Parson, E A and Clark, W C (1991) 'Learning to Manage Global Environmental Change: A Review of Relevant Theory', (unpublished paper), Cambridge, MA ('Parson and Clark').

131 Wendt, A (Spring 1992) 'Anarchy is What States Make of It', *International Organization* 46, p 392. In the book, I consciously limit myself to what Wendt terms a 'rationalist' view in which institutions 'change behavior but not identities and interests'.

132 See Haas, Keohane and Levy supra note 7.

133 Levy supra note 105.

134 Parson and Clark supra note 130.

135 When facing uncertainty, especially in environmental treaties, politicians may defer to scientific experts to define the nation's interests and implement the treaty domestically. These scientists have strong incentives to ensure their country complies with and enforces environmental treaties (Haas supra note 32 at pp 54–63).

136 For two excellent discussions of effectiveness, see Young, 'Effectiveness of International Institutions' supra note 14 and Levy supra note 105.

137 Levy, Osherenko and Young, 'The effectiveness of international regimes'.

138 Wettestad, J and Andresen, S (1991) 'The Effectiveness of International Resource Cooperation: Some Preliminary Findings', Fridtjof Nansen Institute, Lysaker, Norway, cited in Levy supra note 105.

139 Kay, D A and Jacobson, H K (eds) (1983) *Environmental Protection: The International Dimension*, Allanheld, Osmun & Co, Totowa, NJ, p 18.

140 Keohane, Haas and Levy, 'The effectiveness of international environmental institutions', in Haas, Keohane, and Levy supra note 7 at p 7. See also, Kay and Jacobson supra note 139 at p 320.

141 See Parson, E A 'Protecting the ozone layer' in Haas, Keohane and Levy supra note 7.

142 John Kambhu has explored the interaction of these two effects at the domestic level in his excellent article (June 1989) 'Regulatory Standards, Noncompliance and Enforcement', *Journal of Regulatory Economics* 1.

143 This discussion focuses on the relationship of compliance costs to compliance level. The linked problem of the relationship between enforcement costs and compliance has been extensively addressed in attempting to identify optimal levels of regulatory enforcement. For example, see Becker, G S (March/April 1968) 'Crime and Punishment: An Economic Approach', *Journal of Political Economy* 76; Stigler, G J (1970) 'The Optimum Enforcement of Laws', *Journal of Political Economy* 78; and Young, *Compliance and Authority* supra notell in Chapter 7.

144 These include, among others, book manuscripts being written and projects being conducted at, or with funding from, Dartmouth College (Oran Young and Marc

Levy); the European Science Foundation (Kenneth Hanf); the Foundation for International Environmental Law and Development (James Cameron); the Fridtjof Nansen Institute (Steinar Andresen); Harvard University (Abram Chayes and Antonia Chayes); Harvard University (William Clark, Robert Keohane, and Marc Levy); the International Institute for Applied Systems Analysis (David Victor and Eugene Skolnikoff); the Social Science Research Council (Edith Brown Weiss and Harold Jacobson); and the University of Tubingen (Volker Rittberger).

145 On oil pollution, see Mitchell supra note 129; and on endangered species, see Trexler supra note 69.

146 See note 27 in Chapter 1.

147 Edith Brown Weiss of Georgetown University Law Center and Harold Jacobson of the University of Michigan are leading this research team.

148 Center for International Affairs and Center for Science and International Affairs (14 June 1993) 'Developing effective mechanisms for transferring financial resources for environmental protection' (draft proposal), Harvard University, Cambridge, MA.

149 The International Institute for Applied Systems Analysis in Laxenburg, Austria has just begun a project on compliance with international environmental accords that includes a major database module.

150 For example, see Duffield, J S (Autumn 1992) 'International regimes and alliance behavior: explaining NATO conventional force levels', *International Organization* 46:4.

151 An initial effort at this has been made in Ausubel, J and Victor, D (1992) 'Verification of International Environmental Agreements', *Annual Review of Energy and the Environment* 17.

152 On trade, see Kapstein, E (1994) *Governing the global economy: international finance and the state*, Harvard University Press, Cambridge, MA.

153 Lewis, P (7 June 1992) 'Delegates at Earth Summit Plan a Watchdog Agency', *New York Times*; and Glass supra note 107.

154 For historical examples of claims that international environmental studies are new, see Falk, R (1973) 'Environmental Policy as a World Order Problem', in Utton, A E and Henning, D H (eds), *Environmental Policy: Concepts and International Implications*, Praeger Publishers, New York, NY, p 142; and Caldwell, L K (1984) *International Environmental Policy*, Duke University Press, Durham, NC, p 9. Jessica Mathews contends that the environment did not get 'catapulted from the quiet netherworld of "other" concerns to a place among international priorities' until the 1980s ('Introduction and overview', in Tuchman Mathews, J (ed) (1991) *Preserving the Global Environment: The Challenge of Shared Leadership*, W W Norton and Co, New York, NY, 15–16).

155 'We would have difficulties pleading innocence or lack of experience in this field today, considering the amount of international know-how already available' (Sand, P H 'International Cooperation: The Environmental Experience', in Mathews (ed) (1991) *Preserving the Global Environment*, p 239).

2 COMPLIANCE, CITIZENS AND NGOS

1 Ginther, K (1982) 'Redefining International Law From the Point of View of Decolonisation and Development and African Regionalism', 26 *Journal of African Law* 49, p 53.

2 Georgiev, D (1993) 'Politics or Rule of Law: Deconstruction and Legitimacy in International Law', 4 *EJIL* 1 ('Georgiev').

3 Myres, S McDougall, Harold D, Lasswell and Reisman, W. Michael (1968) 'Theories About International Law: Prologue to a Configurative Jurisprudence', 8 *Va J Int'l L* 188, p 296.

4 Lindborg, N 'Future Role of Non-Governmental Organisations in International Environmental Negotiations', in Susskind, L, Dolin, E J and Breslin, J W (eds), *International Environmental Treaty-Making* ('Lindborg').
5 Nanda, V P (1991) 'International Environmental Protection and Developing Countries' Interests: the Role of International Law', 26 *Tex Int'l L J* 497.
6 Lindborg supra note 4.
7 Boyle, A *Saving the World*.
8 Ibid.
9 Koskenniemi, M (1990) 'The Politics of International Law', 1 *EJIL* 4, p 8.
10 Georgiev supra note 2.
11 Id at p 4.
12 Francioni, F (1990) 'Resource Sharing in Antarctica: For Whose Benefit?', 1 *EJIL* 258.
13 UN Charter, Article 71.
14 See Chapters 5 and 6.
15 Lindborg supra note 4.
16 See for example, *Participation by Non-governmental Organisations in the Global Environment Facility* (GEF Administrative Background Paper, 22–23 September 1993), G/PA. 9-22-23 93.
17 GEF Report, p 6, para 2.08.
18 E/1993/L. 18, 11 February 1993.
19 GEF Report.
20 Breckenridge, L P (1992) 'Protection of Biological and Cultural Diversity, Emerging Recognition of Local Community Rights in Ecosystems under International Environmental Law', 59 *Tenn L Rev* 735 ('Breckenridge'), p 763.
21 See Rights Arguments below.
22 Agenda 21, Chapter 27.13.
23 Agenda 21, Chapter 23.2.
24 Agenda 21, Chapter 27.9.
25 Howard, M (then UK Secretary of State for the Environment) (7 June 1992) 'The Talking Must Continue When the Speeches Stop', *The Observer*.
26 Senator Al Gore (20 June 1992) 'Life Beyond the Earth Summit', *The Financial Times*.
27 Extract from presentations by Ms Penny Wensley, Australian Ambassador for the Environment, to the Australian Centre for Environmental Law and Business Council of Australia in November 1993 in Sydney`and Canberra, entitled 'Global trends: the emergence of international environmental law'.
28 Brown Weiss, E (1993) 'Environmentally Sustainable Competitiveness: A Comment', 102 *Yale L J* 2123, p 2137.
29 Report of the Standing Committee on liability for nuclear damage, second session, Vienna 15–19 October 1990, IAEA documents *Doc Scnl/2/lNF2*. Text in 55 *AJIL* 1082 (1961) and 2 ILM 77 (1963), respectively.
30 Id at p67.
31 Id at p 68.
32 Goldberg D J A, Ibarra M, Kiss A C, Kothari M, Ksentini F M, Lador Y, McDonald D C, Parker K, Raman M, Shelton D, Simpson A, Tebourbi M, Thamage T, Cancado Trindade A A and myself.
33 Meeting of Experts on Human Rights and the Environment-UN, Geneva 16–18 May 1994, p 2, Draft Declaration – Final Version.
34 Handl, G (1992) 'Human Rights and Protection of the Environment: A Mildly "Revisionist" View' in Cancado Trindade, A A (ed) *Human Rights, Sustainable Development and the Environment* (Instituto Interamericano de Derechos Humanos, San Jose, p 117 at pp 139–40).
35 Handl supra note 34, at p 140.
36 Breckenridge supra note 20, at 769.
37 Kramer L, Legal Adviser to EC Commission DG Xl, Evidence to Select Committee on the European Communities (Sub-Committee F) 15 October 1991.

38 478 US 221 (1986).
39 (1980), 54 *ALIR* 176.
40 659F, 2d 168 (1981).
41 Text on file with author.
42 In *Lujan* v *Defenders of Wildlife*.
43 Barton and Carter *International Institutions for a New Age* ('Barton and Carter').
44 Cameron, J, Makuch, Z and Ward, H (June 1994) 'Sustainable Development and Integrated Dispute Settlement in GATT 1994', *World Wide Fund for Nature Discussion Paper*.
45 Graham, G, 18 September 1993, *The Financial Times*.
46 Barton and Carter supra note 43.
47 Barnes, J N 'Antarctica, the Politics of Protection', International Union for Conservation of Nature and Natural Resources 16th Technical Meeting, Madrid, 514 November 1984 Symposium B.
48 Beck, P (April 1992) *The Future of the Antarctic Region: Is the Great White Continent Turning Green?* Paper presented at the 33rd Annual Convention of the International Studies Association, Atlanta, Georgia, USA.
49 See Phillips (1992) 'The Management of Science and the Newly Protected Antarctica – The Environmental Angle', 7 *Circumpalla Journal* 1–2 at p139.
50 For a comprehensive account see Lindborg supra note 4.
51 See *ad hoc* Working Group of Legal and Technical Experts with a Mandate to Prepare a Global, Convention on the Control of Transboundary Movements of Hazardous Wastes (Report of the *ad hoc* Working Group on the work of its third session *Doc UNEP WG 189/3*,16 November 1988, 5–6).
52 See Kimball, L 'The Role of Non-Governmental Organisations in Antarctic Affairs' in Joyner, C and Chopra, S (eds), *The Antarctic Legal Regime* 1988.
53 Participation by non-governmental organizations in the global environment facility; *GEF/PA*. 22–23 September 1993.

3 COMPLIANCE WITH INTERNATIONAL ENVIRONMENTAL OBLIGATIONS: EXISTING INTERNATIONAL LEGAL ARRANGEMENTS

1 See Note by the President of the Security Council (1992), 'The Responsibility of the Security Council in the Maintenance of International Peace and Security', 31 January 1992, *UN Doc*. 523500, p 2.
2 As defined by Mitchell, R in Chapter 1.
3 Mitchell supra note 2.
4 See eg Matthews, J T (1989) 'Redefining Security', 68 *Foreign Affairs* 163; Renner, M (1989) 'National Security: the Economic and Environmental Dimensions', *Worldwatch Paper* 89; Timoshenko, A (1990) 'Ecological Security: Global Change Paradigm', 1 *ColJIELP* 127; Vinogradov, S (1990) 'International Environmental Security: The Concept and its Implementation', in Carter, A and Danilenko, G (eds), *Perestroika and International Law*, p 196; Handl, G (1990) 'Environmental Security and Global Change: the Challenge to International Law', 1 *YIEL* 3.
5 See the *Pacific Fur Seals Arbitration (Great Britain* v *United States)* (1893) concerning the issue of whether the United States had the right, on conservation grounds, to stop United Kingdom nationals from taking fur seals in areas beyond national jurisdiction; *Moore's International Arbitrations* (1893), p 755.
6 For example in the *Trail Smelter* Arbitration (*Canada* v *United States* (1941), 3 *RIAA* 1907 (1941), *Lac Lanoux* Arbitration (*France* v *Spain*) (1957) 24 ILR 101; *Gabcikovo-Nagymaros Project Case* (*Hungary/Slovakia*) (1993); *Fisheries Jurisdiction* Case (*United Kingdom* v *Iceland*) (1974); *ICJ Reports* 3 (1974); *Yellow-Fin Tuna* Decision (*Mexico* v *United States*),

(1991), *GATT Doc. DS21/R; Certain Phosphate Lands in Nauru* Case (*Nauru* v *Australia*) *ICJ Report* 240 (1992).

7 See 'Danube dam threatens to open floodgates of hostility,' *Financial Times* 29 October 1992, p 2. A mechanism for consultation and cooperation with regard to emergency situations was adopted by the Berlin Meeting of the CSCE Council, 19–20 June 1991. The mechanism comprises a process of exchange of information between the states involved, which if unsuccessful may lead to a special meeting of the Committee of Senior Officials, who may then refer the matter to a meeting at ministerial level. If the process does not resolve the situation the dispute may be referred to the Procedure for Peaceful Settlement of Disputes, involving the Conflict Prevention Centre: see Sumrnary of Conclusion, 30 ILM 1348 (1991), Annex 2 and Annex 3.

8 Oppenheim, vol 1, p 4.

9 Article 38 of the Statute of the ICJ provides that:

1. The Court, whose function it is to decide in accordance with international law such disputes as are submitted to it, shall apply:

(a) international conventions, whether general or particular, establishing rules expressly recognised by the contesting states;

(b) international custom, as evidence of a general practice accepted as law;

(c) the general principles of law recognised by civilised nations;

(d) . . . judicial decisions and the teachings of the most highly qualified publicists of the various nations, as subsidiary means for the determination of rules of law.

2. This provision shall not prejudice the power of the Court to decide a case *ex aequo et bono*, if the parties agree thereto.

10 ILC Draft Articles on State Responsibility, Part 2, Article 5(1), (1989) Report of the ILC to the United Nations General Assembly, *UN Doc A/44/10*, p 218.

11 Vienna, 23 May 1969, in force 27 January 1980, 8 ILM 679 (1969).

12 Article 2(1)(a). Treaties may also be adopted by international organizations: see 1986 Convention on the Law of Treaties between States and International Organizations, 25 ILM 543 (1986).

13 UN General Assembly Resolution 47/189 recommended that the first substantive session would be held in New York 'without prejudice to the venue of its future session': para 9. The Secretariat to the Commission on Sustainable Development is based in New York, and the normal practice is for a meeting of an institution to be held in the same place as its Secretariat.

14 See eg 1969 Southeast Atlantic Convention, Article X(1); 1972 London Convention, Article VII(1); 1989 Basel Convention, Article 4(4); 1991 Antarctic Environment Protocol, Article 13.

15 1988 CRAMRA, Article 7(1).

16 See eg 1989 Basel Convention, Article 5.

17 1982 UNCLOS, Articles 213, 214, 216 and 222.

18 Article 235(2).

19 1972 Oslo Convention, Article 15(1); 1973 CITES, Article VIII(1); 1974 Paris Convention, Article 12.

20 1946 International Whaling Convention, Article IX(1) and (3); 1969 Southeast Atlantic Convention, Article X(1); 1972 Oslo Convention, Article 15(3);1972 London Convention, Article VII(2); 1989 Basel Convention, Article 4(4).

21 1974 Paris Convention, Article 12 (1); 1989 Basel Convention, Article 9(5); 1991 Bamako Convention, Article 9; see also ILC Draft Articles on State Responsibility (draft Article 19(3)(d)), supra note 10; ILC Draft Articles on the Draft Code of Crimes Against the Peace and Security of Mankind, Draft Articles 22(2)(d) and 26, *Report of the ILC* (1991), *GAOR A/46/10*; see also Resolution on the Role of Criminal Law in the Protection of Nature and the Environment, 8th UN Congress on the Prevention of Crime and the Treatment of Offenders, *UN Doc A/CONF/144/7*, paras 456–62 (1990)

22 See Agenda 21, Chapter 39, para 39.3(d) and (e); EC Commission, 'Towards Sustainability', OJ No C 138,17 May 1993, p 1.

23 Final Report on 'Access to Justice', *ÖKO-Institut*, Darmstadt, Germany, 1992.

24 See EC, 'Fifth Environmental Action Programme' Towards Sustainability, p 82.

25 1982 UNCLOS, Articles 217 to 220.

26 Article 8(10).

27 Article 217(1).

28 Article 218(1). Proceedings in respect of violations taking place in the internal waters, territorial sea or EEZ of another state are, however, subject to certain limitations: see Article 218(2).

29 Article 219.

30 Article 220(1).

31 Article 220(1), (2), (3), (5) and (6).

32 Article 221.

33 Articles 1(1)(1) and 136.

34 Articles 139(1) and 145.

35 See eg 1972 World Heritage Convention, Article 29(1);1989 Basel Convention, Article 13(3)(c); 1992 Climate Change Convention, Article 12(1).

36 See eg 1987 Montreal Protocol, Article 7, as amended.

37 See eg 1946 International Whaling Convention, Article VIII(1).

38 See eg 1972 London Convention, Article VI(4).

39 See eg 1989 Basel Convention, Article 13(2)(c) and (d).

40 See eg 1946 International Whaling Convention, Article VIII(3).

41 Id, Article IX(4).

42 See also 1992 Climate Change Convention, requiring initial reports to be submitted within six months of entry into force by OECD countries, within three years of entry into force or upon the availability of financial resources by developing countries, and at their discretion by least-developed countries: Article 12(5).

43 See United States General Accounting Office, (1992) *International Environment: International Agreements Are Not Well Monitored, Report to Congressional Requesters, GAO/RCED-92-43*.

44 Id, at p 26.

45 Id, at p 25. This high rate of reporting occurred even though the Protocol did not enter into force until February 1991.

46 Id, at pp 24–25. Concern on lack of reporting led to the establishment in June 1990 of an *Ad Hoc* Group of Experts on the Reporting of Data (see Chapter 4, Annex I for further details). Reasons found by the Group for incomplete reporting include lack of financial and technical resources, inability to use customs records to track imports and exports because they do not distinguish between different substances, and confidentiality of information: *GAO Report*, supra note 44 at p 25.

47 Id, at p 26.

48 Id, at pp 26–27.

49 Id, at pp 27–28.

50 Council Decision-Recommendation Concerning the Provision of Information to the Public and Public Participation in Decision-Making Processes Related to the Prevention of, and Response to, Accidents Involving Hazardous Substances, 28 ILM 277 (1988).

51 EC Council Directive on Freedom of Access to Information on the Environment, 7 June 1990, *OJ* 1990 L158/56.

52 Operational Directive 14.70 on Involving Non-Governmental Organizations in Bank Supported Activities.

53 Article I(T) replacing Article 10 of the 1987 Montreal Protocol.

54 Article 4(3). The Convention states that the 'extent to which developing country Parties will effectively implement their commitments under the Convention will depend on the effective implementation by developed country Parties' of their

financial commitments: Article 4(7). Similar provisions may be found in the 1992 Biodiversity Convention, Articles 20(1) to (4), for an analysis of these wordings see Chapter 12.

55 Convention on Civil Liability for Damage Caused during Carriage of Dangerous Goods by Road, Rail and Inland Navigation Vessels, Geneva, 10 October 1989.

56 Convention on Civil Liability for Damage Resulting From Activities Dangerous to the Environment, Lugano, 21 June 1993, 32 ILM 1228 (1993).

57 Communication from the Commission to the Council: A Community Strategy to limit Carbon Dioxide emissions and to improve energy efficiency, *EC Commission Doc XI/626/91*, 22 September 1991, paras 19 to 28 at para 25.

58 Article 4.

59 ILC Draft Articles on State Responsibility, Pt 2, Article 5(1) 'Report of the ILC to the United Nations General Assembly', *UN Doc A/44/10* (1989), p 218.

60 Article 5(2).

61 *Trail Smelter* Arbitration supra note 6.

62 *Lac Lanoux* Arbitration supra note 6.

63 *Nuclear Tests* Case (*Australia* v *France*) (interim Measures) *ICJ Report* 99 (1973), p 103.

64 See *Fur Seals* Arbitration, supra note 5.

65 See eg 'The Wimbledon' (1923) *PCIJ*, Series A, No 1.

66 See eg 1950 ECHR, Article 24.

67 1957 EEC Treaty, Article 170.

68 Case 141/78 *France* v *United Kingdom* [1979] ECR 2923.

69 1989 Basel Convention, Article 19; the information is then to be submitted to the Parties.

70 *South West Africa (Preliminary Objections)* Case, *ICJ Reports* 6 (1966), p 47.

71 *Barcelona Traction Company* Case (*Belgium* v *Spain*) *ICJ Reports* 4 (1970), p 32.

72 *Nuclear Test* Case (*Australia* v *France*), supra note 63 at pp 369–70; *cf* Judge De Castro ('The Applicant has not legal title authorizing it to act as spokesman for the international community and ask the Court to condemn France's conduct'): id, 390. See also Judge Gros (id, 290) and Judge Petren (id 224).

73 See Oppenheim, vol I, 5.

74 See Brownlie, I calling for a liberal approach to the standing issue in such circumstances, (1975) 'A Survey of International Customary Rules of Environmental protection', in Teclaff L and Utton, A (eds), *International Environmental Law* 1 at p 5; Charney, J (1991) 'Third State Remedies for Environmental Damage to the World's Common Spaces', in Francioni, F and Scovazzi, T *International Responsibility for Environmental Harm* 149 at p 157; Leigh, K 'Liability for Damage to the Global Commons', Paper presented at an OECD Symposium on Liability for Nuclear Damage, Helsinki, September 1992, at p 5. On the suggestion that a coastal state is obliged to the world at large to prevent pollution of the territorial sea, see O'Connell, D (1984) *The International Law of the Sea*, vol 2, pp 988–989.

75 Draft Articles on State Responsibility, Article 19 supra note 10.

76 See Oppenheim, 9th ed, vol 1, at p 5, citing the *Reparations for Injuries Case, ICJ Report* (1949), p 185, and the *Namibia* Case, *ICJ Report* (1971), p 56.

77 In the *South West Africa* (*Second Phase*) Case the International Court accepted that *actio popularis* could be established by treaty: supra note 71 at p 47.

78 See Stone C (1972) 'Should Trees Have Standing? – Towards Legal Rights for Natural Objects', 45 *SCalLR* 450.

79 See *Reparations for Injuries* Case, ICJ Report (1949), p 174, where in an Advisory Opinion the International Court of Justice determined that the United Nations had an 'undeniable right' to 'demand that its Members fulfil the obligations entered into by them in the interest of the good working of the Organisation', the capacity to claim adequate reparation for a breach of these obligations, and held that 'fifty States, representing the vast majority of the members of the international

community, had the power, in conformity with international law, to bring into being an entity possessing objective international personality and not merely personality recognised by them alone, together with the capacity to bring international claims . . .'.

80 See 1958 Danube Fishing Convention, Article 12(1), 1969 Southeast Atlantic Convention, Article X(3); 1978 Northwest Atlantic Fisheries Convention, Article XI(5); 1982 Convention for the Conservation of Salmon in the North Atlantic Ocean, Article 4(2),1976 Rhine Chemical Convention, Article 6(3).

81 1973 CITES, Article XIII.

82 1971 Oil Pollution Fund Convention, Article 2(2).

83 1982 UNCLOS, Article 162(2)(a), (u), (v), (w) and (z); the Authority is granted international legal personality and such legal capacity as may be necessary for the exercise of its functions and the fulfilment of its purposes: Article 176.

84 Article 165(2)(i) and (j).

85 Article 7(7) and (8).

86 Article 12(1)(b).

87 Article 21(1)(f) and (x). The 1988 CRAMRA also provides for the establishment of regulatory Committees, the functions of which relate to, *inter alia*, monitoring and inspection of exploration and development activities: Article 31(1)(d) and (f).

88 Article 11.

89 Article 12(1)(a), (d) and (j).

90 Article 10(1) and (2).

91 Article 23(a).

92 Article 23(b).

93 See eg 1971 Nuclear Weapons Treaty, Article III(4); 1972 Biological and Toxic Weapons Convention, Moscow, Article VI.

94 1979 Berne Convention, Article 14(1); 1992 Climate Change Convention, Article 7(2).

95 1957 EEC Treaty, Article 169.

96 From 16 in 1982 to 217 in 1990, see EC Commission, *Eighth Report to the European Parliament on the Enforcement of Community Law* (1991).

97 [1989] *ECR* 2849.

98 2854.

99 2855.

100 See Agenda 21, Chapter 27, para 27.13, and Principle 10 of the Rio Declaration.

101 1974 OECD Council Recommendation on Principles Concerning Transfrontier Pollution, 4 November 1974;1976 OECD Council Recommendation on Equal Right of Access in Relation to Transfrontier Pollution OECD C(76)55 (Final), 18 May 1976, in particular Annex, paras 1 and 2, OECD Council Recommendation for the Implementation of a Regime of Equal Right of Access and non-Discrimination in Relation to Transfrontier Pollution OECD C(77)28 (Final), 23 May 1977.

102 1974 Nordic Environmental Protection Convention, Article 3.

103 Article 4.

104 Article 10.

105 1960 Paris Convention, Article 13;1963 Vienna Convention, Article XI(1).

106 See eg 1969 CLC as amended, Article IX(1); 1971 Oil Pollution Fund Convention, as amended, Article 7(1).

107 See also the 1993 Lugano Convention, 16 September 1988, in force 1 January 1992, *OJ* 1988 319, p 9, also allowing victims a choice of courts.

108 27 September 1968, in force 1 February 1973, *OJ* L 304, p 77 Article 1.

109 Case 21/76, [1976] *ECR* 1735.

110 Id.

111 See supra note 108, p 9; Article X(X) is in the same terms as Article 5(3) of the Brussels Convention.

112 1950 ECHR, Article 25(1); all Parties to the Convention have now accepted the right of individual petition. See also 1969 ACHR, Articles 44 and 45;1981 African Charter on Human and Peoples' Rights, Article 55.

113 Annex to UNGA resolution 2200(XXI) (1966); 993 UNTS 3; in force 3 January 1976.

114 However, under ECOSOC Council Resolution 1988/4 non-governmental organizations in consultative status with the ECOSOC may submit to the Committee on Economic and Social Rights written statements which might contribute to full and universal realization of the rights under the Covenant.

115 Established by the Commission on Human Rights under the authority of ECOSOC Resolution 9(II) (1946).

116 In March 1990 the EC Commission adopted a compromise decision by allowing the proposed subsidies for a limited period of eight years: Case Nos 34/90 and 54/90/ UK: Electricity, *EC Doc IP(90) 267*.

117 See eg 1958 High Seas Conservation Convention, Article 9(1), specifically referring to Article 33 of the United Nations Charter.

118 See eg 1940 Western Hemisphere Convention; 1946 International Whaling Convention.

119 1992 Climate Change Convention, Articles 10, 13 and 14. See also 1985 Vienna Convention, Article 11; 1989 Basel Convention, Article 20; 1992 Biodiversity Convention, Article 27 and Annex II.

120 *Fisheries Jurisdiction* Case, supra note 6.

121 Id, 33. The Court also invoked its earlier statement in the *North Sea Continental Shelf* Cases, that '... it is not a question of applying equity simply as a matter of abstract justice, but of applying a rule of law which itself requires the application of equitable principles', supra note 6.

122 1973 CITES, Article XVIII; MARPOL 73/78, Article 10; 1972 Space Liability Convention, Article IX; 1974 Baltic Convention, Article 18(1); 1979 LRTAP Convention, Article 13;1985 Vienna Convention, Article 11(1) and (2);1992 Climate Change Convention, Article 14;1992 Biodiversity Convention, Article 27(1).

123 By a Protocol dated 2 April 1981 the USSR agreed to pay, and Canada agreed to accept, Canadian $3,000,000 in a final settlement of the claim.

124 *Lac Lanoux* Arbitration, supra note 6 at p 128.

125 See eg 1968 African Nature Convention, Article XIV(3).

126 See eg 1969 CLC, Article III(a).

127 See eg 1972 London Convention, Article V(2).

128 See eg 1974 Paris Convention, Article 9(1).

129 See eg 1974 Nordic Environmental Protection Convention, Article 11.

130 See eg 1976 Pacific Fur Seals Convention Article XII; 1976 ENMOD Convention, Article V(1) and Annex, providing for the establishing of a Consultative Committee of Experts.

131 See eg 1979 LRTAP Convention, Article 5.

132 See eg 1968 African Nature Convention, Article XVIII (referring disputes to the Commission of Mediation, Conciliation and Arbitration of the OAU); 1976 European Convention for the Protection of Animals Kept for Farming Purposes, Article 10; 1982 UNCLOS, Article 284 and Annex V, Section 1; 1985 Vienna Convention, Article 11(2).

133 See eg 1963 Vienna Convention, Optional Protocol Concerning the Compulsory Settlement of Disputes, Article III; 1974 Paris LBS Convention, Article 21 (conciliation by the Commission); 1985 Vienna Convention, Article 11(4) and (5) (providing for the establishment of a conciliation commission); 1992 Biodiversity Convention, Article 27(4) and Annex II, Part 2;1992 Climate Change Convention, Article 14(5) to (7).

134 See eg 1949 FAD Mediterranean Fisheries Agreement, Article XIII; 1951 International Plant Protection Convention, Article IX; 1952 North Pacific Fisheries Convention, Protocol, paras 4 and 5 (special committee of scientists).

135 1909 Boundary Waters Treaty, especially Articles VIII and IX.
136 1950 ECHR, Articles 28 and 31(1).
137 See also dispute settlement under the NAFTA.
138 See *BISD 26S/210, Understanding Regarding Notification, Consultation, Dispute Settlement and Surveillance*, adopted 28 November 1979.
139 1985 Vienna Convention, Article 11;1992 Biodiversity Convention, Article 27.
140 See eg 1982 Jeddah Convention, Article XXIV(2); 1988 Agreement on the Network of Aquaculture Centres in Asia and the Pacific, Article 19(1).
141 Resolution Conference 5.11 (1985) (Definition of the Term 'Pre-Convention Specimen').
142 See *The Haven Incident, Annual Report* 1991, International Oil Pollution Fund, pp 59–62.
143 See Decision II/5 (Non-compliance), Report of the Second Meeting of the Parties to the Montreal Protocol on Substances that Deplete the Ozone Layer, *UNEP/OzL.Pro.2/3*, 29 June 1990; see now Decision IV/5 and Annexes IV and V, adopting the non-compliance procedure; Report of the Fourth Meeting of the Parties, *UNEP/OzL.Pro.4/15*, 25 November 1992, 32 ILM 874 (1993). The 1992 Climate Change Convention, provides for the possible establishment of a 'multilateral consultative process, available to the Parties on their request, for the resolution of questions regarding the implementation of the Convention', Article 13.
144 Articles 11 and 12.
145 Article 8 and Annex 4.
146 Article 3(7).
147 Appendix IV.
148 Supra.
149 1907 Hague Convention on the Pacific Settlement of International Disputes, Article 37.
150 See eg 1958 High Seas Fishing and Conservation Convention, Articles 9 to 12.
151 Article VIII and Annex, Chapter II.
152 See eg 1974 Baltic Convention, Article 18;1985 Vienna Convention, Article 11.
153 See eg 1973 CITES, Article XVIII (to the Permanent Court of Arbitration at The Hague); 1989 Basel Convention, Article 20 and Annex VI.
154 See eg l9B6 Early Notification Convention, Article 11;1986 Assistance Convention,
155 See eg 1992 Biodiversity Convention, Article 27 and Annex II, Part 1;1992 Climate Change Convention, Article 14; 1992 Watercourses Convention, Article 22; 1992 Industrial Accident Convention, Article 21.
156 See eg the International Water Tribunal, based in the Netherlands; the International Court for the Environmental Protection of the Environment (established by the International Juridical Organization for Environment and Development, Rome, in relation to the 1976 Barcelona Convention).
157 In relation to contentious cases it is important to recall that 'only states may be parties in cases before the Court', United Nations Charter, Article 34(1).
158 International Court of Justice, Communique 93/20,19 July 1993. The Chamber was established under Article 26(1) of its Statute; seven Judges (Schwebel, Bedjaoui, Evensen, Shahabudeen, Weeramantry, Ranjeva, Herczegh) were elected by secret ballot for an initial six-month period with effect from 6 August 1993.
159 See eg 1963 Vienna Convention, Optional Protocol Concerning the Compulsory Settlement of Disputes, Article I (not in force).
160 See eg 1959 Antarctic Treaty, Article XI(2); 1974 Baltic Convention, Article 18(2).
161 See eg 1985 Vienna Convention, Article 11(3);1989 Basel Convention, Article 20(3); 1992 Climate Change Convention, Article 14(2); 1992 Biodiversity Convention, Article 27(3);1992 Industrial Accidents Convention, Article 21; 1992 Watercourses Convention, Article 22.
162 Statute ICJ, Article 36(2). As of 1 January 1992 51 States have accepted the Optional Clause.

163 Article 36(3).
164 *River Meuse* Case (1937) PCIJ Ser A/B, No 70.
165 Case concerning the *Territorial Jurisdiction of the International Commission of the River Oder*, Judgment No 16 (1929) PCIJ, Ser A, No 23, p 27.
166 *Corfu Channel (Merits) Case ICJ Report* (1959), p 4.
167 *Fisheries Jurisdiction Case*, see supra note 6, at p 31.
168 See supra note 5.
169 See supra note 6.
170 See supra note 6.
171 Charter of the United Nations, Article 96(1).
172 Article 96(2). ECOSOC, the Trusteeship Council and 15 of the specialized agencies have been authorized by the General Assembly, as has the IAEA, the Interim Committee of the General Assembly and the Committee for Applications for Review of the UN Administrative Tribunal. UNEP and UNCSD have not been so authorized by the General Assembly.
173 Statute ICJ, Article 41.
174 (*Australia* v *France*), *Order re Interim Measures, ICJ Report* (1973), p 99; (*New Zealand* v *France*), *Order re Interim Measures, ICJ Report* (1973), p 135.
175 (*UK* v *Iceland*), *Order re Interim Measures, ICJ Report* (1972), p 12; *Federal Republic of Germany* v *Iceland, ICJ Report* (1972), p 30.
176 (*Finland* v *Denmark*), *ICJ Report* (1991), p 9.
177 1957 EEC Treaty, Article 164. The ECJ also has competence in relation to the interpretation and application of the 1950 ECSC and 1957 Euratom.
178 Cases 30 to 41/81, *EC Commission* v *Italian Republic* [1981] *ECR* 3379; Case 134/86, *EC Commission* v *Belgium* [1987] *ECR* 2415.
179 Cases 96 and 97/81, *Commission of the European Communities* v *Netherlands* [1982] *ECR* 1791 and 1819.
180 Case 291/84 *Commission of the European Communities* v *Netherlands* [1989]1 *CMLR* 479 (concerning the failure to implement into national law Directive 80/68/EEC on the protection of groundwater against pollution by certain dangerous substances).
181 Case 182/89, *Commission of the European Communities* v *France* [*ECR*] where the ECJ held that France had infringed Article 10(1)(b) of Council Regulation 3626/82/EEC (on the implementation of CITES) by granting import licences for skins of certain feline animals originating in Bolivia.
182 Case C-75/91: *Commission* v *Netherlands* (wild birds).
183 1957 EEC Treaty, Article 173.
184 Case C-300/89, *EC Commission* v *Council* (judgement 11 June 1991), declaring void Council Directive 89/428/EEC of 21 June 1989 for harmonizing the programmes for the reduction and eventual elimination of pollution caused by waste from the titanium dioxide industry, on the grounds that the Council adopted the Directive on the basis of the wrong treaty provision; but see more recently Case C-155/91 *EC Commission* v *Council* ECJ, 17 March 1993, (not yet reported).
185 *National Trust for Ireland and WWF UK* v *EC Commission* Case C-407/92 *OJ* C 27, 30.1.1993, p 4.
186 Case 380/87, *Enichem Base et al* v *Commune of Cinisello Balsamo*, [1989] ECR 2491.
187 The relevant courts are the European Court of Human Rights and the Inter-American Court of Human Rights.
188 See eg *Powell and Rayner* v *United Kingdom* (Petition No. 9310/81), Judgement of 21 February 1990.
189 1950 ECHR Articles 44, 45 and 48. All the Parties to the Convention have accepted the compulsory jurisdiction of the Court. Protocol No. 2 to the Convention confers upon the Court competence to give advisory opinions: Strasbourg, 6 May 1963, in force 21 September 1970.
190 Article 47.
191 1982 UNCLOS, Article 287(1).

192 Article 287(3).
193 Article 297(1).
194 Article 297(2).
195 Article 297(3)(a).
196 Article 297(3)(b)(i).
197 Article 298.
198 Articles 186 to 191, and Annex VI, Articles 35 to 40.
199 Article 187. Certain disputes, at the request of the relevant Parties, may be submitted to the International Tribunal for the Law of the Sea, to an *ad hoc* chamber of the Sea-Bed Disputes Chamber, or to commercial arbitration under UNCITRAL rules: ibid, Article 188.
200 Rio Declaration, Principle 10.
201 Principle 26.
202 Agenda 21, Chapter 39, para 39.3(e).
203 Para 39.7.
204 Para 38.22(h).
205 Para 38.24 and 38.25(a).
206 Para 38.13(f).
207 Para 39.3(h).
208 Para 39.9.
209 GA Resolution 47/191 (Institutional arrangements to follow up the UNCED), 22 December 1992, paras 3(c) and (h).

4 DESIGNING A COMPLIANCE SYSTEM FOR THE UN FRAMEWORK CONVENTION ON CLIMATE CHANGE

1 Staff Lawyer, Co-Director, Climate Change and Energy Programme, Foundation for International Environmental Law and Development (FIELD). The author would like to thank Alexandra Keutsch for her invaluable assistance in preparing this chapter.
2 See Chapter 1 of this volume, Mitchell, R *Compliance Theory: An Overview* ('Mitchell').
3 United Nations Framework Convention on Climate Change, 9 May 1992, 31 ILM 849, Article 13.
4 Princen, T (1993) 'International Environmental Conflict Resolution: A Multicentric Perspective', vol 8 no 2 *Natural Reserves & Environment* 11, p 13. Princen refers to this approach as 'country-centric.'
5 See Chapter 4 of this Report for an extensive discussion of the role citizens and non-governmental organizations can play in promoting compliance with international environmental agreements.
6 Birnie, P and Boyle, A (1993) *International Law of the Environment*, Clarendon Press, 1993, p 546 ('Birnie and Boyle').
7 Mitchell supra note 2, p 48.
8 Mitchell questions whether the legal character of international environmental agreements affects state behaviour. As will be discussed below, the legal character of rules is at the very least relevant at the level of procedure, as certain types of compliance mechanisms must be triggered by an alleged breach of law.
9 See Mitchell, for a more detailed discussion on the difference between compliance and effectiveness.
10 'Report of First Session of the Conference of the Parties to the Framework Convention on Climate Change', 7 April 1995 FCCC/CP/1995/7/Add.1 ('Report of COP1'), in which the Parties concluded that the commitments of developed country Parties 'are not adequate' and agreed to begin a process aimed at strengthening these commitments.

11 Article 2; Article 4.2(d); Article 7.2(d).
12 Article 4.2(c).
13 Report to the Ninth Session of the Intergovernmental Negotiating Committee for a Framework Convention on Climate Change by Bert Bolin, Chairman, IPCC, Geneva 7 February 1994.
14 Article 3.3.
15 See Cameron, J and Wade-Gery, W (1993) 'Addressing Uncertainty: Law, Policy and the Development of the Precautionary Principle' in *The Precautionary Principle Conference Papers*, University of New South Wales.
16 Peter Sand has identified this structure of 'differential obligations' in a number of international environmental treaties that aspire to involve countries of differing capacities. He describes this differentiation of obligations as enabling negotiators to avoid bargaining treaties down to the least common denominator of ability to comply. *Lessons Learned in Global Environmental Governance*, World Resources Institute, 1990, p 8.
17 The Convention divides Parties into three general categories of countries (1) 'developed country Parties,' listed in Annex I (2) Annex II countries selected from Annex I and comprising the wealthier OECD countries and (3) developing country Parties, which are those countries not listed in either Annex.
18 It was widely recognized during the negotiations that the industrialized countries are responsible for approximately 75 per cent of historical concentrations and current rates of emissions of greenhouse gases. Mintzer, I (1993) *Implementing the Framework Convention on Climate Change: Incremental Costs and the Role of the GEF*, The Global Environment Facility, ('Mintzer') p 8.
19 Should current patterns of population growth and industrialization continue, developing countries' combined emissions may exceed those of industrialized countries within the next one hundred years. Mintzer p 8.
20 Article 4.7.
21 Mitchell (supra note 2) draws an analytically useful distinction between Primary Rules and provisions related to Compliance Information. It must be noted, however, that at present, the commitment to communicate information can be characterized as the most burdensome obligation under the Convention, and thus must be analyzed as a Primary Rule. It is very likely that any non-compliance response system adopted under the Convention will deal with Parties' difficulties in reporting information before it addresses more substantive commitments such as mitigation and financing. This has indeed been the case of the Montreal Protocol Implementation Committee, which in its first two years of operation has dealt solely with Parties' difficulties in fulfilling their reporting requirements.
22 Article 4.1(a); Article 12.1(a).
23 Article 4.1.(b); Article 12.1(b).
24 Article 12.2 (a) and (b).
25 Article 12.4. See Chapter 12 Jordan and Werksman, *Additional Funds and Incremental Costs: Financing Global Environmental Protection* ('Jordan and Werksman').
26 Article 12.5.
27 Article 4.3; Article 4.7; Article 12.5.
28 Article 12.5.
29 Article 4.1 (b).
30 Article 4.2(a) and (b).
31 Reinstein, R (1994) *The Framework Convention on Climate Change: Developed Country Commitments on Greenhouse Gas Emissions*, (on file with author), p 32.
32 Bodansky, D (1993) 'The United Nations Framework Convention on Climate Change', 18 *Yale Journal of International Law* 2, p 516 ('Bodansky').
33 Sands, P (1992) 'The United Nations Framework Convention on Climate Change', 1 *RECIEL* 270, p 274.
34 Report of COP 1, Decision 1/CP.1. 'The Berlin Mandate'.

35 All Parties to a Protocol to the Convention must also be Parties to the Convention; but not all Parties to the Convention need sign up to the Protocol. Article 17.4.

36 Understandably, as the purpose of financial resource obligations under the Convention is to promote implementation by developing countries, there is no financial obligation placed on these Parties. However, a number of developing countries have contributed nominal funds to the Global Environment Facility in order to purchase political power in its decision-making structure.

37 Article 4.1(a), Article 4.3, and Article 12.1.

38 Article 4.4.

39 Proposals to link the assessment and distribution of developed country Parties' financial contributions to their present or historical share of GHG emissions (eg through a global carbon tax) were rejected by developed country negotiators. The first replenishment negotiations for the GEF were not governed by any assessment of what demand might be generated by the implementation of the Convention. The total amount pledged was a reflection of political will; burden sharing was negotiated on the basis of donors' past contributions to the International Development Agency (IDA).

40 See, for example, the 1985 Vienna Convention for the Protection of the Ozone Layer, which contained no binding restrictions on the production and consumption of Ozone depleting substances (prior to the development of the Montreal Protocol), and yet had a fully developed dispute settlement procedure with annexes on arbitration and conciliation.

41 Széll, P (1994) 'Compliance Regimes' in *Natural Resources and International Dispute Settlement: A Conference Review*, Frere Cholmeley Bischoff and FIELD.

42 1987 Montreal Protocol on Substances that Deplete the Ozone Layer, as adjusted and amended, 25 November 1992, Report of the Fourth Meeting of the Parties, *UNEP/OzL.Pro4/15*. ('Report of MOP4').

43 1994 Protocol to the 1979 UN-ECE Convention on Long-Range Transboundary Air Pollution on Further Reductions of Sulphur Emissions (the Second Sulphur Protocol). References to the Second Sulphur Protocol Process for Reviewing Compliance are made to the final version of the text in *EB.AIR/WG.5/CRP.13*.

44 Resolution of these questions will be complicated further by the involvement of the Global Environment Facility in the operation of the Convention's Financial Mechanism. Although the Convention contains a general assignment of duties between the COP and the GEF, Parties to the Convention and Participants in the GEF Council have yet to clarify how finances available through the GEF, under the Convention, will assist in the Convention's compliance system.

45 The United Nations General Assembly Resolution that launched the Convention negotiations for February 1991, asked that the text be completed by June 1992, in time for the Earth Summit.

46 See Mitchell.

47 Mitchell, R and Chayes, A *Improving Compliance with the Climate Change Treaty*, (on file with author)('Mitchell and Chayes').

48 *A/AC.237/L.23/Add.1*; Proposals for further elements of a Protocol submitted by Germany.

49 United Kingdom Department of the Environment News Release, 116, 8 March 1995, 'UK Calls for Further Commitments to Combat Climate Change'.

50 Mitchell and Chayes, p 2.

51 Article 6(b)(ii). The Training Programme to Promote the Implementation of the United Nations Framework Convention on Climate Change, conducted by the Climate Change Secretariat and United Nations Institute for Training and Research (UNITAR) is an example of such an initiative.

52 This restructuring process follows governmental and non-governmental criticism of the GEF's first three years of operations. 'Instrument for the Establishment of the Restructured Global Environment Facility: Report of the GEF Participants Meeting',

14–16 March 1994. 'Report of the Independent Evaluation of the Global Environment Facility Pilot Phase', UNEP, UNDP, The World Bank, 23 November 1993.

53 Norway, for example, has found it increasingly difficult simultaneously to retain its public opposition to a complete whaling moratorium and remain an active member of the International Whaling Commission. Norway absented itself from the most recent meeting of the IWC and is now facing a consumer boycott organized by Greenpeace. Further whaling sanctuaries imposed by the IWC are likely to make Norway's renegade status even less tenable. (28 May 1994) 'Sanctuary Dooms Japanese Whaling', *The Guardian*, p 6.

54 These were primarily Australia, New Zealand and Austria. The willingness of certain delegations to put forward specific drafts of non-compliance procedures can also be attributed to the enthusiasm and expertise of individual members of the delegations.

55 The use of the words 'monitoring' and 'reporting' are still taboo amongst Parties.

56 Mexico, long time a leader in G-77 politics, has, on the heels of NAFTA, just entered the OECD. It is as yet unclear how this will effect its membership in the G-77, and its status as a non-Annex I 'developing country'. The Convention allows the COP to amend Annex I, and for Parties to adhere unilaterally to Annex I Party obligations. Article 4.2.f; 4.2.g.

57 Since INC 9, Saudi Arabia and Kuwait have led attempts to complicate decision-making within the COP's rules of procedure, they have received the active support of American based industry groups. As Parties to the Convention, this group of oil exporting developing countries was able at COP 1 to prevent the Parties from adopting rules of procedure that would have allowed for majority decision-making on substantive matters. Rules on decision-making remain bracketed.

58 The European Community and the US government have engaged in a game of 'chicken' over the implementation of carbon taxes, neither wanting to risk losing a competitive advantage in a fragile period of economic recovery.

59 See, eg, (11 December 1993) 'A green tinge to corporate Japan' *The Economist*.

60 The Ozone Secretariat, based at United Nations Environment Programme, Nairobi, services both the Vienna Convention and the Montreal Protocol.

61 Report of the Implementation Committee under the Non-Compliance Procedure for the Montreal Protocol on the Work of its Seventh Meeting, 16 November 1993, *UNEP/Ozl .Pro/ImpCom/7/2* .

62 For a detailed analysis of how these processes might work, see Lanchbery, *et al* (1994) 'Reporting and Review Processes in the Climate Change Convention: A Briefing Paper for the INC Delegates and Secretariat' *VERTIC* London ('VERTIC').

63 Article 7.2.e; Article 10.2.a.

64 Article 7.2.a.

65 Article 4.2.d; Article 10.2.b.

66 Article 12.2.b.

67 Article 9.2.b.

68 Article 7.2.1.

69 Report of COP 1.

70 See eg, Susan Subak (April 1994) *A Brief Review of the United Kingdom's 1990 Nations Greenhouse Emissions Inventory*, CSERGE, *Energy, Economics and Climate Change*, challenging the economic assumption of the US Climate Plan, on greennet at gn.climate.forum; *Independent NGO Evaluation of National Plans for Climate Change Mitigation: OECD Countries, Third Review, January 1995*, coordinated by US Climate Action Network and Climate Network Europe.

71 Article 12.3.

72 Article 14.1.

73 See infra, for a more detailed discussion of this proposal.

74 These provisions have their root in Article 33 of the UN Charter, and are modelled on dispute settlement procedures found in the Vienna Convention and in other international environmental agreements.

75 A similar point is made by Bodansky, p 549.

76 Article 14.2. This is in accordance with the Statute of the International Court of Justice, Article 36.2.a. Some delegations suggested that ICJ jurisdiction for the settlement of disputes under the Convention be compulsory. See proposal of Norway (A/237/AC/Misc 5/Add 2, p 14).

77 Article 59 of the Statute of the International Court of Justice.

78 See eg, Vienna Convention for the Protection of the Ozone Layer, Annex on Arbitration, Article 15.

79 The details of these procedures are to be adopted by the COP 'as soon as practicable'.

80 This discussion owes a great deal to the analysis by Martii Koskenniemi (1992) 'Breach of Treaty or Non-Compliance: Reflections on the Enforcement of the Montreal Protocol', 3 *Yearbook of International Environmental Law* 123, ('Koskenniemi').

81 Together, the Vienna Convention and the Montreal Protocol provide for both dispute settlement procedures (Article 11 of the Vienna Convention) and Non-Compliance Procedures. What will be the 1994 Protocol to the 1979 UN-ECE Convention on Long-Range Transboundary Air Pollution on Further Reductions of Sulphur Emissions (the Second Sulphur Protocol), contains both provisions on dispute settlement (Article 9) and provisions for the adoption of a non-compliance procedure modelled on those adopted for the Montreal Protocol (Article 7).

82 Koskenniemi, p 145.

83 Koskenniemi, p 146.

84 With regard to the ICJ, the Statute of the Court limits its jurisdiction to disputes between states.

85 Birnie and Boyle, p 137.

86 Birnie and Boyle, p 137.

87 Birnie and Boyle, somewhat sceptical of what they call 'institutional' dispute resolution, suggest that 'the true role of such bodies may thus be closer to a legitimation of national policies than to acting as a fiduciary for the interests of the environment'.

88 The Parties to the Montreal Protocol, and to the Second Sulphur Protocol, have adopted general statements that the two procedures are separate and that NCP should operate 'without prejudice' to DSPs. The Third Meeting of the Parties to the Montreal Protocol determined that the Protocol's Non-Compliance Procedure and the DSP contained in the Vienna Convention were 'two distinct and separate procedures'. (Dec III/2). Second Sulphur Protocol, Article 7.4.

89 It must be emphasized that a number of these proposals were introduced into the debate at a stage in the negotiations before Parties were certain what shape the Convention's primary rules would take. Although they can be said to represent the type of compliance regime countries might support generally, there has been no indication that these delegations will introduce similar proposals in the future.

90 This discussion is based on the Revised Single Text on Elements Relating to Mechanisms, 30 October 1991, A/AC, 237/Misc.13, presented to delegates at INC 4.

91 The Co-Chairs of Working Group II, which was responsible for negotiating the institutional aspects of the text, were Elizabeth Dowdeswell (Canada) and Ambassador Robert F Van Lierop (Vanuatu).

92 This proposal has a number of aspects in common with dispute resolution procedures established under the General Agreement on Tariffs and Trade (GATT).

93 The COP may 'establish such subsidiary bodies as are deemed necessary for the implementation of the Convention' and to 'exercise such other functions as are required for the achievement of the objective of the Convention' (Article 7.2.i; Article 7.2.m.).

94 Article 7.
95 Article 8.
96 Article 12.9.
97 Article 8.2.b; c and g.
98 The essential difference between the climate change Secretariat's powers and the original mandate of the Ozone Secretariat is the Ozone Secretariat's power to 'prepare' rather than merely 'compile' reports. This hardly seems significant in light of the expansion of Secretariat duties that has since taken place in the Ozone regime. Montreal Protocol, Article 8.
99 Article 10.
100 The MPIC was initially comprised of five members, it now has ten, elected for a period of two years.
101 The present MPIC is divided evenly between the five regional groups that maintain a tenacious hold on UN politics. These are African Group, the Asian Group, the Group of Latin American and the Caribbean, and the Western European and Other Group (WEOG), and the Eastern European and Russian Group. The New Zealand delegation proposed a Committee with a limited membership of 15, again evenly divisible by 5, and based on equitable geographic distribution. (A/237/AC/Misc 5/Add 2 pl2)
102 The recently restructured Global Environment Facility, for example, designed to balance the interests of recipient and donor countries, has formed a governing council composed of 16 developing country members, 14 donor countries and two from former COMECON countries with 'economies in transition'. Individual constituencies were to be formed on the basis of six factors ranging from contributions to the GEF to 'natural resource endowment and environmental vulnerability'. Annex E to the GEF Instrument. The Second Sulphur Protocol, which has a largely Western European membership will have a Committee of eight members, with no formal requirements with regard to geographical representation.
103 To ensure the impartiality of the MPIC's decisions, Parties 'involved in a matter under consideration' are not, however, entitled to take part in the 'elaboration or and adoption of recommendations on that matter'. Report of MOP4, Annex IV, paras 10, 11.
104 UNEP/Ozl.Pro/ImpCom/7/2.
105 Suggestions for the further elaboration of the SBI's powers seemed to be reaching a level of acceptance amongst Parties. In the annex to a draft decision proposed to the first COP, INC 9 delegates suggested that the SBI's duties be extended to include a scientific and technical review of national communications, and the provision of advice on 'issues such as the resolution of questions, dispute settlement and compliance/enforcement mechanisms' Report of INC9, Annex to Decision 9/3. This text was dropped from the final decision of COP 1.
106 Report of MOP4, Annex IV, para 7(c).
107 Report of MOP4, Annex IV, para 7(d).
108 A/AC 237/Misc 5/Add 2, p 12 (Submission of New Zealand).
109 See the submissions of Australia and New Zealand to INC 2; A/AC 237/Misc 5/Add 2 pp 11–12. Australia proposed that the Convention's bodies be given the further power to 'investigate complaints'. A/AC 237/Misc 5/Add 2, p 11.
110 Both the MPIC and the SSPIC will have this power. Report of MOP4, Annex IV para 9. New Zealand supported its inclusion in the Convention's non-compliance response system. Misc 5/Add 2 p 13.
111 Although the language lends itself least to this interpretation, it most closely reflects the Co-Chairs proposal, whereby Parties agree to establish a panel.
112 The MPIC, for example, allows one or more Parties (plural) to raise concerns with regard to another Party (singular).
113 Article 11.3.b.
114 Article 12.9.

115 (7 May 1994) 'The kindness of strangers', *The Economist*, p 21.

116 Some efforts were made toward this end at INC 9, when delegates opened the possibility of giving the Convention's compliance system a role in a 'permanent and feasible system for monitoring the activities of regional and multilateral financial and other institutions relevant to climate change'. Report of INC 9, p 20, para 87. This language was since softened, primarily in response to developing country concerns that such a system might introduce environmental conditionalities on MDB energy lending. At COP 1, Parties decided instead to instruct the Secretariat to monitor bilateral and multilateral financing of just those activities undertaken in implementation of the Convention, in the context of Article 11.5. Report of COP 1.

117 See Report of INC 9, p 21, para 92, seeking advice from the UN Office of Legal Affairs on options for arrangements between the COP and the GEF. At COP 1, the Secretariat was instructed to work with the GEF Secretariat in preparing a draft Memorandum of Understanding to govern the relationship between the COP and the GEF Report of COP 1.

118 There have been indications from a number of developed country Parties at INC9 that any serious increase in commitments would have to be linked to the availability of joint implementation with developing country Parties.

119 See Grubb (1991) 'Pragmatics in the Greenhouse', 354 *Nature* 348, 349; Nitze, W (1990) *The Greenhouse Effect: Formulating a Convention*, Royal Institute of International Affairs; Yamin, F (1993) *The Climate Change Convention and Joint Implementation: Legal, Institutional and Procedural Issues.*

120 At COP 1, Parties agreed to begin negotiations on a protocol or other legal instrument, aimed at strengthening developed Parties' commitments by elaborating policies and measures and by setting quantified limitation and reduction objectives within specific timeframes.

121 The GEF, which is to provide financing for climate change, biodiversity, ozone and international waters projects in developing countries and countries with economies in transition has just been replenished at US$2.2 billion for a three-year period. To place this figure into perspective, if the GEF's funds were spread evenly to 100 countries eligible for funding, and climate change receives 40 per cent of the GEF's total budget, approximately US$2million a year would be available per country per annum over a three-year period.

APPENDIX 2

1 See Ist Report of *ad hoc* Working Group of Legal Experts on Non-compliance.

2 See Ist Meeting of Implementation Committee.

3 Article 11, Montreal Protocol. Article 11(2) also provides a procedure for calling extraordinary meetings of the Parties.

4 Draft Report of the Second Meeting of the Implementation Committee under the Y Non-Compliance Procedure for the Montreal Protocol, para 10.

5 Which was set up and operated during the first Meeting of the Parties to the Montreal Protocol with the aim of finding 'ways of fulfilling the requirements of Article 8 of the Protocol'; Report of the Parties to the Montreal Protocol on the work of their first Meeting, para 53.

6 Id para 54 and 55.

7 Second Meeting of the Parties to the Montreal Protocol on Substances that Deplete the Ozone Layer (*UNEP/Ozl.Pro.2/3*) in Decision II/5.

8 See Second Meeting of the Parties to the Montreal Protocol on Substances that Deplete the Ozone Layer (*UNEP/Ozl.Pro.2/3*), Decision II/5.

9 The non-compliance procedure is established through Decision II/5 on Noncompliance and the IC itself is established in para 3 of Annex III.

10 The IC met once in 1990 and in 1991, twice in 1992, and three times in 1993.

11 Para 5, Annex IV, in the interim NCP up to the fourth MOP, the number of members of the IC was five, see para 3, Annex III, second MOP
12 Two Parties did not appear at the first meeting (which might be an indication of a potential problem for the NCP which has to be addressed), and the latter two states were only elected for one year.
13 Report of the Fourth Meeting of the Parties to the Montreal Protocol on Substances that Deplete the Ozone Layer (*UNEP/OzL Pro.4/15*), Annex IV, para 7.
14 Para 8, NCP.
15 Decision II/9.
16 In Annex IV.
17 Para 2: The Secretariat shall . . . within two weeks of its receiving a submission, send a copy of that submission to the Party whose implementation of a particular provision of the Protocol is at issue. Any reply and information in support thereof are to be submitted to the Secretariat and to the Parties involved within three months of the date of the despatch or such longer period involved as the circumstances of any particular case may require. The Secretariat shall then transmit the submission, the reply and the information provided by the Parties to the Implementation Committee . . . which shall consider the matter as soon as practicable.
18 Para 3.
19 Para 3.
20 Para 4.
21 Para 9.
22 Para 13.
23 Para 14.
24 Fourth MOP, Decision IV/21.
25 Under Decision IV/7 C of the fourth MOP the Secretariat is also under a duty to pass on data on compliance received by non-Parties to the IC. This is important in the context of trade measures which are to be applied to non-Parties under Article 4, especially para 8.
26 Fourth report of the IC, para 8.
27 IC Report IV, para 20.
28 At para 23.
29 Not explained further.
30 Report of the Third Meeting of the *Ad Hoc* Working Group of Legal Experts on Non compliance with the Montreal Protocol at para 23. (Annex IV of Montreal Protocol.)
31 Second Meeting of IC, paras 7 and 9.
32 Para 7.
33 Third Report of the Implementation Committee, paras 11 and 12.
34 See third MOP, Decision III/3b.
35 In the Secretariat's second report on the reporting of data, for example, four Parties reported the following difficulties: Kenya complained of having no records on the individual chemicals as required, Uganda of lack of technical expertise, logistics and adequate financing, the Maldives of lack of expertise to fulfil obligations.
36 Para 25.
37 Fourth Report of IC, paras 16 to 18,
38 Fourth Report of the IC, paras 19 to 21.
39 Seventh Report of IC, para 24.
40 Id.
41 Third report of IC at paragraph 17, relying on Secretariat report on reporting of data. The Secretariat itself cited the *Ad hoc* Group of Experts on reporting difficulties in recommending the following options to facilitate the reporting of data: (a) Import control with the help of customs regulations and the Harmonized Commodity System codes; (b) Licencing of imports and exports of controlled substances; (c) Legislation on the reporting of data; (d) A special survey of consumptions carried

out by a consultant or official body, preferably with the cooperation of industry; (e) A special survey of data as a part of a country study in a developing country; and (f) An international panel of manufacturing companies that can supply data for larger regions consisting of many countries.

42 Sixth Report of the IC, para 7.
43 The international authority responsible for the Harmonized Commodity Description and Coding System.
44 Third Report of IC, para 17.
45 Sixth Report of the IC, para 7.
46 Para 23.

APPENDIX 3

1 See 'Revised single text on elements relating to mechanisms' (*A/AC.237/Misc.13*), pp 30–31.
2 Patricia W Birnie and Alan E Boyle (1992) *International Law and the Environment*, Clarendon Press, Oxford, pp 137–139.
3 See International Environmental Commitments (IEC) Project (1994) 'Design options for Article 13 of the Framework Convention on Climate Change', International Institute for Applied Systems Analysis (IIASA), Laxenburg, Austria.
4 'Note on elaboration of Article 13 of the Climate Change Convention', (May 1992), Verification Technology Information Centre, Carrera House, London, p 3.
5 See IEC/IIASA, supra note 8, pp 13–14.
6 See, in general, IEC/IIASA, supra note 8, pp 3–17.

APPENDIX 4

1 *UNEP/OzL.Pro./4/15.*
2 Report of the Second Meeting of the Parties to the Montreal Protocol on Substances that Deplete the Ozone Layer, *UNEP/Doc.OzL.Pro. 2/3*, 20 June 1990, Annex III, paragraph 7.
3 Annex IV to the Fourth Meeting Report; Article 7(d).
4 Vienna Convention for the Protection of the Ozone Layer (22/3/1985).
5 EB.AIR/WG.5/18, Annex II.
6 ECE/EB.AIR/40.
7 ECE/EB.AIR/12.
8 A special procedure is provided for in the Governing Body Committee on Freedom of Association to examine complaints alleging infringements of trade union rights, whether or not the member state in question has ratified the ILO Conventions on Freedom of Association.
9 Constitution of the International Labour Organisation and Standing Orders of the International Labour Conference, International Labour Office, Geneva, October 1985.
10 General Assembly *Doc A/6316* (1966).
11 For further examples of compliance control procedures under human rights conventions, see:
  - International Covenant on Economic, Social and Cultural Rights (*General Assembly Doc A/6316* (1966))
  - International Convention on the Elimination of All Forms of Racial Discrimination (*660 United Nations Treaty Series 195*)
  - International Convention on the Suppression and Punishment of the Crime of Apartheid (*General Assembly Doc A/9030* (1973))
  - Convention on the Elimination of All Forms of Discrimination Against Women (*General Assembly Resolution 34/180* (1980))

- Convention Against Torture and Other Cruel, Inhuman or Degrading Treatment or Punishment (General Assembly Resolution 39/46 (1984))

12 The 1947 General Agreement on Tariffs and Trade (Basic Instruments and Selected Documents (BISD) vol IV).

13 The main documents constituting the dispute settlement procedure under the GATT are as follows:
- The Understanding regarding Notification, Consultation, Dispute Settlement and Surveillance, adopted on 28 November 1979 (BISD 26 S/210), to which is annexed an Agreed Description of the Customary Practice of the GATT in the Field of Dispute Settlement. They were largely reiterated in the 1982 Ministerial Declaration on Dispute Settlement (BISD 29 S/13)
- The 1989 Improvements to the GATT Dispute Settlement Rules and Procedures (BISD 36 S/61)
- The special regime of disputes in which the plaintiff is a developing country, adopted on 5 April 1966 (BISD 14 S/18)
- The special regimes provided for in some of the non-tariff agreements concluded during the Tokyo Round.

14 The Uruguay Round of the GATT entered into force on 1 January 1995.

15 The United Nations Convention on the Law of the Sea entered into force on 16 November 1994

16 General Assembly *Doc A/Conf 62/122.*

5 COMPLIANCE WITH INTERNATIONAL ENVIRONMENTAL OBLIGATIONS: A CASE STUDY OF THE IWC

1 *UN Doc A/Conf 62/122*, 7 October 1982.

2 LFE Goldie 'Title, Use (and Usufruct) – An Ancient Distinction too Oft Forgot' (1985) 79 *American Journal of International Law*, 689.

3 *UN Doc A/Conf 13/L 52-L*, p 55.

4 The maximum sustainable yield of a stock is the point at which the greatest numbers of that stock can be caught without the stock being adversely affected. This point is calculated by examining each particular stock and seeing how it reacts to being fished. When a stock begins to be fished its size decreases and in order to counteract this it starts growing at a rapid rate in an attempt to reach its original level. The rate of increase is greatest when a stock has been reduced to a particular size. This is the point known as the maximum sustainable yield of that particular stock.

5 Law of the Sea Convention, Article 297.

6 (1992) 'Marine Fisheries and the Law of the Sea: A Decade of Change', *FAO Fisheries Circular* No. 853, Food and Agricultural Organization of the UN, Rome.

7 See Bonnucci, N 'Towards a Code of Conduct for Responsible Fishing'. 2 *Review of European Community and International Environmental Law* (*RECIEL*) 3, p 245.

8 Law of the Sea Convention, Article 65.

9 Law of the Sea Convention, Article 64.

10 See the opening address of the IWC in 1946 when Dean Acheson, USA Acting Secretary of State, said that 'Whales . . . belong to no single nation nor to any group of nations but rather they are the wards of the world . . .'. *IWC* 1st Report 1946 p 1.

11 161 UNTS 72; TIAS No 1849.

12 Id.

13 Hardin, G (1969) 'Tragedy of the Commons', *Science* 1243.

14 Keen, E A (1988) *Ownership and Productivity of Marine Resources*, pp 18–24.

15 Birnie, P W (1985) *The International Regulation of Whaling*, vol 1, Oceana, p 490 ('Birnie 1985').

16 Brown, Gardner M and Crutchfield, J A (eds) (13–16 September 1981) 'Economics of Ocean Resources: a Research Agenda', *Proceedings of National Workshop*, Washington, pp 10–11.
17 Gambell, R (1977) 'Whale Conservation – Role of the International Whaling Commission', 1 *Marine Policy*, pp 301–310.
18 These included the 1959 North East Atlantic Fisheries Convention; the 1959 Convention Concerning Fishing in the Black Sea; and the 1973 Convention on the Conservation of the Living Resources of the Baltic Seas and Belts.
19 ICRW, Article X.
20 IWC Rules of Procedure, Rule 12.
21 Id.
22 Id.
23 ICRW, Article V.
24 ICRW Article V(3)(a).
25 ICRW Article V(3)(b).
26 ICRW Article V(3)(c).
27 Birnie, P W (1989) 'Management and Protection of the Whale', *Natural Resources Journal*, vol 29, p 913 ('Birnie 1989').
28 Smith, G 'The International Whaling Commission: An Analysis of the Past and Reflections on the Future', *Natural Resources Lawyer*, vol XVI, No 3, pp 550–551.
29 Ibid.
30 Id p 559
31 August 1993 *Greenpeace Business* No 14, p 2.
32 *Europe Environment* No 411, Section I, pp 6–7.
33 *Europe Environment* No 413, p 8.
34 Mason, C M (1979) (ed), *The Effective Management of Resources: The International Politics of the North Sea*, at pp 128–131.
35 Underdal, A (1980) *The Politics of International Fisheries Management*, at pp 146–148.
36 Id pp 91–93
37 'Managing Fisheries Resources Beyond 200 Miles: Canada's Options to Protect Northwest Atlantic Straddling Stocks', (January 1990 Report prepared for the Fisheries Council of Canada by the Ocean Institute of Canada).
38 Council Regulation 3760/92, *OJ* 1991 L389/1.
39 Birnie reports that Japan took 250 Bryde's whales under a scientific permit in 1976; Friends of the Earth Manual '78 (p 36) alleged that little information was derived from these specimens. West German authorities seized seven containers of Icelandic whale meat in Hamburg en route to Japan on 20 March 1987 containing 140–75 tons of fin and sei whale meat derived from the 1986 Icelandic scientific programme. The containers were labelled 'frozen seafood'; see Birnie 1989 supra.
40 *IWC 38th Report* (1988) Appendix 1, pp 27–28 (39th Meeting 1987).
41 This requirement has been subject to much criticism, see: van Drimmelen, B 'The International Mismanagement of Whaling', *Pacific Basin Law Journal* vol 10:240 ('Van Drimmelen'), pp 240–159.
42 Id p 244.
43 IWC/45/OS – Denmark.
44 Principle 15, Rio Declaration on Environment and Development, 13 June 1992, *A Conf 151/5/Rev 1*.
45 Hewison, G J 'The Precautionary Principle and its Application to the Management of Straddling Stocks and Highly Migratory Fish' ('Hewison'); a Paper presented to the Greenpeace symposium on high seas fishing on 2 July 1993 at Wellington, New Zealand at p 21.
46 Id p 13.
47 Constable, A (1991) 'The Role of Science in Environmental Protection', *Australian Journal of Marine and Freshwater Research*, cited in Hewison supra note 45.

48 UN General Assembly Resolution 'Large Scale Driftnet Fishing and its Impacts on the Living Resources of the World's Oceans and Seas', reprinted in 29 ILM 1556 (1990).
49 *IWC/44/OS* UK para 7.
50 Hewison supra note 45 at p 18.
51 Greenpeace International Memorandum, 14 December 1992, Greenpeace International.
52 Hewison supra note 45 at p 21.
53 ICRW Schedule, para 10(e).
54 Young, NM (1992) *Understanding the RMP*, Centre for Marine Conservation, Washington DC at p 55.
55 Council Regulation 2241/87.
56 ICRW Schedule, para 2.6.
57 Smith, G 'The International Whaling Commission: An Analysis of the Past and Reflections on the Future', *Natural Resources Lawyer* vol XVI, No 3, 550–551 ('Smith'):
58 *IWC 26th Report* at p 26 (1976).
59 Rose, G L and Crane, S (1993) 'The Evolution of International Whaling Law' in Sands, P (ed), *Greening International Law*, Earthscan, London ('Rose and Crane') at p 171.
60 Voting in favour were Antigua, Australia, Belize, Costa Rica, Denmark, Egypt, France, the Federal Republic of Germany, India, Kenya, Mexico, New Zealand, Oman, St Lucia, St Vincent, Senegal, the Seychelles, Spain, Sweden, the United Kingdom, the United States. Voting against were Brazil, Iceland, Japan, the Republic of Korea, Norway, Peru, the USSR. Chile, China, the Philippines, South Africa and Switzerland abstained.
61 *Eurofish Report* 345 FS/1.
62 Council Regulation 4028/86, *OJ* 1986 L376/7.
63 Churchill, R 'Shared Fisheries Management in the European Community', vol 2 *RECIEL* 3 ('Churchill').
64 Rose, G L (1991) *Community Fisheries Management Legislation in EC Waters*, Greenpeace International, Brussels; ('Rose 1991') at pp 30–34.
66 ICRW, Article IX.
67 ICRW Schedule, para 21(a)(b).
68 *The Guardian*, 12 February 1994.
69 Rose 1991 supra note 64, at p 41.
70 *IWC 24th Report* pp 27–28 (24th Meeting 1972) and IWC 24/12.
71 IWC25/14atp3.
72 *IWC 28th Report* (1978) pp 24–25 (28th Meeting 1976).
73 *IWC 28th Report* (1978) p 24 (28th Meeting 1976) and IWC 28/12.
74 *IWC 30th Report* (1980) Appendix 8, pp 37–38 (31st Meeting 1979) and IWC 31/5/WG.
75 *IWC 38th Report* (1988) p 1 (38th Meeting 1986).
76 Rose and Crane supra note 59, at p 172.
77 Rose, G and Rowland, E (1993) 'Report on Verification and Enforcement under The International Convention for the Regulation of Whaling', in *Verification Report*, Vertic, London.
78 IWC /45 /37.
79 IWC /45 /22.
80 As adopted at CCAMLR-VII (para 124).
81 As adopted at CCAMLR-XI (para 6.11).
82 FAO has estimated that 42 per cent of the total world tuna catch is taken from the South Pacific region (*FAO Fishery Statistics Yearbook*, 1991).
83 Lodge, M 'New Approaches to Fisheries Enforcement', 2 *RECIEL* 3.
84 Id.
85 Id.

86 Id.
87 ICRW Sched/ule, para 25.
88 Churchill R supra note 63.
89 *Pub L 99-61*, 93 Stat 407 (codified at 16 USC 1821(e)(2) Supp V 1981).
90 Smith supra note 57, at p 555.
91 *Pub L* No. 92-219, 85 Stat 786 (codified at 22 USC sec 1978 Supp V 1981).
92 Martin and Brennan (1989) 'Enforcing the International Convention for the Regulation of Whaling: The Pelly and Packwood-Magnuson Amendments', 17 *Den J Int'l L & Pol'y* 293, p 311.
93 (1984) 'Agreement to end Japanese Whaling Announced', *US Dept Comm News NOAA*, p 84.
94 Cherfas, J (1988) 'The Hunting of the Whale: A Tragedy That Must End', *Pacific Basin Law Journal* 110, p 190.
95 See also ECO (1992) No 5 p 1 for 'closed door' US-Japan negotiations, as a result of which 1992 Resolution IWC 44/23 on Japanese research was severely weakened.
96 ICRW, Article VIII(2).
97 Van Drimmelen supra note 41, at p 254.
98 Wilkinson, D M (1989) 'The Use of Domestic Measures to Enforce International Whaling Agreements: A Critical Perspective', 17 *Den J Int'l & Pol'y* 271 ('Wilkinson'), p 285.
99 Van Drimmelen supra note 41.
100 See Chapter 10.
101 Id.
102 Falk, P 'Introduction: Preserving Whales in a World of Sovereign States', 17 *Den Int'l & Pol'y* 249, p 251 (citing unnamed Japanese official) quoted in Sanger, (5 February 1989) 'Japan's Whaling Expedition Stirs Up Old Conflict', *New York Times*.
103 Smith supra note 57, at p 564.
104 In December 1992, Japanese Customs intercepted Bryde's whale meat from Taiwan of an unknown origin. (Personal comment made to Edward Rowland by Dr Ray Gambell, Secretary of the IWC, cited in Rose and Rowland supra note 77.)
105 Scharff, J 'The International Management of Whales, Dolphins, and Porpoises: An Interdisciplinary Assessment', 6 *Ecology Law Review*, p 598.
106 Holt, S (1974) *A Ten-Year Moratorium On All Commercial Whaling*, p 7, cited in Smith supra note 57, supra notes at 120 and 126.
107 *IWC 28th Report* (1978) Appendices 7 and 8, p 31 (27th Meeting 1977). See also *30th Report* (1980) Appendices E and F, pp 8–9 (Special Meeting 1978) and id Appendix 9, p 38 (*31st Meeting* 1981).
108 Wilkinson, D M supra note 98 at pp 282–3; Birnie 1985 supra note 15 in vol I at pp 143–160 and 197–98 at p 505.
109 *IWC 30th Report* (1980) p 32 (*31st Meeting* 1979) and Schedule para 28 (amended 1980). See *Int'l Register of Whaling Vessels* (8th Edn) IWC/44/12 (1992).
110 *IWC 42nd Report* (1992) p 41.
111 Hart, P (15–16 October 1990) 'Review of Legislation Concerning Marine Mammals', *Ad Hoc Working Group on Int'l Legal Arrangements for Marine Mammals* 22, UNEP, Bonn.
112 Draft Global Plan of Action for the Conservation, Management and Utilization of Marine Mammals, para 4.62, FAO/UNEP Project No 0502-78/02, Rome 1981.
113 See Cherfas supra note 94 at pl71.

6 THE ROLE OF THE EC IN IMPLEMENTING INTERNATIONAL ENVIRONMENTAL LAW

1 The question whether the EC should now be referred to as the EU is the subject of some debate and confusion. The author is of the opinion that, for the present at least,

'EC' should be used in the context of this article, which discusses treaty-making and implementing powers.

2 See Nollkaemper (1987) 'The European Community and International Environmental Cooperation: Legal Aspects of External Community Powers', 2 *Legal Aspects of External Community Powers*, pp 55–91.

3 Ruling 1/76, *Physical Protection of Nuclear Materials*, 1978 ECR 2151. See Feenstra (1981) 'A Survey of the Mixed Agreements and their Participation Clauses', in O'Keefe and Schermers, *Mixed Agreements*, Kluwer Deventer, (*'O'Keefe and Schermers'*); Temple Lang (1986) 'The Ozone Layer Convention: A New Solution to the Question of Community Participation', in 'Mixed International Agreements', 23 *CML Rev*, pp 157–176; and Simmonds (1986) 'The Community's Declaration upon Signature of the UN Convention on the Law of the Sea', 23 *CML Rev*, pp 521–544.

4 Case 22/70, *European Road Transport Agreement*, 1971 ECR 263.

5 Treaty of Rome, Articles 110–116.

6 Id, Article 238.

7 Case 41/76, *Donkerwolke* v *Procureur de la Republique*, 1976 ECR 1219; Opinion 1/76, *Understanding on a Local Cost Standard*, 1975 *ECR* 1362; Opinion 1/78, *International Rubber Agreement*, 1979 *ECR* 1362.

8 Opinion 1/76 supra note 7 at pp 1362 and 1364.

9 Krämer and others have warned of this, and it was confirmed in the *Third Fisheries Case*, Case 804/79, *Commission* v *United Kingdom*, 1981 *ECR* 1045.

10 For three interpretations of ERTA, see Temple Lang (1987) 'ERTA and the Case-Law of the Court on Competence and Conflict', *Yearbook of European Law* 6, p 183, and more generally, Cross (1992) 'Preemption of Member State Law in the European Community: A Framework for Analysis', 29 *CML Rev*, pp 447–472; Neuwahl (1992) 'Joint Participation in International Treaties and the Exercise of Power by the EEC and its Member States: Mixed Agreements', 28 *CML Rev*, pp 717–740.

11 ERTA, paras 20–22 and para 31.

12 Joined Cases 3, 4 & 6/76, *Krämer et al*, 1976 ECR 1279.

13 Opinion 1/76, *Laying-up Fund for The Rhine*, 1977 *ECR* 741.

14 *Rhine* Case, supra note 13 at paras 3–4.

15 Opinion 1/91, *European Economic Area Treaty*, [1992] 1 *CML Rev* 245; Opinion 1/92, *EEA Treaty* (*No 2*), [1992] 2 *CML Rev* 217, Opinion 2/91, *ILO Convention No* 170,19 March 1993 (unreported).

16 See Hardy (1977) 'The Rhine Case and the Treaty Making Powers of the Community?', 14 *CML Rev* 561, p 594, and Close, 'Self Restraint by the EEC in the Exercise of its External Powers', 29 *CMLR* 47, p 51. Close speculates that the necessity of Community involvement may be sufficiently clear to mean that a refusal on the part of the Council to ensure this involvement would be a breach of the EC treaty. See also Groux and Manin, 'The European Communities in the International Order' 1984 *ECR* 122 ('Groux and Manin'), and Case 104/81, *Kupfeberg*, 1983 *ECR* 3641, at para 17.

17 See generally Emilou (1992) 'Subsidiarity – An Effective Barrier to the Enterprises of Ambition', 17 *European L Rev*, p 383.

18 Nollkaemper, supra note 2, deals extensively with these and other aspects of the environment policy.

19 Article 189, 'The Regulation, Directive and Decision'.

20 Mastellone, 30 ICLQ (1981), pp 116–117; Leenan (1984/5) 'The EEC in International Environmental Agreements', 93 *Legal Issues of European Integration* (1984/85), and Timmermans (1979) 'The Division of Powers' in Timmermans and Volker (eds), pp 15–28, *CML Rev*, pp 551–553.

21 See Krämer (1992) *Focus on European Environmental Law*, Sweet and Maxwell, pp 62–85, particularly pp 74–76.

22 Opinion 2/91, *ILO Convention No 170*, supra note 15.

23 Id, paras 25–26. Temple Lang speculated that this would be the result; see Lang supra note 10 at pp 203–5.
24 ILO Convention No 170, supra note 15 at para 18.
25 Id, paras 19–21.
26 See The Ottawa Convention on Future Multilateral Cooperation in Northwest Atlantic Fisheries; The London Convention on Future Multilateral Cooperation in Northeast Atlantic Fisheries; and The Reykjavik Convention for the Conservation of Salmon in the North Atlantic Ocean.
27 Opinion 1/78, *Natural Rubber*, 1979 ECR 2871. Member states retained the right to participate in respect of contributions to the buffer funds. Research is another area in which the states claim competence.
28 See London and Reykjavik Fisheries Conventions, supra note 26. Denmark participates in respect of the Faroes.
29 Article 229 supplements this, giving the Commission a general relations power in respect of the UN and its Agencies.
30 See Articles 113–116 and Article 228 and Maastricht amendments to these Articles.
31 Article 228 provides Parliament with a veto in a limited area.
32 Jachtenfuchs 'The European Community and the Protection of the Ozone Layer', 28 *J of Common Market Studies* 261 at p 265.
33 The Presidency has had no formal legal status under the EC Treaty.
34 See Nollkaemper supra note 2 at pp 79–80. ILO Convention No 170, supra note 15, paras 36–38, confirms that such duties exist over the area of potential competence and exclusive competence.
35 In this context the deletion of Article 116 by Maastricht should be noted.
36 *Commission* v *United Kingdom* supra note 9.
37 See Krämer 'The Implementation of Community Environmental Directives Within the Member States: Some Implications of the Direct Effect Doctrine', 3 *J of Envtl L* 1, p 39.
38 Case 106/89, *Marleasing*, 1990 ECR I-4135.
39 Case 213/89, *R* v *Sec State Transport ex p Factortame*, [1990] ECR I-2433.
40 Case 208/90, *Emmott* 25 July 1991 (unreported).
41 See generally Groux and Manin, supra note 16 at p 115 *et seq* and p 122.
42 Case 181/73, *Haegeman*, 1974 ECR 449.
43 Case 87/75, *Bresciani*, 1976 ECR 129, paras 16–18.
44 *Bresciani* supra note 43; *Kziber*, 1991 ECR 119; *Demirel*, 1987 ECR 3719.
45 *Haegeman* supra note 42.
46 Case 21-24/72, *International Fruit*, 1972 ECR 1219.
47 Case 104/81, *Kupfeburg*, para 17.
48 Schermers (1975) 'Community Law and International Law', *CML Rev*, p 1277; Dowrick (1982) 'Overlapping International and European Laws', 88 *ICLQ*.
49 Krämer (1991) 'Community Environmental Law – Towards, a Systematic Approach', 11 *Yearbook of Euro L* 151, at p 155; and Groux and Manin supra note 16 at p 116 *et seq*.
50 There are now direct sanctions for breach of Community commitments in the way of fines which may be levied by the Court under Article 171.
51 The Commission does not generally enforce international agreements to which it is a party. Krämer (1991) 'The Implementation of Community Environmental Law', *German Yearbook of International Law*, p 431.
52 Council Directive 79/409/EEC.
53 *OJ* L638 10.2.82, p 3.
54 The basis upon which the Community claims competence can be gleaned from the Preamble to the decision and associated annex. See The Commission Proposal for Conclusion of the Climate Change Convention, *COM 92 508 final*.
55 This is the logical consequence of the formula upon which the Community accedes to conventions. See Weiler, 'External Relations of Non Unitary Actors' in Timmermans and Volker supra note 20 at pp 78–79.

56 Gaja 'The European Communities Rights and Obligations Under Mixed Agreements' in O'Keefe and Schermers (eds) supra note 3. Gaja speculates that a breach of obligations falling within this portion of the Agreement may be the subject of Community enforcement. See also Balekjian, 'Mixed Agreements: Complementary and Concurrent Competences?', id at p 141; and Tomuschat, id.

57 See Haegeman supra note 42, whlch confirms that an international treaty to which the Community is Party may be the subject of a reference by the national court to the Court of Justice under Article 177.

58 For Maastricht amendments, see Wilkinson, 'Maastricht and the Environment: Implications for the EC's Environment Policy of the Treaty on European Union', 4 *J of Envtl L* 2.

59 Snyder (1993) 'The effectiveness of European Community Law: Institutions, Processes, Tools and Techniques', *Modern L Rev*, p 19.

60 De Burca (1992) 'Giving Effect to European Community Directives', *Modern L Rev* 215, pp 235–239.

61 Common Market Law Review (1995), no 205. For critique, see Bourgeois, (1994) 'The EC in the WTO and Advisory Opinion 1/94; An Echternach Procession', *Common Market Law Review*, 1994.

62 The fact is that the member states and DG XI of the Commission has been successful in securing that such environmental Treaties have been included on Bases other than Article 113. Whatever the controversy with respect to the appropriate Basis (Article 100a or Article 130s since the SEA) for internal measures, the choice has not been unresisted, even if it has never been directly considered by the court. See recently Commission v Council (Waste Framework) 1994 ECR 000, noted by Nicholas de Sadeleer in *Journal of Environmental Law* (1992), and Case 187/93 Regulation of Waste Shipments 1994 ECR 000.

7 A CASE STUDY OF A REGIONAL APPROACH TO COMPLIANCE WITH CITES IN SOUTHERN AFRICA

1 *Major Progress Achieved Towards Setting Up First African Wildlife Task Force* (UNEP News Release 1994/7).

2 Convention on International Trade in Endangered Species of Wild Flora and Fauna, 12 ILM 1088 (1973).

3 Participants included government representatives from Botswana, Kenya, Mozambique, South Africa, Swaziland, Tanzania, Uganda and Zambia, the CITES Secretariat, Interpol, and US Fish and Wildlife Service. NGOs who provided financial, administrative and legal support included Environmental Investigations Agency Tusk Force and the Foundation for International Environmental Law and Development (FIELD). See Proceedings of the First African Wildlife Enforcement Cooperation Conference, December 19–11 1992, at 64 (Rosalind V A Reeve and L A Carter (eds)). The final negotiating seminar took place on 5–6 September 1994, and resulted in the adoption of the Lusaka Agreement on 8–9 September 1994. The text of the agreement can be obtained from UNEP. Its final provisions do not differ substantially from the Initial Negotiating Text discussed in this chapter.

4 Id at 58.

5 Initial Negotiating Text as Revised at the First Expert Group Meeting, 7–11 March 1994, *UNEP/ELI/PAC/LAEGI/7* (attached at Appendix I to this Chapter). The current text is subject to intergovernmental negotiations coordinated by the United Nations Environment Programme (UNEP).

6 This framework has been elaborated by Mitchell to assist identification of how treaties that induce compliance do so. Mitchell, Chapter 1.

7 Mitchell supra note 6.
8 CITES, Article II.
9 The merits and shortcomings of this approach are discussed by Swanson, T M (1992) 'The Evolving Trade Mechanisms in CITES', I *R Eur Community & Int'l Envtl L* 57.
10 For a discussion of the basic objectives and implementation mechanisms of CITES see Chapter 8 and for a general explanation of how CITES operates see Lyster, S (1985) *International Wildlife Law*, ('Lyster') and Wijnstekers, W (1992) 5 *The Evolution Of CITES*.
11 CITES, Articles VI–X.
12 CITES, Article VIII (1).
13 Mitchell supra note 6.
14 CITES, Articles VIII & XII,
15 Mitchell supra note 6.
16 Lyster supra note 10, at p 13.
17 For the importance of negative diplomatic and public opinion in inducing compliance in relation to CITES provisions on elephants and rhinos, see Chapter 8.
18 Mitchell supra note 6.
19 CITES, Article XII.
20 As discussed in Part B of this chapter it has played a critical role in catalysing support for the Lusaka Agreement. See also Gavitt, J D (11–19 December 1992) 'Remarks' ('Gavitt'), in Reeve, R V A and Carter, R A (eds), *Proceedings of the First African Wildlife Enforcement Co-operation Conference*, 'First African Wildlife Enforcement Conference').
21 Sands, P J and Bedecarre A P (1990) 'Convention on International Trade in Endangered Species: The Role of Public Interest Non-Governmental Organizations in Ensuring the Effective Enforcement of the Ivory Trade Ban', 17 *B C Envtl Aff L Rev* 799, p 802 ('Sands and Bedecarre').
22 Id, Chapter 3.
23 Mitchell supra note 6 at p [ ].
24 Lyster supra note 10 at p 12.
25 Lyster supra note 10 at p 247.
26 Swanson supra note 9 at p 61.
27 See Chapter 8.
28 Id at 373.
29 On the effectiveness of CITES trade sanctions, see Jenkins, Chapter 10.
30 Mitchell supra note 6.
31 Thaggert, H L 'Implementing the Convention on International Trade in Endangered Species' in the First African Wildlife Enforcement Conference supra note 20 at p 106 ('Thaggert').
32 Id at 83.
33 Id at 106.
34 Id at 91.
35 Id at 96.
36 Id at 101.
37 Id at 73.
38 Id at 79.
39 Id at 99.
40 Id at 89.
41 Id at 75.
42 Thornton, T and Currey, D (1991) *To Save an Elephant*, p 185.
43 Lyimo, M M 'Remarks' in the First African Wildlife Enforcement Conference supra note 20 at p 22 ('Lyimo').
44 Id at 23.
45 Gavitt, J D 'Remarks' in First African Wildlife Enforcement Conference supra note 20 at p 29.

46 Bashir, A O 'Remarks' in the First African Wildlife Enforcement Conference supra note 20 at p 11 ('Bashir').
47 Id at 49.
48 Bashir supra note 46 at p 10.
49 Colonel Tiroyamodimo, O B 'Remarks', in the First African Wildlife Enforcement Conference supra note 20 at p 8 ('Tiroyamodimo').
50 Nkonga, C C 'Remarks', in the First African Wildlife Enforcement Conference supra note 20 at p 28 ('Nkonga').
51 Bashir supra note 46 at p 10.
52 Major Lategan, P 'Remarks' in the First African Wildlife Enforcement Conference supra note 20 at p 16.
53 Thaggert supra note 31 at pp 81–82.
54 Glennon, M J (1990) 'Has International Law Failed the Elephant?', 84 *Am J Int'l L* 1, p 20 ('Glennon').
55 Tyson, R (19 March 1993) 'Lifting of Ban on Ivory, Horn Sales Urged: Zimbabwe Assailed for Bid to Sell', *Dallas Morning News*, (available on LEXIS/NEXIS).
56 Lyster supra note 10 at p 264.
57 First African Wildlife Enforcement Conference supra note 20 at p 19.
58 Reilly, T E 'Remarks', in the First African Wildlife Enforcement Conference supra note 20 at p 19 ('Reilly').
59 Id.
60 Tiroyamodimo supra note 49 at p 9.
61 Id at 98.
62 Brough, G (23 January 1994) 'Driven out of Africa', *Mail on Sunday*, (available on LEXIS/NEXIS).
63 Lyimo supra note 43 at p 22.
64 Nkonga supra note 50 at p 27.
65 Mitchell supra note 6.
66 Madope, Dr A A 'Remarks' in the First African Wildlife Enforcement Conference supra note 20 at p 12.
67 Reilly supra note 58 at p 18.
68 Glennon supra note 54 at p 23.
69 Ellis, R (12 September 1993) 'Business Booms for Ivory Traders Flouting the Law', *Sunday Times*, (available on LEXIS/NEXIS).
70 Okua, M 'Remarks' in the First African Wildlife Enforcement Conference supra note 20 at p 24 ('Okua').
71 Glennon supra note 54.
72 *Morning Show: African Wildlife Conservation Attitude Shift Needed*, (National Public Radio broadcast, 30 April 1993) (available on LEXIS/NEXIS).
73 Swanson, supra note 9 at p 59.
74 Zimbabwe's National Parks Department could run for two years on the earnings from sales of its stock of ivory and rhino horns. See Remer Tyson (19 March 1993) 'Lifting of Ban on Ivory, Horn Sales Urged Zimbabwe Assailed for Bid to Sell', *Dallas Morning News* (available on LEXIS/NEXIS).
75 Glennon supra note 54 at p 23.
76 See Glennon supra note 54 and 'The Rhino Horn Dilemma', *Christian Science Monitor*, 22 June 1993 (available on LEXIS/NEXIS).
77 See Chapter 5.
78 Opening Address by Lt Gen C S Tembo to the First African Wildlife Enforcement Cooperation Conference, quoted in Executive Summary on *Funding Proposal to Continue Development of the Lusaka Agreement on Cooperative Law Enforcement Operations Directed at Illegal Trade in Wild Fauna and Flora*, Zambian Ministry of Tourism.
79 Tembo 'Remarks' in the First African Wildlife Enforcement Conference supra note 20 at p 5 ('Tembo').

80 Id at 4.
81 Mitchell supra note 6.
82 See First African Wildlife Enforcement Conference supra note 20.
83 Id at 8–27.
84 Id at 35–56.
85 Id at 29 and at 31.
86 Id at 31 and 72–107.
87 Id at 49.
88 Id at 49.
89 Id at 58.
90 Project Description and Funding Request for Development of the Lusaka Agreement on Cooperative Law Enforcement Operations Directed at Illegal Trade in Wild Fauna and Flora from the Office of the Minister, Ministry of Tourism, Lusaka, Zambia 2 (18 July, 1993) (on file with authors).
91 Second Draft Lusaka Agreement, July 1993, attached to the Project Description and Funding Request for Development of the Lusaka Agreement on Cooperative Law Enforcement Operations Directed at Illegal Trade in Wild Fauna and Flora from the Office of the Minister, Ministry of Tourism, Lusaka, Zambia 2 (18 July 1993) (on file with authors).
92 Letter from Lt Gen Tembo (on file with authors).
93 See Executive Summary on *Funding to Continue Development of the Lusaka Agreement on Cooperative Law Enforcement Operations Directed at Illegal Trade in Wild Fauna and Flora* (on file with authors).
94 Letter from Olembo R, Assistant Executive Director of Environment Management, Institutions and Capacity Building, United Nations Environment Programme (8 October 1993) (on file with the authors).
95 Letter from Olembo R, Assistant Executive Director of Environment Management, Institutions and Capacity Building, United Nations Environment Programme (8 February 1994) (on file with the authors).
96 Zimbabwe attended as observers. See Report of the First Expert Group Meeting on the Draft Lusaka Agreement on Cooperative Enforcement Operations Directed at Illegal Trade in Wild Fauna and Flora, Nairobi, 7–11 March 1994, *UNEP/ELI/PAC/LEAG1/5revl*, 20 March 1994.
97 The following donors were represented: Denmark, European Commission, Federal Republic of Germany, Finland, Japan, Norway, Sweden, United Kingdom and the USA.
98 Adopted on 8 September 1994 in Lusaka.
99 See Lusaka Agreement on Cooperative Enforcement Operations Directed at Illegal Trade in Wild Fauna and Flora ('Lusaka Agreement').
100 Lusaka Agreement, Article 5.
101 Lusaka Agreement, Preambular paragraph 5.
102 Lusaka Agreement, Article 4 (1).
103 Lusaka Agreement, Article 6.
104 Lusaka Agreement, Article 5.
105 Lusaka Agreement, Article 5.
106 Lusaka Agreement, Article 4 (3) and (4).
107 Lusaka Agreement, Article 4 (6).
108 Revised Initial Negotiating Text, Article 4 (3), not contained in final Act.
109 Lusaka Agreement, Article 5 (8).
110 Lusaka Agreement, Article 5 (8) and 4 (5).
111 Lusaka Agreement, Article 5 (4).
112 Lusaka Agreement, Article 1, para 6.
113 Lusaka Agreement, Article 7 (8).
114 *Major Progress Achieved Towards Setting Up First African Wildlife Task Force*, (UNEP News Release 1994/7).

115 Lusaka Agreement, Article 8 (3).
116 Lusaka Agreement, Article 8 (4).
117 Lusaka Agreement, Article 8 (3).
118 The GEF has a new governance structure incorporating the concept of 'double-majority decision-making'. This requires a majority of donors and a majority of the overall Participants to make a final decision where consensus has not proved possible. Instrument Establishing the Global Environment Facility, March 1994.
119 Nkonga supra note 50 at p 27.
120 Mitchell supra note 6.
121 Mitchell supra note 6.
122 Nkonga supra note 50 at p 27.
123 Bashir supra note 46 at p 16.
124 Madope supra 66 at p 12.
125 Tiroyamodimo supra note 49 at p 9.
126 Nkonga supra note 50 at p 27.
127 Mitchell supra note 6.
128 Id.
129 Id.
130 Stone 'Defending the Global Commons', in Sands, P (ed), *Greening International Law*, (1993), p 43.
131 Bashir supra note 46 at p 16.
132 Nkonga supra note 50 at p 28.
133 Bowles, I and Prickett, G (1994) *Reframing the Green Window: An Analysis of the GEF Pilot Phase Approach to Biodiversity and Global Warming and Recommendations for the Operational Phase.*
134 Id.
135 See Project Decription for GEF/PRINCE project (on file with author).
136 See Chapter 2.
137 Sands, P J and Bedecarre, A P supra note 21 at p 802.
138 Telephone interview with Allan Thornton, Director of the Environmental Investigation Agency, in London, England (17 March 1994).

8 THE IMPLEMENTATION OF CITES IN CHINA

1 See the Preamble of CITES.
2 In practice Appendix listing often leads to a trade ban, especially when 'particularly strict regulation' is difficult due to lack of adequate knowledge of trade data and conservation standards of species concerned.
3 See Wijnstekers, W (1982) *Evolution of CITES*, Chapter 2.
4 Article 2.3 of CITES.
5 Article 11 of CITES.
6 See Resolution 6.1 adopted by the Sixth COP, 1987.
7 See Article 31 of the 1988 Law and the 1988 Amendment by the Standing Committee of the National People's Congress (NPC) to the Criminal Code of China on punishing the crimes of catching or killing of key, rare or endangered wild animals under state protection.
8 See Article 35 of the 1988 Law and the 1982 Amendment by the Standing Committee of NPC to the Criminal Code of China.
9 See Article 24 of the 1992 Law.
10 According to Article 7 of CITES, Appendix 1, species captive bred for commercial purposes should be considered as Appendix 2 species. However, it is disputable as to how to deal with the captive breeding centre for tigers after the ban on using tiger bone as medicine, imposed by the Notice of the State Council of China of 29 May

1993 on the prohibition of trade in rhino horn and tiger bone, and how to improve the way the gall is obtained from bear.

11 For example, 'Angong Niuhuang Wan', which contains rhino horn as the main ingredient is a very popular medicine in China. It is a traditional habitual medicine used for patients of fatal diseases such as high fever, coma, convulsion, meningitis, toxic cerebrosis, and meningorrhagia.

12 Resolution Conference 6.10 urges all Parties to take primarily the following measures:

(a) prohibition on all sales and trade, internal and international, of rhinoceros parts and derivatives;

(b) the destruction of all government and parastatal stocks of rhinoceros horn.

13 Resolution Conference 8.8.

9 INTERNATIONAL AGREEMENTS AND ENVIRONMENTAL MANAGEMENT: FOLLOW-UP IN BANGLADESH

1 According to the National Planning Commission there has been a steady decline in the man/land ratio. It was 0.23 ha/head in 1949–50 and is forecast to drop to 0.06 ha/head in 2000 when the population is estimated to be 130.3m.

2 Of the multilateral donors, the World Bank has been concentrating on deforestation in hill forests; interior plains and coastal zones; energy efficiency and biomass fuels; flood control and its effect on fisheries; soil nutrients and their transport; and institutional and legislative aspects of resource use and management. The Asian Development Bank has been engaged in agroforestry, coastal rehabilitation and institutional strengthening of the DOE. Of the UN bodies, UNEP has been active in marine and coastal environment problems, while ESCAP produced an environment management plan for the coastal regions of Bangladesh. The bilateral donors have also incorporated environmental issues such as health, rural development and energy into their projects. Needless to say, environmental impact assessments (EIA) figure prominently in such projects.

3 It succeeded the Environment Pollution Control Board, previously an arm of the public health department.

4 This includes the prevention of pollution and degradation; the promotion of environmentally friendly activities; the preservation, protection and promotion of the natural resource base; the strengthening of environmental concerns as a basic requisite of economic development; and the increase of public participation in environmental promotion activities.

5 Recently BCAS has conducted two government commissioned studies: firstly, 'Reconnaissance Study on the Use of the ODS in Bangladesh' (February 1993); and secondly, 'Assessment of the Vulnerability of Coastal Areas to SLR and other Effects of Climate Change' (November 1993).

6 2 *YIEL* (1991), p 294.

7 Khan, A A (1993) 'Freshwater Wetlands of Bangladesh: Opportunities and Options' in Nishat, A, Hussaian, Z, Roy, M K and Karim, A (eds), *Freshwater Wetlands in Bangladesh: Issues and Approaches for Management*, IUCN, Dhaka ('Wetlands').

8 Reza, B 'Wetlands Policies, Rules and Regulations in Bangladesh' in *Wetlands* at p 202.

9 Huq, M F 'Institutional Aspects of Wetlands Management in Bangladesh' in *Wetlands* at p 221.

10 BCAS (1993) 'Reconnaissance Study on the Use of ODS in Bangladesh: Final Report', Dhaka.

11 Ahmed, I (1992) 'Bangladesh Position Paper on Implementation of the Montreal Protocol', Dhaka.
12 2 *Bangladesh Environmental Newsletter* 3.
13 Mahtab, F U (1992) 'Climate Change and Sea Level Rise Due to Green House Effect – Its Consequences on Bangladesh' in *Training Manual on Environmental Management in Bangladesh* DOE, Dhaka, p 160.
14 Warrick, R A and Farmer, G 'The Greenhouse Effect: Climatic Change and Rising Sea Level' in *Transactions of the Institute of British Geographers*, New Series 15, pp 5–20.
15 BCAS (1993) 'Assessment of the Vulnerability of Coastal Areas to Sea Level Rise and Other Effects of Global Climate Change', Dhaka.

10 TRADE SANCTIONS: EFFECTIVE ENFORCEMENT TOOLS

1 See *United States – Restrictions on Imports of Tuna* (unpublished decision) *DS21/R* (3 September 1991), p 48 at p 50. The Panel decision was never adopted by the full GATT Council because Mexico agreed to its withdrawal before it was adopted by the Council.
2 Id at 47.
3 Agenda 21, was adopted by the UNCED Plenary in Rio de Janeiro on 14 June, 1992 (*UN Pub Sales No. E.93.1.11*). Prior to its adoption, four preparatory meetings (Prepcoms) were held to negotiate Agenda 21, during which negotiators endeavoured to agree always by consensus.
4 Id, Chapter 17, 'Protection of the Oceans, All Kinds of Seas, Including Enclosed and Semi-Enclosed Seas, and Coastal Areas and the Protection, Rational Use and Development of Their Living Resources,' *UN Pub Sales No E.93.1.11*.
5 Several provisions offer support for the establishment of strong conservation measures (eg paras 17.62 and 17.76), while others provide for enhanced utilization of marine living resources for food and income (eg para 17.79(g)).
6 Even in the commercial realm, the world community is witnessing the breakdown of consensus as an enforcement mechanism. Certain draft provisions of the GATT Uruguay Round would reduce or eliminate GATT's current reliance upon consensus. Specifically, Article IX of the Agreement Establishing the Multilateral Trade Organization (MTO) provides that 'Decisions of the Ministerial Conference and the General Council shall be taken by a majority of the votes cast, unless otherwise provided in this Agreement or the Multilateral Trade Agreements.' Final Act Embodying the Results of the Uruguay Round of the Multilateral Trade Negotiations, 15 December 1993, Article ix:1.
7 Most IEAs have some sort of governing body such as a commission. Hereinafter, I will refer to such governing bodies as 'IEA organizations.'
8 Restatement (Third) of Foreign Relations Law of the United States (Revised), section 402 (1986).
9 Id, sections 402 and 431.
10 Convention on International Trade in Endangered Species of Wild Fauna and Flora, 12 ILM 1088 (1973).
11 CITES Articles III, IV and X. For a listing of plants and animals specifically regulated, see Appendices I and II.
12 See Chapter 8.
13 See Press Release by CITES Secretariat, 9 September 1993, announcing Decision of the Standing Committee, para 6.
14 161 UNTS 72 (1946).
15 The IWC is currently considering whether to develop an observation and enforcement scheme as part of its revised management scheme. See Resolution on the Revised Management System, *IWC4422 Rev* (1992).

16 See ICRW Schedule, as amended, 3 February 1983.

17 'Pelagic' connotes whaling on the high seas, whereas 'coastal' refers to whaling in an exclusive economic or coastal zone.

18 See ICRW, paragraph 10(e).

19 Although Norway has abided by the ban on commercial whaling since 1987, it claims it is not bound by this provision because it took a timely reservation to this provision at the time it was adopted. See ICRW, footnote to para 10(e).

20 For the IEA see UST 230,1949.

21 See IATTC Report of the Group of Experts, 26 January 1993.

22 IATTC Resolution, La Jolla, California, April 1992.

23 IATTC Background Paper 8, 50th Meeting of the IATTC, 16–18 June 1992.

24 26 ILM 1541 (1987), as amended; 30 ILM 541 (1992) and 32 ILM 878 (1993) (not yet entered into force).

25 See Annex II, Amendment to the Montreal Protocol on Substances that Deplete the Ozone Layer, 30 ILM 541(1991).

26 Article 4 para 1 provides: 'Within one year of entry into force of this Protocol each Party shall ban the import of controlled substances from any State not a party to this Protocol'.

Para 8, however, provides:

'Notwithstanding the provisions of this Article, imports referred to in paragraphs 1, 3 and 4 may be permitted from any State not party to this Protocol if that State is determined, by a meeting of the Parties, to be in full compliance with Article 2 and this Article, and has submitted data to that effect as specified in Article 7.'

27 Article 8 provides: '[t]he Parties, at their first meeting, shall consider and approve procedures and institutional mechanisms for determining non-compliance with the provisions of this Protocol and for treatment of Parties found to be in non-compliance.' At the fourth meeting of the Parties, December 1991, the Parties adopted Annex VII, Non-Compliance Procedures. Paragraph 9 of Annex VII provides . . . 'the Parties may, taking into consideration the circumstances of the matter, decide upon and call for steps to bring about full compliance with the Protocol . . .' Although the Parties to the Protocol have established a comprehensive process for reviewing claims of non-compliance (see, *Handbook for the Montreal Protocol on Substances that Deplete the Ozone Layer, Ozone Secretariat*, (1992)), no enforcement provisions have actually been adopted.

28 Most recently the US threatened to impose trade sanctions against Norway for its resumption of commercial whaling in violation of the IWC ban on commercial whaling. (See Letter from Ronald Brown, US Secretary of Commerce, to President Bill Clinton, dated 6 August 1993.)

29 22 *USC* s 1978 (1988, Supp V).

30 Id s 1978(a)(2).

31 The High Seas Driftnet Enforcement Act of 1992, *Pub L 102–582*, 2 November 1992, 106 Stat 4900 (as amended, 16 USCA s 1826(a)(b) and (c)). The Act directs the Secretary of Commerce to prohibit the importation of all fish, fish products and sport fishing equipment of any nation or nationals which continue to conduct large-scale driftnet fishing beyond the exclusive economic zone of any nation after 31 December 1992, in accordance with UN Resolution 46/215 which calls for a complete worldwide ban on driftnet fishing by that date.

32 *Pub L 101-162*, s 609, 21 November 1989,103 Stat 1037. Commonly known as the Sea Turtle Act, this law prohibits the importation of shrimp and shrimp products from any producing country that does not have an adequate sea turtle conservation programme as defined by the Act and that does not require its shrimp vessels to use turtle excluder devices (TEDs). The purpose of the Act is to promote global protection of five species of endangered sea turtles seriously threatened or endangered by fishing practices of the shrimp industry.

33 The Wild Bird Conservation Act of 1992,16 USCA Section 4901 *et seq* (Supp 1993). The Act directs the Secretary of the Interior to ban or set quotas on the importation of all species of exotic birds (both CITES and non-CITES) from any country that has not implemented a management programme that provides for conservation of the species and its habitat, for humane methods of capture, transport and maintenance of the species, for effective prevention of illegal trade, as well as a variety of other conservation goals. Non-CITES species were included because past trading history demonstrated that if only CITES species were included the commercial community would simply shift the market to non-CITES species, thus putting increased pressure on species that had not been previously imported in large numbers.

34 The International Dolphin Conservation Act, *Pub L 102-523*, s 1, 26 October 1992,106 Stat 3425. The Act, among other things, amends the Marine Mammal Protection Act (MMPA) (16 USC s 1361 *et seq* (1988) (as amended USCA s 1361 (Supp 1993)) and authorizes the tuna embargo to be lifted with respect to those countries that enter into a multilateral agreement with the US to protect dolphins in the Eastern Tropical Pacific Ocean.

35 Note, however, that the Pelly Amendment, the primary US law under which sanctions have been *threatened*, can only be invoked in situations where countries have failed to comply with their obligations under IEA's or are in some way diminishing the effectiveness of an international conservation programme.

36 Pelly sanctions have been threatened at least 12 times. On each of those occasions, the country against whom the threat was made brought its behaviour into compliance with the IEA.

37 The US on 6 August 1993 threatened Norway with trade sanctions under Pelly if it continued to engage in commercial whaling in violation of the IWC ban. On 23 September 1993, The European Parliament Intergroup on Animal Welfare sent President Clinton a letter expressing support for US trade sanctions against Norway under the present circumstances. In addition, on 24 September 1993, the Global Legislators Organization for a Balanced Environment-European Community (GLOBE-EC), which represents 40 members of the European Parliament from diverse political affiliations and all nationalities of the European Community member states, sent President Clinton a letter which similarly expressed strong support for US trade sanctions against Norway.

38 USTR objected to the imposition of an embargo on tuna products on the grounds that it would cause substantial GATT implications. See Opening Brief for Appellants (Nos 92-15126 and 92-15387 at 12-13 and 44-55), *Mosbacher* v *Earth Island Institute,* 929 F 2d 1449 (9th Cir 1991).

39 In 1988, the US Government, Department of Commerce, was sued for its failure to enforce the tuna embargo provisions of the MMPA. See *Earth Island Institute, et al* v *Mosbacher*, 746 F Supp 964 (N D Cal 1990) aff'd in part, *Mosbacher* v *Earth Island Institute,* 929 F 2d 1449 (9th Cir 1991). The embargos against tuna products from Mexico, Venezuela and Vanuatu were only instituted after the US District Court ordered the government to comply with the requirements of the MMPA.

40 See WTO Final Act, Agreement on Technical Barriers to Trade (TBT), Annex 1, para 2.

41 The international community is beginning to realize that destructive processes can cause environmental harm. For instance, Article 4, para 4 of The Montreal Protocol provides: '... the Parties shall determine the feasibility of banning or restricting, from States not a party to this Protocol, the import of products *produced with, but not containing* controlled substances'. (Emphasis added.)

42 GATT, United States – Restrictions on Imports of Tuna, supra note 1 at pp 41–42.

43 CITES,Article IV.

44 See GATT, US – Restrictions on Imports of Tuna supra note 1 at p 50; also GATT Standards Code at 14.25.

45 There is a plausible argument that, if both importing and exporting countries are members of CITES, a waiver has occurred pursuant to Article XXV of GATT. However, the GATT waiver provisions may not apply to non-Parties of CITES.

46 The decision of the CITES Standing Committee would be an example of such 'advice' as CITES currently has no mechanism through which it can vote to 'authorize' sanctions against a member or non-member country.

47 In the tuna-dolphin case, the panel held that the US may not protect dolphins outside of its territorial jurisdiction even though Article XX of GATT provides:
'... Nothing in this Agreement shall be construed to prevent the adoption or enforcement by any Contracting Party of measures ...
(b) necessary to protect human, animal or plant life or health ...'

48 GATT, Article XXV.

11 THE USE OF JOINT IMPLEMENTATION TO INCREASE COMPLIANCE WITH THE CLIMATE CHANGE CONVENTION

1 A limited form of joint implementation is provided for by Articles 2 (5) and 2 (8) (a) of the 1987 Montreal Protocol on Substances that Deplete the Ozone Layer as Adjusted by the Second Meeting of the Parties, London, 27–29 June 1990, Further Amended by the Third Meeting of the Parties, Nairobi, 19–21 June 1991 and the Third Meeting of the Parties, Copenhagen, 23–25 November 1992 (the Montreal Protocol).

2 See Intervention of the Netherlands on Behalf of the European Community and Its Member States: Commitments, 11 September 1991. See, for example, Norwegian Non-Paper, *UN Doc A/AC 237/Misc 1/Add 2*, at 17–19,11 June 1991, and Statement of Prof Angsar Vogel, Federal Ministry for the Environment, Nature Protection and Nuclear Safety of Germany, 4th Session of the INC, 12 December 1991.

3 The relevant provisions are Articles 3.3, 4.2 (a) (b) and (d), 7.2 (c), 11.5 and 12.8.

4 See Annex 1 to this chapter for relevant extracts of the Convention and the decision of COP 1 governing joint implementation.

5 Under the Convention, it is not clear what the legal basis for such entitlement would be but it would have to accord with, inter alia, the principles contained in Article 3, and take into account factors such as population, historical contributions, present needs and financial resources.

6 The Convention's objective, set out in Article 2, is the 'stabilization of greenhouse gas concentrations in the atmosphere at a level that would prevent dangerous anthropogenic interference with the climate system. Such a level should be achieved within a time frame sufficient to allow ecosystems to adapt naturally to climate change, to ensure that food production is not threatened and to enable economic elopment to proceed in a sustainable manner'.

7 For a theoretical discussion of the merits of this approach, see Markyanda, Anil (1991) 'Global Warming: The Economics of Tradeable Permits', in David Pearce (ed), *Blueprint 2: Greening the World Economy*, Earthscan, London.

8 See Markyanda, note 7 above. See also (August 1993) *Joint Implementation: Sustainable Development Through Trade in Environmental Commodities*, Environmental Defense Fund, New York, p 13.

9 A tradable emissions permit system was recently adopted by the United States to control certain emissions of sulphur dioxide under the 1990 Amendments to the US Clean Air Act, 42 United States Code § 7651 *et seq* (1990).

10 See supra note 2.

11 See, eg, United Nations General Assembly (UNGA) Resolution 1803 of 12 December 1962 on Permanent Sovereignty Over Natural Resources which has been recognized

in a number of international arbitral awards and Principal 21 of the Stockholm Declaration.

12 See, eg, UNGA Resolution 3201 of 1 May 1974 on the Declaration on the Establishment of a New International Economic Order, and UNGA Resolution 3281 of 14 December 1974, Charter of Economic Rights and Duties of States. Resolution 3201 provides in relevant part that 'Each State is entitled to exercise effective control over [its natural resources] and their exploitation with means suitable to its own situation, including the right to nationalization or transfer of ownership to its nationals, this right being an expression of the full permanent sovereignty of the State'.

13 See, eg, the *Libyan American Oil Co* (LIAMCO) v *Libya* arbitration, 62 *ILR* 389; 20 ILM 1, 53 (1981).

14 Article 25 (1), Climate Change Convention.

15 See, eg, the tribunal in the *Aminoil* Case statement that 'appropriate compensation' should be determined through an inquiry into all the circumstances relevant to the particular concrete case rather than through abstract theoretical discussion, 21 ILM 1035 (1982).

16 For a general discussion of the difficulties and challenges to public international law which 'guardianship' claims present, see Sands, P (1989) 'The Environment, Community and International Law', 30 *Harv Int'l L J* 2.

17 These, and other legal issues arising from joint implementation will be the subject of future FIELD Working Papers. Some of the institutional and financial aspects of joint implementation have been addressed by Werksman J in a series of FIELD *Working Papers analysing the relationship between the UN Framework Climate Change Convention and the Global Environment Facility* (FIELD, May 1993).

18 Their view is supported by UNGA Resolution 3281 Article 2 (2) (c) on the Charter of Economic Rights and Duties of States which provides that '[i]n any case where the question of compensation gives rise to controversy, it shall be settled under the domestic law of the nationalizing State . . .'.

19 The relevance and utility of public international law as governing law and a source for determining compensation for expropriation is supported by the decisions of a number of arbitral tribunals. See, for example, *BP* v *Libya, 53, ILR* 297; *Texaco/ Calasiatic* v *Libya,* 17 *ILM* 1 (1978); *LIAMCO* v *Libya.*

20 See, for example, the Norwegian Carbon Offset Agreement, drafted as a Memorandum of Understanding between the Norwegian government and the World Bank, 14–15 December, 1992, Washington, D.C.

21 See Newcombe, K and deLucia, R (February 1993) *Mobilizing Private Capital Against Global Warming: A Business Concept and Policy Issues*, Discussion Draft prepared for the GEF Administrator's Office, Environment Department, World Bank (The GEF Discussion Document).

22 Id at p 12.

23 Id at p 10.

24 Id at p 12.

25 In some proposals on joint implementation, the term 'clearing house' is used instead of 'market'. See, for example, Hanisch, T *Joint Implementation of Commitments to Curb Climate Change*, Centre for International Climate and Energy Research-Oslo, Policy Note 1991:2. To the extent that a multilateral clearing house is used to promote, facilitate, monitor and verify joint implementation projects, there would appear to be no significant legal difference between the two concepts.

26 For a discussion of these bodies see Chapter 4.

27 Article 7 (2) (i), Climate Change Convention.

28 Id Article 10.

29 On the role and relationship between the GEF and the COP see generally Werksman, supra note 17.

30 Article 14 provides possible compulsory recourse to arbitration or to the International Court of Justice with the consent of the relevant Parties to a dispute. In

addition, a Party has the right to request the establishment of a conciliation commission that can render a recommendatory award.

31 See Bodansky, D (1993) 'The United Nations Framework Convention on Climate Change: A Commentary'; 18 *Yale J Int'l L* 521, pp 547–9.

32 Article 14 (2) (b) and 14 (7), Climate Change Convention.

33 Article 31, 1969 Vienna Convention on the Law of Treaties (Vienna Convention).

34 Id Article 31 (2).

35 See also the INC Secretariat's Note on Joint Implementation at paragraph 11 which states that 'it is important to distinguish between, on the one hand, joint implementation of measures or commitments, as provided for in Article 4 (2) (a) and (b), and on the other hand, various kinds of financial and/or technical assistance that may be provided by Annex I Parties to other Parties (as noted by the phrase 'may assist other Parties' in Article 4 (2) (a) and that Annex II Parties are explicitly committed to provide by Article 4.3, 4.4 and 4.5'.

36 The only general reference to joint activities is contained in Article 3 (3) of the Convention which states in relevant part '[e]fforts to address climate change may be carried out cooperatively by interested Parties' (emphasis added). It is relevant to note that in stark contrast to the mandatory and exhortatory language, such as 'shall' or 'should', contained in the Principles, the 'joint implementation' language in Article 3 (3) is permissive only. This is also the case for the joint implementation language in Article 4 (2) (a) and (d). Despite the permissive nature of such language, some observers have interpreted the Convention as 'endorsing' the concept of joint implementation; see, eg Bodansky supra note 31, at 521.

37 On this point, *cf* paragraph10 of the Secretariat's Note on Joint Implementation.

38 The full text of Article 4 (1) (b) requires all Parties to '[f]ormulate, implement, publish and regularly update national and, where appropriate, regional programmes containing measures to mitigate climate change by addressing anthropogenic emissions by sources and removal by sinks and of all greenhouse gases not controlled by the Montreal Protocol, and measures to facilitate adequate adaptation to climate change'.

39 Under international law the territorial scope of treaty obligations extends to a state's own territorial area unless there is contrary indication; Article 29, Vienna Convention.

40 The footnote to Article 4 (2) makes clear that national policies 'includes policies and measures adopted by reglonal economic integration organizations'.

41 Article 31 (4), Vienna Convention.

42 Article 3 (1), Climate Change Convention.

43 Id Article 3 (1).

44 Id Preambular paragraph 14.

45 Id Preambular paragraph 6 and Article 3 (1).

46 Id Article 3 (2).

47 Id Article 3 (4).

48 See also text at note 8.

49 The full provision requires the COP to '[a]ssess, on the basis of all information made available to it in accordance with the Convention, the implementation of the Convention by the Parties, the overall effects of the measures taken pursuant to the Convention, in particular environmental, economic and social effects as well as their cumulative impacts, and the extent to which progress towards the objective of the Convention is being achieved'.

50 Council Directive 88/609, *OJ* 1988 L 2336/1.

12 FINANCING GLOBAL ENVIRONMENTAL PROTECTION

1 The UNCED Secretariat calculated that the North would need to provide the South with US$125bn of additionality each year between 1992 and 2000 to implement Agenda 21 (World Resources Institute, 1994, 226). Jordan (1994a) discusses other estimates made of the total amount of additionality needed to implement sustainable development.

2 Patlis, J M (1992) 'The Multilateral Fund of the Montreal Protocol', 25 *Cornell International Law Report* 1, pp 181–230.

3 Bodansky, D (Summer 1993) 'The United Framework Convention on Climate Change', 18 *Yale Journal of International Law* 2 ('Bodansky'), p 492.

4 Sand, P (1990) *Lessons Learned in Global Environmental Governance*, World Resources Institute, Washington.

5 UNEP, 'Interpretations of Phrases "Adequate, New and Additional, New and Additional, and Adequate and Additional"', *Intergovernmental Negotiating Committee for a Convention on Biological Diversity*, Fourth Session, 23 September–2 October; (*Unep/Bio Div/Inc 4/4*,16 August), UNEP, Nairobi, 1991.

6 UNEP, 'Interpretations of Phrases', supra note 5.

7 Kohona, P (1992) 'UNCED: The Transfer of Financial Resources to Developing Countries', 1 *RECIEL* 3, pp 307–313.

8 Jordan, A J (1994) 'Financing the UNCED Agenda: The Controversy over Additionality', 36 *Environment* 3, pp 16–20 and 26–34.

9 Jordan, A J and Werksman, J (1994) 'Power, Money and the Global Environment Facility', *EcoDecision*, Vol 14, pp 68–70, ('Jordan and Werksman'). Developed country Parties to the Montreal Protocol recently agreed to provide between $300–500m to the Multilateral Ozone Fund in the period 1994–6, Rowlands, I (1993) 'The Fourth Meeting of the Parties to the Montreal Protocol', CSERGE *Working Paper* vol GEC 93–18, CSERGE, London and Norwich.

10 OECD (1992) *Development Cooperation 1992 Report*, OECD, Paris, p 79. Net North-South Financial Transfers (US$) amounted to 54bn in 1980 and 34bn in 1991; in 1985 and 1986 they were minus 13bn and minus 3bn respectively (id, p A-25) ('OECD, *Development Cooperation* 1992 Report').

11 UNEP, UNDP, World Bank (1993) *Report of the Independent Evaluation of the Global Environment Facility*, GEF, Washington, Part VIII.

12 World Resources Institute (1994) *World Resources 1994–5: A Guide to the Global Environment*, Oxford University Press, Oxford, p 227.

13 OECD, *Development Cooperation 1992 Report* supra note 10 at p 25.

14 MacNeill et al (1991) *Beyond Interdependence*, Oxford University Press, Oxford, p 104. Note also that Switzerland and the US do not accept this target.

15 Norway, Denmark, Sweden, Netherlands, Finland (OECD, *Development Cooperation 1992 Report*, supra note 10).

16 Kjorven, O and Sydnes, A (1992) *Funding for the Global Environment: The Issue of Additionality*, Working Paper 1992/4, Norway Fridjtof Nansen Institute, Lysaked, p 12.

17 Government of Sweden (1991) *Proposition 1990/1: 100, bilga 5, Submission to the Swedish Parliament of Budget Proposals for 1991–2*, Ministry for Foreign Affairs, Stockholm.

18 Benedick, R (1991) *Ozone Diplomacy*, Harvard University Press, Cambridge, Mass ('Benedick').

19 This was the interpretation of additionality pushed by the US in negotiations to revise the Montreal Protocol, but pressure from other states subsequently forced it to back down (Benedick supra note 18).

20 In 1991 private flows of money made up 42 per cent of total resource flows from North to South. (OECD, Development Cooperation 1992 Report supra note 10.)
21 Quoted in Holmberg, J (1992) 'Financing Sustainable Development' in Holmberg, J (ed), *Policies for a Small Planet*, Earthscan, London.
22 The term 'compensation' is used here to describe a payment in return for a service (ie the provision of global environmental 'services'), and not a payment by way of acknowledgment of liability for damage (ie as demanded by a strict legal interpretation of the term).
23 Benedick supra note 18.
24 Wood, A Study Three (1993) 'The Interim Multilateral Fund for the Implementation of the Montreal Protocol' in Reed, D (ed), *The GEF: Volume II*, WWF International, Washington.
25 More definite arrangements will be discussed at the first meeting of the COP in 1995.
26 Bodansky supra note 3 at p 524.
27 In the last (March, 1992) draft of the Convention prior to it being signed, references to the scope of funding still appeared thus: '[full]/[agreed] incremental costs' (See: A/AC/237/18 (Part I), 10 March 1992. A compromise (ie to include agreed and full) was only reached at INC 5 (8 May 1992) when the final text was adopted. This was only a month before the UNCED (see: A/AC.237/L.14).
28 See Jordan and Werksman supra note 9.
29 Sharma, R 'Debate on PRINCE likely to Delay Progress on GEF', 2 *Climate Action Network – South Asia (CANSA) Newsletter* 3, p 8, and Werksman, J (1993) *Incremental Costs under the Climate Change Convention: The International Legal Context*, FIELD Working Paper, FIELD, London.
30 Johnson, I 'Incremental Costs and the GEF', Letter to workshop invited participants (GEF Letter); 'Attachment 1: PRINCE', 10 November 1992, GEF, Washington, p 2.
31 GEF (1993) *GEF Replenishment Paper*, GEF, Washington, p 18 ('GEF Replenishment').
32 *Approaches To The Determination Of Agreed Full Incremental Costs*: Note by the Interim Secretariat to the Convention on Climate Change. *A/AC 237/50/Add 1*, 21 December 1993.
33 Werksman, J (1993) *Incremental Costs under the Climate Change Convention: The International Legal Context*, FIELD Working Paper, FIELD, London.
34 Pearce, D and Barrett, S (1993) *Incremental Costs and Biodiversity Conservation*, Paper prepared for a GEF Seminar on Incremental Costs and the Global Environment, Washington, 21 September 1993, CSERGE, London and Norwich, ('Pearce and Barrett') .
35 Group of 77 and China (draft decision) (15–20 March 1993) *Matters Relating To Arrangements For the Financial Mechanism*. INC 7. *A/AC.237/L.18*.
36 Oberthur, S (1993) 'Discussions on Joint Implementation and the Financial Mechanism', 23 *Environmental Policy and Law* 6, p 248.
37 GEF, *The GEF Replenishment Paper* supra note 31.
38 Pearce and Barrett supra note 34.
39 GEF (1993) *The GEF and the Evaluation: Learning from Experience and Looking Forward*, GEF, Washington, p 18. '[T]he . . . incremental cost concept [provides] an analytical framework for a structured dialogue between a potential recipient country, or institution, and an Implementing Agency' (GEF, id, p 5).
40 King, K (1993) *Issues to be Addressed by the Program Measuring Incremental Costs*, Working Paper 8, GEF, Washington.
41 *A/AC 237/50/Add 1*, p 2.

13 THE UN FRAMEWORK CONVENTION ON CLIMATE CHANGE: THE EUROPEAN CARBON/ ENERGY TAX AND ITS INTERNATIONAL TRADE LAW IMPLICATIONS

1 This objective is stated in Article 2 of the Convention which provides as follows: 'The ultimate objective of this Convention and any related legal instruments which the Conference of the Parties may adopt is to achieve, in accordance with the relevant provisions of the Convention, stabilization of greenhouse gas concentrations in the atmosphere at a level that would prevent dangerous anthropogenic interference with the climate system. Such a level should be achieved within a time frame sufficient to allow ecosystems to adapt naturally to climate change, to ensure that food production is not threatened and to enable economic development to proceed in a sustainable manner.'

2 See Chapters 4 and 11 for an in-depth discussion of the important provisions of the Climate Change Convention.

3 The Community's First Action Programme on the Environment, *OJ* 1973 C112/1.

4 The EEC actively participated in the first negotiations of the Intergovernmental Negotiating Committee (INC) for a Framework Convention on Climate Change which took place in Washington DC in February 1991, and all subsequent negotiating sessions.

5 See Commission of the European Communities, SEC (91) 1744 Final, 14 October 1991.

6 Proposal for a Council Directive Introducing a Tax on Carbon Dioxide Emissions and Energy. Commission of the European Communities. COM (92) 226 Final. Brussels, 30 June 1992.

7 See *Europe Energy*, No 415 – January 1 1994, part 1 – energy policy at p 7.

8 Personal Communications with Commission officials.

9 Article 3.

10 Article 5.

11 In an effort to gain support for the tax, Philippe Maystadt, current President of the Finance Council, has suggested that the figure be $3 per barrel without any automatic increase.

12 Article 7.

13 Article 1.

14 Japan's Ministry of International Trade and Industry, has published a policy document entitled 'Fourteen Proposals for a New Earth', outlining Japan's preferred options for reducing carbon dioxide emissions. These are mainly 'promotive measures'. Their reason for rejecting a unilateral tax is that it would 'invite the international migration of industry', and that the 'quite high rates' required might reduce economic growth and cause inflation. The US Climate Change Action Plan (October, 1993) does not include an energy tax. As well, President Clinton recently failed to secure the safe passage of the BTU Tax (proposed on 17 February 1993) through Congress.

15 Montreal Protocol on Substances That Deplete the Ozone Layer, September 1987, 26 ILM 1541 (1987). London Revisions, 29 June 1990, Copenhagen Revisions, 25 November 1992.

16 Benedick, R E (1991) *Ozone Diplomacy*, Harvard University Press, pp 199–211.

17 General Agreement on Tariffs and Trade, opened for signature, 30 October 1947, 61 *Stat A3, 55 UNTS 187* (GATT). See also section 'GATT Article XX exceptions' of this chapter.

18 The experience of negotiating the Convention confirms the fact that this provision is intended to apply to the EC.

19 Border tax adjustments have been defined by the OECD as: 'any fiscal measures which put into effect, in whole or in part, the destination principle (ie which enable exported products to be relieved of some or all of the tax charged in the exporting country in respect of similar domestic products sold to consumers on the home market and which enable imported products sold to consumers to be charged with some or all of the tax charged in the importing country in respect of similar domestic products).'

20 Explanatory Memorandum to the Proposal for a Council Directive introducing a tax on carbon dioxide emissions and energy, p 6.

21 Article II concerns Schedules of Concessions and allows, for example, a charge equivalent to an internal tax to be levied consistent with Article III.2 in respect of a like domestic product or in respect of an article from which the imported product has been manufactured or produced in whole or in part. Article III deals with national treatment on internal taxation and regulation and the issue of protection to domestic production. Article IV allows for anti-dumping and countervailing duties and therefore a controlled exception to Article II, see in particular Article VI.2 and VI.3. On the other side of the issue is Article XVI on subsidies.

22 See Working Party Report on 'Border Tax Adjustments', L/3464, 2 December 1970, *BISD 18S/97*, 101, para 15. See also Thaggert, H (1994) 'Like Products: Production and Process Methods in the Trade and Environment Context', FIELD conference paper, Cameron, J and Demaret, P (eds), *Trade, Treaties and the Environment* Cameron-May Publishers, London ('Thaggert').

23 Id, 101.

24 See Thaggert supra note 22.

25 United States – Taxes on Petroleum and Certain Chemical Products (Superfund), *BISD 34S/136*.

26 *Pub L No 99-499*, 515(a) adding 26 *USC* 4671–4672.

27 See also section on 'Like products' of this chapter for a discussion.

28 Supra note 19 at p 163.

29 See section on 'Nullification and impairment' in this chapter.

30 Article 10 of the Convention.

31 'United States – Taxes on Petroleum and Certain Imported Substances; Report of the Panel, adopted on 17 June 1987 (L/6175),' GATT, 34th *Supp BISD 137* (1988).

32 See supra 98.

33 Id.

34 Explanatory Memorandum, p 12.

35 Under Article XVI, contracting Parties shall not 'grant either directly or indirectly any form of subsidy on the export of any product other than a primary product which subsidy results in the sale of such product for export at a price lower than the comparable price charged for the like product to buyers in the domestic market'.

36 See the 'Declaration Giving Effect to the Provisions of Article XVI' paragraph 4, 9th *Supp BISD 32* (1961), 445 *UNTS* 294 (1962).

37 Article VI(2) provides, in part, that: 'In order to offset or prevent dumping, a contracting party may levy on any dumped product an anti-dumping duty not greater in amount than the margin of dumping in respect of such product'.

38 GATT Article VI.4.

39 Articles 10 and 11 contain the four tax measures mentioned herein.

40 See GATT Article XVI(4).

41 Id.

42 See the Panel Report entitled, Operation of the Provisions of Article XVI, 10th *Supp BISD 201*, 206–207 (1962).

43 Article VI (6) (a) provide as follows: 'No contracting party shall levy any anti-dumping or countervailing duty on the importation of any product of the territory of another contracting party unless it determines that the effect of the dumping or subsidization, as the case may be, is such as to cause or threaten material injury to

an established domestic industry, or is such as to retard materially the establishment of a domestic industry'.

44 According to Article VI (4): 'No product of the territory of any contracting party imported into the territory of any other contracting party shall be subject to anti-dumping or countervailing duty by reason of the exemption of such product from duties or taxes borne by the like product when destined for consumption in the country of origin or exportation, or by reason of the refund of such duties or taxes'.

45 Supra note 33.

46 See Article XX, 61 Stat at A60-61.

47 Demaret, P 'Trade Related Environmental Measures (TREMs) in the External Relations of the European Community' in *Trade, Treaties and the Environment*, supra note 10.

48 Hazardous products bans are still susceptible to trade challenges as disguised restrictions on trade. They would be evaluated according to the components of the necessity test which are identified in this section of the paper. A GATT ACTIVITIES report [1989 at 100-01 (1990)] commenting on a US ban on Chilean grapes is also informative in this regard.

49 See Article XX, 61 Stat at A60–61.

50 See *Tuna-Dolphin Panel Report, GATT Doc DS21/R 93* September 1991, pp 45–46.

51 See Charnovitz, S (1991) 'Exploring the Environmental Exceptions in GATT Article XX', 25 *Journal of World Trade* 37, 38–47 (providing an excellent discussion of the negotiating history of Article XX). Since the *Tuna-Dolphin* panel report (supra note 50) has not been adopted by the contracting parties the decision is not binding. However, it is to be noted that its principles are being codified in the text being negotiated at the GATT Uruguay Round. For an analysis of those areas of text which have been influenced by the *Tuna-Dolphin* panel report referring to Makuch, Z (1992) *Environmental and Natural Resource Implications of the Final Text of the GATT Uruguay Round*, Canadian Environmental Law Association Publications.

52 See *Thailand – Restrictions on Importation of and Internal Taxes On Cigarettes*, Report of the Panel Adopted 7 November 1990, BISD (37th Supp) 200–223 para 74 (1990). This trade dispute involved a Thai government prohibition on exports and imports without a licence granted by the Thai Tobacco Monopoly.

53 The panel accepted that smoking constituted a serious risk to health. Consequently, measures to reduce smoking would normally fall within the Article XX exception were it not for the discriminatory nature of the regulation. On this basis, and in view of other less trade restrictive but still effective alternatives, the panel found the prohibition to be GATT-inconsistent.

54 See *Tuna-Dolphin* report (supra note 50). The panel also failed to recognize that the United States and other nations have been involved in efforts to reach a multilateral agreement on dolphin conservation for upwards of 15 years.

55 See GATT Secretariat, Trade and the Environment (1992). Here, the Secretariat discusses unilaterally implemented environmental regulations or threats thereof all of which are identified as having some success.

56 See *Tuna-Dolphin* panel report supra note 50, p 46. The MMPA provides a maximum incidental dolphin taking rate, that foreign fleets must meet during a particular period, which is the same as the rate recorded by US domestic fishing fleets during the same time. In the panelists' view, this did not allow Mexican fleets to determine whether their harvesting was in line with MMPA standards at any given time. As a result the US could not persuade the panel that this limitation on trade was 'necessary'. The unpredictable nature of the limitation weakened the US argument of necessity.

57 A timely example of a threat whose mitigation could be hindered by a required degree of scientific uncertainty is the greenhouse effect. Although scientists agree that global warming is taking place, the complexity of the problem makes the prediction of environmental results prone to controversy and a significant

divergence of scientific opinion. If Article XX's necessity requirement demands scientific certainty contracting Parties seeking to abate global warming will have difficulty in doing so. This may occur for virtually any environmental circumstance requiring the use of the precautionary approach.

58 Cameron, J (1994) 'The Status of the Precautionary Principle in International Law', in O'Riordan, T and Cameron, J (eds), *Interpreting the Precautionary Principle*, Cameron-May Publishers.

59 It is interesting to note that the panel did not use the term territorial in its deliberations concerning Article XX(b). The panel does not speak decisively on the matter of the limits of the Party's jurisdictional ability to act. The question to be answered is whether an action taken extraterritorially, but within the jurisdiction of a contracting party, falls within Article XX.

60 *United States – Prohibition on Imports of Tuna and Tuna Products from Canada*, Report of the Panel adopted on 22 February 1982 (L/5198), GATT, *29th Supp BISD 91* (1983), p 96.

61 This is implied in the Preamble to the Directive and the Introduction contained in the Explanatory Memorandum which accompanies the Directive.

62 UNG A Resolution 44/215,12 February 1990.

63 See GATT Article XX(g), 61 Stat at A61.

64 See supra note 60.

65 *Canada – Measures Affecting Exports of Unprocessed Herring and Salmon*, Report of the Panel adopted 22 March 1988 (*L/6268*), GATT, *35th Supp BISD 98* (1988), p 114.

66 Ibid.

67 As per the *Tuna-Dolphin* panel report on Article XX(b), the decision does not explain whether the exception is limited to domestic actions concerning the protection of national resources, or whether an action taken beyond one's jurisdiction to protect a domestic resource is still permitted through the use of Article XX(g).

68 16 *USC* 1371. The decision concerning this EC challenge is due to be handed down in March 1994.

69 Parliament Resolution A3-0329/92. 'EC Parliament Proposes Two-Year Moratorium on GATT Panel Environmental Decisions', 10 *International Trade Reporter* 136 (1993).

GLOSSARY

ACC	–	(UN) Administrative Coordination Committee
ASOC	–	Antarctic and Southern Ocean Coalition
ATS	–	Antarctic Treaty System
BACT	–	Best Available Control Technique
BCAS	–	Bangladesh Centre for Advanced Studies
BRAC	–	Bangladesh Rural Advancement Committee
BWUs	–	Blue Whale Units
CAA	–	Clean Air Act
CAC	–	Command-and-Control
CAFE	–	Corporate Average Fuel Economy
CARDMA	–	Coastal Area Resource Development and Management Association
CCAMLR	–	Convention on the Conservation of Antarctic Marine Living Resources
CCAS	–	Convention on the Conservation of Antarctic Seals
CCP	–	Common Commercial Policy
CFP	–	Common Fisheries Policy
CIDIE	–	Committee of International Development Institutions on the Environment
CITES	–	Convention on International Trade of Endangered Species
CLA	–	Catch Limit Algorithm
CLASP	–	Centre for Law and Social Policy
CONABIO	–	National Biodiversity Use and Documentation Commission
COP	–	Convention of the Parties
CPRE	–	Council for the Protection of Rural England
CRAMRA	–	Convention for the Regulation of Antarctic Mineral Resource Activities
CSD	–	Commission on Sustainable Development
CSCE	–	Conference on Security and Cooperation in Europe
CWA	–	Clean Water Act
DPCSP	–	Department for Policy Coordination and Sustainable Development
DSP	–	Dispute Settlement Procedures

DSU – Dispute Settlement Understanding
EA – Environmental Assessment
EBRD – European Bank for Reconstruction and Development
EC – European Community
ECE – Economic Commission for Europe
ECJ – European Court of Justice
ECOSOC – UN Economic and Social Council
ECR – European Court Reports
EIA – Environmental Impact Assessment
EIA – Environmental Investigation Agency
ENMOD – Convention on the Prohibition of Military or Other Hostile Use of Environmental Modification Techniques
EPA – Environmental Protection Agency
FAO – Food and Agriculture Organization
FEPA – Federal Environmental Protection Agency
FFA – Forum Fisheries Agency
FIFRA – Federal Insecticide, Fungicide, and Rodenticide Act
FM – Financial Mechanism
GAO – General Accounting Office
GATS – General Agreement on Trade in Services
GATT – General Agreement on Tariffs and Trade
GEF – Global Environmental Facility
GESAMP – Joint Group of Experts on the Scientific Aspects of Marine Pollution
GOLE – Group of Legal Experts
HLW – High Level Waste
IAEA – International Atomic Energy Agency
IATTC – Inter-American Tropical Tuna Commission
IBRD – International Bank for Reconstruction and Development
IBWC – International Boundary and Water Commission
IC – Implementation Committee
ICJ – International Court of Justice
ICJ Reps – Reports of the International Court of Justice
ICRC – International Committee of the Red Cross
ICRW – International Convention for the Regulation of Whaling
ICSU – International Council of Scientific Union
IDA – International Development Association
IEA – International Environmental Agreement
IFC – International Finance Corporation
IGPRAD – Intergovernmental Panel of Experts on Radioactive Wastes
IGY – International Geophysical Year
IIED – International Institute for Environment and Development
ILO – International Labour Organization
ILW – Intermediate Level Waste
IMO – International Maritime Organization
INC – Intergovernmental Negotiating Committee
IOS – International Observer Scheme
IPCC – Intergovernmental Panel on Climate Change
ITF – International Transport Federation
ITQ – Individual Transferable Quotas

IUCN – World Conservation Union
IWC – International Whaling Commission
LC 72 – London Convention 1972 (previously known as LDC)
LDC – London Dumping Convention
LLW – Low Level Wastes
LTRAP – Long Range Transboundary Air Pollution
MAGP – Multi-Annual Guidance Programmes
MIGA – Multilateral Investment Guarantee Agency
MLS – Monthly Official Summary
MMPA – Marine Mammal Protection Act
MPIC – Montreal Protocol Implementation Committee
MPMF – Montreal Protocol Multilateral Fund
MSY – Maximum Sustainable Yield
MTO – Multilateral Trade Organization
NACEC – North American Commission on Environmental Cooperation
NACOM – National Conservation Movement
NAFO – North Atlantic Fisheries Organization
NAFTA – North American Free Trade Organization
NAMMCO – North Atlantic Marine Mammals Conservation Organization
NCCP – National Climate Change Plan
NCP – Non-compliance Procedures
NEA – Nuclear Energy Agency
NEAFC – North East Atlantic Fisheries Commission
NEPA – National Environmental Protection Agency
NGO – Non-Governmental Organization
NMP – New Management Procedures
NOAA – National Oceanic and Atmospheric Administration
NPWS – National Parks and Wildlife Services
NRDC – Natural Resources Defence Council
NUS – National Union of Seamen
OAU – Organization of African Unity
ODA – Overseas Development Agency
ODA – Official Development Assistance
ODS – Ozone Depleting Substances
OEA – Office of Environmental Affairs
OECD – Organization of Economic Cooperation and Development
OPEC – Organization of Petroleum Exporting Countries
OSPAR – Convention for the Protection of the Marine Environment of the North-East Atlantic
PA – Participants' Assembly
PCIJ – Permanent Court of International Justice
POTW – Publicly Owned Treatment Works
PPM – Process and Production Methods
PREP – Protocol on Environmental Protection
PRINCE – Programme for Measuring Incremental Costs for the Environment
RECIEL – Review of European Community and International Environmental Law
RIAA – Reports of International Arbitral Awards
RIIA – Royal Institute of International Affairs

RMP	–	Revised Management Procedures
RUCN	–	International Union for Conservation of Nature and Natural Resources
SBI	–	Subsidiary Body for Implementation
SBSTA	–	Subsidiary Body for Scientific and Technical Advice
SCAR	–	Scientific Committee on Antarctic Research
SEDESOL	–	Social Development Secretariat
SPC	–	South Pacific Commission
SPREP	–	South Pacific Regional Environmental Programme
SSPIC	–	Second Sulphur Protocol Implementation Committee
STAP	–	Scientific and Technical Advisory Panel
TAC	–	Total Allowable Catch
TBT	–	Technical Barriers to Trade
TDR	–	Transferable Development Sites
TREMs	–	Trade Related Environmental Measures
TRIPs	–	Agreement on Trade Related Intellectual Property Rights
UBINIG	–	Policy Research Development Alternatives
UNCED	–	United Nations Conference on Environment and Development
UNCHE	–	United Nations Conference on the Human Environment
UNCLOS	–	United Nations Convention on the Law of the Sea
UNESCO	–	United Nations Education Scientific and Cultural Organization
UNDP	–	United Nations Development Programme
UNEP	–	United Nations Environment Programme
UNGA	–	United Nations General Assembly
WCED	–	World Commission on Environment and Development
WHO	–	World Health Organization
WICEM	–	World Industry Conference on Environmental Management
WWF	–	World Wild Fund for Nature
YIEL	–	Yearbook of International Environmental Law

AFTERWORD TO CHAPTER 5, *A CASE STUDY OF THE INTERNATIONAL WHALING COMMISSION*

In August 1995, over a hundred states, participating in three years of intergovernmental negotiations, adopted an *Agreement for the Implementation of the Provisions of the United Nations Convention on the Law of the Sea of 10 December 1982 Relating to the Conservation and Management of Straddling Fish Stocks and Highly Migratory Fish Stocks* (1995 Fish Stocks Agreement). The text will be opened for signature at the fiftieth session of the United Nations General Assembly. While the implications for this forward looking text are likely to be far reaching, and cannot be analyzed fully here, it is possible to make some initial observations of relevance to the setting of primary rules for the conservation and management of marine living resources within and beyond national jurisdictions, and in promoting compliance with these rules.

Upon entry into force, the 1995 Fish Stocks Agreement will require that the conservation and management measures established for the high seas are compatible with those adopted for areas under national jurisdiction. Parties will be required to apply a precautionary approach, as set out in Annex II of the Agreement, and to implement agreed conservation and management measures when precautionary reference points are exceeded. Parties are to ensure that the risk of exceeding such reference points is very low and are to take into account scientific uncertainties when setting their fisheries policies.

States parties to the Agreement will be obliged to collect and share information on such matters as vessel position, catch of target and non-target species, and fishing effort. Data provided are to be timely, complete and accurate, as set out in the standards in Annex I of the agreement. It is sobering to note, however, that many of these standards are recommendatory rather than mandatory.

With regard to inspection, the 1995 Fish Stocks Agreement introduces a traditional regime, but innovates considerably by making it generally applicable on the high seas. Flag states are to permit boarding and inspection of their vessels, irrespective of whether the flag state participates in the regional organization or arrangement governing the area in which the inspection takes place.

The rights and duties of port states to take measures to promote the effectiveness of international fisheries conservation measures are emphasized by the Agreement. Although language in the Agreement is permissive, rather than obligatory, it beats a new path forward for port states to enforce internationally set standards. The Agreement provides that, when a fishing vessel is in port, the port state may inspect documents, gear and catch, and may prohibit landings or transshipments where it has been established that the catch has been taken illegally. We may expect that this approach to cooperative enforcement will be developed by the elaboration of common duties, incumbent upon port state inspectors. Such common duties have already been elaborated successfully to promote regional cooperation in the enforcement of international vessel safety and pollution control standards.

INDEX